Success for College Students with Learning Disabilities

Susan A. Vogel   Pamela B. Adelman
Editors

Success for
College Students with
Learning Disabilities

With a Foreword by Janet W. Lerner

With 21 Illustrations

Springer-Verlag
New York Berlin Heidelberg London Paris
Tokyo Hong Kong Barcelona Budapest

Susan A. Vogel, Ph.D.
Northern Illinois University
Department of Educational Psychology,
   Counseling and Special Education
DeKalb, IL 60015-2854
USA

Pamela B. Adelman, Ph.D.
Department of Education
Barat College
Lake Forest, IL 60045
USA

Library of Congress Cataloging-in-Publication Data
Success for college students with learning disabilities/Susan A.
   Vogel, Pamela Adelman, eds.
         p.   cm.
   Includes bibliographical references and index.
   ISBN 0-387-97763-5
   1. Learning disabled—Education (Higher)—United States.
   2. Learning disabled—Services for—United States.   I. Vogel, Susan
Ann.   II. Adelman, Pamela.
   LC4704.75.S83   1992
   371.9'0474—dc20   91-41399

Printed on acid-free paper.

Production managed by Natalie Johnson; manufacturing supervised by Jacqui Ashri.
Typeset by Best-set Typesetter Ltd., Hong Kong.
Printed and bound by Hamilton Printing Co. Rensselaer, NY.
Printed in the United States of America.

9 8 7 6 5 4 3

ISBN 0-387-97763-5 Springer-Verlag New York Berlin Heidelberg
ISBN 3-540-97763-5 Springer-Verlag Berlin Heidelberg New York

This book is dedicated to our husbands, Manfred and Steven, and sons, Evan, Henry, David, and Robert. No matter how busy and immersed in our work we became, we could always count on their love and understanding.

Foreword

JANET W. LERNER

This timely volume explores issues pertinent to the emerging subject of college education for adults with learning disabilities. The inspiration for the book was a conference held at Barat College in Lake Forest Illinois on April 7, 1990, entitled *College Students with Learning Disabilities: Reviewing the '80s and Planning for the '90s*. The occasion was the celebration of the tenth anniversary of Barat College's program for college students with learning disabilities. Papers presented at this conference, plus several additional invited chapters, and those of the co-editors are included in this much needed publication.

Only a few years ago, college was out of the question for most adults with learning disabilities. It is heartening to note that this situation has changed substantially over the last 15 or so years, with great strides in opportunities for adults with learning disabilities to acquire a college level education. From a slow beginning with programs such as the one at Barat College, there are today programs and support services in a variety of settings at a growing number of colleges and universities. Many individuals with learning disabilities can look forward to experiencing college and better preparing themselves for the future. The collection of papers in this book offers a comprehensive review of this exciting and challenging field.

The 13 chapters in this publication are divided into four parts: Part I, *Introduction*; Part II, *Making the Transition to College*; Part III, *Meeting the Needs of College Students with Learning Disabilities*; and Part IV, *Research on the Cutting Edge*. Selected chapters include a case study on a specific student that exemplifies the program, setting, policies, intervention approach, and/or accommodations.

Part I, *Introduction*, consists of two chapters. In Chapter I, Susan A. Vogel, who originated the Barat College program, reviews the historical development of college programs during the 1980s. Vogel analyzes the nature of learning disabilities in adults and identifies the major concerns of college and university faculty, staff, and administrators. Suggested teaching and evaluation modifications and accommodations are described as well as a proposed support services and research agenda for the decade of the 1990s.

In Chapter II, Laura F. Rothstein explores the legal requirements and interpretation of the law as they relate to students with learning disabilities. Rothstein examines the implications of the U.S. Constitution, federal statutes (especially Section 504 of the Rehabilitation Act of 1973 and the Americans with Disabilities Act), regulations of the law, and judicial interpretation. Important precedent cases of the law are discussed relative to higher education's requirements for individuals with disabilities.

Part II, *Making the Transition to College*, also has two chapters. In Chapter III, Sara Cowen considers the importance of the high school years in making the transition to college. During the high school years, students with learning disabilities should (1) understand the nature of their problem, (2) get appropriate counseling, (3) give thought to career options, (4) develop independence, and (5) select the college or university setting that will best serve their needs. The transition process requires a team consisting of the student, parents, and secondary school personnel. Cowen also outlines transition activities for the four years of high school. It is important for the student and parents, if appropriate, to visit the campus of the selected colleges prior to applying. An extremely valuable part of this chapter is a listing and description of college guides for students with learning disabilities.

Chapter IV, by Connie Dalke, expands the discussion of transition by describing the high school to college transition program at the University of Wisconsin–Whitewater. Entering college students with learning disabilities need an orientation to become aware of new behaviors that are needed in college. Major differences between high school and college are: (1) less student-teacher contact, (2) long range assignments and infrequent evaluation rather than day-to-day monitoring that occurs in high school, (3) lack of the support network of family and friends that was available during high school, (4) more unstructured time to manage, (5) the need for self-advocacy, (6) an expansive physical environment with classes in different buildings, and (7) adjustment to roommates and to the eating and sleeping patterns of life in the dormitories. This chapter offers a detailed account of the University of Wisconsin–Whitewater's summer program, which is designed to provide transition activities before the student enrolls in the university. The five components of this summer transition program cover college study skills, campus and community awareness, psychosocial skills enhancement, fall course advisement and registration, and career awareness exploration. Students who participated in this transition program made better grades, they stayed in the college program longer, and they judged the program to be beneficial.

Part III, *Meeting the Needs of LD College Students*, is the most extensive section of the book, consisting of seven chapters. In Chapter V,

Susan A. Vogel examines the diverse array of responses of colleges and universities to Section 504 of the Rehabilitation Act for students with learning disabilities. Although the federal law mandates accessibility to postsecondary education for students with disabilities, colleges and universities differ in their responses to the requirements of this law. Vogel conceptualizes the wide spectrum of responses of institutions in terms of a continuum, from a minimum level of response to a maximum level. The colleges are judged on compliance with Section 504 in terms of several factors: availability of information about services, the petition process, faculty and staff awareness, the application and admission process, eligibility for services, support services available, staff training, the student-staff ratio, the availability of diagnostic services, and curriculum modification. To illustrate, a college that provides a maximum response would have a student-staff ratio of 12 or 15:1, while a college with a minimum response would have a student-staff ratio of 100 or more to one.

In Chapter VI, Doris J. Johnson discusses the professional preparation of specialists to work in postsecondary LD programs. Competencies recommended for personnel include a Master's Degree in Learning Disabilities with certification at the secondary level, an understanding of the characteristics of adolescents and adults with learning disabilities, proficiency with the diagnostic/assessment procedures for this population, understanding the principles of remediation and teaching needs of college students, competencies in counseling, advising, and guidance, knowledge of the college rules and regulations, and skills in helping students make the transition to the world of work.

In Chapter VII, Ernest Rose highlights the need to educate faculty. One of the greatest challenges faced by college students is gaining and maintaining the acceptance and cooperation of the academic faculty. The research shows that faculty members are often not supportive of the concept of providing accommodations for students with learning disabilities. In-service programs are needed to help faculty understand the needs of students with learning disabilities and to become familiar with accommodations that can be made. Rose discusses questions that are typically asked by faculty such as: the nature of learning disabilities, the college's responsibilities under the law, and methods of providing reasonable accommodations. Several instruments to survey and evaluate the faculty attitude, knowledge, and needs are included in this chapter.

In Chapter VIII, Margaret M. Policastro discusses assessing and developing metacognitive attitudes in college students with learning disabilities. Her concern is helping students develop a strong metacognitive awareness base and become responsible for their own learning. Policastro first describes the Learning and Support Services Program at Roosevelt University (located in a large urban center), then she discusses metacognition in individuals with learning disabilities in terms of history, reading, writing, social/emotional functioning, and assessment. Finally, she links the two by discussing the procedures used at Roosevelt University to teach metacognitive skills to college students with learning disabilities.

Chapter IX, by William D. Bursuck and Madhavi Jayanthi, analyzes programming for independent study skills usage. The purpose of this chapter is to present a technology for teaching study skills that draws from the learning strategies literature. The goal is to maximize independence in study skills. Training for independence is discussed within the context of four major aspects of the instructional process: assessment, curriculum design, skill acquisition and fluency, and skill generalization.

Chapter X, by Pamela B. Adelman, Jody O'Connell, Dee Konrad, and Susan A. Vogel, discusses methods of integrating remediation and subject-matter tutoring. The goal is to use students' course work to help them acquire skills that help them succeed in current situations and generalize to new learning situations. The authors note that for some individuals, college is the most appropriate time in their education to receive remediation. The impact of the challenge of college courses and motivation to succeed, combined with the increased emotional, social, and cognitive growth often leads to a more receptive attitude. This chapter focuses on the integration of remediation and subject-matter tutoring as the primary type of support. It contains several sections: a review of research on cognitive abilities and achievement levels of college students with learning disabilities; key components for developing an individualized education plan for the student; and instructional approaches that integrate remediation and subject-matter tutoring.

Chapter XI, by Marshall H. Raskind and Neil G. Scott, reports on the use of technology for college students with learning disabilities. The authors (1) examine technologies available to help college students with learning disabilities achieve academic success, (2) provide criteria for selecting and evaluating technology, and (3) offer guidelines for instructing with technology. The Learning Disability Program and Computer Access Lab of the Office of Disabled Student Services at California State University at Northridge have been using technology with college students with LDs for the past four years. The technologies (and the skills area) which are described in this chapter include word processing (written language); spell-checkers (written language); proofreading programs (written language); outlining/"brainstorming" (written language); abbreviation expanders (written language); speech recognition (written language); speech synthesis/screen review (written language/reading); optical character recognition systems/speech synthesis (reading); personal data managers (organization, memory); free-form databases (organization, memory); variable speech control tape recorders (listening, memory, reading); listening aids (listening); and talking calculators (math). A valuable resource is a Technology Product Resource List, which shows products that have been successfully used with college students with LDs.

Part IV, *Research on the Cutting Edge*, consists of 2 chapters. Chapter XII, by Leonore Ganschow and Richard Sparks, deals with the topic of "foreign" language learning disabilities. For certain students, their learning disability is most troublesome in the college foreign language class. Ganschow and Sparks, who have been studying foreign language learning disabilities, report on the nature of such a disability, provide a historical review of this problem, review the research, and offer an analysis of the factors related to a foreign language learning disability. In particular, the chapter examines the hypothesis of a linguistic decoding deficit, methods of assessment and evaluation, and teaching methodology. Other important issues are waivers and substitutions for foreign language courses and accommodations that can be made in the foreign language classroom.

The subject of the last chapter, Chapter XIII, by Pamela B. Adelman and Susan A. Vogel, is program evaluation. The authors specify two different approaches to evaluating programs. The first is an objective-oriented approach, the purpose of which is to assess accomplishments of general program goals. The second approach is a naturalistic and participant-oriented approach to evaluation, the purpose of which is to assess the perspectives and reactions of various program participants. To measure outcomes, the chapter reviews the evaluation of academic performance, improvement of basic skills, social-emotional adjustments, and career attainments. To assess a program in terms of participant evaluation, the measurement should include the perspectives of students, faculty, administrators, and service providers. The authors present examples of measures designed to evaluate program services and needs. Results of student and faculty evaluations are presented to exemplify how program goals can be validated and ongoing support for the program and/or services can be ensured.

Acknowledgments. Acknowledgments for this useful collection of papers on college students with learning disabilities are due to Barat College for holding the conference which provided the impetus for this publication, to the editors, Susan A. Vogel and Pamela B. Adelman, for conceptualizing this conference and supplementing the original collection with many additional worthwhile chapters, and to the authors who contributed to this publication. The book will be of particular benefit for several groups. For college faculty who are starting or expanding programs or preparing professionals to work with college students with LDs, it will serve as a practical guide. For researchers, the comprehensive reviews of literature and research agenda will be thought provoking. The discussions of the law, teaching methodology, and program evaluation will prove useful to all readers, but especially so for university administrators, service providers, and faculty.

Janet W. Lerner
Northeastern Illinois University

Acknowledgments

We want to thank the many people who in some way contributed to this book. Since its founding in 1980, Barat College administrators, faculty, and trustees have supported the Learning Opportunities Program. One person in particular stands out. Dee Konrad, director of the Communication Skills Program, has worked closely with us since the inception of the Learning Opportunities Program. She has shown extreme sensitivity and has used her expertise to develop curricula for improving the written language skills of students.

We have also been fortunate to work with highly skilled and dedicated LD specialists who have developed innovative learning strategies that meet the specific needs of college students with learning disabilities. In addition, special appreciation and thanks go to the many students who participated in the program. Through their hard work and perseverance they helped us gain a better understanding of how learning disabilities are manifested at the college level and how best to ameliorate them.

Very special thanks to our contributors. We are extremely fortunate that so many outstanding professionals contributed scholarly and thought-provoking chapters. Many also participated in the Tenth Anniversary Conference of the Learning Opportunities Program.

We are also grateful to the Lloyd A. Fry Foundation and to the Thorn River Foundation for their generous support of our research and assistance in program development and evaluation.

Susan A. Vogel   Pamela B. Adelman
Northern Illinois University   Barat College

Contents

Contributors

PAMELA B. ADELMAN, PH.D. Department of Education, Barat College, Lake Forest, IL 60045, USA

WILLIAM D. BURSUCK, PH.D. Department of Educational Psychology, Counseling, and Special Education, Northern Illinois University, DeKalb, IL 60115, USA

SARA COWEN, ED.D. Educational Counseling Service, 50 Lakewood Circle, St. Charles, IL 60174, USA

CONNIE DALKE, PH.D. College of Education, University of Wisconsin-Whitewater, 800 West Main Street, Whitewater, WI 53190-1790, USA

LEONORE GANSCHOW, ED.D. Department of Educational Psychology, Miami University, Oxford, OH 45056, USA

MADHAVI JAYANTHI, ED.D. Department of Educational Psychology, Counseling, and Special Education, Northern Illinois University, DeKalb, IL 60115, USA

DORIS J. JOHNSON, PH.D. Learning Disabilities Center, Northwestern University, Evanston, IL 60201, USA

DEE KONRAD, M.A. Department of English, Barat College, Lake Forest, IL 60045, USA

JANET LERNER, PH.D. Department of Special Education, Northeastern Illinois University, 5500 N. St. Louis Avenue, Chicago, IL 60625, USA

JODY O'CONNELL, M.A. Department of Education, Barat College, Lake Forest, IL 60045, USA

MARGARET M. POLICASTRO, PH.D. Learning and Support Services, Roosevelt University, Chicago, IL 60605, USA

MARSHALL H. RASKIND, PH.D.[1] Learning Disability Program and Computer Access Lab, Office of Disabled Student Services, California State University–Northridge, 18111 Nordhoff Street, Northridge, CA 91330, USA

ERNEST ROSE, PH.D. School of Education and Human Services, Eastern Montana College, Billings, MT 59101-0298, USA.

LAURA F. ROTHSTEIN, J.D. Law Center, University of Houston, Houston, TX 77204-6391, USA

NEIL G. SCOTT, B.E. (hons)[2] Office of Disabled Student Services, California State University–Northridge, 18111 Nordhoff Street, Northridge, CA 91330, USA

RICHARD SPARKS, ED.D. Education Department, College of Mount St. Joseph, 5701 Delhi Road, Mount St. Joseph, OH 45051, USA

SUSAN A. VOGEL, PH.D. Department of Educational Psychology, Counseling, and Special Education, Northern Illinois University, DeKalb, IL 60115, USA

---

[1] *Present address:* The Frostig Center, 971 N. Altadena Drive, Pasadena, CA 91107, USA.
[2] *Present address*: Center for the Study of Language and Information, Stanford University, CSLI/Stanford, Venture Hall, Stanford, CA 94305, USA.

Part I
Introduction

I
A Retrospective and Prospective View of Postsecondary Education for Adults with Learning Disabilities

Susan A. Vogel

The field of learning disabilities, as we know it today, is a relatively young field. Moreover, our understanding of adults with learning disabilities is only in its infancy. In the 1980s, we witnessed significant changes in our awareness of the chronicity of learning disabilities. We have yet to examine systematically the effects of intervention and maturation on cognition, language, academic achievement, employment, and psychosocial development by gender and type of learning disability. Moreover, we are only in the seminal stages in systematically identifying the factors that can have a significant impact on educational and employment attainments and life satisfaction.

Revisions to the Definition

The recency of our awareness and understanding of the chronicity of learning disabilities can be seen by examining the development of alternative definitions of learning disabilities. The first, and the most widely accepted formal definition of learning disabilities, was formulated by the National Advisory Committee on Handicapped Children (1968) and was later incorporated into the Education for All Handicapped Children Act of 1975, Public Law 94-142. It states:

Children with special learning disabilities exhibit a disorder in one or more of the basic psychological processes involved in understanding or using spoken or written languages. These may be manifested in disorders of listening, thinking, talking, reading, writing, spelling, or arithmetic. They include conditions which have been referred to as perceptual handicaps, brain injury, minimal brain dysfunction, dyslexia, developmental aphasia, etc. They do not include learning problems which are due primarily to visual, hearing, or motor handicaps, to mental retardation, emotional disturbance or to environmental disadvantage. (Federal Register, 1977, Sect. 121a.5.)

This definition refers specifically to "children" and served us well in the 1970s to identify and educate hundreds of thousands of children with

3

learning disabilities who were previously unidentified and underserved. It has since been revised several times to reflect the increase in awareness that learning disabilities do not disappear in adulthood (Hammill, 1990).

A second change in the revised definitions was the fact that it was no longer necessary to refer to previous nomenclature such as minimal brain dysfunction or developmental aphasia. Moreover, as the children with learning disabilities identified in the 1970s reached adulthood, they themselves, their parents, and professionals came to realize that a learning disability is neither only a childhood disorder nor just a "school" disability (ACLD, 1985). This realization led to the necessity of revising other aspects of the definition.

The most widely accepted revision (Hammill, Leigh, McNutt, & Larsen, 1981) was developed in 1981 by the National Joint Committee on Learning Disabilities (NJCLD). It states:

Learning disabilities is a generic term that refers to a heterogeneous group of disorders manifested by significant difficulties in the acquisition and use of listening, speaking, reading, writing, reasoning, or mathematical abilities. These disorders are intrinsic to the individual, presumed to be due to central nervous system dysfunction, and may occur across the life span. Problems in self-regulatory behaviors, social perception, and social interaction may exist with learning disabilities but do not by themselves constitute a learning disability. Although learning disabilities may occur concomitantly with other handicapping conditions (for example, sensory impairment, mental retardation, serious emotional disturbance) or with extrinsic influences (such as cultural differences, insufficient or inappropriate instruction), they are not the result of those conditions or influences (NJCLD, 1981).

Chronicity

In this definition, it is clearly stated that a learning disability (LD) is a lifelong condition that continues to affect the manner in which individuals take in information and retain and express the knowledge and understanding they possess. The most common deficits in adults with LD are in reading rate, spelling, and mechanics of writing. Frequent, and no less troublesome, are problems in organizational skills, time management, and self-esteem. For most adults with LD, perceptual problems are also still evident. The most commonly reported perceptual problems, sometimes referred to as psychological processing deficits, include difficulties in discrimination (e.g., in perceiving differences between two similar but unlike sounds, words, or visual symbols) and in retaining what is heard, read, or seen (Houck, Engelhard, & Geller, 1989; Johnson & Blalock, 1987; Vogel, 1987).

Some Common Misconceptions

Lack of experience and knowledge about learning disabilities among college and university personnel, especially in the 1970s and 1980s, caused some individuals to confuse those with learning disabilities with mentally retarded persons. The learning disabled are not mentally retarded. They range in intelligence from low-average to gifted. In post-secondary settings, the range in IQ scores of students with LD will vary depending on the competitiveness of the admissions criteria. Students with LD accepted to the most highly selective colleges and universities would be in the superior range in intelligence, would be only minimally impaired in academic achievement, and probably would have had en-riched home environments and educational experiences (Dalke, 1988; Gajar, Salvia, Gajria, & Salvia, 1989; Hughes & Osgood-Smith, 1990; Leonard, 1991; Shaywitz & Shaw, 1988; Vogel, 1986). It may be helpful to keep in mind that Albert Einstein, Thomas Edison, Woodrow Wilson, and Nobel Prize winners Niels Bohr and Baruj Benat Ceraf, among other eminent individuals, were all learning disabled. In addition, Brown, Dartmouth, and Harvard have become nationally visible in their sponsor-ship of an annual conference for invited representatives from other selec-tive institutions interested in meeting the needs of gifted college students with learning disabilities on their campuses (President and Fellows of Harvard University, 1990).

A second common misperception is that the learning disabled are unmotivated or lazy and, therefore, do not achieve to the level of their potential. In fact, this is not the case for most college students with LD who often work twice or three times as hard as their non-LD classmates to achieve the same goals. In fact, for some, taking longer to complete reading assignments, papers, and/or exams is a result of a slower rate of processing, one of their continuing information-processing deficits.

Causes of Learning Disabilities

The cause of learning disabilities is addressed in the NJCLD definition, based on preliminary research findings reported in the early 1980s. The definition states: "These disorders are . . . presumed to be due to central nervous system dysfunction . . ." The choice of the word "presumed" will, no doubt, require modification based on the anatomical abnormalities in the brains of dyslexics found by Galaburda at the Harvard Brain Research Laboratory, and based on the genetics of reading disabilities based on the twin studies of DeFries and his colleagues at the Colorado Institute of Behavioral Genetics and of Lubs at the University of Miami School of Medicine (Lubs et al., 1990, 1991).

Galaburda's research (1983; 1985; 1989; 1991) describes the presence of microscopic changes in the cortex (the outer layer) of the brain. These changes include poor organization; misplaced nests of cells in the outermost layer of the cortex, referred to as focal cortical dysgenesis; and the presence of deeper enfoldings in the cortex or polymicrogyria. Through his research and that of others using animal models, Galaburda determined that these changes occurred in fetal life within the first half of pregnancy. This finding is an important one because the earlier anomalies occur in brain development, the more likely it is that higher level language functioning will be affected (see Duane & Gray, 1991 for an in-depth review).

A second major area of Galaburda's investigations is the study of the two halves (or hemispheres) of the brain and of the anatomic asymmetries and symmetries in the language area of the brain that may relate to the linguistic (oral language, reading, and writing) deficits of dyslexics. Galaburda found symmetry in 100% of the dyslexic subjects studied in an important language area in the cerebral cortex, the planum temporale. In contrast, symmetry is present in about 16% to 25% of nonaffected individuals. This finding was confirmed by Larsen, Høien, Lundberg, and Ødegaard (1990), who used magnetic resonance imaging (MRI) techniques, and found symmetry in 70% of dyslexic children as compared to 30% of the controls in a study in Norway.

The second body of research that has helped us understand the etiology of learning disabilities is the study of twins and their families by DeFries (1985); DeFries and Fulker (1985 & 1988); DeFries, Fulker, and LaBuda (1987); DeFries and Gillis (1991); and Smith, Kimberling, Pennington, and Lubs (1983). Through these twin studies involving complex analyses (i.e., segregation and linkage analysis), researchers have been able to identify heritable familial factors in 25% to 50% of those with a reading disability. In those families with three generations of affected individuals, the chromosomes that have been implicated to date are 6 and 15.

Confirmation and new information will inevitably result from research, still at an explorative stage, on wakeful children and adults with reading disorders. It includes electrophysiologic studies using neurometrics and event-related potentials and MRI and brain electrical area mapping (BEAM) studies. The 1990s, referred to as the "Decade of the Brain," may in reality transform our understanding of the way the brain of those with learning disabilities develops, why it develops differently, and eventually of the functional correlates of these anomalies.

Incidence of Learning Disabilities in Adults in Postsecondary Settings

We have witnessed in the 1980s a dramatic increase in the number of students with learning disabilities attending colleges and universities. According to the Higher Education and Adult Training for People with

Handicaps (HEATH) Resource Center of the American Council on Education (ACE), the proportion of first-time, full-time freshmen with disabilities attending college increased threefold between 1978 and 1985, from 2.6% in 1978 to 7.4% in 1985, for example (Astin, Green, Korn, Schalit, & Berz, 1988). Among the 2.6% in 1978, 4.7% reported having a learning disability as compared with 14.3% in 1985.

In 1986, the U.S. Department of Education's National Center for Education Statistics began collecting and analyzing data on all handicapped students (both full-time and part-time) enrolled in two-year or four-year colleges, graduate schools, and doctoral degree-granting postsecondary institutions (U.S. Department of Education, 1987). Because the U.S. Department of Education did not limit the sample to full-time, first-time freshmen, the data are not completely comparable with that reported by ACE. However, some interesting information and patterns emerged. For example, 10½%, or 1.3 million out of 12.5 million students in post-secondary institutions (PSIs), reported having one or more disabilities. Of that number, 12.2% (approximately 160,000) reported having a specific learning disability, 39% had a visual handicap, 20% were hard of hearing, and 17.6% had an orthopedic handicap. These data highlight the trend in the 1980s for the sensorially and motorically impaired to report their disabilities in much larger numbers than the learning disabled.

In contrast, in the late 1980s, a shift in the proportion of students with learning disabilities as compared to other groups of disabled students requesting services occurred. In the 1989–1990 academic year in the greater Washington, DC, area, service providers in public and private highly selective universities as well as community colleges reported being overwhelmed by the number of students with LD requesting services. Approximately half of the students registered in the Disabled Student Services (DSS) office had a diagnosed learning disability (W. Scales, Personal Communication, 1990).

A second trend reported in the 1987 data provided by the U.S. Department of Education is that a larger number of students with disabilities are attending two-year colleges as compared to doctoral degree-granting institutions and graduate and professional schools. At two-year institutions, 11.8% of the student body reported having one or more handicaps; at four-year schools, 10.8%; at the graduate-school level, 8.4%; and in professional schools, 7.3% reported having one or more disabilities. In a survey of graduate and professional school administrators, Parks, Antonoff, Drake, Skiba, and Soberman (1987) found that many graduate-school administrators were less responsive to the needs of the handicapped, especially the learning disabled, than undergraduate-school administrators. There are signs that this trend also may begin to reverse itself in the 1990s as pressure from advocates and students with learning disabilities who are attending graduate school is brought to bear. For example, entrance examinations to medical and law schools, the medical boards, and the bar exam are now available in a format with modified examination procedures for individuals with LDs (Guyer, 1988). A new handbook (Adelman & Wren, 1990) in the series by Wren and her colleagues (Wren, Adelman, Pike, & Wilson, 1987; Wren & Segal, 1985) is addressed to students with LD attending graduate school.

The Law and the Learning Disabled

The significant increase in the number of students with learning disabilities attending postsecondary institutions has been the result of various pressures, not least among them the passage of Public Law 93–112 of The Rehabilitation Act of 1973; and, in particular, The Rehabilitation Act Regulations, Section 504, Subpart E (34 C.F.R., part 104).

As a result of Section 504, qualified handicapped students, including the learning disabled, were guaranteed that they would not be subjected to discrimination in admissions solely on the basis of their handicap. Neither would they be denied the opportunity to participate in programs receiving federal funds. Section 504, though brief, played a significant role in the 1980s in providing previously unavailable opportunities for higher education to the learning disabled.

A comprehensive review of Section 504 and of the legal issues relating to college students with learning disabilities can be found in Chapter II, by Laura Rothstein. This chapter and current practices that have evolved in the 1980s address the questions that follow from the perspective of admissions officers, faculty, and administrators.

Admissions Concerns and Questions

1) When students disclose in the admissions process that they have a learning disability, what should be the response?

First, if there is personal contact with the applicant, the student should be thanked because this openness has given admissions staff the opportunity to interpret the applicant's information more accurately. Second, supplementary information, such as documentation from previous evaluations, should be requested.

2) How can non-LD specialists be expected to understand psychoeducational diagnostic reports?

They should not be expected to interpret technical reports. Specialists with expertise in learning disabilities can be enlisted to review and interpret diagnostic reports for the admissions staff and to assist in the decision-making process.

3) Should admissions test results be interpreted the same way for non-LD and LD applicants?

Because commonly used admissions tests such as the Scholastic Aptitude Test (SAT), American College Testing Program (ACT), and Law School Admissions Test (LSAT) may unduly reflect the handicapped individual's disability, Section 504 mandates that universities accept scores from tests administered under nonstandardized procedures. Test results should be examined to determine if nonstandardized administration procedures were used. If so, questioning the applicant about the specific modifications provided would be a good indication of those needed for exams.

Admissions staff should look for and expect unevenness in subtest scores (e.g., Verbal higher than Quantitative on the SAT or vice versa) and note if the student's highest subtest scores are within the range of scores for successful applicants on their campus. Because predictive validity of such test results is presently unknown, low scores should be interpreted cautiously and supplementary information such as portfolios, albums, tape recordings, videotapes, newspaper clippings, and so on that are indicative of special talents should be requested. Each institution has to determine how to interpret and weight the standard and supplementary information provided in the application process. (See Chapter V on the continuum concept for an in-depth description of some universities' alternative responses.)

4) Must all students with learning disabilities be accepted to the institution once they self-disclose?

No. Only qualified applicants should be accepted. "Qualified" refers to a handicapped person who meets the "academic and technical standards" required for admission or participation in an educational program or activity. The intent of Section 504, therefore, has been to ensure that handicapped individuals are not denied admission solely on the basis of their disability while at the same time ensuring program integrity.

5) Can a limit be set on the number of students with learning disabilities who are accepted into the institution?

No. Section 504 mandates that an institution may not limit the number of or proportion of qualified handicapped students who are accepted to the institution. However, if the students are not "qualified" and are accepted into a special program, these regulations do not apply.

6) How can we be sure that students with learning disabilities will be successful on a specific campus?

Predicting success is difficult for non-LD students and even more so for students with learning disabilities. To aid in this process, institutions should track self-identified students with learning disabilities on their campus and develop profiles of those who have been successful (i.e., who graduated or maintained a strong GPA), as well as of those who have not, to enable a more accurate interpretation of the information presented in the admissions process. Until such profiles are readily available, descriptive follow-up studies may be helpful (Adelman & Vogel, 1990; Adelman & Vogel, 1991; Vogel & Adelman, 1990a; Vogel & Adelman, 1990b).

Administrators' Concerns and Questions

From the administrators' point of view, the questions most frequently asked are:

1) Are any institutions or programs within an institution exempted from Section 504?

No. All institutions, programs, and activities are to be accessible to individuals with learning disabilities.

2) How should institutions disseminate information about available services?

In order to assist administrators, faculty, advisors, staff, and students in locating available services, institutions should have a university "map" which identifies available services and their location, and service providers' names, offices, and phone numbers. This information could be incorporated into university publications including those for new students, the academic handbook, the student newspaper, new student orientation packets, and so on. Some institutions have also published separate booklets or brochures on services for students with learning disabilities (for example, the Office of Disabled Student Services at Harvard University, Marshall University, or Davis and Elkins College).

3) Academic issues and concerns about the curriculum are often raised. They include:

a) How should an institution respond to a request to change the time limits to complete a degree for students with learning disabilities?

Institutions have had to alter the requirement for full-time study for some students with disabilities. This provision for undergraduates has not presented as much of a challenge as it has in completion of professional degrees in the fields of law and medicine. Creative solutions, however, have been devised in dentistry (Parks, Antonoff, Drake, Oliver, Sedita, Weiss, & Daddi, 1982).

b) How should institutions respond to requests for a modification of major or degree requirements such as course(s), competencies, or experiences?

Modifications, substitutions, or waivers of major or degree requirements may be necessary to meet the needs of some students with learning disabilities. Modifications are determined on a case-by-case basis and are granted after considering the type and severity of learning disability, the student's specific needs, program of studies, experiences, and attempts or past failure to meet the requirements. However, procedural guidelines for students and administrative procedures for processing requested modifications have to be developed. Institutions should not only develop but also publish and publicize policies describing the petition process for students who request modifications.

Students with learning disabilities frequently request a modification of the university's foreign language requirement. A commonly provided modification to this requirement is to substitute courses on foreign culture or literature in translation. In the institutions that have developed procedures, students must provide appropriate documentation and follow the prescribed time line (see Freed, 1987). Students are often also requested to provide documentation showing that they have made a sincere effort in the past to learn a foreign language (preferably in high school so that the student's college academic record is not compromised).

Students with learning disabilities may request and be provided with a modification to the list of required courses in the student's major except when the course is essential to the program of study. The most common modification is to substitute a course that accomplishes the same objectives as the one in which the student is experiencing difficulty. For example, the main objective of the statistics course usually is to enable students to read, interpret, and evaluate research in a specific field to study. In one university, a student majoring in social work was allowed to substitute for statistics a course on questionnaire construction and interview strategies, research procedures frequently used in that field. (See Scheiber & Talpers, 1987, 102.)

    c) Do accommodations and modifications ever involve watering down or changing course objectives for students with learning disabilities?

No. Mandated accommodations and individually determined modifications address modifying ways in which faculty provide information to the student with learning disabilities and the method used to evaluate student mastery and/or accomplishment of the course objectives.

4) Are there cocurricular implications that entail nonacademic modifications that institutions have made in response to Section 504?

Yes. Some students with learning disabilities need to take a part-time load, rather than full-time study, just as do students with neurological disorders such as multiple sclerosis. These students may also need housing in the "quiet" dormitory, a single room, or a carrel in the library, which may be difficult to obtain. The Dean of Students' office may become involved in making such accommodations.

Faculty Concerns and Questions

1) What aspects of Section 504 pertaining to students with learning disabilities are particularly relevant for faculty?

Faculty should know that no student can be excluded from any course, major, or program solely on the basis of a handicap. Moreover, modifications, substitutions, or waivers of a major or degree requirement may be necessary to meet the needs of some students with learning disabilities.

2) What academic adjustments or accommodations are mandated by Section 504 for students with learning disabilities?

It is generally accepted that Section 504 mandates accommodations defined as those measures that provide the individual with learning disabilities access to postsecondary programs or activities. There are two basic types of accommodations for the learning disabled that faculty can provide: (1) those that relate to teaching methods such as the way in which faculty provide information; and (2) those that relate to evaluation methods, that is, how faculty measure student mastery.

The academic adjustments described below, though they are designed for students with learning disabilities, are not "magical" or highly technical. Rather, they employ principles of the psychology of learning, and they have been found to be beneficial for all students.

Suggested teaching accommodations include:

a) Making the syllabus available four to six weeks before the beginning of class and, when possible, being available to discuss it with students considering taking the course.

b) Beginning lectures with a review of the previous lecture, an overview of topics to be covered that day, and/or an outline of the lecture.

c) Using the chalkboard or overhead projector to outline and summarize lecture material, being mindful of legibility and of the necessity to read aloud what is written.

d) Explaining technical language, specific terminology, or foreign words.

e) Emphasizing important points, main ideas, and key concepts orally in lecture and/or highlighting them with colored pens on the overhead.

f) Speaking distinctly and at a relaxed pace, pausing occasionally to respond to questions or for students to catch up in their note taking.

g) Noticing and responding to nonverbal signals of confusion or frustration.

h) Trying to diminish if not eliminate auditory and visual classroom distractions such as noise in the hallways or a flickering fluorescent light.

i) Leaving time for a question–answer period and/or discussion periodically and at the end of each lecture.

j) Trying to determine if students understand the material by asking volunteers to give an example, summary, or response to a question. Also note that students with learning disabilities ofren have difficulty reading aloud in spite of good silent reading comprehension. Calling only on students who volunteer to read aloud will avoid unnecessary embarrassment.

k) Providing periodic summaries during lecture emphasizing key concepts.
l) Giving assignments in writing as well as orally and being available for clarification.
m) Providing a suggested time line when making long-range assignments and suggesting appropriate checkpoints.
n) Being available during office hours for clarification of lecture material, assignments, and readings.
o) Selecting a textbook with a study guide, if available, offering question and answer sessions, review sessions, and quiz sections.
p) Helping students find study partners and organize study groups.
e) Providing study questions for exams that show the format that will be used as well as the content.
r) Asking the student who self-discloses how the instructor can facilitate his or her learning.
s) Discussing in private with the student suspected of having a learning disability, describing what was observed, and if appropriate, referring the student to available support services.

3) What is the most commonly provided testing or evaluation accommodation?

The most commonly provided testing accommodation (except when such an alteration would result in a modification to course objectives) is to allow extended time.

4) If a student with learning disabilities gets extra time, are not students without learning disabilities placed at a disadvantage?

Research has shown that giving extended time resulted in improved reading comprehension scores for the college students with learning disabilities whereas the non-LD students' scores showed no change in performance (Runyan, 1991). This research demonstrated that this modification reduced the effect of the learning disability on performance and improved the students' chances of entering the examination on an equal footing, just as does the concept of "handicap" in golf tournaments.

5) What other evaluation accommodations can be used?

The specific evaluation or testing accommodations provided will be determined on an individual basis after considering the student's type and severity of learning disability, the specific course content, and the course objectives to be measured. Suggested evaluation accommodations include:

a) Allowing a reader or a taped version of an objective exam.
b) Providing the exam in an alternate format if appropriate to subject matter (e.g., objective instead of essay or vice versa).
c) Allowing students to take exams in a separate room that is distraction free.
d) Allowing for oral, taped, or typed exams (using a word processor) instead of a written exam.

e) Allowing a student to clarify or rephrase a question in his or her own words as a comprehension check before answering an exam question.

f) Analyzing the process as well as the final solutions (as may be appropriate in solving math, chemistry, or physics problems).

g) Allowing alternative methods of demonstrating mastery of course objectives (e.g., a project, demonstration, oral presentation, research project, or paper).

h) Allowing students to use computational aids such as a multiplication table or simple calculator and various spelling aids such as a secretary's desk reference, Franklin Speller, a spell checker on a word processor, or a misspeller's dictionary during examinations.

i) Avoiding double negatives, unduly complex sentence structure, and embedding questions within questions in composing examinations.

j) Providing adequate scratch paper, lined paper, or a word processor to aid students with overly large, cramped, laborious, or illegible handwriting.

k) Providing alternatives to computer-scored answer sheets such as allowing students to indicate their answers directly on the examination.

l) Discounting spelling errors when determining a grade for written work done in class without spelling aids, unless this is one of the objectives of the course.

A Support Services Agenda for the 1990s

The following recommendations are made for the 1990s in order to enhance successful undergraduate, graduate, and professional school degree completion for students with learning disabilities:

1) Postsecondary planning and preparation should begin in high school and continue in college. During this process, an updated, in-depth assessment and one-on-one counseling should be provided to help students understand their learning disability, strengths and affected areas, ways they learn best, ways teachers can help them learn, and ways to compensate. While in high school, LD students should also learn about Section 504, accommodations, and services commonly provided in postsecondary settings, and how to access them. (For an in-depth discussion on this subject, see Chapter III by Sara Cowen.)

2) Institutions should have a university "map" that identifies available services and their location, and service providers' names, offices, and phone numbers.

3) Institutions should have written, well-publicized petitioning procedures for students who need some university policies and/or require-

ments, such as a foreign language requirement, to be modified. (See Chapter XII by Leonore Ganschow and Richard Sparks.)

4) At the beginning of each semester, faculty and staff workshops, films, videotapes, speakers, student panels, and printed materials about learning disabilities should be provided. (See Chapter VII by Ernest Rose).

5) Information about services for students with disabilities should be included in the orientation held for new students at the beginning of each semester. (See Chapter IV by Connie Dalke.)

6) A drop-in center staffed by LD specialists; subject-matter tutors; reading, writing, and math teachers; and word-processing instructors should be open whenever the library is open, with staff increased during peak times.

7) A faculty mentoring program for students with learning disabilities should be instituted to provide guidance and encouragement to students with LD throughout their degree program.

8) Job shadowing and internship experiences should be provided to allow students to test their hypotheses about career choices and determine if and how their learning disability may interfere with performance.

9) Assistance in the job-application process, résumé writing, and interviewing techniques should be available. The instructor should have special understanding of the impact of learning disabilities on these tasks.

A Research Agenda for the 1990s

A comprehensive, prospective research program, integral to the LD support services, should be designed. Research should occupy a critical role in providing a mechanism for ongoing program development and refinement as well as in contributing to the overall knowledge and understanding of learning disabilities in adults. The provision of support services to learning disabled students offers a unique opportunity to acquire new information about learning disabilities in adults. Out of more than 100 articles about LD adults published in the 1970s and 1980s, less than one-third were data-based (Hughes & Osgood-Smith, 1990). In a recent review of those studies pertaining to college students with learning disabilities, they found that 13 studies reported on cognitive abilities; 10 on reading and math abilities; 8 on written expressive language; and 5 addressed foreign language learning difficulties. However, none of the studies examined intervention effectiveness. Relatively few data-based studies have been conducted on gender differences in this population (see Vogel & Walsh, 1987) or on social-emotional functioning (see Saracoglu, Minden, & Wilchesky, 1989).

Some Research Questions to Address in the 1990s

1) How many students with learning disabilities who enter postsecondary schools complete a certification/licensing program, associate, undergraduate, graduate, or professional school degree compared to their nondisabled peers? How many fail? What are the risk and resilience factors that contribute to their success or failure?
2) What services and accommodations are the most effective in enhancing the chance of successful outcomes?
3) How knowledgeable are faculty, administration, and staff about learning disabilities? How best can information be provided to them?
4) How willing are faculty to provide accommodations? How can negative attitudes be changed?
5) How can effective planning take place in postsecondary settings to best assist individuals with learning disabilities to make appropriate career decisions and to ensure a smooth transition to successful employment? What are the employment attainments and career paths of adults with learning disabilities who complete a postsecondary degree?
6) Do problems in social-emotional functioning and self-esteem persist into adulthood and, if so, how are they manifested? What intervention has been effective in ameliorating these difficulties?
7) What effect, if any, does postsecondary degree completion have on cognitive abilities, academic achievement, social-emotional functioning, employment, and life satisfaction?

In order to address these and other questions in a systematic way, a prospective research program should be designed based on collaborative efforts involving faculty from departments such as special education, English, math, research and evaluation, psychology, and counseling. The Office of Disabled Students should be an integral participant in this research. Such an effort could provide this office with important input for program evaluation as well as assist other offices dealing with student advisement, retention, graduate follow-up, and affirmative action. Essential in this prospective study is the availability of a comparison group and the collection of consistent data at entrance, annually, and at exit. For this purpose, each student with learning disabilities could be paired at entrance with a similar nondisabled peer matched according to gender, age, ethnicity, socioeconomic status (SES), and year in school at entrance.

An identical or partial battery could be administered to a control group randomly selected from the nondisabled peers. In addition, the groups should be compared on entrance examination test scores, high-school preparation and performance, and college performance (Vogel & Adelman, 1990a; Vogel & Adelman, 1990b). The importance of a control, or comparison, group is central in understanding and interpreting findings. The following recommendations are made for those planning descriptive, longitudinal, and/or follow-up studies of adults with learning disabilities in postsecondary settings:

1) The definition, criteria for determining the presence of a learning disability, and eligibility criteria for the specific setting should be carefully determined and described.

2) If not all students with learning disabilities registered with the DSS office were included in the sample, the selection criteria should be specified (e.g., no known brain damage, hearing loss, primary emotional disorder, uncorrected visual impairments, or language other than English spoken in the home).

3) Demographic information should be provided and used in interpreting the findings in light of previous studies regarding the importance of age at first evaluation, retesting, or follow-up, gender, and socio-economic status.

4) Intellectual functioning, language abilities, as well as aptitude-achievement discrepancy in the sample should be described as an indication of the severity of the learning disability considering the fact that severity has been found to be one of several important variables influencing educational, occupational, and academic achievement levels in adulthood. The methods of quantification of severity should also be described as well as the rationale for the selection of a specific model.

5) The etiology of the learning disability can have a significant impact on later achievement. Individuals whose learning disability is the result of known trauma to the brain comprise a distinct subgroup within the learning disability population and should be provided with different services and accommodations and studied as a comparison group.

6) Longitudinal and follow-up studies should be conducted to determine outcomes, program effectiveness, and factors contributing to success. In these studies, researchers should determine whether or not the resultant sample has the same characteristics as the original sample as well as the reasons for nonparticipation. In the discussion of findings, researchers can then provide documentation on whether the reasons for subject withdrawal have biased the results of the study.

7) Selection of reliable and valid instrumentation appropriate to adults with learning disabilities is an important factor in designing the research program. Recently, several measures have been revised, and they include adults at various educational attainment levels in the standardization sample. However, use of informal measures may be required to supplement the available diagnostic tests.

By making a research program an integral part of support services on every campus, new information about learning disabilities will be acquired that will enhance our understanding of learning disabilities, and, more importantly, enhance the effectiveness of intervention on academic success, employment attainments, life adjustment, and satisfaction.

References

Adelman, P.B., & Vogel, S.A. (1990). College graduates with learning disabilities—Employment attainment and career patterns. *Learning Disability Quarterly*, *13*(3), 154–166.

Adelman, P.B., & Vogel, S.A. (1991). The learning disabled adult. In B. Wong (Ed.), *Learning about learning disabilities*, (pp. 564–594). New York: Academic Press.

Adelman, P.B., & Wren, C.T. (Eds.). (1990). *Learning disabilities, graduate school, and careers: The student's perspective*. Lake Forest IL: Barat College.

Astin, A., Green, K., Korn, W., Schalit, M., & Berz, E. (1988). *The American freshman: National norms for 1988*. Los Angeles: University of California.

Board of Directors Association for Children and Adults with Learning Disabilities ACLD (1985). Definition of the condition of specific learning disabilities, *Newsbriefs*, *153*, 1–3.

Dalke, C. (1988). Woodcock-Johnson psycho-educational test battery profiles: A comparative study of college freshmen with and without learning disabilities. *Journal of Learning Disabilities*, *21*(9), 567–570.

DeFries, J.C. (1985). Colorado reading project. In D.B. Gray & J.F. Kavanaugh (Eds.), *Behavioral Measures of Dyslexia*, (pp. 107–122). Parkton, MD: York Press.

DeFries, J.C., & Fulker, D.W. (1985). Multiple regression analysis of twin data. *Behavior Genetics*, *15*, 467–473.

DeFries, J.C., & Fulker, D.W. (1988). Multiple regression analysis of twin data: Etiology of deviant scores versus individual differences. *Acta Geneticae Medicae et Gemellologiae: Twin Research*, *37*, 205–216.

DeFries, J.C., Fulker, D.W., & LaBuda, M.C. (1987). Evidence for a genetic etiology in reading disability in twins. *Nature*, *329*, 537–539.

DeFries, J.C., & Gillis, J.J. (1991). Etiology of reading deficits in learning disabilities: Quantitative genetic analysis. In J.E. Obrzut & G.W. Hynd (Eds.), *Advances in the neuropsychology of learning disabilities: Issues, methods and practice* (pp. 29–47). Orlando, FL: Academic Press.

Duane, D.D., & Gray, D.B. (Eds.). (1991). *The reading brain: The biological basis of dyslexia*. Parkton, MD: York Press.

Federal Register (August 23, 1977). *Education of handicapped children: Implementation of part B of the Education of the Handicapped Act. Federal Register, Part II*. Washington, DC: U.S. Office of Education; U.S. Department of Health, Education, and Welfare.

Freed, B. (1987). Exemptions from the foreign language requirement: A review of recent literature, problems, and policy. *Association of Departments of Foreign Language Bulletin*, *18*(2), 13–17.

Gajar, A., Salvia, J., Gajria, M., & Salvia, S. (1989). A comparison of intelligence achievement discrepancies between learning disabled and non-learning disabled college students. *Learning Disabilities Research*, *4*(2), 119–124.

Galaburda, A.M. (1983). Developmental dyslexia: Current anatomical research. *Annals of Dyslexia*, *33*, 41–55.

Galaburda, A.M. (1985). Developmental dyslexia: A review of biological interactions. *Annals of Dyslexia*, *35*, 21–33.

Galaburda, A.M. (1989). Ordinary and extraordinary brain development: Anatomical variation in developmental dyslexia. *Annals of Dyslexia*, *39*, 67–80.

Galaburda, A.M. (1991). Anatomy of dyslexia: Argument against phrenology. In D.D. Duane & D.B. Gray (Eds.), *The reading brain: The biological basis of dyslexia* (pp. 119–131). Parkton, MD: York Press.

Guyer, B. (1988). Dyslexic doctors: A resource in need of discovery. *Southern Medical Journal*, *81*(9), 1151–1154.

Hammill, D.D. (1990). Defining learning disabilities: The emerging consensus. *Journal of Learning Disabilities*, *23*, 74–84.

Hammill, D.D., Leigh, J., McNutt, G., & Larsen, S.C. (1981). A new definition of learning disabilities. *Learning Disability Quarterly*, *4*, 336–342.

Houck, C.K., Engelhard, J., & Geller, C. (1989). Self-assessment of learning disabled and nondisabled college students: A comparative study. *Learning Disabilities Research*, *5*(1), 61–67.

Hughes, C.A., & Osgood-Smith, J. (1990). Cognitive and academic performance of college students with learning disabilities: A synthesis of the literature. *Learning Disability Quarterly*, *13*(1), 66–79.

Johnson, D., & Blalock, J. (Eds.). (1987). *Adults with learning disabilities*. Orlando, FL: Grune & Stratton.

Larsen, J.P., Høien, T., Lundberg, I., & Ødegaard, H. (1990). MRI evaluation of the size and symmetry of the planum temporale in adolescents with developmental dyslexia. *Brain and Language*, *39*, 289–301.

Leonard, F.C. (1991). Using Wechsler Data to predict success for learning disabled college students. *Learning Disabilities Research and Practice*, *6*(1), 17–24.

Lubs, H.A., Duara, R., Levin, B., Jallad, B., Lubs, M.L., Rabin, M., Kushch, A., & Gross-Glenn, K. (1991). Dyslexia subtypes: Genetics, behavior, and brain imaging. In D.D. Duane & D.B. Gray (Eds.), *The reading brain: The biological basis of dyslexia* (pp. 89–117). Parkton, MD: York Press.

Lubs, H.A., Rabin, M., Carland-Saucier, K., Wen, X.L., Gross-Glenn, K., Duara, R., Levin, B., & Lubs, M.L. (1990). Genetic bases of developmental dyslexia: Molecular studies. In J. Obrzut & G. Hynd, (Eds.). *Neuropsychological Foundations of Learning Disabilities: A Handbook of Issues, Methods and Practice*. Orlando, FL: Academic Press, Inc.

National Advisory Committee on Handicapped Children. (1968). *Subcommittee on education of the committee on labor and public welfare: First annual report*. Washington, DC: U.S. Government Printing Office.

National Joint Committee on Learning Disabilities. (1981). *Learning disabilities: Issues on definition*. Unpublished manuscript. (Reprinted in *Journal of Learning Disabilities*, *20*, 107–108, 1987.)

Parks, A.W., Antonoff, S.. Drake, C., Oliver, C., Sedita, J., Weiss, I., & Daddi, B. (1982). Screening for specific learning disabilities among dental students. *Journal of Dental Education*, *46*, 586–591.

Parks, A.W., Antonoff, S., Drake C., Skiba, W.F., & Soberman, J. (1987). A survey of programs and services for students with learning disabilities in graduate and professional schools. *Journal of Learning Disabilities*, *20*, 181–188.

President and Fellows of Harvard University. (1990). *The next step: An invitational symposium on learning disabilities in selective colleges* (Proceedings). Cambridge, MA: Author.

The Rehabilitation Act of 1973, §504, 29 U.S.C. §794 (1977).

The Rehabilitation Act Regulations, 34 C.F.R. part 104.

Runyan, M.K. (1991). The effect of extra time on reading comprehension scores for university students with and without learning disabilities. *Journal of Learning Disabilities*, *24*(2), 104–108.

Saracoglu, B., Minden, H., & Wilchesky, M. (1989). The adjustment of students with learning disabilities to university and its relationship to self-esteem and self-efficacy. *Journal of Learning Disabilities*, *22*(9), 590–592.

Scheiber, B., & Talpers, J. (1987). *Unlocking Potential: College and other choices for learning disabled people—a step-by-step guide*. Bethesda, MD: Adler & Adler.

Shaywitz, S.E., & Shaw, R. (1988). The admissions process: An approach to selecting learning disabled students at the most selective colleges. *Learning Disabilities Focus*, *3*(2), 81–86.

Smith, S.D., Kimberling, W.S., Pennington, B.F., & Lubs, M.A. (1983). Specific reading disability: Identification of an inherited form through linkage analysis. *Science*, *219*, 1345–1347.

U.S. Department of Education. (1987). *Profile of handicapped students in postsecondary education*. National Center for Education Statistics, 1987 National Postsecondary Student Aid Study (Report No. 065-000-00375-9). Washington, DC: U.S. Government Printing Office.

Vogel, S.A. (1986). Levels and patterns of intellectual functioning among LD college students: Clinical and educational implications. *Journal of Learning Disabilities*, *19*, 71–79.

Vogel, S.A. (1987). Issues and concerns in LD college programming. In D. Johnson & J. Blalock (Eds.), *Adults with learning disabilities: Clinical studies* (pp. 239–275). Orlando, FL: Grune and Stratton.

Vogel, S.A., & Adelman, P.B. (1990a). Extrinsic and intrinsic factors in graduation and academic failure among LD college students. *Annals of Dyslexia* (Orton Dyslexia Society), *40*, 119–137.

Vogel, S.A., & Adelman, P.B. (1990b). Intervention effectiveness at the postsecondary level for the learning disabled. In T. Scruggs & B. Wong (Eds.), *Intervention research in learning disabilities* (pp. 329–344). New York: Springer-Verlag.

Vogel, S.A., & Walsh, P.C. (1987). Gender differences in cognitive abilities in learning disabled females and males. *Annals of Dyslexia* (Orton Dyslexia Society), *371*, 142–165.

Wren, C.T., & Segal, L. (1985). *College students with learning disabilities: A student's perspective*. Chicago: DePaul University.

Wren, C.T., Adelman, P.B., Pike, M.B., & Wilson, J.L. (1987). *College and the high school student with learning disabilities*. Chicago: DePaul University.

II
Legal Issues

Laura F. Rothstein

Introduction

The late 1980s brought a dramatic increase in the number of students with disabilities on college campuses, particularly students with learning disabilities. This increase was predictable because the Education for All Handicapped Children Act of 1975 had been in effect for long enough that a large population of students had gone through public education having been identified and provided with special education.

What has also been predictable is the increase in litigation and awareness of the legal requirements with respect to college students with disabilities. Whereas the major relevant law—Section 504 of the Rehabilitation Act of 1973—and the implementing regulations have been in place for over a decade, there was little litigation in this area until the late 1980s. There are probably two major reasons for the increase in litigation. First, students with disabilities now reaching college age, who have gone through the public schools receiving services, are accustomed to procedural safeguards and to using the legal system to receive protection. Second, the increased awareness of disability rights issues brought by the passage of the Americans with Disabilities Act (ADA) in 1990 has led to a greater willingness to use the legal system to enforce rights.

There have not been many legal developments relating to college students and learning disabilities (LDs) specifically, but the legal requirements and the interpretations of the law relating to individuals with

A complete overview of the legal requirements relating to higher education and individuals with disabilities can be found in L. Rothstein, *Disabilities and the Law*, Chapter 7 (Shepard's/McGraw-Hill, 1992 and cumulative supplements). The material contained in the chapter of Programming for Success for College Students with Disabilities is adapted from material included in *The Next Step: An Invitational Symposium on Learning Disabilities in Selective Colleges, Proceedings*, November 17, 1989, Cosponsored by Barnard, Dartmouth, Harvard, and Wellesley Colleges. Permission to adapt is gratefully acknowledged.

disabilities can provide general legal guidance. As this is a developing area of law, it is difficult to define with absolute certainty what the law requires. This chapter, however, provides as much guidance as is possible at this time.

Legal Overview

Four sources of law are relevant to the rights of college students with LDs and to the obligations of colleges toward them. These are the U.S. Constitution, statutes, regulations, and judicial interpretation of the Constitution, statutes, and regulations.

United States Constitution

The U.S. Constitution is not the primary authority of relevance in this area. The Fourteenth Amendment of the Constitution would be relevant in situations where a state or state agency (such as a state college or university) treats individuals in a discriminatory manner without a good justification. The test that courts would apply in evaluating whether a student with LDs or applicant had been treated unfairly by a college would be what is known as the *rational basis test* (*San Antonio v. Rodriguez*, 1973). This would mean that substantial deference would be given to the college's decision making. For example, whereas requiring a certain level of academic achievement for admission to a college may have an adverse impact on students with LDs, if the college can show that there is a rational basis for the requirement, the courts will probably defer to that decision.

Statutes

Of much greater significance are statutes, primarily two federal statutes. Section 504 of the Rehabilitation Act of 1973 prohibits recipients of federal financial assistance (such as colleges) from discriminating on the basis of handicaps (including learning disabilities). The Americans with Disabilities Act of 1990 provides for broader coverage. Not only are recipients of federal financial assistance prohibited from discriminating, but providers of public services and accommodations and virtually all employers will also be required not to discriminate on the basis of disability. In reality, the ADA adds little to the legal requirements affecting college students with LDs. Its passage, however, is a factor in the increased awareness of these issues in general. Some states may have legal requirements that would apply to students with LDs, but the major impact is from the Rehabilitation Act.

Regulations

Section 504 of the Rehabilitation Act is fairly minimalist in its language. The details of its requirements are spelled out in the model regulations that were promulgated by the Department of Health, Education, and Welfare in 1977 (Rehabilitation Act Regulations, 1977). It is in the regulations under a special section devoted to postsecondary education that one can find more specifically what colleges are required to do to assist students with disabilities (Rehabilitation Act Regulations, subpart 104, 41–47).

Judicial Interpretation

Neither statutes nor regulations can provide complete guidance as to what is required in a given situation. The courts are the forum for interpreting what statutes and regulations require. They use legislative history, other similar laws, and the language of the statutes and regulations themselves to provide insight as to what is required in a particular circumstance. Although their rulings are limited to the controversy before them, the general commentary included in judicial opinions (known as *dicta*) is often an indication of how courts will decide other controversies on related issues or with similar factual backgrounds.

With this general overview as background, a more extensive review of the requirements of Section 504 of the Rehabilitation Act and of the ADA can be provided.

Section 504 of the Rehabilitation Act: The Statute, the Regulations, and the Judicial Interpretations

Section 504 of the Rehabilitation Act provides that otherwise qualified individuals with handicaps may not be discriminated against by recipients of federal financial assistance (Rehabilitation Act, 1973). Virtually all colleges are recipients of federal financial assistance in some department or other. A 1987 amendment to the Rehabilitation Act (Civil Rights Restoration Act, 1987) clarified the definition of assistance, stating that if any part of a program or activity receives federal financial assistance, then all the operations of the program are subject to Section 504.

The second issue of relevance is whether the individual is handicapped according to the statute. The statute defines a handicapped individual as one who has an impairment that substantially limits one or more major life activities, has a record of such an impairment, or is regarded as having such an impairment (Rehabilitation Act of 1973, §706(7)(B)). Under Section 504 regulations, learning disabilities are included as a category of impairment (Rehabilitation Act Regulations, §104.3(j)(2)(i)).

The individual must be qualified to perform the essential requirements of the program "in spite of" the handicap (*Southeastern Community College v. Davis*, 1979). The regulations state that for postsecondary and vocational education services, a qualified handicapped person is one who meets the academic and technical standards required for admission or participation in the program or activity (Rehabilitation Act Regulations, §104.3(k)(3)). Although Section 504 requires "reasonable accommodation," it does not require any fundamental alteration to the nature of the program (*Southeastern Community College v. Davis*, 1979, p. 410). Whether accommodations *must* be provided in a particular situation will be decided on a case-by-case basis. It should also be noted that the law does not require that accommodations and services be provided to students for their personal use.

Undue Hardship

In determining whether a particular accommodation is reasonable, judicial interpretations have recognized two major defenses for refusing to provide particular accommodations. First, if a college can demonstrate that it would be unduly burdensome, either financially or administratively, to provide a particular accommodation, the college may refuse to do so (*United States v. Board of Trustees of the University of Alabama*, 1990). Relevant factors in assessing the cost issue will include the overall size of the program and the type of operation. Colleges may be reluctant to raise this defense because for political reasons they may not wish to have their overall budget examined by the courts. It is important to recognize that financial hardship is not the only consideration. If, for example, a college could demonstrate the administrative hardship of providing certain accommodations, it might be exempt from doing so.

Safety

The second major defense is that of safety. If safety concerns are genuine, the college will usually be successful in raising them (*Doe v. New York University*, 1981). This is particularly true for medical programs such as nursing, medical school, optometry, and so on. For example, courts will probably be less likely to second-guess a requirement in pharmacy school that students be able to do certain mathematical computations in order to prescribe medication appropriately.

Admissions

The previous material focused on some general legal standards. There are within the Section 504 regulations several requirements of particular relevance to students with LDs. These include issues relating to admissions and recruitment and academic adjustments (Rehabilitation Act Regulations, 1977, §104.42). Of relevance in the admissions area is the prohibition against using tests or criteria for admission that have disproportionate, adverse impact on individuals with a disability or a particular type of disability unless these tests have been validated as a predictor of success and alternate tests are not available. In addition admissions tests must reflect the applicant's relevant abilities. It is also prohibited to make preadmissions inquiries about a disability unless such an inquiry is intended to correct past discrimination. The response must clearly be optional. Validity may be based on first-year grades, but periodic validity studies should be made to relate to overall success.

As a response to the admissions requirements of the Section 504 regulations, virtually all of the major higher education testing services have evaluated whether accommodations in the testing procedure could be made. As a result of these evaluations, higher education admissions standardized tests are usually available with accommodations such as additional time, separate exams rooms, etc. Because of the testing services' concern about the validity of scores obtained under nonstandard conditions, the Department of Education adopted an interim policy in 1978 that permits testing services to "flag" the fact that a test was taken under nonstandard conditions (*Recruitment, Admissions, and Handicapped Students*, 1978). In effect this allows a college to make a preadmissions inquiry. In spite of this the Department of Education has not discontinued its interim flag policy. The major testing services have continued on an ongoing basis to monitor their practices relating to accommodating test takers and reporting their scores to the institutions of higher education.

The preadmissions inquiry restrictions within the regulations permit colleges to ask about a disability, so long as it is clear that the response is voluntary and that the purpose behind the inquiry is for remedial or voluntary action reasons. Information obtained is to be kept confidential. The applicant must be advised of this and of the fact that refusal to provide such information will not result in adverse action.

Academic Adjustments

The entire section of the regulations relating to academic adjustments is of relevance to students with LDs (Rehabilitation Act Regulations, 1977, §104.44). It provides that modifications such as changes in the length of time for degree completion, course substitution, and adaptation of the manner in which specific courses are conducted are modifications that should be made if necessary, unless the college can demonstrate that the requirement is essential to the program of instruction. For example, if a college could demonstrate that an ability to respond quickly in a debate class is an essential requirement, a student with LDs need not be given extra time to write down thoughts before responding. A law student who has an inability to process complex material need not have the exam questions simplified so as not to be so complex because what lawyers must do is to analyze and synthesize complex material.

Colleges must ensure that auxiliary aids such as taped texts are available to students with LDs. According to at least one judicial interpretation, whereas it is legitimate for the college to request that a student seek assistance for payment for auxiliary services through state vocational rehabilitation services and volunteer organizations before the college provides the services, colleges may not use financial need of the student as the basis for determining whether to provide the service (*United States v. Board of Trustees of the University of Alabama*, 1990). The college must demonstrate its own undue hardship instead. In this case, which involved services for students with disabilities at the University of Alabama, the court referred to the 1979 Supreme Court decision in *Southeastern Community College v. Davis*. The decision established that under Section 504, recipients of federal financial assistance are required to make only reasonable accommodations that do not cause "undue financial or administrative burdens" (*Southeastern Community College v. Davis*, 442 U.S. at 397).

Although neither the *University of Alabama* nor the *Davis* case provided extensive guidance as to what "undue burden" means, the ADA, which is to be interpreted similarly to the Rehabilitation Act, refers to several factors that are relevant in determining whether an undue hardship exists. These include the nature and cost of the accommodation, the overall financial resources of the program, the type of operation, and the impact on the operation of the program. Although these provisions are in the employment portion of the ADA, it is reasonable to expect that a similar interpretation would apply to a college setting. In the *University of Alabama* case the court held that the University could reasonably accommodate students needing accessible campus bus transportation when the cost was approximately $15,000 out of an annual university transportation budget of $1.2 million.

The academic adjustment portion of the regulations also refers to course examinations. Colleges must provide methods of evaluation of achievement that represent the student's achievement rather than reflecting the impairment, except where such skills are the factors that the test purports to measure (See Chapter 5 on evaluation modifications that can be made).

Participation

The regulations require that rules that limit participation of students with disabilities are not allowed. For example, a prohibition on the use of tape recorders would limit participation by some students with LDs. Whereas the instructor could require the student to sign a statement limiting the use of the tape recording to study purposes in order to protect the instructor's intellectual property, in most circumstances a complete prohibition would not be acceptable.

Career Counseling

Counseling students with LDs to restrictive career options is prohibited by the regulations (Rehabilitation Act Regulations, 1977, §104.46). Whereas it is permissible to inform individuals of the requirements of a profession and of the difficulties an individual with a learning disability might have in a particular career, it is not permissible to counsel the student away from an area of interest simply because of the learning disability.

Documentation

While the regulations do not make specific reference to the issue of documentation, the fact that a student must be otherwise qualified to perform the essential aspects of the program would seem to make it permissible for a college to require appropriate documentation of a disability when the student puts the disability at issue. When a student who claims to have a learning disability seeks special consideration in the admissions process or accommodations upon enrollment, it is legal for the college or a standardized testing service to request that the student provide documentation of the disability. While each college and testing service may have its own specific requirements, it would not be unreasonable for such a requirement to specify that the documentation be done by a professional, be relatively recent, and include specific tests. It is also permissible to expect that the student with LDs pay for the cost of such documentation. Although some students may have documentation from their public school years, and this may be acceptable for undergraduate education, it may well be viewed as unacceptable in a graduate or professional program. This is the case because the mental processes and effects can change significantly from childhood to adulthood. For that reason, it should be considered reasonable to require recent documentation (within the past three years, for example).

Litigation

There has been little case law directly relating to students with LDs that has interpreted the statutes and regulations. Only two cases involving college students with LDs have been resolved by the courts in reported decisions. That does not mean that there has not been other litigation, because other lawsuits may have been settled before court resolution.

One of the cases is *Salvador v. Bell*, 1986. In that case it was decided that a university does not violate the Rehabilitation Act when it does not know that an individual is learning disabled. The student claimed that he had not been admitted to college because of his learning disability. Because the college did not know of his learning disability, there could not have been any discrimination.

The second case raises some difficult questions that have not yet been fully resolved by the decision that was reached. In *Wynne v. Tufts University School of Medicine*, 1991, a medical student with LDs claimed that he had not been provided reasonable accommodation in the exam format because he failed a multiple choice exam several times. The federal circuit court held that he had stated a claim under the Rehabilitation Act. The court also held that if the medical school refuses to provide multiple choice tests in another format, it must demonstrate that it considered alterative means, their feasibility, cost, and effect. The refusal would be justified if it would lower academic standards or require substantial program alteration to provide the accommodation. In most instances a university will have to provide reasonable accommodations such as additional time, a reader, or similar accommodations. It is more difficult to determine whether it is reasonable to expect that a different test format be made available to a specific student. It is likely that there will be more cases addressing this type of issue.

An unresolved issue that relates to liability is whether the college is responsible when an instructor refuses to allow a reasonable accommodation. In a case that never resulted in a reported opinion, a math student whose instructor refused to allow additional time, although the handicapped student service office recommended it, sued both the instructor and the university (*Dinsmore v. University of California, Berkeley*, 1990). It seems that a university has an obligation to have a grievance procedure in place to ensure that conflicts between the disabled students service office and a faculty member are appropriately resolved. The failure to have such a system in place puts the college at risk of liability.

There are a number of other cases involving higher education and the Rehabilitation Act that indicate how the courts are likely to address certain issues relating to students with LDs. These cases, however, do not involve learning disabilities directly, but they are nonetheless relevant for interpreting the Rehabilitation Act of 1973 as it applies to colleges. In subsequent portions of this chapter, the statute, regulations, and case law interpretations will be applied to a number of frequently raised issues, but the previous discussion provides the current framework for such an application.

The Americans with Disabilities Act of 1990

The Americans with Disabilities Act of 1990 was passed because most services, programs, and employers were not covered by the Rehabilitation Act. The ADA in many respects mirrors the Rehabilitation Act, and it is clear that the courts will interpret the ADA using precedents set under the Rehabilitation Act. Because colleges were already subject to the Rehabilitation Act, the ADA adds little substantively to what they are required to do.

The one provision of the ADA that probably has the greatest specific impact on students with learning disabilities is Section 309 that provides that those parties offering examinations or courses relating to secondary or postsecondary education, professional, or trade purposes must offer them in a place and manner accessible to persons with disabilities or make alternative arrangements. This provision has been in effect since January, 1992. It also applies to standardized test services and licensing boards. It is not clear what is meant by accessible "manner." It may mean only that extra time, readers, or similar accommodations are required. What is not clear is whether an exam must be changed from a multiple-choice format or some other format to a different format in a given situation.

The fact that the Rehabilitation Act has already been in effect for so long and covers most major issues relating to colleges will probably mean that the ADA will not have major substantive impact on colleges.

State Laws

It is beyond the scope of this chapter to go into what the various states require relating to higher education and disabled students. Colleges and students with LDs, however, should be aware that some states mandate support services for students with disabilities, and these mandates may be an additional source of law that should be considered.

Legal Requirements:
Some Frequently Asked Questions

This section focuses on responses to legal questions frequently asked about college students with LDs. It is essential to remember that the responses are generally based on what the courts are *likely* to hold in a particular instance. Only when the Supreme Court, a statute, or regulation *specifically* addresses a question is the answer conclusive. Most of the questions raised below have not been specifically answered in this way, and therefore the likely outcomes are based on lower court cases, legislative history, *dicta* from relevant Supreme Court opinions, and Department of Education interpretations.

1) What learning disabilities will be considered handicaps or disabilities under the Rehabilitation Act and the Americans with Disabilities Act?

From kindergarten through twelfth grade there has been much controversy in public education about whether children with certain conditions should be considered learning disabled within the Education for All Handicapped Children Act of 1975. Debate about whether attention deficit disorder and other conditions should be included has not yet been resolved. Because of the increased awareness of learning disabilities as a handicap or disability entitling individuals to accommodations and special consideration, it is becoming increasingly important for colleges and related institutions such as testing services to determine when an individual is entitled to protection.

The Rehabilitation Act regulations do not separately define learning disabilities, although they are included as a handicap generally. By incorporating the requirement that a disability be one that substantially impairs a major life activity (such as learning), it is possible that the definition of the Education for All Handicapped Children Act of 1975 for learning disabilities could offer guidance. That definition provides coverage for individuals who have

. . . a disorder in one or more of the basic psychological processes involved in understanding or in using language, spoken or written, which may manifest itself in an imperfect ability to listen, think, speak, read, write, spell, or to do mathematical calculations. The term includes such conditions as perceptual handicaps, brain injury, minimal brain dysfunction, dyslexia, and developmental aphasia. (§1401(1))

Learning problems primarily the result of visual, hearing, or motor handicaps, mental retardation, emotional disturbance, or environmental, cultural, or economic disadvantage are not considered to be learning disabilities. There is no case holding that this definition can be incorporated into the Rehabilitation Act, but it provides at least a minimum inclusion of learning disabilities. Section 504 may be even broader in coverage if a certain learning disability is deemed to be a substantial limitation on a major life activity.

It should also be noted that the fact that an individual may have school records that indicate qualification for special education services under this definition during grade or high school does not necessarily mean that the same degree of impairment continues to exist. Just as motor or health or other impairments can change over time, so can learning disabilities. For that reason, it will be reasonable for a college to require recent documentation establishing that the individual currently has a learning disability. Refusal to provide consideration for an individual who is not thought to have a learning disability may result in a dispute through a grievance procedure or through the legal system. This is an area where little direct guidance is available from the courts.

2) Should a student with LDs self-identify in the admissions process?

College applicants with LDs face a dilemma when deciding whether to take an accommodated standardized admissions test (which may be flagged) or to self-identify through a personal statement or voluntary check-off on an application form. The learning disability may be a significant factor to explain why grades or the standardized test scores are not accurate predictors of the student's ability. Some colleges, however, may illegally discriminate against individuals who are known to have learning disabilities. They may do so because of lack of information about legal requirements, because they are concerned that they lack resources to provide accommodations, or simply because they are skeptical about whether a learning disability is a *real* handicap. Such illegal discrimination is very difficult to prove, and because of that the student who self-identifies takes a risk.

If the ability to perform well on a standardized test will be significantly impaired without taking an accommodated test, it is probably better to take the chance and allow the self-identification through flagging. In addition, if the learning disability is the basis for poor performance in some areas, the applicant will need to explain that to justify the poor performance.

If the college is one known to do a good job of providing accommodations to students with learning disabilities, the student may be well served to self-identify because the admissions office probably uses the expertise of the disabled student service office in its evaluation process.

Applicants may need to be reminded that colleges are not required to accept students who do not meet the academic standards or other requirements. Therefore, a college will not have to accept a student with a poor record simply because the student has a learning disability.

3) Are mandatory standardized tests permissible and what accommodations are provided for these tests?

A 1982 study criticized many standardized tests for admission to educational programs (*Ability Testing of Handicapped People*, 1982). Because of that study, virtually all of the standardized test services have provided testing with accommodations. Such accommodations vary from test to test, but they may include additional time, separate rooms, readers, or other accommodations appropriate to individuals with learning disabilities. The burden on the testing services, however, as a result of the increased number of individuals requesting accommodations is likely to create an increase in the documentation requirements. While the testing services are not themselves subject to the Rehabilitation Act, the fact that they serve colleges that are has caused the testing services to provide the accommodations that the college would probably be required to provide.

The college may require that the standardized test be taken if accommodations are available so as to eliminate any unfair, disproportionate, or adverse impact, and if the test has been validated as a predictor of overall success in the education program (Rehabilitation Act Regulations, 1977, §104.42(b) & (d)). The college, however, as a matter of good policy, should probably take into account other factors even when the validity study has been done.

4) Whose responsibility is it to identify a student as learning disabled?

A student with LDs who has self-identified in the admissions process should not assume that the college will automatically provide reasonable accommodations to the enrolled student. The individual within the college who is responsible for such accommodations may not have direct access to the information in the application relating to the disability. In addition, colleges are allowed to make preadmissions inquiries only for remedial purposes and only if the information is voluntarily provided. It is legal for a college to make a postadmissions inquiry about a disability, but colleges are not *required* to do so. For all these reasons, it is the obligation of students with LDs to take the initiative to self-identify after admission if they are seeking reasonable accommodations or modifications because of their learning disabilities.

Upon receiving a request for accommodation, it is reasonable for a college to require appropriate documentation of the disability, a reasonable amount of time to evaluate the documentation, and a reasonable amount of time to arrange for the accommodations. The student who, the day before the exam, requests arrangements for additional time on a final exam at the end of a semester probably does not have a strong case of discrimination when the college administrator refuses to make such arrangements.

A related situation is the student who is academically disqualified from a college but who did not request any accommodations and now seeks readmission on the basis that these should have been provided. If the student knew of the learning disability and of the probability that accommodations would be necessary and failed to request them, the college probably has no obligation to readmit the student. When the learning disability is unknown, what is legally required becomes less clear. If the college can demonstrate that the student would probably not have met the requirements even with accommodations, then refusal to readmit is legal. If the college cannot provide such proof, good policy would probably be for the college to allow a conditional or probationary readmission, although it is not clear that the college *must* do so within current legal requirements.

5) What accommodations will the college be required to make?

As noted previously, accommodations that are required in a given situation must be determined on a case-by-case basis, taking into account whether the accommodation is unduly burdensome financially or administratively and whether the requested accommodation involves a fundamental requirement of the program. Although the college has the responsibility of demonstrating an undue burden or a fundamental requirement will be on the college, courts have traditionally given colleges a great deal of deference on these issues.

The types of accommodation that should be considered include additional exam time, and other exam modifications such as readers and separate rooms, lightened courseloads, taped texts, and permission to tape-record classroom lectures and discussion. Substitution of coursework and waiver of some requirements should also be considered in appropriate cases. One area in which a number of students with LDs have difficulty is foreign languages. The college should consider allowing substitution of a foreign culture course, a computer language course, or even sign language, unless it can demonstrate that a foreign language is a fundamental aspect of the program. For an academic program for foreign service, a foreign language is probably fundamental. For a liberal arts degree it may be less important. If the student *wants* to complete a foreign language course and requests special tutoring, it is not clear what is legally mandated. Because the regulations do not require assistance for *personal* use, the issue here is to determine whether this type of assistance represents personal use. The college may have to demonstrate that it would be unduly burdensome to provide individual tutoring in such an instance; particularly when it is willing to allow a reasonable substitution or waiver, it may be deemed reasonable to deny individual tutoring.

Allowing students to use computers and word processors can raise difficult issues. If the word processor enables the student to use a spell check so as not to be unduly penalized for misspelling, then this option should be considered. Colleges may, however, have legitimate concerns about the difficulty of monitoring cheating because of the memory that could allow storage of information such as notes for an exam. The college will probably need to demonstrate that it is unduly burdensome to monitor computer-taken exams if it decides to deny this as an accommodation.

6) Can the college note that accommodations have been provided on a student's transcript?

Unless a college notes all accommodations for all students on transcripts, it clearly violates the Rehabilitation Act of 1973 because it would be discriminatory to note only accommodations provided to students with disabilities. Thus if allowing extra time or lightened courseloads, and so on is noted only on the transcripts of students with disabilities, that would be illegal. If the college notes all course work accommodations or waivers for all students, the situation is different.

7) What about noncooperative faculty?

If an appropriate administrative decision has been made to allow a particular student an accommodation such as additional time, the instructor who refuses to permit the accommodation on the basis of academic freedom nonetheless violates the Rehabilitation Act of 1973. While the instructor should be provided an opportunity to explain the reason for the refusal, the college that does not require the instructor to comply if it is determined that accommodation requirements outweigh the individual instructor's concerns is itself acting illegally (*Dinsmore v. University of California, Berkeley*).

While it is probably not appropriate to give an office for disabled student services unilateral authority to require accommodations, such an office should be given deference in the decision-making process. Colleges should implement procedures for deciding when accommodations should be required and grievance procedures to resolve disputes when accommodations cannot be agreed upon.

8) What level of confidentiality about a student's learning disability is required?

The Family Educational Rights and Privacy Act of 1974, popularly known as the Buckley Amendment, provides for protection of individual student records. Only the agency or institution maintaining the records may have access to them, and the information should be made available only to those who need to know. Unfortunately, in higher education there is little guidance as to who that is. While technically instructors, as agents of the college, are obligated to maintain confidentiality, there is little enforcement in this area. Thus, students with learning disabilities are understandably concerned about stigmatization. This is one of the reasons that they are often reluctant to self-identify. In recognition of this legitimate concern, colleges should implement practices and procedures that ensure as much confidentiality as possible in this regard.

In developing a policy on confidentiality it should be recognized that there are instances in which some university employees need to know of the disability, but that the disabled student's concern about privacy, discrimination, and stigma may justify nondisclosure under some circumstances. The policy should address the following issues: Who *can* be informed, who *should* be informed, who *must* be informed, who *should not be* informed, and when and how *waivers* from the student should be obtained.

Conclusion

The denial of full participation in educational programs for students with LDs is not only illegal, but it is also a waste of an important resource. For that reason, colleges would do well to develop creative, flexible, and sensitive policies and practices relating to students with LDs. The result will thus not only be the avoidance of litigation, but the assurance that a bright and energetic group of individuals will participate in our society.

References

Sherman, S., & Robinson, N. (Eds.) (1982). *Ability testing of handicapped people: Dilemma for government, science, and the public.* Americans with Disabilities Act of 1990, 42 U.S.C. §§12101 *et seq.*

Civil Rights Restoration Act of 1987, 29 U.S.C. §794(a)(2)(A).

Dinsmore v. University of California, Berkeley (N.D. Cal., September 23, 1990).

Doe v. New York University, 666 F.2d 761 (2d Cir. 1981).

Education for All Handicapped Children Act, 20 U.S.C. §1401 *et seq.* (now known as the Individuals with Disabilities in Education Act).

Family Education Rights and Privacy Act of 1974, 20 U.S.C. §1232g, and Regulations, 34 C.F.R. part 99.

Recruitment, Admissions, and Handicapped Students: A Guide for Compliance with Section 504 of the Rehabilitation Act. (April 1987). Published by the American Association of Collegiate Registrars and Admissions Officers and the American Council on Education under contract with the Office for Civil Rights, Department of Health, Education, and Welfare.

Rehabilitation Act Regulations, 34 C.F.R. part 104 (1977).

Salvador v. Bell, 622 F. Supp. 438 (N.D. Ill. 1985), *aff'd,* 800 F.2d 97 (7th Cir. 1986).

San Antonio v. Rodriguez, 411 U.S. 1 (1973).

Section 504 of the Rehabilitation Act, 29 U.S.C. §794.

Southeastern Community College v. Davis, 442 U.S. 397 (1979).

United States v. Board of Trustees of the University of Alabama, 908 F.2d 740 (11th Cir. 1990).

Wynne v. Tufts University, School of Medicine, 732 F.2d 19 (1st Cir. 1991).

Part II
Making the Transition to College

III
Transition Planning for College-Bound Students with Learning Disabilities

Sara Cowen

Introduction

Transition planning is an exciting process for all college-bound students. The preparation begins prior to the freshman year in high school when students choose their curriculum. Those who choose college preparatory classes will have more options in the 1990s than in the past. The process continues throughout the high-school years. Academic interests, extra-curricular activities, hobbies, and work experiences help students identify their interests and aptitudes. High-school counselors help them integrate these into the exploration of career options, which guide them toward choosing a major area of study in college.

During the junior year, college-bound students begin to gather information about colleges. With more than 3,000 colleges and universities to choose from, they work with their parents and counselors to narrow their preferences. Location, size, major offerings, admission requirements, campus environment, cost, financial aid, campus housing, and other personally valued factors receive consideration. Once choices are narrowed, students and parents may visit several campuses and compare the positive features of each one. Preferences that emerge lead to applications to one or more colleges. If admitted to more than one college, the student selects the preferred college.

College-bound students with learning disabilities must go through the same process as their non-learning-disabled peers. However, their learning disabilities require that attention be directed to several additional issues.

First, many college-able students with learning disabilities do not understand the nature of their disability. As a result, they lack the confidence to consider attending a traditional college program. They do not recognize their learning strengths. Experience has taught them to focus on their learning weaknesses. They often develop a low self-concept and become less motivated to succeed academically (Deshler, 1978). Such students need help understanding their disability and recognizing their learning strengths (Aase & Price, 1987; Ness & Price, 1990; Vogel, 1982).

Other students need guidance in accepting their disability. They need to overcome such characteristics as denial or overconfidence (Ness & Price, 1990). They require counseling to develop an awareness of the impact of their disability on their learning and daily living skills. They need aid in identifying support services to bypass or accommodate their learning weaknesses.

Second, many college-able students with learning disabilities lack academic preparation to succeed in college (Dalke & Franzene, 1988; Dowdy, Carter, & Smith, 1990; Harris, 1985; Johnston, 1984). Some have not taken appropriate classes (McGuire, Norlander, & Shaw, 1990; Seidenberg, 1986); they need counseling to take course work that will keep their postsecondary options open. Others have not developed adequate study skills to succeed in college preparatory classes (Dexter, 1982; Seidenberg & Koenigsberg, 1986); they need instruction from their special education and mainstream teachers in developing learning strategies (Deshler & Schumaker, 1986).

Third, many students with learning disabilities have not participated in career exploration (Biller, 1985) that provides a basis for setting a goal to go to college. In order to establish realistic career interests, they need career decision-making guidance (Biller, 1988; Rosenthal, 1986). They need to integrate knowledge of their learning strengths and weaknesses into their career exploration.

Fourth, many students with learning disabilities have not developed the independence needed to adjust to college (Manganello, 1990). They seem ill-prepared to deal with the flexible environment they will encounter on a college campus (Dalke and Schmitt, 1987; Davis, Dollahan, Jacobs, Jaeger, & Marici, 1986). Some lack the social skills necessary to adjust to living away from home (Barbaro, Christman, Holzinger, & Rosenberg, 1985; Blalock & Dixon, 1982). They need counseling to enhance their interpersonal skills and personal independence (Cowen, 1988; Evelo & Price, 1991; Price, 1988).

Fifth, they need guidance finding college programs that match their interests and abilities. The programs must offer adequate support services for their needs (Cowen, 1985; Cowen, 1991; Dalke & Franzene, 1988). The proliferation of services available in colleges and universities requires an extensive search, which requires knowledge of (1) how to read and evaluate the many guides available; (2) how to locate services in colleges not listed in guides; and (3) how to evaluate the located services. Finally, they need help gathering the material needed to complete the application process.

For college-bound students with learning disabilities, the need for systematic transition planning that incorporates these issues is recognized by professionals in the field (Aase & Price, 1987; Aune, 1991; Baker &

Blanding, 1985; Evelo & Price, 1991; Getzel, 1990; Michaels, 1987; National Joint Committee on Learning Disabilities, 1987; Scheiber & Talpers, 1985; Vogel & Adelman, 1990). However, usually it is not available (Seidenberg, 1986; Dowdy et al., 1990).

The purpose of this chapter is to describe key characteristics of the transition process that address all five issues. Researchers have identified these characteristics as essential to successful transition planning. They include the establishment of a transition team and a timeline for specific activities. If implemented, these features will improve the transition of students with learning disabilities from high school to four-year colleges or universities.

The Transition Process

The transition planning process for college-bound students with learning disabilities develops over a period of time (Aase & Price, 1987; Getzel, 1990; Evelo & Price, 1991). The process is developed by a transition team. The team, comprised of secondary personnel, parents, and the student, should be formed when the student enters high school. Postsecondary personnel need to become part of the team during the student's senior year in high school. Members of the team perform specific activities each year the student progresses through high school (Seidenberg, 1986).

The Roles of the Transition Team

Transition planning is specific to each student. Throughout the process the student should participate in every team activity and every team decision (National Joint Committee on Learning Disabilities, 1987). The student's participation in the decision-making process appears to contribute to his or her sense of identity and of competence as a learner (Phillips, 1990).

Parents are also an intrinsic part of the team (Evelo & Price, 1991). Parental encouragement influences student success (Bruck, 1987; Haring, Lovett, & Smith, 1990; Scheiber & Talpers, 1985). Parents can help students identify their areas of cognitive strength and they can encourage their child to develop interests through participation in extracurricular activities. Students who participate in extracurricular activities are more likely to seek a postsecondary education (Miller, Snider, and Rzonca, 1990). Parents can foster good study habits by providing a quiet study environment. Their interest can stimulate career exploration (Biller, 1985; Dowdy et al., 1990). They can nurture independence by respecting their child's opinions.

The psychologist contributes to the team by interpreting the results of psycho-educational evaluations. He or she interprets the results for the student, parents, LD specialist, and counselor. The interpretation helps them understand the specific nature of the student's learning disability and forms the basis for helping the student and parents recognize that the student is college-able.

The counselor encourages the student to choose classes that will keep postsecondary options open and guides the student's career explorations. The counselor provides information on postsecondary education opportunities and arranges for the administration of college admissions tests such as the Scholastic Aptitude Test (SAT) or the American College Testing Program (ACT). The counselor helps the student evaluate college information, contact college personnel, arrange for campus visits, and complete applications.

The LD specialist helps the student understand the impact of his or her disability on academic success and daily living skills. The specialist then helps the student develop strategies for bypassing or overcoming academic weaknesses. Learning disability specialists may also encourage students to learn to use accommodations such as textbooks on tape. The special education resource room may provide a setting for developing social skills. The specialist and the student need to work together to identify support services the student will need in college. (See Chapter I by Susan A. Vogel)

Mainstream teachers are important team members who help the student validate learning strengths and may encourage the student to use accommodations or strategies in order to succeed in their classes. They are also an important source of letters of recommendation when the student applies to college programs.

Postsecondary service providers become team members during the actual selection process. They help students recognize whether or not their program meets their needs. They also facilitate the student's preparation for the educational, social, and emotional differences that students will encounter as they move from high school to college.

The Time Line for Transition Activities

Freshman Year

Four goals that will smooth the transition process are first addressed in the freshman year; they are (1) to develop an understanding of the nature of the student's disability; (2) to prepare academically for college; (3) to explore career options; and (4) to develop independence. The approach begins when the student and parents work with high school personnel who will be members of the transition team.

A meeting with the school psychologist helps the student and parents understand the nature of the student's learning disability. The purpose of the meeting is to review recent assessment information. Such information clarifies the specific nature of the student's learning disability. The review should be presented in nontechnical language. It should emphasize the cognitive and academic strengths that indicate that the student is college-able. Students with average to above-average intellectual functioning are more likely to be accepted in traditional four-year college and university programs (Vogel, 1985; 1986). The information on cognitive and academic strengths serves as an important step toward improving self-image and self-esteem (Vogel, 1982). The review should also indicate the cognitive and academic weaknesses that need to be remediated or accommodated in the years ahead. The student's understanding and acceptance of his or her strengths, weaknesses, and learning disability form the foundation for all other transition activities (Aune, 1991).

Academic preparation begins with the selection of appropriate classes. If the student enters high school with basic competencies in reading and math (e.g., functional literacy skills at the fifth or sixth grade level), the counselor should encourage the student to take college preparatory classes. The student should work with the LD specialist to remediate any basic-skill deficits (Miller et al., 1990).

The counselor should also encourage the student to participate in a career exploration program. Biller (1985) believes that career exploration programs should develop the following abilities:

1) awareness of the need to plan ahead and of the relationship between present and future events;
2) awareness of information necessary for career planning and knowledge of how and where to get it;
3) understanding of how to make decisions;
4) knowledge of general career-development information;
5) knowledge of specific information about a variety of occupations and the organization of the world of work;
6) and knowledge of specific information about the clusters of occupations.

The move toward independence requires instruction in strategies. Strategy instruction fosters success in the college preparatory curriculum. An LD specialist in a resource room usually delivers the instruction. Mainstream teachers help the student generalize such instruction. They encourage the student to use accommodations (i.e., taped textbooks, extended time for tests) and learning strategies that will enable the student to succeed in their classes (Cowen, 1988; Dexter, 1982).

Parental participation in the process is supportive. Parents will be more effective if they understand the nature of their child's learning disability. Understanding will enable them to counsel their child realistically, which in turn will help their child deal with feelings of inadequacy or periods of denial. They should encourage their child to participate in extracurricular activities and to develop hobbies. They should provide positive feedback to the student's interest in class work and career exploration.

Sophomore Year

The focus of transition activities is on clarifying the nature of the student's disability. This occurs through the continued development of academic skills, the exploration of career options, and the growth of independent skills.

The counselor may need to advise the student about the importance of continuing to take college preparatory classes. A retreat to lower-track classes at this point will limit the student's postsecondary options (McGuire et al., 1990). Further, some postsecondary service providers consider the quality of high-school course work more important than grade point average (Vogel, 1989). The student should supplement college preparatory course work with elective courses that appear interesting. Exploration of academic interests helps the student identify academic strengths.

The LD specialist should continue to work with the student to remediate basic skill deficits. They should also work together to develop learning strategies for academic success (Dalke, 1988). Learning strategies foster the student's ability to cope with cognitive and academic weaknesses (Cowen, 1988).

The student should continue career exploration through participation in extracurricular activities, hobbies, and work experiences. Evaluating interests in these experiences contributes to career maturity (Miller et al., 1990). Identified interests, aptitudes, values, and opportunities provide a basis for tentative occupational decisions. The interests and aptitudes need to be related to the world of work. Knowledge of the relationship encourages further exploration (Biller, 1985).

The parents, LD specialist, counselor, and mainstream teachers need to help the student develop academic and personal independence. They should provide constructive feedback to the student's efforts. Constructive feedback facilitates learning (Zigmond, Sansone, Miller, Donahoe, & Kohnke, 1986) and helps the student develop a positive attitude toward teachers and the learning process. Such an attitude is characteristic of students with learning disabilities who are successful in college (Vogel & Adelman, 1990).

Junior Year

During this year, transition planning focuses on matching the student's interests and abilities to an appropriate college choice. The first step is to evaluate the student's progress in the four goals of the preceding years. Those goals were (1) to understand the nature of the learning disability;

(2) to prepare academically; (3) to explore career options; and (4) to grow toward independence. The process of evaluating these characteristics will lead to the identification of an area of study and the services needed to succeed in that area of study. Verification of the area of study and needed services directs the search for a college preference.

The psychologist needs to do an updated psycho-educational evaluation. He or she should review the results with the student and parents. The review should reinforce their understanding of cognitive and academic strengths and residual weaknesses. The psychologist should recommend services that would benefit the student in a postsecondary setting. The LD specialist also needs to identify services that would benefit the student. The student and parents should acknowledge the need for the identified services. Their agreement demonstrates an understanding of the specific learning disability.

College achievement tests provide a measure of academic preparation. In the fall, the student should register and take the Preliminary Scholastic Aptitude Test (PSAT). The results of the PSAT will provide a basis for determining future course work the student should take to prepare for college. They may also suggest that the student would benefit from taking a course to prepare for the SAT or the ACT.

In the spring, the student should take the SAT or the ACT. Markel, Bizer, and Wilhelm (1985) recommend the use of test accommodations such as extended time, large-print test materials, or large block answer sheets. The psychologist or LD specialist must verify the need for accommodations. If the results are unsatisfactory, the student and LD specialist may want to analyze them. They can then develop a plan that addresses the problems (e.g., tutoring in a content area, reduction of test anxiety). After dealing with the problem, the student can retake the test.

Next, a tentative goal for seeking a postsecondary education should be established. Career exploration activities seldom lead to a specified career goal in high school. However, interests in an occupational area often crystallize (Biller, 1985). Such interests identify a preferred area of study in postsecondary education. The student, parents, and counselor should work together to establish a tentative career goal. They should then determine an area of study in college consistent with the career goal.

Those students who understand the nature of their learning disability need to acquire self-advocacy skills. Such skills will foster independence (Aune, 1991; Evelo & Price, 1991). The LD specialist or the counselor should help the student develop them. For those students still lacking understanding, Ness and Price (1990) describe two strategies that have proven effective with high-school students, namely, group counseling and individual disability awareness training. They suggest that group counseling sessions address such topics as time management, defining and understanding learning disabilities, study skills, assertiveness training, stress management, and preparing for final exams. Individual counseling strategies are recommended to develop disability awareness. The LD specialist or counselor provides the counseling. Ness and Price recommend that students who exhibit inappropriate behavior and negative feelings seek professional help.

The counselor and student are now ready to gather information about college programs. Exposure to resources affects the type of postsecondary experience the student selects (Miller, Rzonca, & Snider, 1991). Therefore, it is important that counselors inform students with learning disabilities about opportunities in four-year colleges and universities.

As with all students who choose to participate in a traditional college program, the choices will rapidly decrease. Colleges will be eliminated based on location, size, major offerings, campus environment, cost, financial aid, campus housing, and other personally valued factors. Students will realize that they do not meet the admissions requirements of some colleges they might otherwise like to attend. Although admissions criteria vary from one institution to another, they generally include a minimum class rank, grade point average (GPA), SAT or ACT Score, and prerequisite coursework.

In addition to these factors, the student with learning disabilities who meets the minimum admissions requirements may want to consider the average academic qualifications of the student body of an institution. He or she may want to eliminate institutions that appear too competitive (Cowen, 1991; McGuire & Shaw, 1987).

The most important consideration for a student with learning disabilities is finding a college that provides needed services. Services available in various programs include academic or program advisement; remediation of basic skills; subject-area tutoring; special courses in English, reading, or study skills; auxiliary aids and services such as taped textbooks or testing accommodations; and counseling services (Mangrum and Strichart, 1984). Since the student, psychologist, and LD specialist have identified services the student needs, the search can be very specific. Only those programs that offer the identified services will be considered.

The search usually begins by perusing directories of colleges that offer services for students with learning disabilities (see the annotated bibliography at the end of the chapter). Before using a directory, the student and counselor should evaluate it. They should consider the following factors: (1) the date of publication; (2) the source of the information in the entries; (3) the number of entries; (4) the organization of the entries; and (5) the content of the entries. Newer publications will include both established programs and newer programs. Information that was systematically gathered will be more reliable. Those with fewer entries will not identify as many programs as those with larger numbers of entries. Organized entries make it easy to locate information about specific institutions. Student and counselor should distinguish between comprehensive programs and those with limited services. Listings that do not make this distinction are misleading. The content of the entries should be comprehensive. Comprehensive entries provide an indication of the types and quality of services available. They also list the cost of the services and a contact person.

A comprehensive directory rapidly helps the student and counselor target potentially appropriate programs and services. Those institutions listing services the student needs will form a starting point for further investigation. Each listing must be verified, however, as programs are continually changing (Lerner, 1989; McGuire & Shaw, 1987).

Services have proliferated rapidly. Even the most comprehensive directory will not have a complete listing of all institutions that offer services (Cordoni, 1982; Cowen, 1990). An active search of other sources of information must supplement the use of directories. The student should talk with college representatives who visit the high school. The student and parents should attend a college night. They should ask the college representatives about services for the learning disabled available at their institutions. When potential programs are identified, the counselor should contact the service providers. The service providers must verify the services available. The counselor should describe the nature of the student's disability. The service provider may indicate whether or not the student should pursue his or her inquiry about the program.

Senior Year

Academic preparation for college continues through participation in college preparatory classes. English and mathematics courses are particularly important. Further development of study skills and advocacy skills should continue in the resource program.

During this year, activities center on choosing a college. The student and parents visit those campuses under consideration. Letters must be written to admissions officers and service providers requesting a visit to their campuses. The counselor or LD specialist helps the student write the letters.

Prior to the visit the student and counselor should prepare a transition packet. The packet should contain recent psycho-educational evaluations, the Individual Education Plans (IEPs), ACT or SAT scores, high school transcript, psychological or psychiatric report if available, medical record if appropriate, and a sample of the student's written expression. The packet should also contain letters of recommendation from mainstream teachers and the LD specialist.

The student and parents should visit those campuses under consideration early in the year. As part of the preparation, they should develop questions that will help them evaluate the services available. Vogel (1987) suggested that the following questions might be appropriate:

1) What are the requirements for admission?
2) How many LD students are on campus? What year are they in? Are they part-time, full-time, residents, commuters, traditional age or older? Men? Women?
3) What are the goals and objectives of the program?
4) What services are provided?
5) Who provides these services?
6) What specialized training in learning disabilities do these individuals have?
7) Is remediation and/or support provided on a one-to-one basis or in a group?
8) What supervision is provided for noncertified instructors or tutors?
9) How long is service provided? One year only, or longer?
10) How is the duration of service determined?
11) Who will be the academic advisor and what training does this individual have in learning disabilities?
12) Do LD students take the regular college courses?
13) Are there any course or programs unavailable to LD students?
14) What modifications have faculty or administrators been willing to make for LD students on this campus?
15) Are there additional courses required of LD students? If so, do they carry college credit and does the credit count toward graduation?
16) Has the program or services been evaluated? If so, are the goals and objectives being accomplished, and how well?

Role playing with the LD specialist or counselor helps prepare the student for the personal interviews that occur during campus visits (Dexter, 1982).

During the campus visit, the service coordinator will interview the student and the parents. Questions will be asked about the specific nature of the learning disability. The student's level of motivation, maturity, and social appropriateness may be assessed (Vogel, 1987). The student may be asked to complete a case history or to take some tests.

The coordinator and staff try to help the student understand some of the important differences between high school and college. Dalke and Schmitt (1987) suggest that service providers discuss such differences as academic environment, grading, knowledge acquisition, support, stress, and responsibility. Academic environment is less structured and less concrete. Classes meet less frequently. Grading may be based on just two or three test scores. There are more major writing assignments. Knowledge acquisition is dependent on reading comprehension and note-taking skills. Students must seek clarification of information. Even with comprehensive support programs, the support system changes significantly. There is less contact with instructors. The environment is often impersonal. The extrinsic encouragement to achieve provided by parents and high-school personnel is removed and must be replaced by student motivation. Stress often results from the increased work load and faster pace of classes. Students must assume more responsibility for monitoring their progress.

The student and parents will also evaluate the coordinator and members of the staff. It is important that the student feel comfortable with the support system that will be available on campus. The student should try to meet college students receiving support services. These students can evaluate the effectiveness of the services they have received.

The student and parents will want to meet with the admissions officer. The officer will provide information about financial aid opportunities and admissions procedures. He or she will indicate when the student will be informed of the status of the application.

Following the visit, the coordinator and staff will review the transition packet materials, the results of any additional testing, and their impressions of the student's ability to succeed with their services. If the student's needs match their services, they will encourage the student to enroll at their institution.

The student and parents will compare the various campuses they visited. They will evaluate the overall campus environment during the visit. Jarrow, Baker, Hartman, Harris, Lesh, Redden, and Smithson (1986) suggest that the student and parents appraise the housing, the leisure activities available, and the social and learning climate. The most important comparisons will be their comfort level with the service coordinator and staff and the comprehensiveness of the needed services. Based on their comparisons, they will predict which programs will most likely enable the student to enjoy academic success.

The student will apply to two or more of the preferred colleges. The counselor should help the student gather the information requested in the application process and complete the application forms. Once the application process is completed, the student should wait for an acceptance letter. If there is no response within four to six weeks of the date the admissions officer said the decision would be made, the student should phone to check on the status of the application.

If the selected campus has a preadmission summer program, it is highly recommended that the student attend it. Dalke and Schmitt (1987) described such a program at the University of Wisconsin-Whitewater. The program helps high-school students with learning disabilities adjust to the university setting and is designed to meet the following goals:

1) to afford an opportunity for a prospective student to deal with the change that occurs in support system;
2) to furnish an educational experience similar to college;
3) to acquaint students with the layout of the campus;
4) to introduce students to procedures of the college system;

5) to develop an awareness of organizational agencies and related services available to students;
6) to review prerequisite skills for academic success in college;
7) and to provide direct instruction in study skills, time management, note-taking skills, and library usage.

Conclusion

The need for comprehensive, systematic planning for students in transition from high school to college is well established in the literature. It requires the collaborative effort of a team comprised of the student, parents, LD specialist, counselor, mainstream teachers, and postsecondary personnel.

The planning is most effective if it begins as early as the freshman year in high school. Early planning gives the student more time to prepare adequately for college. Preparation includes the development of an understanding of his or her learning disability, acquisition of academic skills, knowledge of career options, and growth in independence.

Planning then centers on choosing an appropriate college. An informed choice requires knowledge of the student's educational goals and support services needed to reach those goals. It requires access to information about programs and services available at the postsecondary level. As part of the information-gathering process, the student and parents visit campuses under consideration. They then apply a decision-making process to determine their college preference. They predict which program will best support the student's academic progress. They weigh their personal values regarding the overall campus environment. Then they choose their college preference.

As with all decisions, even the most careful planning does not guarantee complete satisfaction with the choice. For students with learning disabilities, however, an informed choice decreases the chances of failure. Those concerned with transition planning will find the procedures recommended in this chapter helpful in increasing the student's opportunity to succeed in a college or university setting.

References

Aase, S., & Price, L. (1987). Building the bridge: LD adolescents' and adults' transition from secondary to postsecondary setting. In D. Knapke & C. Lendman (Eds.), *Capitalizing on the future* (pp. 126–139). Columbus, OH: AHSSPPE.

Aune, E. (1991). A transition model for postsecondary-bound students with learning disabilities. *Learning Disabilities Research and Practice, 6*(3), 177–187.

Baker, B., & Blanding, M. (1985). Bridging the gap: College preparation for disabled students. In J. Gartner (Ed.), *For tomorrow is another day*. Columbus, OH: AHSSPPE.

Barbaro, F., Christman, D., Holzinger, S., & Rosenberg, E. (1985). Support services for the learning-disabled college student. *Journal of the National Association of Social Workers, 30*(1), 12–18.

Biller, E.F. (1985). *Understanding and guiding the career development of adolescents and young adults with learning disabilities.* Springfield, IL: Charles C. Thomas Publisher.

Biller, E.F. (1988). Career decision-making attitudes of college students with learning disabilities. *Journal of Postsecondary Education and Disability, 6*(4), 14–20.

Blalock, G., & Dixon, N. (1982). Improving prospects for the college-bound learning disabled. *Topics in Learning and Learning Disabilities, 2*(3), 67–78.

Bruck, M. (1987). The adult outcomes of children with learning disabilities. *Annals of Dyslexia, XXXVII*, 252–263.

Cordoni, B. (1982). A directory of college LD services. *Journal of Learning Disabilities, 15*(9), 529–534.

Cowen, S.E. (1985). College choice for LD students: Know your "SWIS." *Academic Therapy, 21*(1), 77–81.

Cowen, S.E. (1988). Coping strategies of university students with learning disabilities. *Journal of Learning Disabilities, 21*(3), 161–164.

Cowen, S.E. (1990). [Review of *Peterson's guide to colleges with programs for learning disabled students*]. *Learning Disabilities Focus, 5*(2), 124–126.

Cowen, S.E. (1991). *How to choose a college: Helpful strategies for students with learning disabilities.* Unpublished manuscript.

Dalke, C. (1988). Woodcock-Johnson Psycho-Educational Test Battery profiles: A comparative study of college freshmen with and without learning disabilities. *Journal of Learning Disabilities, 21*(9), 567–570.

Dalke, C., & Franzene, J. (1988). Secondary-postsecondary collaboration: A model of shared responsibility. *Learning Disabilities Focus, 4*(1), 38–45.

Dalke, C., & Schmitt, S. (1987). Meeting the transition needs of college-bound students with learning disabilities. *Journal of Learning Disabilities, 20*(3), 176–180.

Davis, C.L., Dollahan, J., Jacobs, M., Jaeger, A., & Marici, T. (1986). *A guide for parents of college-bound learning disabled high school students* (Document No. 7). Long Island University Transition Project.

Deshler, D.D. (1978). Psychoeducational aspects of learning disabled adolescents. In L. Mann, L. Goodman, & J. L. Wiederholt (Eds.), *Teaching the learning disabled adolescent* (pp. 47–74). Boston: Houghton Mifflin.

Deshler, D.D., & Schumaker, J.B. (1986). Learning strategies: An instructional alternative for low-achieving adolescents. *Exceptional Children, 52*(6), 583–590.

Dexter, B.L. (1982). Helping learning disabled students prepare for college. *Journal of Learning Disabilities, 15*(6), 344–346.

Dowdy, C.A., Carter, J.F., & Smith, T.E.C. (1990). Differences in transitional needs of high school students with and without learning disabilities. *Journal of Learning Disabilities, 23*(6), 343–353.

Evelo, S., & Price, L. (1991). The transition of students with learning disabilities: A case study. *Journal of Postsecondary Education and Disability, 9*(1 and 2), 207–218.

Getzel, E.E. (1990). Entering postsecondary programs: Early individualized planning. *Teaching Exceptional Children, 23*(1), 51–53.

Haring, K.A., Lovett, D.L., & Smith, D.D. (1990). A follow-up study of recent special education graduates of learning disabilities programs. *Journal of Learning Disabilities, 23*(2), 108–113.

Harris, R. (1985). Has 94–142 failed the college-bound disabled student? In *Support services for LD students in postsecondary education: A compendium of readings* (pp. 8–11). Columbus, OH: AHSSPPE.

Jarrow, J., Baker, B., Hartman, R., Harris, R., Lesh, K., Redden, M., & Smithson, J. (1986). *How to choose a college: Guide for the student with a disability.* Columbus, OH: AHSSPPE.

Johnston, C.L. (1984). The learning disabled adolescent and young adult: An overview and critique of current practices. *Journal of Learning Disabilities, 17*(7), 386–390.

Lerner, J. (1989). *Learning disabilities: Theories, diagnosis, and teaching strategies (Fifth Edition).* Boston, MA: Houghton Mifflin.

Manganello, R. (1990, spring). The learning disabled college student: Balancing the 3 Rs and the 3 Ds. *Latest developments: A publication for the learning disabilities special interest group.* Columbus, OH: AHSSPPE.

Mangrum, C., & Strichart, S. (1984). *College and the learning disabled student.* New York: Grune & Stratton.

Markel, G., Bizer, L., & Wilhelm, R.M. (1985). The LD adolescent and the SAT. *Academic Therapy, 20*(4), 397–409.

McGuire, J.M., Norlander, K.A., & Shaw, S.F. (1990). Postsecondary education for students with learning disabilities: Forecasting challenges for the future. *Learning Disabilities Focus, 5*(2), 69–74.

McGuire, J.M., & Shaw, S.F. (1987). A decision-making process for the college-bound learning disabled student: Matching learner, institution, and support program. *Learning Disability Quarterly, 10*(2), 106–111.

Michaels, C.A. (1987). Assisting students with learning disabilities in transition from high school to college. In D. Knapke & C. Lendman (Eds.), *Capitalizing on the future* (pp. 140–150).

Miller, R.J., Rzonca, C., & Snider, B. (1991). Variables related to the type of postsecondary education experience chosen by young adults with learning disabilities. *Journal of Learning Disabilities, 24*(3), 188–191.

Miller, R.J., Snider, B., & Rzonca, C. (1990). Variables related to the decision of young adults with learning disabilities to participate in postsecondary education. *Journal of Learning Disabilities, 23*(6), 349–354.

National Joint Committee on Learning Disabilities. (1987). Adults with learning disabilities: A call to action. *Journal of Learning Disabilities, 20*(3), 172–175.

Ness, J., & Price, L.A. (1990). Meeting the psychosocial needs of adolescents and adults with LD. *Intervention in School and Clinic, 26*(1), 16–21.

Phillips, P. (1990). A self-advocacy plan for high school students with learning disabilities: A comparative case study analysis of students', teachers', and parents' perceptions of program effects. *Journal of Learning Disabilities, 23*(8), 466–471.

Price, L. (1988). Effective counseling techniques for LD adolescents and adults in secondary and postsecondary settings. *Journal of Postsecondary Education and Disability, 6*(3), 7–16.

Rosenthal, I. (1986). New directions for service delivery to learning disabled youth and adults. *Learning Disabilities Focus, 2*(1), 55–61.

Scheiber, B., & Talpers, J. (1985). *Campus access for learning disabled students.* Washington, DC: Closer Look, Parents' Campaign for Handicapped Children and Youth.

Seidenberg, P.L. (1986). *The high school-college connection: A guide for the transition of learning disabled students* (Document No. 8). Long Island University Transition Project.

Seidenberg, P.L., & Koenigsberg, E. (1986). *A comparison of the perceptions of high school and college faculty: Implications for program development for secondary learning disabled students* (Document No. 1). Long Island University Transition Project.

Vogel, S.A. (1982). On developing LD college programs. *Journal of Learning Disabilities, 15*(9), 518–528.

Vogel, S.A. (1985). Learning disabled college students: Identification, assessment, and outcomes. In D.D. Duane & C.K. Leong (Eds.), *Understanding learning disabilities: International and multidisciplinary views* (pp. 179–204). New York: Plenum Press.

Vogel, S.A. (1986). Levels and patterns of intellectual functioning among LD college students: Clinical and educational implications. *Journal of Learning Disabilities, 19*(2), 71–79.

Vogel, S.A. (1987). Issues and concerns in LD college programming. In D. Johnson & J. Blalock (Eds.), *Adults with learning disabilities: Clinical studies* (pp. 239–275). Orlando, FL: Grune & Stratton.

Vogel, S.A. (1989, February). *Successful and unsuccessful LD college students.* Paper presented at the meeting of the ACLD International Conference, Miami Beach, FL.

Vogel, S.A., & Adelman, P.B. (1990). Extrinsic and intrinsic factors in graduation and academic failure among LD college students. *Annals of Dyslexia, XXXX*, 119–137.

Zigmond, N., Sansone, J., Miller, S.E., Donahoe, K.A., & Kohnke, R. (1986). Teaching learning disabled student at the secondary school level: What research says to teachers. *Learning Disabilities Focus, (1)*2, 108–115.

Bibliography: College Guides for Students with Learning Disabilities

BOSC Directory for Facilities for Learning Disabled
Compiled and edited by Irene Slovak

Date of Publication:	1985
Source of Information:	Responses to mailed questionnaires
Organization of Entries:	Three sections: schools and independent living programs, colleges and vocational training programs, agencies; entries in each section listed alphabetically by state
Number of Entries:	53 College and Vocational Training Programs, numerous entries in other sections

Content of Entries:	Minimal content; no distinction made between extensive services and limited services; contact person listed; cost listed
Cost:	$20.00
Address:	BOSC
	Dept. F, Box 305
	Congers, NY 10920

College Guide for Students with Learning Disabilities
By Annette Joy Sclafani and Michael J. Lynch

Date of Publication:	1988
Source of Information:	Not Given
Organization of Entries:	Three sections: four-year colleges with programs (i.e., comprehensive services), two-year colleges with programs, and list of colleges offering limited services; entries in each section listed alphabetically by state
Number of Entries:	Approximately 200
Content of Entries:	Program features and entrance requirements described; contact person listed; cost of program listed
Cost:	$24.95
Address:	SPEDCO Associates, Inc.
	P.O. Box 120
	Farmingville, NY 11738

A Guide to Colleges for Learning Disabled Students
By Mary Ann Liscio

Date of Publication:	1984
Source of Information:	Not given
Organization of Entries:	One section: colleges listed alphabetically by state; no heading to indicate where list of one state ends and a new state starts; difficult to locate information on a particular institution
Number of Entries:	Approximately 600
Content of Entries:	Description of colleges and services, no distinction made between comprehensive services and limited services; contact person not consistently listed by name; cost of services not listed
Cost:	$24.95
Address:	Academic Press
	Harcourt Brace Javonavich, Publishers
	Orlando, FL 32887

Guide to Colleges with Programs or Services for Students with Learning Disabilities
By Midge Lipkin, PhD

Date of Publication:	1990
Source of Information:	Surveys mailed to more than 3,000 colleges and universities; telephone conversations with responding schools

Date of Publication:	1990
Organization of Entries:	Two sections: colleges with programs (i.e., comprehensive services) and colleges with services; entries in each section listed alphabetically by state
Number of Entries:	Approximately 600
Content of Entries:	comprehensive information on each college and program; contact person listed; cost of program not listed
Cost:	$29.95
Address:	Schoolsearch Press
	127 Marsh Street
	Belmont, MA 02178

Lovejoy's College Guide for the Learning Disabled (Second Edition)
By Charles T. Straughn, II

Date of Publication:	1988
Source of Information:	Response to questionnaires mailed to every college listed in *Lovejoy's College Guide*
Organization Entries:	One section: capsule descriptions of the colleges; entries listed alphabetically by state
Number of Entries:	Approximately 270
Content of Entries:	Comprehensive information on colleges and programs; three levels of services (full services, partial services, limited services) coded in the entries; contact person listed; cost of program listed
Cost:	$12.95
Address:	Monarch Press
	Simon & Schuster, Inc.
	1230 Avenue of the Americas
	New York, NY 10020

National Directory of Four Year Colleges, Two Year Colleges and Post High School Training Programs for Young People with Learning Disabilities (Sixth Edition)
P.M. Fielding, Editor and Dr. John R. Moss, Directory Consultant

Date of Publication:	1989
Source of Information:	Questionnaires mailed to 3,000 institutions
Organization of Entries:	One section: entries listed alphabetically by state
Number of Entries:	Approximately 170
Content of Entries:	Description of services varies, some entries fairly comprehensive and others have minimal information; no distinction made between comprehensive services and minimal services; contact person listed, cost of services not listed
Cost:	$21.95
Address:	Partners in Publishing
	Box 50347
	Tulsa, OK 74150

Peterson's Guide to Colleges with Programs for Learning-Disabled Students (Second Edition)
By Charles T. Mangrum, II, EdD and Steven S. Strichart, PhD

Date of Publication:	1988
Source of Information:	Questionnaires mailed to all accredited two-year and four-year colleges and universities
Organization of Entries:	Two sections: colleges with comprehensive programs and colleges with special services; entries in each section listed alphabetically by state
Number of Entries:	900
Content of Entries:	Description of college and comprehensive description of program or services in each entry; contact person listed; cost of services listed
Cost:	$19.95
Address:	Peterson's Guides 5710, 166 Bunn Drive P.O. Box 2123 Princeton, NJ 08540

IV
Making a Successful Transition from High School to College: A Model Program

CONNIE DALKE

Making a successful transition from high school to college may be difficult for all students. However, the ability to easily integrate oneself into new settings can be particularly troublesome for students with learning disabilities. For these students, the changes they face as they move from high school to college can be dramatic. Adjusting can be so overwhelming for students that they may, in fact, find themselves failing almost as soon as they have begun. Therefore, it is critical that support programs in higher education for students with learning disabilities (LDs) address the need that incoming students have for support in helping them realize a smooth and successful transition into college life.

This chapter discusses the high school-to-college transition program developed at the University of Wisconsin-Whitewater (UW-W) through the Project Assist program, a support program for UW-W students with learning disabilities. It includes the rationale underlying the need for a specific transition program, the key components of the Project Assist transition model, and the significant qualitative and quantitative outcomes that have been derived from the transition program. This chapter concludes with a case study that follows the college career of one student enrolled at UW-W from the time she entered the transition program to her first semester of her senior year at the university. This case study also provides insight from her perspective as to the benefit of transition programs for students with learning disabilities.

Rationale for Transition Programs

University student service personnel have long recognized that there are many changes facing students as they move from high school into higher education. It has become commonplace for colleges to offer some sort of

Parts of this chapter are excerpted from *Support Programs in Higher Education for Students with Disabilities: Access for All*, by Connie Logan Dalke with permission of Aspen Publishers, Inc., 1991.

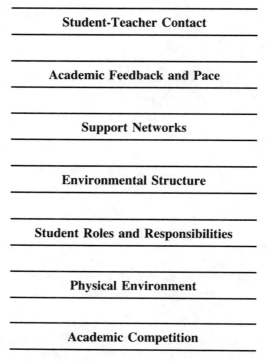

FIGURE 4.1. Major Differences Between High School and College.

orientation program for incoming freshmen. During these one- or two-day events, new students and their parents get a "preview" of university life. These types of program are often sufficient for the average new-comer, but for students with learning disabilities, this brief orientation may not be enough. According to Dalke and Schmitt (1987), as students with learning disabilities move from high school to college, they may be confronted with many more challenges than are their peers without learning disabilities. Although there are many challenges that all students face, there are five major differences between high school and college that require new behaviors from students with learning disabilities (see Figure 4.1).

Student–Teacher Contact

Contact between the students and their teachers is frequent in high school, usually occurring five times per week for each subject. In college, this contact decreases significantly and may occur only one to three times per week. Classroom size also may be variable. High-school classes have a typical student-to-teacher ratio of 1 to 25 or 30, and if the student is enrolled in a special education class, this ratio may be even lower. However, in college the student-to-teacher ratio increases and may range anywhere from 1 to 20 to 1 to 500. In high school, the teachers get to know their students on an individual basis and can easily keep track of their progress. In college, instructors may not get to know the students on an individual basis and may not be aware of each student's progress in the course. In high school, students have ample opportunity to converse with their teachers and need not seek out their instructors outside of the classroom. In college, there may not be an opportunity for students to discuss concepts and ask the instructors questions during class time. Students may need to seek out instructors after class in order to clarify concepts or to get additional assistance.

Academic Feedback and Pace

Homework usually is assigned on a day-to-day basis in high school, and students are expected to complete and turn in their homework on a regular basis, thus making it easier for teachers to assess student progress and for students to monitor their performance. In college, long-range comprehensive assignments are often given out at the beginning of each term. Students are expected to work independently to complete all assignments. Student progress, therefore, is not monitored on a frequent basis. The amount of work assigned outside of the classroom is limited in high school. Typically, students read only their textbooks and complete an occasional project. In college, however, the amount of work assigned outside of the class is extensive. Students are expected to supplement information presented in class with additional activities such as independent readings, papers, and projects.

When students with learning disabilities are enrolled in special education classes or basic-level courses in high school, the pace of the classes is often determined by the individual student's ability, often resulting in a much slower pace than the traditional classroom. However, in college, students must complete the course at the pace set by the instructor. Many universities now have what are called "developmental courses" that are designed to provide students with a review in areas such as math, written language, English literature, and reading. Although these courses focus on assisting the students to gain a better foundation for college work, they still move at a much faster pace than high school courses.

Support Networks

During high school, students typically live at home and have a network of friends and family who can lend them support when necessary. People who want to foster the students' success are readily available and there is an on-going, day-to-day system of support. This may change significantly once the person leaves home to attend college. Their friends may not be attending the same institution and their family is not around on a daily basis to lend support. Students are not sought out if problems occur. Rather, they must seek out people who can help them solve their difficulties.

Environmental Structure

At the secondary level, the students' time is fairly structured between school, home, and perhaps work. There are many people available to make certain that students attend classes regularly and turn assignments in on time. However, once in college, students' time is not structured and it is up to them to manage their time. This is a critical difference between the two settings. The amount of free time during the day that students have in high school as compared to college is significantly different, and it is up to the students themselves to manage their time effectively and efficiently.

Student Roles and Responsibilities

In high school, the students' advocates are their families, teachers, counselors, and friends. Students may or may not be actively involved in advocating for their needs. Once students reach college, it becomes essential that they be able to advocate for themselves.

Physical Environment

Most high schools are housed in one building in which the students move from room to room during the day, and, therefore, there is not much time or effort involved in getting from class to class. However, in college, the buildings are numerous and may be spread far apart; thus the students must negotiate a much larger campus. In high school, students may have set eating and sleeping patterns that can be adhered to without much deviation in routine. They may even have their own room in which to retreat. However, in college they may be living in a communal setting such as a residence hall. Sleeping and eating patterns can be altered depending on the roommate situation and the residence hall routines. Students may be faced with making compromises and adjustments to their usual patterns in order to accommodate this new living situation.

Academic Competition

In high school, students may be competing for grades with students whose abilities range from very low to very high. In college, however, students are competing for grades with the higher achieving high-school graduates. In high school, students with learning disabilities may have been graded based on indicators such as effort or level of improvement and, therefore, their grades may not have reflected their actual achievement. In college, students are graded primarily on their level of mastery of content and as such may receive significantly lower grades than expected.

It is evident that there are many differences between the academic and social environment of high school and that of a college setting. Due to the nature of the academic and psychosocial difficulties that many students with learning disabilities have, these changes can present substantial obstacles.

In the 1980s, professional literature and research have begun to identify some of the major areas in which college students with learning disabilities display difficulties. Although studies show that university students with learning disabilities have average or above average intelligence (Cordoni, O'Donnell, Ramaniah, Kurtz, & Rosenshein, 1981), research also shows that these students have deficits in reading (Ingram & Dettenmaier, 1987), writing (Gajar, 1989; Vogel, 1985; Vogel & Moran, 1982), math (Ganschow and Sparks, 1986), and an overall lack of general knowledge (Dalke, 1988).

After reviewing numerous research studies, Hughes and Smith (1990) concluded that ". . . college students with learning disabilities demonstrate a variety of problems that adversely affect their academic performance" (p. 76). Some of the specific difficulties observed were in comprehending college-level textbooks; reading materials at a slow rate; solving math word problems; performing basic math skills such as computing multiplication tables; and having poor writing skills such as spelling, punctuation, and grammar errors and lack of sentence complexity.

In addition to the persistence of academic deficits, students with learning disabilities also continue to have difficulties in other areas such as social immaturity (Haig & Patterson, 1980), time management skills, completing tasks, study skill habits (Kahn, 1980), overall self-esteem, and displaying an external locus of control orientation (Peterson, 1989).

Considering the many changes that occur for students with learning disabilities as they move from high school to college in light of their persistent social and academic difficulties, it becomes apparent that support programs need to provide assistance to them so that they can make a smooth and successful transition. An ideal vehicle to introduce and prepare students for these changes is a specific transition program. Moreover, it is important that the transition activities occur *before* students are confronted by the many academic and social demands placed on them as they enter college. Therefore, a high school-to-college transition program should occur during the summer prior to the students' first freshman-level semester.

The Project Assist Transition Program

The Project Assist transition program at UW-W was implemented in 1985. Each year, the program was evaluated and refined. The transition program lasts five weeks during which students experience a taste of college life prior to their freshman year. They participate in a variety of activities designed to help them prepare for the changes they will experience as they move from the high school to the college environment. The model is comprised of three stages that include an orientation program held in the spring, the five-week summer transition program, and a follow-up program held in the fall of the students' freshman year. Figure 4.2 presents a model of the summer transition program.

The following is a discussion of each of these three stages of the Project Assist transition program along with descriptions of the activities that occur within each stage.

Spring Orientation Program

During the spring semester of the students' senior year in high school, an orientation program for prospective students and their parents or guardians is held on the UW-W campus on a Saturday. The purpose of this orientation program is to

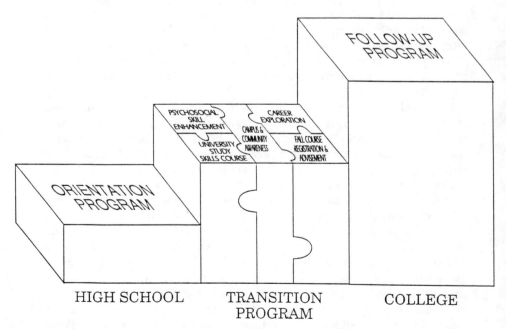

FIGURE 4.2. High School-to-College Transition Program Components.

- provide an overview of the goals and objectives of the summer transition program;
- provide information concerning the costs and payment schedule for the summer program;
- discuss the activities that will take place during the summer program;
- discuss the expectations of the staff in regard to student participation;
- address any specific concerns or issues of the students and their parents.

The students have an opportunity to meet and interact with the program staff as well as with other students who will be attending the summer program. Two or three students who are currently enrolled at UW-W and who receive support services from Project Assist attend the orientation session. In addition, parents of present students are also invited to participate. These students and their parents act as hosts and hostesses for the day, give tours of the campus, and answer any questions that the prospective students or parents may have about the program or the university.

During this orientation session, the staff conducts a learning style inventory assessment on each new student using the Center for Innovative Teaching Experience (undated) Learning Style Instrument. This learning style inventory identifies the major and minor styles of learning preferred by the students from among the following nine areas: visual language; visual numerical; auditory language; auditory numerical; auditory/visual kinesthetic; social individual; social group; expressive oral; and expressive written. The inventory is scored and added to the information obtained from each student prior to admission into Project Assist.

The primary reason for this orientation session is, of course, to acquaint the students with the summer program and to give them a head start in thinking about what will be happening in the summer. Another reason is to help parents gain an understanding of what will be occurring in the summer session and to help them think about the upcoming transition that their sons and daughters will be making. Just as students with learning disabilities have many changes taking place in their lives, so do parents. Parents may need to make their own adjustments and, thus, Project Assist staff try to be sensitive to their needs by including them in the transition process.

Because of the need to know about legal guidelines and regulations, parents of students with learning disabilities are actively involved in their children's education. They are continually consulted and asked to participate in activities such as attending yearly or bi-yearly multidisciplinary team meetings designed to discuss their children's progress and to determine individual education plans.

Suddenly, their "children" reach the age of 18 and the guardianship is supposed to automatically end and responsibility to be transferred from the parents to the child. This is a difficult adjustment for some parents to make. Even if their minds tell them to let go, their hearts might be telling them not to. Once the students are enrolled in college, the Project Assist staff does not contact the parents unless there is serious concern about the students' personal well-being. Therefore, it becomes important to help orient parents to their changing roles as their sons and daughters come of age and leave home to enter college. The goals for parent activities include

- providing them with information on the differences between high school and college;
- answering their questions and addressing their concerns about their children's new educational setting;
- sharing with them strategies on how they might help their sons and daughters make a smooth transition into college;
- offering ideas and advice on how to keep in contact with their sons and daughters without seeming as if they are constantly watching over their shoulders.

Parents who have a child with learning disabilities enrolled in Project Assist are part of the parent orientation program and share their experiences with one another. Parents get an opportunity to talk to other parents who have been through the transition from high school to college and offer suggestions and advice from a first-hand and personal perspective. The parents realize that they are certainly not alone in feeling concern and worry about their sons and daughters going away to college. They learn how others have coped with letting go of their children.

The orientation session for both the students and their parents ends with an invitation to join the staff for a meal at one of the residence hall dining rooms. Tours also are provided for any of the families who would like to see the campus.

Summer Transition Program

The second and most comprehensive stage in the Project Assist transition model occurs in the summer prior to the students entering as college freshmen. The program lasts five weeks during which the students live on campus in a residence hall. There are five components to the summer program:

1) a college study skills course;
2) campus and community awareness;
3) psychosocial skill enhancement;
4) fall course advisement and registration;
5) career awareness and exploration.

College Study Skills Course

The first component of the summer transition program is a three-credit course entitled Study and Academic Survival Skills. This course is offered during the academic year to any student enrolled in UW-W. During the summer program, the faculty member who normally teaches this course during the academic year offers a special section for the transition program students. This course is designated as a developmental studies course; the grade received for the class goes on the students' transcripts, but the three credits do not count toward graduation.

The goal of this course is to provide students with direct instruction in learning how to learn and how to improve their ability to study more effectively and efficiently. The following objectives are included in the sessions:

- organizing efficient approaches to classes;
- taking lecture and reading notes that are clear and useful;
- accurately summarizing information from textbooks and lectures;
- efficiently using the library;
- effectively preparing for examinations;
- writing clear answers to questions, including essay exam questions;
- developing an effective time management system.

The students are given carefully designed writing assignments that are based on the expectations for written language competencies at the college level. For example, the students work through the process of writing a research paper including deciding on a topic, narrowing down the topic, researching sources in the library, writing drafts, participating in peer editing, and writing the final draft. An introduction to the word processors is included in order to prepare the students better for their future English courses. Students also participate in discussion groups, oral presentations, and debates with an emphasis on critical thinking.

Campus and Community Awareness Activities

For students with learning disabilities, part of making a successful transition from high school to college is learning to feel comfortable in the new environment. The physical dissimilarities between high school and college can often be a formidable obstacle for students as they adjust to the new setting. Typically, high schools are comprised of one or two buildings whereas in college the physical size increases to a multiacre campus. Students may enter college feeling overwhelmed by the size of the school. Therefore, a primary focus of this component is to ensure that students become familiar with the physical layout of the campus and know where different buildings and offices are located. The staff make certain that the students know where facilities such as the library, book-store, book rental office, health center, and so forth are located. Students are given miscellaneous information such as where to go to sign up for ride sharing, how to get parking permits, and where to buy tickets for campus cultural and sporting events.

A second aspect of this component is helping the students become familiar with the community at large. Tours are arranged that explore the community and point out places such as public parks, shopping areas, restaurants, churches, community centers, and theaters as well as recreational activities in the nearby area.

A third aspect of this program segment focuses on making certain that students are aware of the other support services or agencies available on campus such as financial aid, health care, counseling, career planning and placement, and tutorial services. The staff involves representatives from these services in the transition program events so that the students can meet and interact with them on a personal level.

An entertaining activity that acquaints students with the UW-W campus and surrounding community is a scavenger hunt in which they must locate specific information or services. The staff asks for participation from various personnel around campus. For example, tasks include asking students to

- locate the registrar's office and to obtain the secretary's signature;
- determine where a specific book or journal is located in the library and check it out;
- locate the cashier's office;
- find out what hours the swimming pool is open;
- locate a specific professor's office and write down the office hours.

Psychosocial Skill Enhancement

The third component of the summer transition program addresses the psychosocial concerns of individuals with learning disabilities. The emotional adjustments that the students are required to make as they move from high school to college settings can be considerable. In some cases, this type of adjustment may be the most difficult one for students to make. Therefore, the summer transition program addresses specific concerns and issues at the personal level including

- exploring feelings concerning change in support networks;
- talking about issues related to living in a semi-independent communal-type setting;
- understanding one's learning disability and its implications for academic and social life;
- learning and practicing strategies for self-advocacy.

To assist students in the last area, values clarification workshops are held in which students begin to identify and articulate how they are feeling about their new environment. They discuss their worries and concerns about both the social and academic expectations that will soon be placed upon them.

During this segment of the transition program the staff also works with the students to ensure that they clearly understand their own learning disability and how the disability will affect them in their personal and academic life at the university. It is not uncommon for persons with learning disabilities to have an unclear or uncertain picture of their own abilities. Often they are told by their teachers and parents that they have problems learning and need special classes. Unfortunately, they may have not internalized what this disability means to them in their daily lives. For example, some students may have difficulty with math and understand that they will need extra support help with their math courses. However, they may not understand why they are having math problems. Is it because of poor abstract reasoning skills? Is it because of visual sequencing difficulties? Or is it because they process information at a slower pace than their peers and therefore have not progressed to a level commensurate with their grade in school? Whatever the reason for their learning difficulties, they need to know.

In order to accomplish this task, the staff first meets on an individual basis with each student. The student's records are made available and, along with the student, the staff member goes through the file. Formal and informal diagnostic information is explained and testing reports are summarized. This information is discussed verbally with the student as well as written down in summary form by the staff person, who assists the student to understand both strengths and weaknesses in how he or she learns. It is important that the students internalize what their abilities are and understand how these might affect them in and out of the classroom. To check to see whether students are understanding themselves better, they are asked to write a one- to two-page summary of their learning profile.

In addition to understanding their own learning disability, students also need to learn to self-advocate. They must be able to articulate their needs to others as the occasion arises. For example, if students would like to have extended time on their examinations in math class, they must be able to explain the nature of their disability to the professors and articulate how this disability impedes taking tests under a time limit.

In order to assist students with this task, the Education Planning Strategy (Van Reusen, Bos, Deshler, & Schumaker, 1987) is taught. According to its authors, it is ". . . a motivation strategy that students can use when preparing for and participating in any type of education planning conference. The steps in this strategy provide students with a way of getting organized before a planning conference and with techniques for effectively communicating during the planning conference" (p. 2). The acronym for the strategy is *I-PLAN* and includes five specific steps of instruction.

Step 1 is *I*nventory in which the students are required to complete a self-perceived profile of their strengths and weaknesses and to identify their goals for learning including vocational, social, and academic goals. Step 2 is *P*rovide your inventory information in which the students are taught how to actively provide input into the education planning conference. Step 3 is *L*isten and respond, a technique that helps the students learn how to be effective listeners and, in turn, how to respond to others' statements and questions made during the education planning conference. Step 4 is *A*sk in which the students learn how to ask their own questions of others during the conference. Finally, Step 5, *N*ame your goals, helps the students in learning how to restate and summarize what goals were set and agreed upon during the conference.

Once students master this strategy, they have the tools to effectively participate in any type of education planning conference, whether it be planning sessions held with support service personnel, meetings with vocational and career counselors, or individual conferences with course instructors. As Goldhammer (1990) points out, the more individuals know about themselves and how to articulate their needs to others, the easier and more effective self-advocacy becomes. These skills are critical ones for students to possess if they are going to advocate for themselves. For example, if a student requires extra time on a biology exam, the student must not only understand his or her learning disability but also be able to explain the disability to the instructor, to articulate how this disability affects test taking, to answer any questions the instructor might have, and to achieve some sort of closure to the request.

Once students become proficient at this strategy, the staff asks course instructors to participate in role playing sessions. A mock meeting is set up between professors and students during which they explain their learning disability and needs in relation to a particular course.

In order to provide the Project Assist staff with information regarding how well students interact on a personal level in social situations, several prearranged social activities take place. Once or twice a week the students attend a social activity such as swimming or bowling parties, barbecues, volleyball games, or theater performances.

Other activities that take place during this segment of the summer transition program are geared to general information on topics such as drug and alcohol abuse, eating disorders, and AIDS. Guest speakers are invited in to talk about these issues of concern to university students.

Fall Course Advisement and Registration

The fourth component of the summer transition program focuses on the students' registration for their fall courses. The staff work with the students to help them set up a realistic balance of first-semester classes. For example, if students have a lot of difficulty in math, the staff may recommend that the students postpone taking their math courses until they have had a semester or two at the university; or they may advise them to take the math course, but keep the rest of their schedule fairly light so that most of their efforts can be focused on the more difficult subject.

The Project Assist staff advise students not only on what classes to take but also work with them to set up a schedule that is compatible with the students' learning styles. For example, if the student is a person who likes to sleep late in the morning, the staff would advise the individual not to register for any morning classes but to schedule their courses in the afternoon. If the student is a visual learner, then the staff would try to recommend classes taught by professors who frequently use visuals such as overheads and handouts.

Career Awareness and Exploration

The fifth and final component of the summer transition program is career exploration. The Project Assist staff works with the students to help them begin to make a match between their interests and abilities and the career training options open to them at UW-W. Several assessments and questionnaires are used for this purpose including the Career Occupational Preference System (Knapp & Knapp, 1984), the Career Ability Placement Survey (Knapp & Knapp, 1976), the Career Orientation Placement and Evaluation Survey (Knapp & Knapp, 1981), the Strong Vocational Interest Blank (Hansen & Campbell, 1985), and the Discover System for College and Adults (American College Testing, 1987).

In addition to these formal assessment instruments, the students participate in a career exploration activity. In this activity, they investigate possible career choices by calling and talking to people who are currently employed in whatever area the students are interested. They talk to the employees about the specifics of their job such as how they like it, what type of education they had to have to get the job, and the possibilities for advancement. The students also make appointments to talk to faculty and staff on campus who are associated with the particular training programs.

At the end of the summer transition program the students participate in an exit conference with the Project Assist staff. This conference is a way to ascertain if the students are feeling comfortable on campus and if the goals and objectives of the program were met from the students' perspective. Figure 4.3 presents a sample exit interview form that is used in Project Assist. This form helps structure the exit interview and provides information that will be useful to the staff once the academic year begins.

Sample Transition Program Exit Interview Form

Name: _____   Date: _____

1. Do you have any questions regarding services from our support program for this fall?

2. Is there anything that our staff needs to know in order to help you when you return to school this fall?

3. Do you have any questions or concerns about: Your classes:

   Your course schedule:

   Other support services on our campus:

4. Do you feel comfortable on campus?

5. Do you feel comfortable within this community?

6. Do you feel that you fully understand your learning disability and how it might and might not affect you in your studies?

7. Do you feel comfortable in being able to go to your course instructors to discuss your learning disability with them?

8. Are there any specific academic concerns you have for this fall?

9. Are there any specific nonacademic concerns you have for this fall?

Staff Follow-Up Notes:

FIGURE 4.3.

At the end of the summer transition program the students return home for approximately three weeks before coming back for the fall for their first semester at the university.

Follow-Up Program

In order to assess the effectiveness of the summer transition program in preparing students with learning disabilities for college life, follow-up activities occur during the fall semester. All students who attend the summer transition program are automatically enrolled for services in Project Assist. It is a fairly easy task for the staff to gather quantitative and qualitative information about these students throughout their first semester at UW-W. The follow-up information includes:

- assessing how well the students did in their first semester;
- talking to the students to see if they have any concerns after being in school for one semester;
- having the students answer a follow-up evaluation questionnaire in which they rate the effectiveness and appropriateness of the summer transition program.

Follow-along data are kept on the students' progress for as long as they are enrolled in the university. These data are compiled for the students who participated in the summer transition program as well as for those individuals who did not. It is of interest to the staff to compare these two groups of students in order to discover whether the summer transition program has an impact on the success of the students.

Over the past five years, 27 (19%) of the incoming freshmen with learning disabilities did not participate in the summer transition program while 117 (81%) did participate. Of the group of 27 nonparticipants, 17 students did not participate because they were unaware of Project Assist prior to their first semester on campus, 5 students had summer jobs that made it impossible for them to attend, and 5 chose not to attend for personal reasons.

In order to determine whether there were any significant cognitive or academic differences among the participants and nonparticipants, individual test scores on the American College Test (American College Testing Program, 1981), the Wechsler Intelligence Scale for Children-Revised (WISC-R) (Wechsler, 1974) or the Wechsler Adult Intelligence Scale-Revised (WAIS-R) (Wechsler, 1981), and the Woodcock-Johnson Psycho-Educational Battery (WJPEB), Parts I and II (Woodcock & Johnson, 1977) were compared. A summary of the mean scores of the two groups are presented in Table 4.1. The paired t-tests indicate that there were no significant differences between the participants and non-participants on these standardized measures.

TABLE 4.1. Comparisons of mean performance scores of summer transition program participants and nonparticipants.

Test	Participants			Nonparticipants			t^a	p
	N	Mean	SD	N	Mean	SD		
ACT								
English	109	11.63	4.81	26	12.19	3.29	−.71	.48
Math	109	9.81	5.88	26	8.31	6.42	1.09	.28
Social Studies	109	13.16	6.54	26	11.69	5.15	1.13	.22
Natural Science	109	17.52	5.60	26	15.69	4.91	1.66	.10
Composite	111	13.18	4.43	26	12.15	3.57	1.26	.22
WAIS-R								
Verbal	48	98.81	14.02	12	92.50	14.94	1.32	.20
Performance	48	99.10	14.32	12	92.83	16.00	1.24	.23
Full Scale	48	98.10	12.78	13	92.85	12.02	1.38	.18
WISC-R								
Verbal	35	97.86	10.65	8	94.38	14.23	.66	.53
Performance	35	105.46	11.98	8	98.25	15.14	1.26	.24
Full Scale	35	101.77	10.57	8	95.25	11.96	1.42	.19
WJPB								
Full Scale Broad								
Cognitive Ability	112	92.68	15.99	26	93.46	12.54	−.27	.79
Verbal Ability	112	99.43	16.30	26	96.15	16.35	.92	.36
Oral Language	112	96.55	16.00	26	92.92	14.87	1.15	.26
Reasoning	112	92.44	18.67	26	88.26	25.01	.80	.43
Broad Reasoning	112	93.71	16.23	26	89.77	18.82	.99	.33
Visual Perceptual								
Speed	112	88.73	18.81	26	92.08	26.14	−.62	.54
Memory	112	92.00	21.53	26	95.38	19.62	−.78	.44
Reading Aptitude	112	99.38	14.32	26	94.65	12.99	1.64	.11
Math Aptitude	112	92.08	16.51	26	89.62	20.87	.56	.58
Written Language								
Aptitude	112	94.90	14.64	26	94.50	15.44	.12	.91
Knowledge Aptitude	112	96.58	14.89	26	93.88	13.19	.92	.37
Reading Achievement	112	91.39	13.97	26	94.52	8.48	−1.45	.15
Math Achievement	112	91.57	14.89	26	92.56	13.34	−.29	.77
Written Language								
Achievement	112	88.44	15.18	26	90.72	9.81	−.94	.35
Knowledge								
Achievement	112	96.09	15.92	26	91.04	18.69	1.25	.22

[a] Separate variance estimate

In order to compare the academic success of the students who did and did not attend the summer transition program, the staff looked at the retention rate of the two groups. Of the 117 students who attended the program, 68 (58%) have remained at the university while 49 (42%) have left school. The mean length of time the students who attended the transition program have remained at the university is 4.25 semesters with

TABLE 4.2. Summary of Reasons for Exit.

Reason for Exit	Participants (N = 49)	Nonparticipants (N = 17)
Transferred to another university	5	2
Transferred to a community college	8	1
Transferred to a technical or vocational school	9	3
Joined the military	3	1
Academic dismissal	15	6
Unknown	9	4

TABLE 4.3. Comparison of grade point averages.

Variable	Participants			Nonparticipants			t^a	p
	N	Mean	SD	N	Mean	SD		
First-Semester GPA	117	2.18	.77	27	1.84	.63	2.45	.02
Current cummulative GPA (retainees)	68	2.49	4.54	10	2.10	.32	3.25	.004

[a] Separate variance estimate

a range of 1 to 10. Of the 27 individuals who did not participate in the transition program, 10 (37%) have remained whereas 17 (63%) have left the university. The mean length of time that these students remained at the university is 3.85 semesters, with a range of 1 to 8. Of those students who attended the summer transition program and were successful at UW-W, two have graduated. None of the students who did not attend the summer program have yet to graduate. Table 4.2 presents a summary of the reasons other than graduation for exiting school.

To examine further the differences between those students who did and did not attend the summer transition program, the staff compared the first semester grade point averages of both groups. The paired t-test indicates that those students who did participate in the program received a significantly higher first semester grade point average ($p < .02$) than those who did not. The staff also compared the students' current cumulative grade point averages and noted a similar finding; the students who attended the program have significantly higher overall grade point averages ($p < .004$) than those students who did not participate. Table 4.3 presents a comparison of the grade point averages between both groups of students.

In addition to these quantitative data, Project Assist staff have collected extensive qualitative data on the effectiveness of the summer transition program. The overwhelming majority of the students indicated that they felt the program was very worthwhile and recommend it to any college freshman. Their statements typically reflect that they felt more comfortable on the campus and never felt lost or confused by the size of the school. They also commented on how they learned a lot about their own disability and realized that they were not "dumb" or "stupid" but that they learn differently and that it is okay to be different. They frequently noted that they were pleased with the variety of effective study strategies that they learned in the summer and feel that these helped them succeed in their first semester.

Although a summer transition program appears to be very beneficial to students with learning disabilities, it is important that service providers continue to collect data and study the effectiveness of such a program. It would be useful to identify specific components of a transition program for further study. For example, the issue of self-advocacy may be one area to investigate further. What skills that they find the most useful once they get into college do students learn? How might a transition program help foster these skills in a direct and purposeful manner, and how might support service providers continue to foster these skills once the students are enrolled on campus? Longitudinal studies may prove enlightening in order to determine whether direct instruction in areas such as intrinsic locus of control, motivation, and self-esteem building not only fosters behavioral change but encourages personal growth and development as well.

Another area for further research and program development for service providers is to consider the transition needs of students as they move from the university environment into the world of work. Just as the new and unfamiliar setting of college presented challenges to the students, so will their future work setting. Support services might want to consider establishing specific school-to-work transition programs to meet the students' need for their next transition stage.

In summary, it is evident that transition programs for students with learning disabilities who are entering college are beneficial. These students will be faced with many changes and challenged with numerous obstacles. An effective way for support services to address the needs and concerns of these students as they make their way into higher education is to provide a summer transition program.

Case Study: Maggie

Maggie entered UW-W in the summer before her freshman year at age 17. Upon entering the university, she knew that she wanted to major in accounting. Maggie was born and reared in a small community in central Wisconsin. Her father is a truck driver who dropped out of school after ninth grade but then went on to receive a GED certificate. Her mother received her high-school diploma and works in a leather goods factory assembling wallets.

Her mother reported that her pregnancy with Maggie was normal with no complications during birth. She also noted a normal developmental history for Maggie. However, as an infant, Maggie began to have significant allergies to many foods, animals, and environmental factors. These allergies have remained persistent, and Maggie continues to receive monthly allergy shots from her doctor.

Maggie's mother reported that the school noticed academic problems early in her school career. In kindergarten the teachers commented that she did not follow directions and seemed more interested in playing. The teachers became concerned that Maggie would become a behavior problem in first grade if she did not learn to attend to the tasks at hand.

In first grade, Maggie continued to have problems. She was excellent in her verbal expression skills, but when it came time to accomplish visually orientated tasks such as learning to read and write, Maggie showed significant delays. She was able to compute math problems verbally, but when asked to complete workbook pages, Maggie did not do well. Upon reflection, Maggie says that she believes she had trouble relating to visual materials. She recalls dreading everytime a dittoed worksheet was handed out because it was inevitable that she would somehow confuse the directions. For example, she would cross out the items that were wrong instead of the ones that were right, or she would circle when she should have crossed out, or she would color the "r" words green instead of red or the "p" words blue instead of purple.

Maggie also experienced trouble outside of school when she was enrolled in her church catechism classes. Since she could not read, Maggie reported that she simply refused to do so and, consequently, became labeled as a behavior problem in her church. Her instructor contacted her parents and told them that he felt she was unwilling to learn about religion. Maggie noted that, "I had to read words like Jerusalem—when I couldn't even tell the difference between big, dig, and pig, I didn't have a prayer with Jerusalem!"

Maggie was assessed at the end of third grade and was diagnosed as having a learning disability in reading. She also had significant difficulties in math, particularly when she computed on paper. Maggie could add and subtract in her head, but had difficulty doing the written work. In thinking back, she feels certain that, "It must have been due to my frequent reversal of letters and numbers. Give me a problem to do in my head and I could answer it in a flash, but put it on paper—no way!" Maggie was placed in a self-contained special education classroom in fourth grade where she remained for three years.

In seventh grade, Maggie decided that she wanted to go to college. Her parents were very supportive of her goal and encouraged her to look toward a college career. In order to do so, she had to enroll in college-bound classes. Her teachers wanted her to remain in the self-contained special education classroom, but Maggie and her parents wished to remove her from the special program in seventh grade so that she might pursue a college-bound curriculum. A compromise was reached and Maggie attended the college-bound classes but continued to receive resource help from the school's learning disabilities specialist. Maggie also was able to get extra help before and after school from the special education teacher.

Reflecting back upon her public school experience, Maggie felt that, although her teachers tried to assist her, she still felt very stupid. She reported feeling very poorly adjusted socially, and had trouble making and keeping friends. She characterized herself as being very aggressive and "tough," often getting into physical confrontations.

Upon applying to college, Maggie was tested by her school disctrict's psychologist, and her test scores revealed a Verbal Scale IQ of 107; a Performance Scale IQ of 129, and a Full Scale IQ of 118 as tested on the Wechsler Intelligence Scale for Children-Revised; a reading recognition grade level of 4.5, a reading comprehension grade level of 10.2, a written language grade level of 12.5 in grammar, a 3.5 in spelling, and a math grade level of 12.9 as tested on the Woodcock-Johnson Psycho Educational Tests of Achievement. On her ACT college entrance exam, which was administered under an extended time accommodation, Maggie scored a composite score of 21 which included 17 in English, 21 in Math, 20 in Social Studies, and 26 in Science.

Maggie entered the summer transition program prior to her first semester as UW-W. During the program, the staff were able to observe and gather information about Maggie in terms of her strengths and needs in the cognitive, academic, and social areas. In the cognitive realm, Maggie definitely performed better when she received auditory input. If tasks were presented totally through the visual channel, Maggie would not do as well. For example, in the study skills class, when asked to silently read a paragraph and then summarize it, Maggie had difficulty. However, when the paragraph was read to her, she did quite well. Maggie's reasoning and critical thinking skills were excellent. When she was engaged in a discussion or a debate, she was quick to grasp the issues and to articulate her response.

Academically, Maggie performed as would be expected considering the test results on the Woodcock-Johnson. With her poor word attack skills, she read very slowly and laboriously, but when she was done, her comprehension of what she had read was quite good. In the area of written language, Maggie tended to procrastinate on the assignments. She reiterated time and time again that she was not a good writer, could not spell, would never be able to spell, and simply did not like writing.

Socially, Maggie experienced some of her greatest difficulties. She tended to be very aggressive with the other students in the program as well as the staff. If things were not done the way she thought they should be, she became somewhat angry. Maggie recalls that her attitude in the summer transition program was not good. "I was a real jerk. I didn't think I could make any friends and that everyone was smarter than me. I just pushed people away as soon as they came close."

In order to address some of Maggie's immediate needs, the staff introduced her to several strategies. In the cognitive area, Maggie began to understand her own unique learning style. As an outcome of this knowledge, Maggie learned that she was not "stupid," as she once thought but that she has her own unique template for learning. She also realized that all the other students in the group also had their own unique style and that no one way was necessarily better than another one. Maggie was able to not only tell the staff what her style is, but she was also able to put it down in words. The following is what Maggie wrote during the summer transition program (unedited).

I learn best from verbal communication. When teachers hold class discussions, I learn more than if I were to read the same material. Working with someone I can comprehend more than if I work alone. When I participate in class discussions, my responses to the questions are very intelligent.

When I speak, many people are impressed with my articulation and cannnot [sic] tell that I have a learning disability. I speak with good diction and grammar. However, when I write, I sound like a little kid. This can be seen on my sentence structure and spelling. I tend to leave out some words and as I proof my work I will read the missing words as if they are there. With my spelling problems, I feel that I cannot spell past the third grade even though I can recognize misspelled words beyond those words in my written vocabulary.

I feel one of my strengths is in math. It was a developed strength, instead of a natural ability. When I first started school, I could only do math problems that were read to me in my head. As I progressed through school, I started to do math using manipulative aids to determine the answers. Over the years I have been able to learn to do math problems on paper as well as if I did them in my head.

Maggie was introduced to and had a chance to use taped textbooks during the summer program. She thrived on this compensatory tool. She was able to get through her text much faster than when she tried to read it on her own at her laboriously slow pace. Maggie also felt that, in addition to helping her finish quicker, the tapes actually helped improve her reading skills. She commented that, "Instead of trying to sit and sound out a word, the reader told me the word right away. Sometimes I would stop the tape and say to myself, 'Yes, that's what that word is—now I get it.'"

Maggie found the use of computers and word-processing programs to be her most important discovery in the program. The arduous task of writing became less stressful, especially when she realized how easy rewrites could be, not to mention the built-in spell checker. Maggie observed, "Word processors are a lifesaver for me. It's so nice to be able to write my ideas down and not worry about spelling for now, and also I don't have to worry anymore about my penmanship. It's so easy to fix things later. I may use up a lot of paper, but it's so much easier than before."

Upon entering her first semester in college, Maggie achieved a 3.0 grade point average. Maggie felt that the summer program had really prepared her for college, especially in understanding the pace at which classes move and the necessity to keep up with the assignments. Maggie also reported that she felt she had learned how to talk to her professors and was not afraid to do so. She also felt that she was approaching her instructors in a more assertive, rather than aggressive, manner.

Today, Maggie summarizes the significance of her transition program experience in this way: "I didn't want to go to the program in the first place, but boy am I glad now! I learned that I am not stupid, that there are a lot of people with learning disabilities that make it okay. I learned that I do not have to face things alone and that there are people to help me if I need it. I like myself today a whole lot more than I did four years ago. I feel that I just keep learning more and more about myself and that I like what I see. If I didn't have the summer program, I think I might have had some big problems my freshman year and maybe I wouldn't even be here now. It was a big step for me to come to college and I believe that the transition program helped make that step a whole lot easier."

Maggie is a senior with a 2.64 grade point average and is majoring in accounting. She is well liked by her professors and has a good support network of friends on campus. In fact, Maggie was elected president of her residence hall her sophomore year and continues to be active in student government. She is employed in Project Assist as a student worker and has set up an effective and efficient accounting system for monitoring the program's budget. Maggie plans to graduate in another year, at which time she hopes to find a job as an accountant.

References

American College Testing Program. (1981). *American College Test*. Iowa City: Author.

American College Testing. (1987). *Discover System for College and Adults*. Iowa City: Author.

Cordoni, b., O'Donnell, J., Ramaniah, N.V., Kurtz, J., & Rosenshein, K. (1981). Wechsler adult intelligence score patterns for learning disabled young adults. *Journal of Learning Disabilities, 14*(7), 404–407.

Dalke, C. (1988). Woodcock-Johnson Psycho-Educational Test Battery profiles: A comparative study of college freshmen with and without learning disabilities. *Journal of Learning Disabilities, 21*(9), 567–570.

Dalke, C., & Schmitt, S. (1987). Meeting the transition needs of college-bound students with learning disabilities. *Journal of Learning Disabilities, 20*(3), 176–180.

Gajar, A.H. (1989). A computer analysis of written language variables and a comparison of compositions written by university students with and without learning disabilities. *Journal of Learning Disabilities*, *22*(2), 125–130.

Ganschow, L., & Sparks, R. (1986). Learning disabilities and foreign-language difficulties: Deficits in listening skills? *Reading, Writing, and Learning Disabilities*, *2*(4), 305–319.

Goldhammer, R. (1990, Fall). I-PLAN: Implications for teaching self-advocacy skills to college students with learning disabilities. *Latest Developments*, 2–5. Association on Handicapped Student Service Programs in Postsecondary Education.

Haig, J.M., & Patterson, B.H. (1980, March). *An overview of adult learning disabilities*. Paper presented at the Annual Meeting of the Western College Reading Association, San Francisco.

Hansen, J.C., & Campbell, D.P. (1985). *Strong Vocational Interest Blank-Strong-Campbell Interest Inventory* (4th Ed.). Stanford, CA: Stanford University Press.

Hughes, C.A., & Smith, J.O. (1990). Cognitive and academic performance of college students with learning disabilities: A synthesis of the literature. *Learning Disability Quarterly*, *13*(1), 66–79.

Ingram, C.F., & Dettenmaier, L. (1987). LD college students and reading problems. *Academic Therapy*, *22*(5), 513–518.

Kahn, M.S. (1980). The learning problems of the secondary and junior college learning disabled student: Suggested remedies. *Journal of Learning Disabilities*, *13*(8), 445–449.

Knapp, R.R., & Knapp, L. (1976). *Career Ability Placement Survey*. San Diego, CA: EdITS/Educational and Industrial Testing Service.

Knapp, R.R., & Knapp, L. (1981). *Career Orientation Placement and Evaluation Survey*. San Diego, CA: EdITS/Educational and Industrial Testing Service.

Knapp, R.R., & Knapp, L. (1984). *Career Occupational Preference System*. San Diego, CA: EdITS/Educational and Industrial Testing Service.

Ness, J. (1990). Essential skills in the transition process. *LD Forum*, *15*(2), 22–23.

Peterson, J. (1989). *Self-concept and locus of control orientations of college freshmen with and without learning disabilities*. Unpublished master's thesis, University of Wisconsin-Whitewater.

Van Reusen, A.K., Bos, C.S., Deshler, D.D., & Schumaker, J.B. (1987). *The education planning strategy*. Lawrence, KS: Edge Enterprises.

Vogel, S. (1985). Syntactic complexity in written expression of college writers. *Annals of Dyslexia*, *35*, 137–157.

Vogel, S., & Moran, M. (1982). Written language disorders in learning disabled college students: A preliminary report. In W. Cruickshank & J. Lerner (Eds.), *Coming of age: The best of ACLD 1982* (Vol. 3). Syracuse, NY: Syracuse University Press.

Wechsler, D. (1974). *Wechsler Intelligence Scale for Children-Revised*. Psychological Corporation.

Wechsler, D. (1981). *Wechsler Adult Intelligence Scale-Revised*. San Antonio, TX: Psychological Corporation.

Woodcock, R., & Johnson, M.B. (1977). *Woodcock-Johnson Psycho-Educational Test Battery*. Allen, TX: DLM Teaching Resources.

Part III
Meeting the Needs of College Students with Learning Disabilities

V
The Continuum of University Responses to Section 504 for Students with Learning Disabilities

Susan A. Vogel

When postsecondary services for students with learning disabilities (LDs) were initiated in the 1970s, they repeated the history of the development of services and programs for elementary-age children with learning disabilities. Prior to Public Law 94-142 (PL 94-142), these early services for children with learning disabilities (nomenclature at that time included, for example, minimally brain injured, perceptually handicapped, or aphasic) could be found in private schools. Modeled after the best practices of the day, in the mid-1970s a handful of LD specialists in small private colleges developed comprehensive programs for college students with learning disabilities. Diagnostic testing formed the basis for individually designed programs. Most of these programs had a strong remediation emphasis, and LD specialists provided the instruction, delivered mainly on a one-to-one basis or in small groups. These services are described in the first available directory of postecondary services for the learning disabled published by a learning disabilities self-advocacy and support group called Time Out to Enjoy, Inc. (Ridenour & Johnston, 1981). The programs described in this directory provide an excellent historical perspective on the available services and programs in the late 1970s and early 1980s.

All of the earliest programs were centralized, that is, services were provided within a learning center or the special education department rather than in the Disabled Students Services (DSS) office. Some programs were housed in their own building (e.g., at Curry College or at the American International College). Regardless of its physical location, each program had its own special emphasis. For example, the emphasis was on social skills at Adelphi University, on problem solving at Curry College, and on improvement in basic skills at College of the Ozarks.

There were a few notable exceptions to the rule of thumb that services were initiated in small private colleges. Conspicuous among them were the programs that were initiated at Southern Illinois University (SIU) (Cordoni, 1979) and at the University of Wisconsin-Oshkosh (UW-Oshkosh) (Nash, 1989). The latter program has as its special strength a very structured program in reading and spelling for students who are significantly impaired in knowledge of grapheme-phoneme correspondences.

A third program at a public university, very different in character from SIU and UW-Oshkosh, was at the University of Virginia (UVA), a highly selective institution that requires a 1200 or greater Scholastic Aptitude Test (SAT) combined score for admission. This program, housed within the Learning Assistance Center, provides comprehensive diagnostic evaluation in order to determine if the referred student is learning disabled, and then counsels the student with identified LD to use subject-matter tutors, general support services, compensatory strategies, and reasonable accommodations. The students in these three institutions most probably represent three distinct subgroups of students with learning disabilities who differ in their academic achievement and cognitive abilities.

A very unique response, for its time, to the specific needs of students with learning disabilities was devised in the 1970s at the Harvard Counseling Center (Dinklage, 1971). Dinklage observed that otherwise successful, bright, hard-working students were having specific problems passing the foreign language requirement. He then coined the term, foreign language disability. In response to these students' difficulties, the University agreed to waive the foreign language requirement, but only after students had made multiple attempts to satisfy the requirement. In spite of the hardship incurred on students prior to receiving a waiver, this accommodation was revolutionary in concept and significantly ahead of its time.

Just as PL 94-142 made special education available through the public schools, beginning in 1977, PL 93-112, Section 504, Subpart E 34 C.F.R. part 104 was passed in 1973 with implementing regulations in 1978. Section 504 mandated accessibility to postsecondary education for students with handicaps. The first response was to eliminate physical barriers for those with mobility impairments. However, Section 504 also protects students with learning disabilities from discrimination in admission and in program participation. (See Chapter II by Laura Rothstein for an in-depth review.) The impact of Section 504 has been felt quite dramatically in higher education in the 1980s and resulted in, among other responses, a proliferation of a diverse array of programs and services for students with learning disabilities. It is this array of services that is the focus of this chapter.

The Continuum Concept

Rationale

Because programs and services emerged in a naturalistic setting and institutions differ, programs may appear unique. Their uniqueness resulted from the differences inherent in each postsecondary institution's location, student body, size, mission, curriculum, degree offerings, financial resources, as well as faculty, staff, and administration. (See Vogel, 1982 for an in-depth discussion.) Often ignored is the very important factor of admissions policies (open versus selective), degree of selectiveness or competitiveness, quality and robustness of the applicant pool, and yield (i.e., how many students who apply and are accepted actually enroll). These factors have a direct bearing on the profile and range of abilities and deficits of students with learning disabilities who apply to a specific postsecondary institution. All of the above factors determine the services students will require in order to enhance their chances of successful degree completion. This mosaic of factors resulted in the diversity of responses to the needs of students with learning disabilities in the 1970s and in the 1980s.

The advantage of a retrospective overview is that it provides the opportunity to identify trends, similarities, and contrasts among programs initially thought to be heterogeneous and to place them within a framework that may prove useful to both consumers, present and future program directors, and service providers. This perspective also allows students to compare and select from among the diverse institutions that fall within their geographic area and economic constraints, that offer degree programs and majors of interest, and also that meet their needs for accommodations and services.

We have conceptualized this framework as a continuum of responses that institutions have made to the needs of students with learning disabilities. The responses range from those made by institutions in compliance with Section 504 to responses that entail comprehensive, highly coordinated programming (Vogel, 1988; see Figure 5.1). Within this continuum, there is no one best or correct response. In fact, we would like to suggest that the availability of this diversity of responses and variety of programs and services on different campuses serves college students with learning disabilities better than if there were only one model because it allows for the developmental differences and preferences of individual students. Students with learning disabilities (like other individuals) develop at different rates; specifically germane to this discussion is the development of self-understanding, recognition of needs, and willingness to accept help (Polloway, Smith, & Patton, 1984). Some of the determinants that impact on the rate of development are age at diagnosis, cognitive abilities, type and degree of severity of the learning disability, and former intervention. For example, students whose learning disability is first identified in college at highly selective institutions such as Brown University (Shaw, 1988) and Dartmouth College (Pompian & Thum, 1988) have to go through a series of stages in a highly compressed time frame to achieve understanding and acceptance of their learning disability. For these students, the process includes: (1) acceptance/denial of the learning disabilities diagnosis; (2) overcoming the sense of loss of their

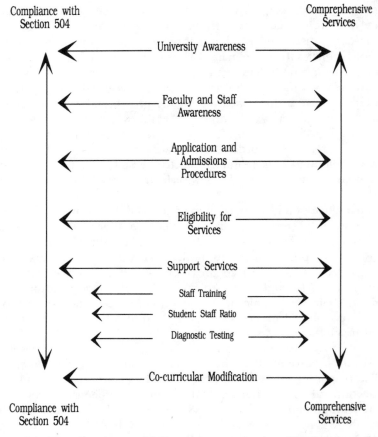

FIGURE 5.1. The Continuum of Responses to Section 504 for Students with Learning Disabilities.

former self and the accompanying assumption of "normalcy;" (3) over-coming the anger for having struggled in the past without assistance; (4) understanding of the results of testing; (5) learning about the impact of Section 504 and the learning disabled; (6) dealing with the resultant low self-esteem and scars from past failures; (7) understanding the implica-tions for themselves and their progeny; and (8) finally coming to the realization that what caused them to have a learning disability may also have given them some special talents, perhaps even giftedness, and a special empathy and ability to help others. This process has to occur while they simultaneously have to make the adjustment to college life and to struggle to keep up with the heavy demands of a highly competitive academic environment.

For those students identified in earlier years, seeking out services they may need prior to experiencing the demands of college may be unrealistic, since some students with learning disabilities have difficulty learning vicariously or in anticipatory behavior. These students need to work with a knowledgeable counselor, need to participate in a summer pre-college transition program and/or need to experience college life first-hand to know what services they need. (See Chapter III by Sara Cowen and Chapter IV by Connie Dalke.) Moreover, the demands of college life will vary based on the student's year in school, level of courses, whether or not the courses are in the area of the student's strengths or weaknesses, how the courses are taught, the reading load, number of required papers, and how the student is evaluated such as the type and frequency of exam.

University Awareness

No matter how responsive faculty and/or staff are or want to be to the needs of students with disabilities, someone in the university's top echelon of administrators or senior faculty such as the president of the institution, provost, academic dean, or a highly respected chair of an academic department has to be sensitive to their needs, want to be in compliance with Section 504, be willing to take a leadership role, be successful in securing financial resources and space, and/or compete successfully for grants.

Information About Services

Institutions that are in compliance with Section 504 provide information about services for students with disabilities in university publications. In order to examine how institutions provide information about LD services, institutions that were either listed in a widely used directory of college programs for students with learning disabilities (Mangrum & Strichart, 1988b) or had well-established services, were sent a letter requesting literature about their LD support services and the institution. Only 49 (29%) of the 170 institutions that responded had an identifiable entry in the catalog's Table of Contents or Index. Of these 49, 20 (41%) had one or more entries in the Table of Contents and 34 (69%) had one or more entries in the Index. Thirteen (27%) listed the services under "handicapped," 23 (47%) under "disabilities or disabled," and four (8%) had a specific reference to either "learning disabled" or "learning disabilities."

More than twice as many of the references (64 versus 29) appeared in the Index as compared to the Table of Contents and of those 64 institutions that included a reference in the Index, 8 (28%) also listed one or more entries in the Table of Contents. Only 1 entry was made in the Index by 13 (25%) institutions, while 20 (31%) institutions included multiple entries in the Index. Of the 20 institutions making multiple entries in the Index, 2 entries were made by 14 (70%) of the institutions;

TABLE 5.1. Number of references to LD services in table of contents and/or index of the catalog by college or university.

College or University	Table of contents	Index
Adelphi University	2	2
Arizona State University	1	
Barat College		1
Boston University		1
Brenau		1
California State University	1	
College of Lake County		1
The College of Wooster	2	
Columbus State Community College	1	
Community College of Denver	2	
East Texas State University		1
Elgin Community College		4
George Mason University	1	2
Hofstra University		1
Illinois State University	2	1
Indian Hills Community College	1	
Joliet Junior College	2	2
Lake Land College		3
Marshall University		5
Mesa College		2
Metropolitan State College		2
Montgomery College	1	1
Moorpark College		2
Northeastern University	2	2
Northern Illinois University		3
Northern Kentucky University		3
Oakton Community College		1
Penn State		2
Roosevelt University		1
Salisbury State University		4
Seminole Community College		1
Seton College	1	1
Southern Illinois University	1	
Southwest State University	1	
Tarrant County Junior College	2	
Technical Institute of Hutchinson	2	
Towson State University		2
Union College		2
Unity College in Maine	1	4
University of Colorado	1	
University of Kentucky		2
The University of Vermont		2
University of Wisconsin—Superior	2	
William Paterson College		1
York University		2

three entries were made by 2 institutions (10%); 4 entries were made by 3 (15%), and 5 entries were made by 1 (5%) institution. It appears that the most common practice is for two different entries to appear in the Index, although information retrieval is facilitated when at least one entry appears in the Table of Contents, since one or more entry was made by 41% of the institutions. Given the students' reading, word retrieval, and skimming and scanning difficulties, multiple entries using a variety of terminology appears to be practiced and is highly recommended. Names of the institutions, alternative entries, frequency, and placement appear in Tables 5.1 and 5.2.

Making information about support services for students with disabilities readily available in university publications is considered a minimal response. However, proactive administrators on a variety of campuses have sometimes done more. For example, when professor Harriet Sheridan was dean of the College of Arts and Sciences at Brown University, she provided faculty and staff with the National Institutes of Health one-page defintion of dyslexia at the beginning of every semester in order to raise faculty awareness, dispel misconceptions about students with dyslexia, and to minimize attitudinal barriers (Sheridan, 1984).

TABLE 5.2. College or university catalog references to LD services.

Reference	Table of Contents	Index
Academic support services	2	
Center . . .	1	1
Clinical services		1
Counseling		4
Developmental Skills . . .		1
Disabilities . . . or Disabled . . .	4	21
Disadvantaged	1	
Handicapped	1	12
Health Services	1	
Learning disabilities . . . or Learning disabled . . .		4
Learning . . . (center, opportunities, assistance, resource, etc.)	2	7
Physically disadvantaged	1	1
Special programs by specific names, i.e. PLUSS, Mach III.		1
Special . . . (services, programs, needs, options, student, etc.)	4	5
Speech . . .		1
Student services	10	4
Student, disabled		2
Support services		1
Teaching learning		1
Tutoring		1

Petition Process

Another aspect of academic concern usually under the purview of the academic dean is to establish a college curriculum that ensures fulfillment of the institutional mission, that is, to nurture well-rounded, liberally educated individuals. In such institutions, core requirements may include, for example, mastery of a foreign language or written language competency. Such requirements may be met by successful completion of a series of courses or by examination.

Some students with learning disabilities have found that their language and/or auditory processing deficits significantly interfere with mastery of a foreign language. (See Chapter XII by Leonore Ganschow and Richard Sparks.) Universities have responded in different ways to student requests for modifications of all-college requirements. Some universities respond on an ad hoc basis whereas on other campuses committees have been created to deal with such requests. The committee's procedures and response will vary on a continuum based on, among other factors, its composition and understanding of learning disabilities. The variety of procedures developed have to be made known to staff, advisors, faculty, administrators, and students. How this task will be accomplished will also vary on a continuum from limited dissemination of the information to wide exposure.

Faculty and Staff Awareness

College and university instructors may have limited knowledge about learning disabilities gleaned from the popular press. What little information they do possess may be dated or at worst inaccurate (Prater & Minner, 1986). Although not mandated by Section 504, some colleges and universities have been proactive to various degrees in providing faculty and staff with information and workshops about learning disabilities. (See Chapter VII by Ernest Rose.)

One of the easiest, inexpensive, and far-reaching methods to disseminate information to faculty is through university newspapers and student publications that can be used as vehicles for basic information (e.g., services, locations, hours, staff names, and telephone numbers). In addition, students, faculty, and staff can produce and contribute to special publications or feature articles in the weekly newspaper or the alumni bulletin. (See Appendix 5.1 for a listing of sample articles and publications.)

Below are additional suggestions for institutions that want to improve faculty and staff awareness.

1) Educate the faculty and staff regarding the requirements of Section 504 through presentations, workshops, and films or videos at the beginning of every semester. The U.S. Department of Education's

Civil Rights Offices will provide at no cost the videotape "Equality in Education: Section 504 in Postsecondary Programs." (See Appendix 5.2 for a list of addresses and Chapter II by Laura Rothstein.) The executive director of the Association on Higher Education and Disability (AHEAD) at (614) 488-4972 can provide awareness training and also recommend local speakers.

2) Provide the faculty and staff with written information regarding learning disabilities. A collection of readings can be put on reserve in the library. (See Appendix 5.3 for a list of suggested readings.)

3) Offer awareness training to minimize attitudinal barriers and eliminate misconceptions. (See Chapter VII by Ernest Rose.)

4) Provide information through videos and films about college students with learning disabilities and the causes of learning disabilities (e.g., "Strengths and Weaknesses: The College Student with a Learning Disability," available from Lawren Publications, P.O. Box 666, Mendocino, CA 95460; "Dyslexia: The Hidden Disability," available from the Orton Dyslexia Society national headquarters at 800-ABCD-123).

5) Provide funding to arrange colloquia or symposia featuring prominent people in the field of learning disabilities as well as nationally known individuals from a wide variety of fields who themselves are learning disabled such as scientists, medical doctors, artists, architects, bankers, financial consultants, and politicians. (The Orton Dyslexia Society at 800-ABCD-123 can provide a list of suggested speakers.)

6) Organize college student panel presentations in which successful students with learning disabilities share autobiographical information that will help the faculty and staff to understand the nature of learning disabilities and how these students succeeded in spite of them.

Application and Admissions Procedures

The most frequently asked question when students with learning disabilities apply to a specific college is about the application procedures and admissions requirements. Section 504 mandates that:

1) Admissions inquiries as to an applicant's disability are prohibited unless the information is requested on a voluntary basis and is for purposes of taking remedial steps or voluntary actions to correct the effects of past discrimination. In addition, the applicant must be told:
   a) the reason for requesting the information;
   b) that the information is requested on a voluntary basis;
   c) that the information will be kept confidential;
   d) and that refusal to provide the information will not result in any adverse treatment.

2) Institutions may not limit the number of or proportion of qualified applicants with disabilities who are accepted.

3) Institution must accept results of college entrance admissions testing administered with nonstandardized procedures. (See Chapter II by Laura Rothstein for an in-depth discussion.)

Many institutions apply the same admissions criteria and have identical application procedures for all students. However, if an institution so desires, it can modify the application procedures, admissions criteria, and/or decision-making process for applicants with learning disabilities who self-disclose. The rationale for modifications has been the lack of adequate information regarding the interpretation and/or predictive validity of admissions information (e.g., SAT or ACT scores, high-school grade point average, previous college transcripts for applicants with learning disabilities).

Modified application procedures have been implemented in a variety of public and private universities, at open admissions institutions, as well as at institutions that represent different levels of selectivity. Generally, however, the more selective the institution, the fewer the modifications.

Regardless of the degree of selectivity, colleges and universities that have well-developed LD support services or programs have frequently asked students to supplement the standard information provided in the application process. When this information is submitted, the admissions committee often consults with personnel who have expertise in learning disabilities. Some institutions go even further and involve LD experts in a cooperative decision-making process.

A variety of types of supplementary information is requested and different researchers have found that preferences vary across studies. Yarwood (1988) surveyed 90 Pennsylvania institutions and found that college admissions personnel considered the distribution of courses as well as high-school achievement more important than admission test results. When admissions test scores were considered, admissions personnel preferred untimed over timed administration. The respondents indicated that letters of recommendation and interviews also provided valuable supplementary information.

In a survey sent to members of the LD Special Interest Group (SIG) of the Association on Handicapped Student Service Programs in Postsecondary Education (AHSSPPE), Bursuck, Rose, Cowen, and Yahaya (1989) found that, unlike the respondents to Yarwood's survey, for AHSSPPE LD SIG members psychoeducational reports and personal interviews were the most preferred data, whereas letters of recommendation and autobiographical statements were of secondary importance, with no mention of high-school performance. However, these contradictory findings may be a result of the lack of a clear distinction between decision-making procedures regarding admission to the institution versus eligibility for services. Neither was a clear distinction made among the respondents from open versus selective admissions institutions.

The admissions decision-making process varies on a continuum from autonomous decision making of the Admissions Office to autonomous decision making of the director of the LD program which bypasses the Admissions Office completely. In such case, the director of the LD support services usually requests that applicants provide extensive developmental, educational, and family history information, as well as reports from past teachers, medical specialist, or other institutions. In addition, the student may be involved in a series of interviews, medical examinations, or partial psychoeducational evaluations. Some institutions require minimal testing during the application process, and once the student is admitted to the college, conduct a complete evaluation. Whether the evaluation is completed before or after admissions, this information then forms the basis for program planning, developing self-knowledge, and compensatory strategies. (See Appendix 5.4 for a sample of a complex application process.)

Institutions that require a complete evaluation often consider not only the profile of test and subtest scores, but also the pattern of performance in high-school courses, special talents, awards, accomplishments, study habits, and work methods. Vogel and Adelman (1990) found that motivation for college-level work and attitude toward teachers and the teaching-learning process contributed significantly to successful degree completion, and, though difficult to achieve, recommended including assessment of these attributes in the application process.

At institutions with comprehensive programs, the program director often functions autonomously in making admissions decisions regarding applicants with LD who self-disclose in the initial stages of the application process. In preparing a directory describing LD support services in both two-year and four-year public and private postsecondary institutions, Kravetz and Wax (1991) asked each institution to respond to the question, "Does acceptance into the LD program mean acceptance into the college?" Of the 102 four-year public and private institutions listed, 29 (28%) indicated that acceptance into the LD program means acceptance into the college, which indicates autonomous decision making of the director of the LD program. Upon examination of the list of these 29 institutions, it appears that slightly more than half have nationally known, comprehensive programs. It is also interesting to note that for 34 (31%) of the institutions acceptance into the program was independent of acceptance to the college, that is, admissions to the institution and eligibility for services are two distinct processes. Six (6%) institutions indicated that decisions regarding acceptance into the college are made jointly by the director of the support services or special program and the admissions office (i.e., a cooperative decision-making process). In contrast, Bursuck et al. (1989) found that 23% of the LD SIG members responding to their survey used a cooperative decision-making process, perhaps reflecting some special attributes of the LD SIG members who responded in this study.

Eligibility for Services

In the early development of programs and services, the major hurdle for students with learning disabilities was acceptance to the institution; once accepted to the university, eligibility for LD services was automatic. As services evolved and the number of students with learning disabilities increased, service providers had to spread limited resources more and more thinly to meet the needs of larger and larger numbers of students. Simultaneously, a growing trend emerged in the late 1980s whereby institutions began to require documentation such as a high-school Individual Educational Plan (IEP) or previous diagnostic report confirming the diagnosis of a learning disability to establish or verify the diagnosis in order for a student to be eligible for support services.

In some institutions, there was also a concern about the recency of testing; others requested specific tests be administered, and still others specified that eligibility was based on the specific results of testing. For example, at some colleges and universities (e.g., Montgomery Community College in Rockville, MD [J. Hermanson, personal communication, September, 1989] and California State University-Northridge [J. Zvi-Collins, personal communication, May, 1990]), students have to score at or above a minimum IQ cutoff score based on observational data that indicate that students scoring below this cutoff have been unable to benefit from LD support services, and that moreover, providing these students with support services can give students unrealistic expectations. In institutions with open admissions or where students qualify for admissions because they have completed an AA degree, but are not found eligible for LD support services, counseling and other types of support services are made available. Other eligibility criteria that have been adopted are based on the aptitude-achievement (a-a) discrepancy model and information-processing theory (e.g., University of Georgia-Athens. See Gregg & Hoy, 1989). These criteria are very infrequently used to date perhaps because of the continuing controversy regarding the quantification of a-a discrepancy, information-processing deficits and learning disabilities, the nature of learning disabilities in adults, the impact of educational intervention, and the inadequacy of the data base regarding developmental factors that may alter the profile, type, and degree of deficits in adults with learning disabilities (Mellard, 1987; Polloway, Smith, & Patton, 1984; Vogel, 1987).

The California Community College (CCC) system is the only statewide effort to date to develop criteria in an attempt to ensure greater uniformity and consistency across diagnosticians within the same institution or on different campuses within the state. Because this model is unique, it will be described in detail below.

The CCC eligibility model has three features: an ability cutoff score, intraindividual discrepancy among abilities (scatter), and aptitude-achievement discrepancy as measured by aptitude or intelligence tests as compared to academic achievement measures. In addition, in accordance with the recommendation of the National Joint Committee on Learning Disabilities (NJCLD) on assessment and diagnosis (NJCLD, 1987), diagnosis and eligibility are not determined solely on the basis of quantitative data, standardized test results, or discrepancy formulas. In regard to each of these three features, there is a provision for override based on informal procedures, qualitative information, and professional judgment.

The California Assessment System for Adults with Learning Disabilities (Mellard, 1990) implemented in October 1987 was developed by the CCC system in conjunction with the Kansas Institute of Learning Disabilities between 1982 and 1987. It was designed as a data-based eligibility model to provide guidelines for the diagnosis of LD in such a way as to minimize inequities and biases. The system was developed with comprehensive input from college administrators, faculty, LD specialists, ancillary staff, students, the Board of Governors, legislators, and vocational rehabilitation personnel. Experts from many fields, including special education, measurement, psychology, policy analysis, decision theory, and speech and language composed task forces, responded to questionnaires, and became consultants on various aspects of the system. This is a highly complex model designed for implementation specifically within the community college population of California, a population that presents a significant diagnostic challenge.

The eligibility model was based on a survey of the literature and data from questionnaires given to LD experts and other service providers. Specific procedures that measure the identified characteristics of adults with LDs were used, and normative data were collected on a random stratified sample of 900 nonhandicapped CCC students and 900 previously clinically diagnosed students with LDs. These samples provided baseline data and allowed for data manipulation and computer simulations of alternative eligibility models. Statewide local norms were then generated from these data and cutoff scores selected, followed by trial implementation, revision, and finally implementation in October 1987.

Based on specific guidelines and on the CCC definition of LD, the eligibility model relies on formal and informal evaluation procedures providing information on present problems; educational, family, medical, and vocational history; language abilities; academic and vocational achievement; expected achievement level; and academic processing skills.

There are seven components to the CCC eligibility model using the above information and clinical judgment:

1) *Intake screening.* The first component is the intake screening during which the student provides information on questionnaires and in an interview regarding present difficulties, history, career goals, and employment experiences. During the interview, the diagnostician as-

sesses the student's language proficiency, academic attributes, or skills based on self-report or prior testing such as oral or written language abilities or the student's attitude toward these skills (Kanter, Halliday, Mellard, & Howard, 1987).

2) *Measured achievement.* The second component is to determine if the student has achieved a certain degree of success in either an academic or employment setting that would differentiate the individual with LDs from the low achiever. Performance below a certain level in academic achievement areas would indicate this student may not be able to benefit from the CCC curriculum even with LD support services. Measured achievement may be demonstrated on formal testing, college entrance or placement exams, academic success in high school or college, or a successful employment experience at least part-time for 6 consecutive months.

3) *Adaptive behavior.* The third component, adaptive behavior, refers to the area of social competence and social maturity as reflected in the student's behavior in personal and professional life, whether within or outside the classroom. Measures used follow a self-report or interview format (e.g., Adaptive Behavior Scale and Scales of Independent Behavior).

4) *Ability level.* The fourth component provides an indication of sufficient intellectual ability to succeed in the community college setting. This aspect of the eligibility criteria follows the most widely accepted federal guidelines and includes individuals with an intelligence quotient (IQ) of 80 or above on either verbal, performance, or full scale IQ of the Wechsler Adult Intelligence Scale-Revised (WAIS-R) (Wechsler, 1981), or the broad cognitive ability full scale cluster on the Woodcock-Johnson Psycho-Educational Battery (WJPEB), Part I (Woodcock & Johnson, 1977). This component also allows for two groupings of subtests on the WAIS-R (perceptual organization and verbal comprehension factors) and the reading, math, or written language aptitude clusters of the WJPEB. Kanter et al. (1987) reported that 34% of the 900 randomly selected clinically diagnosed students with LDs on CCC campuses who provided the data base fell below the 78 IQ level (Mellard, 1987). This finding relates to the earlier statement regarding some of the reasons for determining definition, diagnostic procedures, and eligibility criteria.

5) *Processing deficit.* The fifth component evaluates the student's ability to acquire, integrate, store, retrieve, and express information as exemplified in the WAIS-R factor scores and WJPEB cluster scores. The specific discrepancies (i.e., strengths and weaknesses) among these grouped scores are used as the criteria for distinguishing low and underachievers from individuals with LDs.

6) *Aptitude-achievement discrepancy.* The sixth component is based on information and data collected while determining if the student has

met some of the previous components. A significant discrepancy between aptitude and reading, math, or written language achievement is determined based on the local CCC norms generated from the data base. These norms take into account the correlation of subtests and regression effects and range in different age bands from 18 to 40 and over. In the development of these components, Mellard (1987) reported that this component was the most consistent descriptor of the 900 clinically diagnosed students with LDs as well as the best discriminator between the LD and randomly identified nonhandicapped sample. However, among the random sample, 32% also had met this criterion, that is, one in three non-LD students had met the criterion as having a significant aptitude-achievement discrepancy (Mellard, 1987). This finding confirms that if eligibility for service was based solely on a discrepancy formula, many non-LD individuals would be identified as LD and would be eligible for service (Mellard, 1987; Reynolds, 1985; Sinclair & Alexson, 1986).

7) *Eligibility recommendation.* At the completion of each step in the six components, there is a criterion component check; the examiner must indicate whether the interview or test-administration procedures, or both, are appropriate, as well as whether they were valid and accurately completed (Mellard, 1987). If not, the clinician has the option to use secondary procedures and in such cases must state why the primary procedures were invalid and describe the alternate method. Clinicians can use an alternate method with no more than 0.1% of the total number of students with LDs on their campus. If that number is exceeded, the chancellor's office must be notified. This provision allows the chancellor's office to monitor problems that may arise in the eligibility model or in its implementation.

After completing the procedures for each component, the LD professional indicates whether the criterion has been met. In the seventh component, all of the information must be integrated and clinical judgment used to make a final determination, assuming the student met the criteria for each of the six components.

Support Services

To date, no nationally representative random stratified sample of institutions has been surveyed. However, in the survey by Bursuck et al. (1989), they divided support services into three categories: 504 Access Services, Special Services, and Remedial Services. This division seems to relate well to the continuum concept in that programs that have more full-time staff, a lower student-staff ratio, and more staff with specific training in the field of learning disabilities, also provide all three types of services.

The support services included under 504 Access Services were assistance in ordering taped textbooks, allowing tape recording of lectures, providing notetakers, and assistance in arranging for modified examination procedures. The second type of services, Special Services, included academic advising, tutoring, counseling, advocacy, IEPs, special classes, and monitoring of progress. Lastly, Remedial Services included instruction in reading, written language, math, and study habits. Whereas 504 Access Services do not seem to vary from campus to campus, except perhaps in degree of ease in accessing the services, Special Services such as academic advising, counseling, and tutoring as well as staff training and student-staff ratio can vary from campus to campus and can also be conceptualized as falling along a continuum.

Staff Training

One of the parameters that can be used to place support services on a continuum is the level of expertise in LD of the service providers. Disabled students service providers, academic advisers, and counselors may have very limited knowledge, training, and experience in learning disabilities (Norlander, Shaw, & McGuire, 1990). No one group is to be blamed for this. The significant increase in the number of students with learning disabilities requesting services at postsecondary institutions created staffing dilemmas in the 1980s. Offices of Disabled Student Services have had difficulty not only funding, but also finding qualified individuals to meet the needs of the growing number of college students with learning disabilities.

The LD experts who developed the first programs did not initially provide training for others. However, when support staff with limited background in LD began to work with students with learning disabilities in other service centers such as DSS offices and Educational Opportunity Programs and these service providers and LD specialists began to interact on behalf of the students, cross-fertilization began to occur.

Some of the non-LD specialists had received adult or developmental education and/or vocational rehabilitation training. Only 9% of directors of DSS offices had training in special education according to a survey conducted by Blosser (1984) whereas fewer than 5% of learning lab staff were thought to have any formal training in LD (Markham, 1983). These specialists extended the model of accommodations and compensatory strategies used by the hearing impaired, visually and/or physically disabled to the learning disabled. Learning disability experts were thus exposed to a different conceptualization of service delivery while at the same time, the LD specialists were asked to provide LD training and in-service programs, preconference, and conference workshops for non-LD professionals working with the learning disabled (Bursuck et al., 1989; Norlander, Shaw, & McGuire, 1990). Norlander et al. (1990) found that for learning specialists the most desired competencies were in assessment of students with learning disabilities, cognitive interventions, and instructional skills. Konrad (1984) also reported that this type of collaboration was mutually beneficial to composition instructors who gained insight into the student's learning disability, strengths, weaknesses, and appropriate teaching strategies while LD specialists learned strategies for improvement in written language. In some programs, LD specialists also provided training and supervision for subject-matter peer tutors (Adelman & Olufs, 1986; Vogel & Adelman, 1981).

In some instances, the LD specialist provided workshops for freshmen and transfer students' academic advisors or served as the student's advisor until he or she declared a major. During a transition period, the LD specialist sometimes functioned as the coadvisor with the faculty in the student's major. Working closely with specific faculty members within academic departments led to the development of the faculty liaison concept and enabled a sharing of expertise and a smooth transition once the student declared a major (Vogel, 1982). In an examination of college performance, Vogel and Adelman (1990) found the academic failure rate and number of failing grades, incompletes, and withdrawals significantly lower for students with learning disabilities as compared to a sample matched on ACT composite scores and attributed this, at least in part, to the shared advisement responsibility.

Institutions with highly developed postsecondary programs in place also became the natural training sites for graduate students to acquire skills and experience in providing LD support services and in administering programs, and later these students used their skills in developing new programs on other campuses. Thus far, however, only one institution (University of Connecticut) has developed a formal doctoral program designed to prepare LD specialists to direct college programs (Shaw, Norlander, & McGuire, 1987). (See Chapter VI by Doris Johnson for an in-depth discussion of the important components of such programs.) In addition, one state in the nation, California, developed minimum qualifications for LD specialists working in community colleges (Kanter et al., 1987). It is hoped that the University of Connecticut and the California models will be catalysts for the development of other formal training programs to prepare college-level LD specialists, program directors, evaluators, and directors.

Student–Staff Ratio

Student–LD specialist ratios vary widely. In the two largest postsecondary institutions in this country (University of Ohio and University of Minnesota), the student–staff ratio is more than 100 to 1. In contrast, in settings such as Southern Illinois University, Barat College, Curry College, and The College of the Ozarks, the ratio is between 12 and 20 to 1. This large discrepancy in caseload has a profound impact on the amount, type, and delivery of services, the monitoring of student academic progress, and communication and coordination of effort on behalf of the student. On campuses with a high student–staff ratio, staff responsibility includes referral to other services on campus, Access Services, and accommodations (e.g., note takers, books on tape, and examination modifications). In contrast, on campuses with a low student–staff ratio, Access Services, Special Services, and Remedial Services are usually provided (Bursuck et al., 1989).

Diagnostic Testing Services

One of the most expensive services for postsecondary institutions (PSIs) to provide (and therefore usually not provided) is diagnostic testing for students referred (by themselves and others) for first-time assessment, or those in need of updating or verifying previous diagnostic evaluations. In the 1980s, institutions referred students to private clinics, diagnosticians, or hospitals or have charged for testing done on campus, often at a fee much lower than what testing could be obtained for elsewhere but still prohibitive for some. Brown University, Southern Illinois University, and Barat College are examples of these three alternatives. A rare exception is Ohio State University, where full evaluations are available to students at no charge through the DSS office (L. Block, personal communication, July, 1988). Another exception is the State of New Jersey, where regional centers have been established to provide diagnostic evaluations (Kress, 1990).

An interesting third alternative used at Brown University (Shaw, personal communication, March, 1990) is to offer students a health coverage plan that pays for diagnostic testing. It is yet to be seen if this type of benefits package will be offered to students at other institutions. If assessment does become readily available, the cost to the student or the institution will no longer be an obstacle to identification and provision of services for students with LDs in the 1990s.

Cocurricular Modification

Although academic success is the primary reason for making instructional and testing accommodations, cocurricular modifications may be indirectly but equally critical to academic success. This type of modification provides a physical environment conducive to the learning needs of individuals with learning disabilities. Although not all institutions have been requested to make such modifications, they are always based on individual needs and fall within the mandates of Section 504.

A very frequent response to students with disabilities required institutions to allow part-time undergraduate study without financial penalty to the student. This modification, originally provided for students with certain medical conditions (e.g., multiple sclerosis), recognized that part-time undergraduate study for some students with disabilities could demand the same or more expenditure of effort as full-time study. Because of slower processing rates affecting mainly reading and writing, and because college students with LDs often find it necessary to take developmental courses simultaneously with college courses, they frequently need to take a part-time load. In a time-to-complete-degree study, Vogel and Adelman (1992) found that college graduates with learning disabilities had carried an average of 10.5 credit hours per semester (12 to 15 is considered full time) and had taken a little more than six years to complete their Bachelor's degree, one year longer than their non-LD peers matched on ACT composite scores.

Modifying the lock-step law and medical school curricula has been more problematic. Creative use of summer school programming or extending the degree program by one year have been advocated by Parks, Antonoff, Drake, Oliver, Sedita, Weiss, and Daddi (1982). More commonly, all students carry a full load, and those with learning disabilities often earn lower grades or fail one or more courses. If they are fortunate enough and still motivated, they will be allowed to repeat the semester or year. Often the second-time-around exposure, combined with perhaps tutoring, study groups, shared notetaking, familiarization with test format, and completion of more practice exams, they manage to succeed, sometimes with flying colors (Guyer, 1988).

Another response to the physical needs of resident students with learning disabilities who often reported being distracted by background noise (Vogel, 1985) is to provide them with a single room in the "quiet dormitory," or a study carrel in the library, even though they would not have qualified for either of the above by the method in use. Such modifications have been found to be facilitative for students with dyslexia at Brown University where an associate dean has the responsibility for responding to such requests.

The Range of Responses to Section 504

Although it is difficult, if not impossible, to place each institution on the continuum in regard to each type of response, it is relatively easy to identify the extreme poles. First, it is important to state that to make no response to Section 504 is not in compliance with Section 504 and, therefore, is not considered to be part of the continuum. However, there are fewer and fewer institutions that can afford to take this risk. Therefore, at the very least, institutions assign a person whose major responsibilities are typically within the Affirmative Action Office or Dean of Students Office (less often within the Provost or Dean of Academic

Affairs Office) to respond on an ad hoc basis to the needs of students with learning disabilities. This person usually has limited knowledge, experience, time, staff, and resources to meet the needs of students with learning disabilities and primarily provides Access Services or refers students to generic services on campus.

Depending on the level of the academic demands of the institution, the rigidity or flexibility of individual faculty encountered, the type and severity of LD, and their own self-advocacy skills, among other factors, some students with learning disabilities at such institutions begin to flounder soon after enrollment. In frustration, some students may seek out sympathetic faculty, the university ombudsman, or other students with learning disabilities on their campus, other campuses, or at local, regional, or national conferences. Such networking sometimes results in the establishment of student self-help groups (Johnson, 1988) that have served a variety of functions. At some universities they have been effective in providing workshops for faculty, conferences for high-school students and their parents and teachers (Javorsky, 1990), or in acting as pressure groups to improve support services. A summary of minimal responses to Section 504 is given in the following list:

Individual in Student or Academic Affairs office is given the responsibility for and responds on a case-by-case basis to the needs of students with disabilities. The person has limited knowledge, experience, time, staff, and resources.

Access Services are provided including
- assistance ordering books on tape;
- note takers;
- assistance arranging for modified examination procedures;
- referral to generic support services on campus.

Staff providing services may have background in adult education, educational administration, or reading, writing, and math instruction.

Students are referred to other services on campus such as tutoring, group instruction, computer-assisted instruction in basic skills, subject-matter tutoring, personal counseling, and career counseling.

The staff-student ratio may be 100 to 1 or higher.

At the other pole on this continuum, maximal responses to Section 504, the institution publishes information regarding its policies and services in a variety of university publications including those targeted at students. University policies and procedures are well developed and have been established in response to student requests for modifications to academic and cocurricular university requirements. In addition, the university provides faculty and staff awareness training on Section 504 and learning disabilities through a variety of regularly offered activities, print, and audio-visual materials.

When a student with learning disabilities self-discloses in the application process, the admissions staff frequently requests supplementary information. An individual with LD expertise (usually the director of the LD services) is often involved in the interpretation of the standard and supplementary information and provides input in the admissions decision-making process. At some institutions cooperative decision making is standard practice; at others, the director of the LD program makes an autonomous decision to accept or reject a student to the program that automatically extends to the institution as well.

Implied in this discussion regarding admissions decisions is the concept of eligibility criteria for LD services. These criteria usually include a recent, comprehensive psychoeducational evaluation that forms the basis for the development of an IEP. This program includes a statement of goals and objectives based on strengths and weaknesses identified in testing, student interests, possible major, career goals, college graduation, and credentialing requirements.

The director and staff have expertise in learning disabilities, have to work well as a team, and have to be able to provide one-on-one assistance. The student–staff ratio is approximately 15 to 1, enabling staff to work with students initially one to two hours per week, to confer with faculty, and to provide training and ongoing support for advisors, subject-matter tutors, basic skills instructors, and personal and career counselors. The staff also have to have time to monitor academic progress and recommend program modifications as needed. Frequency and duration of meetings between the student and LD specialist are determined based on academic record of success, specific course load, student goals, and need for emotional support among other factors.

Program development and monitoring program effectiveness are an integral part of the director's responsibilities. One method for accomplishing this is the establishment of an advisory committee composed of universitywide representation of faculty, administration, staff, and students. (See Chapter XIII by Pamela Adelman and Susan Vogel for an in-depth discussion.) Follow-along and follow-up studies are other methods and data collected regularly include students' academic progress, graduation and attrition rate, special honors, dismissals, graduate and professional school degree completion, and employment attainments (Adelman & Vogel, 1990; Adelman & Vogel, 1991). A summary of this type of response to Section 504 is listed in the following:

Information regarding services appears in university publications.
University has well-developed policies and procedures for students requesting modifications to university requirements.
Faculty and staff awareness training and materials are provided.
Supplementary information is requested in the application process when students self-disclose.

Cooperative admissions decision making or autonomous decision making by director of LD services are not uncommon.

Current and comprehensive testing is required for student to be eligible to receive services and accommodations.

Director and staff have expertise in LD.

IEPs are developed for each student.

LD staff provide one-on-one assistance to students.

LD staff provide training and ongoing support to non-LD specialists such as advisors, faculty, subject-matter tutors, and counselors.

Student–LD staff ratio is approximately 15 to 1.

LD staff monitor academic progress of students regularly.

The Director implements ongoing program evaluation and follow-up studies of students that include monitoring academic performance, graduation and attrition rate, employment attainments, and graduate and professional school degree completion.

Concluding Remarks

The goal of this chapter was to be suggestive by presenting the wide spectrum of responses that have been made to Section 504 in the 1980s. In light of this array of responses, institutions can examine or reexamine the needs of their students, their curriculum, mission, and institutional resources to determine or refine and implement their own unique response. No matter what the response may be, it is incumbent on each institution to formulate its response and disseminate it in order to provide access to qualified students with disabilities. Providing information about the institution's response allows informed students to select from among the various institutions those that provide the services, accommodations, or modifications they need to succeed and, thus, enable them to accomplish their intended goal in the spirit of Section 504.

References

Adelman, P.B., & Olufs, D. (1986). Assisting college students with learning disabilities. Columbus, OH: Association on Handicapped Student Service Programs in Postsecondary Education.

Adelman, P.B., & Vogel, S.A. (1990). College graduates with learning disabilities—Employment attainment and career patterns. *Learning Disability Quarterly*, *13*(3), 154–166.

Adelman, P.B., & Vogel, S.A. (1991). The learning disabled audlt. In B. Wong (Ed.), *Learning about learning disabilities* (pp. 563–594). New York: Academic Press.

Blosser, R.E. (1984). *The roles and functions and the preparation of disabled student services directors in higher education. Dissertation Abstracts International*, *45*, 2396A. (University Microfilms No. 84–25, 117).

Bursuck, W.D., Rose, E., Cowen, S., & Yahaya, M.A. (1989). Nationwide survey of postsecondary education services for students with learning disabilities. *Exceptional Children*, *56*(3), 236–245.

Cordoni, B. (1979). Assisting dyslexic college students: An experimental design at a university. *Bulletin of Orton Society*, *29*, 263–268.

Dinklage, K. (1971). Inability to learn a foreign language. In G. Blaine & C. McArthur (Eds.), *Emotional problems of the student* (2nd ed., pp. 185–206). New York: Appleton-Century-Crofts.

Gregg, N., & Hoy, C. (1989). Coherence: The comprehension and production abilities of college writers who are normally achieving, learning disabled, and underprepared. *Journal of Learning Disabilities*, *22*(6), 370–372; 390.

Guyer, B. (1988). Dyslexic doctors: A resource in need of discovery. *Southern Medical Journal*, *81*(9), 1151–1154.

Javorsky, J. (1990). Orton Dyslexia Society College Affiliates. *Perspectives*, *16*(2), 2.

Johnson, J. (1988). *Learning disabilities academic support group manual*. Minneapolis: University of Minnesota.

Kanter, M., Halliday, K., Mellard, D., & Howard, R. (1987). *What LD is, not what it isn't*. Paper presented at the 1987 AHSSPPE Conference, Washington, DC.

Konrad, D. (1984). The Barat writing lab. In W.M. Cruickshank & J.M. Kliebhan (Eds.), *Early adolescence to early adulthood: The best of ACLD* (Vol. V, 177–182). Syracuse: Syracuse University Press.

Kravetz, M., & Wax, I. (1991). *The Kravetz and Wax Guide to Colleges and the Learning Disabled Student*. Deerfield, IL: Kravetz, Wax.

Kress, J.E. (1990). Higher education services for special needs students program FY 1986–FY 1989. *New Jersey Department of Higher Education*.

Mangrum, C., & Strichart, S. (1988). *Peterson's guide to colleges with programs for learning disabled students* (2nd ed.). Princeton, NJ: Peterson's Guides.

Markham, S. (1983). Characteristics of learning center staffing two- and four-year colleges. *Journal of Developmental and Remedial Education*, *3*, 108–113.

Mellard, D.F. (1987). Educational issues surrounding severe discrepancy: A discussion. *Learning Disabilities Research*, *3*(1), 50–56.

Mellard, D.F. (1990). The eligibility process: Identifying students with learning disabilities in California's community colleges. *Learning Disabilities Focus*, *5*(2), 75–90.

Nash, R.T. (1989). *Project success—A remedial program for postsecondary learning disabled students* (Report No. HE 022 617). Washington, D.C. American Association of State Colleges and Universities; Wisconsin University, Oshkosh (ERIC Document Reproduction Service No. ED 306 893).

National Joint Committee on Learning Disabilities. (1987). Learning disabilities: Issues on definition. *Journal of Learning Disabilities*, *10*(2), 107–108.

Norlander, K.A., Shaw, S.F., & McGuire, J.M. (1990). Competencies of postsecondary education personnel serving students with learning disabilities. *Journal of Learning Disabilities*, *23*(7), 426–432.

Parks, A., Antonoff, S., Drake, C., Oliver, C., Sedita, J., Weiss, I., & Daddi, B. (1982). Screening for specific learning disabilities among dental students. *Journal of Dental Education*, *46*, 586–591.

Polloway, E.A., Smith, J.D., & Patton, J.R. (1984). Learning disabilities: An adult development perspective. *Learning Disability Quarterly*, *7*, 179–186.

Pompian, N.W., & Thum, C.P. (1988). Dyslexic/learning disabled students at Dartmouth College. *Annals of Dyslexia, 38*, 276–284.

Prater, G., & Minner, S. (1986). Factors inhibiting the performance of learning-disabled students in postsecondary settings. *Reading, Writing, and Learning Disabilities, 2*, 273–277.

Reynolds, C.R. (1985). Critical measurement issues in learning disabilities. *Journal of Special Education, 18*, 451–475.

Ridenour, D., & Johnston, J. (1981). *A guide to postsecondary educational opportunities for the learning disabled.* Oak Park, IL: Time Out to Enjoy, Inc.

Shaw, R. (1988). *Effective college and graduate programs for dyslexic students.* Paper presented at the 39th Annual Conference of the National Orton Dyslexia Society, Tampa, FL.

Shaw, S.F., Norlander, K.A., & McGuire, J.M. (1987). Training leadership personnel for learning disability college programs: Preservice and inservice models. *Teacher Education and Special Education, 9*, 77–81.

Sheridan, H. (1984). *Making one's way at the university.* Paper presented at the 35th Annual Conference of the National Orton Society, Winston Salem, NC.

Sinclair, E., & Alexson, J. (1986). Learning disabilities discrepancy formulas: Similarities and difference among them. *Learning Disabilities Research, 1*, 112–118.

Vogel, S.A. (1982). On developing LD college programs. *Journal of Learning Disabilities, 15*(9), 518–528.

Vogel, S.A. (1985). Learning disabled college students: Identification, assessment, and outcomes. In D.D. Duane & C.K. Leong (Eds.), *Understanding learning disabilities—An international perspective* (pp. 179–203). New York: Plenum.

Vogel, S.A. (1987). Eligibility and identification considerations in postsecondary education: A new but old dilemma. In S. Vaughn & C.S. Bos (Eds.), *Issues and future directions for research in learning disabilities* (pp. 121–137). Boston: College-Hill Press.

Vogel, S.A. (1988). *Problems of LD college students and programs to meet their needs.* Paper presented at the New York Branch of the Orton Dyslexia Society 12th Annual Conference, New York.

Vogel, S.A., & Adelman, P. (1981). College and university programs designed for learning disabled adults. *ICEC Quarterly, 30*(1), 12–18.

Vogel, S.A., & Adelman, P.B. (1990). Extrinsic and intrinsic factors in graduation and academic failure among LD college students. *Annals of Dyslexia, 40*, 119–137.

Vogel, S.A., & Adelman, P.B. (1992). The success of college students with learning disabilities: Factors related to educational attainments. *Journal of Learning Disabilities, 25*(7), 430–441.

Wechsler, D. (1981). *Wechsler Adult Intelligence Scale-Revised.* New York: Psychological Corp.

Woodcock, R., & Johnson, M. (1977). *Woodcock-Johnson Psychœducational Battery.* Hingham, MA: Teaching Resources.

Yarwood, W.F. (1988). *Perceptions of college admissions decision makers concerning students with learning disabilities.* Unpublished doctoral dissertation, Temple University, Philadelphia.

Appendix 5.1: University and Student Publications About Learning Disabilities and Higher Education

Access to learning at New York University. New York: New York University Public Affairs Department for the Henry and Lucy Moses Center for Students with Disabilities.

Barry, K., Brinckerhoff, L., Keeney, L., & Smith, N. (1983). *College students with learning disabilities*. Madison: University of Wisconsin System/McBurney Resource Center.

Blackmore, N., Jahiel, R., Keeney, E., Mosher, S., Oberlin, A., & Tampkin, D. (1991). *Learning disabilities at Harvard: A pamphlet written by students with learning disabilities for students with learning disabilities at Harvard*. Cambridge, MA: Harvard University Office of Disability Resources.

Cain, C., Gasti, R., Keen, S., Lewis, M., & Quinn, H. (1984). *Dyslexics at Brown: A student perspective*. Providence, RI: Brown University.

Chisolm, A. (1988, May 20). Coping with Dyslexia: Finding New Ways to learn. *Harvard University Gazette, 83*(36), 1; 5.

Higher education for learning problems. Huntington, WV: Marshall University.

U.S. Department of Health and Human Services. *Facts about dyslexia*. Washington, DC: National Institute of Child Health and Human Development.

Appendix 5.2: U.S. Department of Education Regional Civil Rights Offices

Region I:
(Connecticut, Maine, Massachusetts, New Hampshire, Rhode Island, Vermont)

U.S. Department of Education
Office for Civil Rights, Region I
John W. McCormack Post
Office and Courthouse
Building, Room 222
Boston, MA 02109
(617) 223-9662
(617) 223-9695 (TDD)

Region II:
(New Jersey, New York, Puerto Rico, Virgin Islands)

U.S. Department of Education
Office for Civil Rights,
Region II
26 Federal Plaza, 33rd Floor
New York, NY 10278-0082

(212) 264-4633
(212) 265-9464 (TDD)

Region III:
(Delaware, District of Columbia, Maryland, Pennsylvania, Virginia, West Virginia)

U.S. Department of Education
Office for Civil Rights,
Region III
3535 Market Street,
P.O. Box 13716
Gateway Building, 6th Floor
Philadelphia, PA 19104-3326
(215) 596-6772
(215) 596-6794 (TDD)

Region IV:
(Alabama, Florida, Georgia, Kentucky, Mississippi, North Carolina, South Carolina, Tennessee)

U.S. Department of Education
Office for Civil Rights,
Region IV
101 Marietta Tower, NW,
27th Floor
P.O. Box 1705
Atlanta, GA 30301-1705
(404) 331-2954
(404) 331-7236 (TDD)

Region V:
(Illinois, Indiana, Michigan,
Minnesota, Ohio, Wisconsin)

U.S. Department of Education
Office for Civil Rights,
Region V
300 South Wacker Drive
8th Floor
Chicago, IL 60606
(312) 353-2520
(312) 353-2540 (TDD)

Region VI:
(Arkansas, Louisiana
New Mexico, Oklahoma, Texas)

U.S. Department of Education
Office for Civil Rights,
Region VI
1200 Main Tower Building,
Suite 2260
Dallas, TX 75202
(214) 767-3936
(214) 767-3639 (TDD)

Region VII:
(Iowa, Kansas, Missouri,
Nebraska)

U.S. Department of Education
Office for Civil Rights,
Region VII
10220 N. Executive Hills Blvd.

8th Floor
Kansas City, MO 64153
(816) 891-8026
(816) 374-7607 (TDD)

Region VIII:
(Colorado, Montana, North
Dakota, South Dakota, Utah,
Wyoming)

U.S. Department of Education
Office for Civil Rights,
Region VIII
Federal Office Building
1961 Stout Street, Room 342
Denver, CO 80294-3608
(303) 844-5695
(303) 844-3417 (TDD)

Region IX:
(Arizona, California, Hawaii,
Nevada, Guam, Trust Territory
of the Pacific Islands, American Samoa)

U.S. Department of Education
Office for Civil Rights,
Region IX
221 Main Street, 10th Floor
San Francisco, CA 94105-1925
(415) 556-7000
(415) 227-8124 (TDD)

Region X:
(Oregon, Washington, Alaska)

U.S. Department of Education
Office for Civil Rights,
Region X
915 Second Avenue
Room 3310, 10-9010
Seattle, WA 98174-1099
(206) 553-6811
(206) 553-4542 (TDD)

Appendix 5.3: Suggested Readings

Adelman, P.B., & Vogel, S.A. (1990). College graduates with learning disabilities—Employment attainment and career patterns. *Learning Disability Quarterly*, *13*(3), 154–166.

Adelman, P.B., & Vogel, S.A. (1991). The learning disabled adult. In B. Wong (Ed.). *Learning about learning disabilities*, (pp. 563–594). New York: Academic Press.

Adelman, P.B., & Wren, C.T. (Eds.). (1990). *Learning disabilities, graduate school, and careers: The student's perspective*. Lake Forest, IL: Barat College.

American Association of Community and Junior Colleges. (1988). *Community colleges and students with disabilities*. Alexandria, VA: Author. (Available from AACJC, 80 South Early Street, Alexandria, VA 22304, 1-800-336-4776.)

Association on Handicapped Student Service Programs in Postsecondary Education. (1986). *Support services for LD students in postsecondary education: A compendium of readings*. Columbus, OH: Author.

AHSSPPE (1987). *Unlocking the doors: Making the transition to postsecondary education*. Columbus, OH: Author.

Aune, B., & Ness J. (1988). *Supplement to transition curriculum: Preparing learning disabled students for postsecondary education*. Minneapolis: University of Minnesota, LD Transition Project.

Cowen, S. (1985). College choice for LD students: Know your "SWIS." *Academic Therapy*, *21*(1), 77–82.

Dalke, C., & Schmitt, S. (1987). Meeting the transition needs of college-bound students with learning disabilities. *Journal of Learning Disabilities*, *20*(3), 176–180.

Fielding, P., & Moss, J. (Eds.). (1989). *A national directory of four year colleges, two year colleges and post high school training programs for young people with learning disabilities* (6th ed.). Tulsa, OK: Partners in Publishing.

Gajar, A.H. (1986). *Assisting the learning disabled: A program development and service delivery guide for university service providers, diagnosticians, tutors, counselors, and learning disabled students*. University Park: Pennsylvania State University.

Garrett, M.K., & Welch, E.L. (1987). *Serving the student with a learning disability: A manual for SUNY faculty and professional staff*. Albany: State University of New York.

HEATH Resource Center. (1987, Spring). *Learning disabled adults in postsecondary education*. Washington, DC: Author. (Available free from HEATH, One Dupont Circle, NW, Suite 800, Washington, DC 20036 or call 1-800-544-3284.)

HEATH Resource Center. (1987, Fall). *Young adults with learning disabilities and other special needs*. Washington, DC: Author. (See ordering information Under HEATH, 1987.)

HEATH Resource Center. (1989a). *Resources for adults with learning disabilities*. Washington, DC: Author. (See ordering information Under HEATH, 1987.)

HEATH Resource Center. (1989b). *Software for LD writers*. Washington, DC: Author. (See ordering information Under HEATH, 1987.)

Human Resources Center. (1988). *The successful college student's handbook*. Albertson, NY: Author.

Johnson, J. (1988). *Learning disabilities academic support group manual.* Minneapolis: University of Minnesota.

Liscio, M. (Ed.). (1986). *A guide to colleges for learning disabled students.* Orlando: Academic Press.

Mangrum, C., & Strichart, S. (1988a). *College and the learning disabled students* (2nd ed.). New York: Grune & Stratton.

Mangrum, C., & Strichart, S. (Eds.). (1988b). *Peterson's guide to colleges with programs for learning disabled students* (2nd ed.). Princeton, NJ: Peterson's Guides.

Michaels, C.A., Thaler, R., Zwerlein, R., Gioglio, M., & Apostoli, B. (1988). *How to succeed in college: A handbook for students with learning disabilities.* Albertson, NY: Vocational Rehabilitation Services Division of the National Center on Employment and Disability, Human Resources Center.

Minskoff, E.H., Hawks, R., Steidle, E.V., & Hoffmann, F.J. (1989). A homogeneous group of persons with learning disabilities in vocational rehabilitation. *Journal of Learning Disabilities, 22*(8), 521–528.

National Association of Trade and Technical Schools. *How to choose a career . . . and a career school for the student with a disability.* Washington, DC: Author. (To order write: NATTS, 2251 Wisconsin Ave., NW, Washington, DC 20007, or call 202-333-1021.)

Neault, L. (1990). *Life directions for young adults with learning disabilities and other special needs.* East Sandwich, MA: (To order write: Riverview School Corporation, Route 6A, East Sandwich, MA 02537, or call 508-888-0489).

Price, L., & Johnson, K.E. (1986). *The secondary to postsecondary transition process for learning disabled adolescents and adults: An annotated bibliography.* Minneapolis: University of Minnesota.

Scheiber, B., & Talpers, J. (1987). *Unlocking potential: College and other choices for learning disabled people: A step-by-step guide.* Rockville, MD: Adler & Adler.

Shaywitz, S.E., & Shaw, R. (1988). The admissions process: An approach to selecting learning disabled students at the most selective colleges. *Learning Disabilities Focus, 3*(2), 81–86.

Skyer, R., & Skyer, G. (1986). *What do you do after high school? The nationwide guide to residential, vocational, social, and collegiate programs serving the adolescent, young adult, and adult with learning disabilities.* Rockaway Park, NY: Skyer Consultation Center. (To order write: ACLD Bookstore, 4156 Library Rd., Pittsburgh, PA 15234.)

Straughn, C.T. (Ed.). (1988). *Lovejoy's college guide for the learning disabled* (2nd ed.). New York: Monarch Press.

Vogel, S.A. (1982). On developing LD college programs. *Journal of Learning Disabilities, 15*(9), 518–528.

Vogel, S.A. (1985). Learning disabled college students: Identification, assessment, and outcomes. In D.D. Duane & C.K. Leong (Eds.), *Understanding learning disabilities—an international perspective* (pp. 179–203). New York: Plenum.

Vogel, S.A. (1986). Levels and patterns of intellectual functioning among LD college students. *Journal of Learning Disabilities, 19*(2), 71–79.

Vogel, S.A. (1987a). Issues and concerns in LD college programming. In D. Johnson & J. Blalock (Eds.), *Adults with learning disabilities: Clinical studies* (pp. 239–275). Orlando: Grune & Stratton.

Vogel, S.A. (1987b). Eligibility and identification considerations in postsecondary education: A new but old dilemma. In S. Vaughn & C. Box (Eds.), *Issues and future directions for research in learning disabilities* (pp. 121–137). Boston: College-Hill Press.

Vogel, S.A. (1988). Creating safety nets in residential settings. *Journal of Postsecondary Education and Disability*, 6(3), 3–6.

Vogel, S.A. (1989a). Adults with language learning disabilities: Definition, diagnosis, and determination of eligibility for postsecondary and vocational rehabilitation services. *Rehabilitation Education*, 3, 77–90.

Vogel, S.A. (1989b). Special considerations in the development of models for diagnosis of LD adults with learning disabilities. In L. Silver (Ed.), *The assessment of learning disabilities: Preschool through adulthood* (pp. 111–134). Boston: College-Hill Press.

Vogel, S.A. (1990). *College students with learning disabilities: A handbook for college LD students, university admissions officers, faculty, and administration* (3rd ed.). (Available from ACLD, 4156 Library Road, Pittsburgh, PA 15234.)

Vogel, S.A., & Adelman, P.B. (1990a). Extrinsic and intrinsic factors in graduation and academic failure among LD college students. *Annals of Dyslexia*, 40, 119–137.

Vogel, S.A., & Adelman, P.B. (1990b). Intervention effectiveness at the postsecondary level for the learning disabled. In T. Scruggs & B. Wong (Eds.), *Intervention research in learning disabilities* (pp. 329–344). New York: Springer-Verlag.

Vogel, S.A., & Adelman, P.B. (1992). The success of college students with learning disabilities: Factors related to educational attainments. *Journal of Learning Disabilities*, 25(7), 430–441.

Vogel, S.A., & Konrad, D. (1988). Characteristic written expressive language deficits of the learning disabled: Some general and specific intervention strategies. *Journal of Reading, Writing, and Learning Disabilities International*, 4, 88–99.

Vogel, S.A., & Moran, M.R. (1982). Written language disorders in learning disabled college students: A preliminary report. In W. Cruickshank & J. Lerner (Eds.), *The best of ACLD 1981, Volume III, Coming of age* (pp. 211–225). Syracuse: Syracuse University Press.

Wren, C., Adelman, P., Pike, M.B., & Wilson, J.L. (1987). *College and the high school student with learning disabilities.* (To order write: ACLD Bookstore, 4156 Library Road, Pittsburgh, PA 15234.)

Wren, C., & Segal, L. (1985). *College students with learning disabilities: A student's perspective.* Chicago: DePaul University. (To order write: ACLD Bookstore, 4156 Library Road, Pittsburg, PA 15234.)

Appendix 5.4

Barat College, Lake Forest, Illinois, Learning Opportunities Program

Application Procedure Checklist

This checklist is designed to help you complete the necessary steps in applying for admission to the Learning Opportunities Program at Barat. The application procedure has been divided into two stages: After Stage 1, we will notify you whether or not you are eligible to complete Stage 2. Please note which items and fees should be sent to the Admissions Office and which should be sent to the Learning Opportunities Program.

Stage 1

Date Completed

1. *Application for Admission*
   Complete the entire application form including the Student's Personal Statement and send it with the required application fee (non-refundable) to the *Admissions Office*.   _____

2. *Recommendations*
   Using the forms included with the application, ask two former teachers or one teacher and your counselor to write letters of recommendation. Their recommendations are to be sent directly to the Admissions Office.   _____

3. *Transcripts*
   Have your high school (and any college you have previously attended) send an official copy of your transcript to the Admissions Office.   _____

4. *SAT or ACT*
   Take the SAT or ACT (the untimed versions are acceptable) and ask that your scores be sent to the *Admissions Office*.   _____

5. *Case History*
   Complete the Case History form and return it to the Learning Opportunities Program.   _____

6. *Testing*
   Have the Wechsler Adult Intelligence Scale (WAIS) administered and ask the examiner to send the results and a copy of the protocol to the Learning Opportunities Program. If the WAIS has not been administered, the Wechsler Intelligence Scale for Children (WISC) is acceptable, if taken within the last four years. Your high school counselor may be able to help you arrange for the WAIS to be administered. For further assistance, contact the Learning Opportunities Program.   _____

After you completed Stage 1, the Learning Opportunities Program will notify you about completing Stage 2 of the application process.

Date
Completed

Stage 2
The required $50 fee (non-refundable) applies to the $500
diagnostic fee, if the student is accepted. Send fee to the
Learning Opportunities Program.   _____

1. *Past Evaluations*
   Write to all specialists who have evaluated and/or worked
   with you (e.g., psychologists, neurologists, psychiatrists) and
   request that they send the Learning Opportunities Program
   a report regarding their findings and/or your progress.   _____

2. *LD Teacher, Counselor, or Specialist Report*
   Ask a learning disabilities teacher who has helped you in
   high school to fill out the form called "LD Teacher,
   Counselor, or Specialist's Report" and mail it to the
   Learning Opportunities Program.   _____

3. *Release Form*
   Give the Program Director permission to telephone the
   specialists if further information or clarification is needed
   (by listing on the blue Release Form the names, positions,
   addresses, and telephone numbers of the professionals
   whom you have contacted who will be sending reports to the
   Program Director). Return this blue form to the Learning
   Opportunities Program.   _____

4. *Health Information*
   a. Have your family doctor send the reults of a physical
      examination, using the Health Service Form to the
      Learning Opportunities Program.   _____
   b. Have your hearing checked by the school nurse, your
      community hospital, or an audiologist (sometimes
      affiliated with an ear, nose, and throat doctor). A report
      with the results of the audiometric exam should be sent
      to the Learning Opportunities Program (no special form
      provided).   _____
   c. If you have not had your eyes examined within the last
      two years, have them checked by an opthalmologist.
      Have the results of your most recent exam sent to the
      Learning Opportunities Program (no special form
      provided).   _____

5. *Placement Tests and Interviews*
   After all information required in Stage 2 has been
   forwarded, telephone the Learning Opportunities Program
   to make an appointment for Placement Tests and an
   interview with the Program Director, an Admissions
   Couselor, and the Director of Counseling. If you wish, you
   may also schedule a tour of the campus and stay overnight in
   the dorm.   _____

VI
Professional Preparation of Specialists to Work in Postsecondary Learning Disability Programs

Doris J. Johnson

Introduction and Rationale for Professional Preparation

The purpose of this chapter is to identify several areas of competence to consider when preparing special educators to work in postsecondary programs for learning disabilities (LDs). During the 1980s there had been a significant increase in the number of students with learning disabilities who wished to enroll in postsecondary education. As a result, more personnel with expertise in program development, assessment, intervention, and administration are needed. In addition, more graduate students are expressing an interest in working in postsecondary programs. While the nature of these programs vary, a common body of knowledge is needed for specialists to work with college-level students. Fortunately, there is now a considerable amount of literature that can be used as the basis for personnel preparation and future research. Books such as that by Mangrum and Strichart (1984), chapters by Vogel (1987a,b), and many articles reviewed in this volume provide the basic coursework and practicums for students in training.

In an excellent article on postsecondary education for students with learning disabilities, McGuire, Norlander, and Shaw (1990) summarized several issues that should be considered in professional preparation. Their data from a survey of administrators and direct services personnel indicated that the ability to interpret standardized tests of academic achievement was perceived as the most desired competency. Personnel also wanted to achieve competence in pinpointing learners' strengths and weaknesses, in interacting with faculty and administrators, in acquiring management and leadership skills, and in providing cognitive interventions. They also emphasized the need for research on program evaluation. This chapter includes a summary of recommended competencies for professional preparation programs. These are based on reviews of the literature and experiences of individuals who work with this population.

Broad Overview of the Curriculum

Unlike current programs for elementary and secondary special education, there are no state certification requirements or established criteria for specialists working in postsecondary settings. However, it is recommended that such personnel have, at the very minimum, a master's degree in learning disabilities with certification that extends through the secondary level. The reason for the MA degree is the fact that work with postsecondary students requires a level of maturity and experience as well as coursework beyond the traditional K-12 curriculum in special education. Students need coursework and supervised practicums with adults as well as the sensitivity and objectivity necessary to assist college students with problems.

As in many other areas of professional preparation in special education, it is assumed that the coursework will include theories regarding normal and atypical development; characteristics of the handicapping condition; and courses in assessment, intervention, and model programs. In diagnostic practicums students should have supervised experience in taking case histories; administering, scoring, and interpreting tests; opportunities to participate in multidisciplinary staffings; and final conferences with adults and their families. They also should have intervention practicums that include teaching many types of cases under supervision. In such courses they should learn how to measure progress and make appropriate recommendations for accommodation. They should have an opportunity to see various types of programs designed to provide both accommodations and intervention. Discussions with college professors as well as with special educators help students learn about the need for ongoing realistic planning and adjustments that may be needed for individuals with learning disabilities.

Students working toward a PhD should have research experience including program evaluation. Whenever possible, doctoral candidates should be given opportunities to supervise undergraduates or MA students in practicums and to do college teaching. Although they might not be assigned to teach entire courses, students who plan to work in leadership positions should learn how to organize and present lectures to future teachers. As the number of postsecondary programs increase, more teacher trainers and researchers will be needed to generate and disseminate knowledge. Given this broad overview, the next section is devoted to more specific content in the curriculum.

Characteristics of the Population

Preparation programs should help students understand the symptomatology and heterogeneity of the population (Ackerman, McGrew, & Dykman, 1987). Often individuals with learning disabilities at the postsecondary level are thought to have problems only in reading, writing, and spelling. Although these frequently are the chief concerns, evidence from several follow-up studies, including those of Rogan and Hartman (1990), indicate that other areas such as language and mathematics are of equal concern.

Strichart (1990) reported that Mangrum and Strichart (1984) identified 134 characteristics of postsecondary students from reports in the literature. Their broad categories included difficulties in cognition, spoken and written language, perceptual-motor skills, academics, work and study habits, and social and affective behaviors. Johnson and Blalock (1987) identified problems in listening comprehension, vocabulary, pronunciation of multisyllabic words, syntax, oral formulation, and pragmatics (i.e., language usage). In addition, they found that many college students with LDs were performing below expectancy even in practical mathematics such as the use of money, time, and measurement. On the other hand some were very strong in mathematics but had reading and spelling difficulties. Stone (1987) identified some with concept formation and abstract reasoning difficulties. Such problems often interfere with all subject matter as well as with listening and reading comprehension.

Some students with LDs have difficulty with social skills and nonverbal communication that impact on their overall life on campus. Others may have residual attention problems that interfere with their ability to focus and maintain attention span, either in the classroom or when doing homework.

In general, anyone working with college-level students with LDs should be prepared for a heterogeneous population, though perhaps not as diverse as those in elementary and secondary programs. While the same types of problem may be identified across a wide age range, the overall intellectual and achievement levels should be somewhat higher among college students. Motivation is often better among university students, although some have difficulty sustaining the motivation because of the time it takes to complete assignments and because of negative feedback. The latter frequently has an impact on self-esteem. Disabilities among college students may be more subtle. Therefore, students should be prepared to investigate higher level thinking and language problems than those they might see in elementary and secondary schools.

If one accepts the standard definition of learning disabilities (Federal Regiser, 1977), students with LDs can be expected to present a discrepancy between potential and achievement in listening, speaking, reading, writing, and/or mathematics. If one accepts the definition of the National Institutes of Health (NIH), they may also have problems with social skills and attention (Kavanagh & Truss, 1989). Reviews of the literature also suggest that this older population may have problems with time management, organization, rate of processing, and other skills that cannot always be measured by highly structured standardized tests. Therefore observations and analysis of college assignments will be needed.

Despite the heterogeneity, problems rarely occur in isolation (Johnson & Blalock, 1987). For example, students with problems in conceptualization or concept formation often have difficulty with higher level listening, reading comprehension, math reasoning, and certain social skills. Similarly, listening comprehension problems typically interfere with oral expression and reading comprehension. Most dyslexics have spelling and written language difficulties; many also have other verbal deficits as indicated by the research on subtypes. By noting patterns of problems that tend to co-occur, the special educator or guidance worker can make better informed decisions about course selections and work loads. Such patterns of problems also should be considered when helping students plan for future occupations and when conducting research. Often, subtypes of problems can be obscured if one calculates only means and standard deviations. While there is research on subtypes of dyslexics and other school-age students with LDs (Lyon, 1983), studies should be conducted among the postsecondary population to determine more about patterns of problems that co-occur. However, subtypes may vary with the nature of the institution (i.e., junior college, four-year college, graduate school), the type of major, entrance requirements, and other factors. For example, in our clinic population, which is drawn from many colleges and universities in the Chicago metropolitan area and the Midwest, the mean intelligence question (IQ) for a group of 125 college students who had been evaluated was 106. However, the levels of ability varied considerably from low average to gifted. If we eliminate all those in community and junior colleges, the scores are higher. Therefore, research on subtypes should include data regarding age, both verbal and nonverbal mental ability, achievement in all areas, type of institution, entrance requirements, and many other descriptors.

The Diagnostic Process

Some college programs for learning disabilities have established standard, routine test batteries for entrance criteria (e.g., California Community College system cited in Mellard, 1990). Others rely on the special educator to select appropriate tests. In certain instances, colleges and universities require psychoeducational testing to be done before the student is admitted. Nevertheless, postsecondary special educators should be familiar with the diagnostic process and the many assessment procedures in order to critique tests, interpret results, and administer other tests as needed. Vogel (1989) offers an excellent discussion of models for assessment.

The diagnostic process involves both standardized testing and observation as well as a case history. Therefore, students in personnel preparation programs should learn how to obtain information from many sources. The case history is one of the most valuable aspects of the diagnostic process (Johnson, 1987). From the history one gains information about the adult's concerns and perceptions of the problems. The questions raised during the history should, to a certain extent, guide the selection of tests for the evaluation, though all areas of learning should be screened. During the discussion one learns about the adult's communication skills including vocabulary, grammar, articulation, and pragmatics. One can also learn about nonverbal communication, turn taking, and social skills. The students' descriptions of the history of their learning problems are revealing and important for the final diagnosis. Some may have had no formal diagnosis prior to college but struggled throughout school, with or without tutoring, counseling, and other forms of treatment. During the history, many describe their work habits and display remarkable coping skills. While the literature often highlights problems with strategies and study skills, we are impressed with many who have learned, on their own, to complete their assignments even though they needed longer and more circuitous routes to do the work. Many exert double the effort of the average student. On the other hand, some talk about their loss of motivation and inability to stay on task when they faced content they could not master. All of their comments provide relevant information to use along with formal tests, informal measures, and observations.

In certain instances, self-assessment scales are beneficial. For example, Houck, Engelhard, and Geller (1989) conducted a study of LD and non-disabled college students and found the former group perceived themselves to have greater problems in reading, written expression, visual processing, and short-term memory. While self-reports are not always verified with standardized tests, in many cases, adults are quite accurate in defining their problems.

During the evaluation, we are always concerned about those students who have no history of learning difficulties prior to college. If they have had no prior problems, and experience difficulty only with a foreign language or certain advanced courses, they may not have a specific learning disability. In order to be eligible for special services, there should be evidence of a discrepancy between potential and achievement some processing deficits, and a history of chronic learning problems. There are, of course, certain students in LD postsecondary programs who have acquired disorders that were not evident in early childhood. For example, people who had closed head injuries or illnesses such as encephalitis or meningitis may have specific learning disabilities. Those with closed head injuries frequently have problems with attention, initiative, planning, and self-monitoring. Such cases require careful multidisciplinary planning.

As stated above, it is rare to find a single area of underachievement. Usually clusters of problems interfere with several areas of learning. For example, the student with visual spatial problems may have difficulty with some aspects of geometry, chemistry, graphic arts, or personal skills. Dyslexics may have phonological processing problems that interfere with repeating and remembering multisyllabic words, word-retrieval problems, and spelling difficulty.

Areas of Assessment

Knowledge of assessment procedures for adults is essential. Special educators should be familiar with standardized tests for oral language, reading, written language, mathematics, cognitive processes, adaptive behavior, and screening measures for self-esteem, and be able to administer, score, and interpret the results. In addition, they should become familiar with criteria for eligibility and with the various approaches used to calculate discrepancies between achievement and ability (Gajar, Salvia, Gajria, & Salvia, 1989).

However, we have stated elsewhere (Johnson, 1987) that all tests assess multiple functions. Therefore, even the most valid and reliable measures may not always test what they purport to measure among the disabled. For example, a low reading comprehension score may be related to faulty decoding, poor abstract thinking, or verbal comprehension. Low visual motor scores may result from faulty visual processing skills, inability to plan a motor sequence, or lack of visual motor integration. Hence students should be taught to regard the diagnostic study as a problem-solving activity (Vogel, 1986). They should learn to analyze error patterns and formulate hypotheses about problems and to relate case history information to the test results.

Intelligence

Although most learning disabilities specialists will not be trained to give individualized IQ tests such as the Wechsler Scale (1981), they should be familiar with the tasks and be able to hypothesize how certain disabilities might interfere with achievement.

Students also should be familiar with the literature on the cognitive profiles of college students with learning disabilities (Cordoni & Goh, 1989; Vogel, 1986) as well as those that might predict college success. Leonard (1991), for example, found that the Wechsler Adult Intelligence Scale-Revised (WAIS-R) results did not predict success, but comprehension and similarities were correlated with GPA. One must, however, be aware of differences in demands at various colleges (see Chapter III by Sara Cowen).

Personality

Most LD specialists will not be prepared to give individual personality tests; however, discussions with psychologists may be helpful in determining whether any processing or linguistic deficits were manifested in the student's performance, particularly on projective tests.

Cognitive Ability

Specialists in learning disabilities should be prepared to give tests of cognitive ability such as the Woodcock-Johnson-Revised (1989) and should be familiar with the studies using these measures (Cuenin, 1990; Dalke, 1988; Gregg & Hoy, 1985; Hoy & Gregg, 1986). Tests such as Concept Formation and Analysis and Synthesis are particularly interesting because they measure nonverbal reasoning problems that may not be identified on the WAIS-R. On the other hand, students with visual spatial problems sometimes score much higher on concept formation than on the Wechsler. Other cognitive measures such as Piagetian formal operations tasks are useful for studying problem solving in adults (Stone, 1987) and may be useful in identifying various subtypes.

Processing Skills

Since some colleges attempt to identify specific processing deficits for eligibility, students in training should be familiar with various measures for assessing attention, perception, memory, and concept formation. Tests such as the Woodcock-Johnson-Revised (1989) have subtests for spatial relations, visual matching, and similar skills. However, clinicians also use error patterns as indicators of possible processing deficits. For instance, spelling errors may reflect problems in auditory or phonological processing (e.g., *rember* for remember) whereas others may be related to visual memory, recall of orthographic features, or visual monitoring (*lihgt* for light). Rate of processing may be evident on certain types of timed tasks. Thus, diagnosticians will want information that might be relevant to recommend accommodations and specific types of intervention. The student with very slow processing skills might require more repetition or additional time to complete assignments.

Language

Learning Disability specialists should be able to evaluate many parameters of both receptive and expressive language. However, there are a limited number of tests for adults. Furthermore, standardized tests rarely include the quantities and levels of information required of most college students. Consequently we often give simulated lectures or read portions of students' texts aloud to them to determine more about their listening comprehension, vocabulary, and recall of content. Naturalistic observations in various contexts are also helpful in making judgments about linguistic competence and flexibility. We are interested in knowing whether the student with LDs has the ability to respond in class, to give well-organized reports, and to communicate with both professors and peers.

To evaluate receptive vocabulary we usually give the Peabody Picture Vocabulary Test-Revised (PPVT-R) (Dunn & Dunn, 1981) or a similar measure that requires no verbal expression. Sometimes college students score below expectancy on normed reference tests, yet they have relatively high-level domain specific knowledge. Their low scores on tests such as the Peabody may reflect lack of exposure to broad content areas or lack of reading. In contrast, some students score within the expected range on standardized tests, but they have only vague notions about word meanings. Hence, diagnosticians may need to develop informal measures in content subjects. This might be done in collaboration with professors from various subject areas such as science, literature, mathematics, and the arts.

The Woodcock-Johnson-Revised Psycho-Educational Battery (WJPEB-R) (1989) can be used as a measure of listening comprehension, but, as stated above, the paragraphs are not as long as the extended discourse college students will need to master.

We are particularly concerned about listening comprehension ability when a student requests tape-recorded examinations. Some think their major problems are in reading comprehension, when, in reality, they have equal difficulty comprehending spoken language. If they are not aware of these problems, they could perform just as poorly, if not worse, on auditory tasks because of the memory component.

In the area of expressive language, diagnosticians should be prepared to look for problems of word retrieval, pronunciation of multisyllabic words, syntax, and organization of ideas. As one listens to the oral summaries and explanations given by many students with LDs, their language difficulties become very evident. Word retrieval and syntax problems often result in false starts and reformulation of sentences. Sequencing errors can be detected in faulty pronunciations of long words, particularly among dyslexics with phonological coding disorders. These same mistakes may be reflected in faulty spelling.

Information regarding expressive vocabulary and definitions can be obtained from the WAIS-R and other IQ tests. However, a more linguistic evaluation of definitions can be done by using procedures recommended by Litowitz (1987). She found many adults with LDs had good verbal intelligence and knowledge, as indicated by standardized test scores, but the scores did not reveal their subtle oral language and conceptual difficulties.

The problems in pragmatics, language usage, and sense of audience seen in children with learning disabilities may persist and even increase at the college level when students are required to communicate with a wide range of people in both formal and informal settings. Tape recordings of language samples can be transcribed and analyzed to study vocabulary (including type-token ratios), syntax, organization, coherence, and cohesion.

Reading

Students in training should be prepared to give a variety of tests for both oral and silent reading. In our program we try to obtain information about both single-word and contextual reading since there are often rather wide discrepancies in performance. Standardized tests of word-attack skills provide an indication of a student's ability to decode unfamiliar words. Unfortunately, many standardized tests do not have enough difficult items that are comparable to college-level reading. Therefore, we typically investigate the students' ability to read word lists and passages from various textbooks to see how well they can use their background knowledge and word recognition skills. Some report they cannot read (decode) words until they hear professors use them in class. Often, there are significant differences in their abilities to deal with familiar and unfamiliar material. Thus, diagnosticians should be cautious when making predictions about reading performance from a single test of word recognition. It is not unusual to see as much as a three to five grade-level difference between oral reading of single words and silent-reading comprehension. Adults with decoding problems often use their good intelligence and background knowledge when reading in context. Others read single words adequately but do not comprehend them. Often, the latter have generalized thinking problems and more serious problems in college. Students in training should be taught how to administer various comprehension tests including those that measure both literal and inferential comprehension, skimming, and scanning. In practicums they should construct informal reading inventories and passages that allow them to see whether the person can read for many purposes. Diagnostic teaching may be helpful to evaluate long-term recall of information.

Written Language

Since written language problems are among the most prevalent of all the disabilities, professionals in training should become familiar with various standardized tests and scoring systems to evaluate written language as well as the literature on the most common writing problems (Englert, Raphael, Anderson, Gregg, & Anthony, 1989; Gregg, 1983). The Woodcock-Johnson-Revised (1989) offers new measures of writing fluency but none is comparable to the demands of college. Therefore, students should learn to use informal checklists to investigate skills such as handwriting, legibility, cohesion, coherence, syntax, and sense of audience. They should become familiar with the work of Shaughnessey (1977), Vogel (1986), and others who studied writing problems among college students.

They should also be familiar with tests and research on spelling (Frith, 1980; Leuenberger & Morris, 1990) because of the many persistent problems. A review of corrected term papers or examinations will provide data for instruction. We recommend the analysis of spontaneous spelling as well as recognition and dictated tests since they provide information about possible processing deficits and rule application (Johnson, 1987). Students with LDs frequently perform much better on highly structured dictated tests and may appear to be ineligible for services until one inspects their spontaneous writing.

Mathematics

Mathematics is frequently underassessed, but an evaluation is important for making decisions about selecting college courses and for life skills. Measures of computation and reasoning including speed and accuracy are helpful. While tests are necessary for eligibility criteria, they may be insufficient for planning a program. Therefore, students in training should learn to do error analyses along with curriculum-based assessments. They should be aware of performance on timed and untimed tests. Many students with LDs have better math skills than they can demonstrate on measures such as the Wide Range Achievement Test (WRAT) (Jastak & Wilkinson, 1984) because of the time factor. In these instances, they may need accommodations for their slow speed. Some do well on math reasoning but have poor computation scores because of poor memory for facts and lack of automaticity. Students with attention disorders often fail to notice signs and make errors when required to switch from one process to another. Hence, they may need more time for monitoring. Still others may need help with basic algorithms and operations. Given the multiple reasons for low scores, the clinician must go beyond test scores to make specific recommendations.

Adaptive Behavior

In certain instances adaptive behavior also should be assessed. Tests such as the Scales of Independent Behavior (Bruininks, Woodcock, Weatherman, & Hill, 1985) may be useful. Occasionally students with nonverbal learning disabilities have problems with time, money, and orientation that ultimately interfere with independence. These people usually have high verbal skills but are deficient in visual-spatial thinking and in social perception.

Self-Esteem

There is a growing body of literature on self-esteem among college students with LDs (Saracoglu, Minden, & Wilchesky, 1989). Scales such as the Tennessee Self-Concept Scale-Revised (Fitts & Roid, 1988) and others may provide quantitative measures for evaluation and research. However, informal discussions are equally valuable. Many of our own students feel that a course in counseling is helpful, particularly if the instructor has had experience with adults who have learning disabilities.

Diagnostic Teaching

As a part of the assessment process some students need a period of diagnostic teaching prior to the final diagnosis. For example, one might want to know whether performance changes with (1) additional time; (2) a change of response mode; or (3) modifications of rate of input. Whereas most schools require a discrepancy between ability and achievement for eligibility, clinical observations may also be used in making the final diagnosis.

Explanation of Test Results

Professionals should make certain that test results are interpreted clearly to students with learning disabilities. They should clarify any technical terms or diagnostic labels and try to help the students understand how their problems might interfere with learning and occupation. For example, students who are told they are performing below average on measures of receptive language should understand how such problems might interfere with listening to lectures or certain social situations. Written reports without technical jargon should be prepared so the student with LDs can review the results and ask further questions.

In general, the professional who is involved in the assessment process should be able to choose appropriate tests, analyze and interpret the results, administer and score tests properly, prepare informal measures, integrate all of the information, and communicate the findings clearly both orally and in writing. Students in training should have supervised practicum experiences that allow them to observe and participate in all phases of the evaluation. In most instances, theory and certain lecture courses should precede practicums; however, we recommend the integration of theory and practice as early as possible. For example, graduate students in our program begin with lecture courses and observations the first quarter. Thereafter, they take two lecture courses and a practicum each term. There are divided equally between diagnostics and intervention. During the last quarter, MA students take a seminar on research and trends in the field.

Direct Services and Intervention

All professionals working with postsecondary students should have supervised practicum in remediation. This means that they should be prepared to help students with each potential area of underachievement, although some problems may be more prevalent than others.

A review of the literature as well as of diagnostic profiles from over 100 college students with LDs in our clinic indicates that all had problems with written language. Our most recent studies indicate they had particular problems with cohesion, coherence, grammar, and spelling. Whereas some colleges reduce the demands for writing and permit oral examinations, we recommend that such accommodations be considered as temporary and that instruction in writing be provided. Because writing is a powerful aid for memory and organization, it should not be avoided. The use of technology, including word processors and spell checkers, should be encouraged (see Chapter XI by Marshall H. Raskind and Neil G. Scott and Collins & Price, 1986).

The professional preparation program should include methods of teaching reading. Our data suggest that many college students are not decoding at a college level. Their scores on word-attack skills and phonetic analysis often indicate that they have not learned the graphic representations for various phonemes. This disability also causes severe problems in spelling. Despite these weaknesses, many struggle through their textbooks by relying on background knowledge. However, when asked to read individual words, they cannot do so. Although such deficits may be temporarily bypassed with tape-recorded texts, there is evidence to suggest that adults can make progress and that efforts should be made to remediate the deficits, perhaps in summer school or at times when there are fewer academic pressures. Many college students with LDs can read at a post high-school level but they lack automaticity. Consequently, they may need intervention and additional time to complete assignments.

Comprehension problems are often more pervasive and are manifested in both listening and reading. Students in training should learn effective techniques for building vocabulary, understanding relationships between words and sentences, teaching figurative language, and procedures for self-questioning. In the area of expressive language, they should learn how to help adults with problems of word retrieval, syntax, organization and preparation of oral reports, and pragmatics.

Whatever the philosophy, personnel should be prepared to help with both accommodations and direct intervention. Because of the heterogeneity of the LD population, students in training should become familiar with many approaches to instruction. For example, in the area of decoding and spelling, some methods stress explicit rule learning, whereas others emphasize implicit rule acquisition. Some studies show that direct instruction is needed whereas others focus on reciprocal teaching and guided instruction. Professional preparation should include more than descriptions of methods. Rather, in remediation practicums, students should observe master teachers and videotapes, and do role playing or simulated intervention with peers. Working with adults requires a large repertoire of techniques and finesse. Most adults with LDs are quick to tell the teacher what procedures are helpful or not. Specialists at the college level must be skilled in the use of multiple procedures. Whereas some need assistance with time management and organizational strategies, most need remediation to improve their deficits.

Advising and Guidance

Special educators often need to help LD students make the transition from secondary to postsecondary programs. However, that transition is a problem for many college-bound students, not just those with problems. Whereas many students need to learn how to manage time and develop study skills, others work so hard that they have little time for recreation and social interaction. Advisors should attempt to help them achieve a proper balance.

The college special educator does not necessarily serve as an advisor but should communicate with others to help students select the most appropriate courses. Efforts should be made to create a balanced load so a student does not have many reading and writing courses in one term if those present significant problems. Vogel (1987a) provides several important suggestions for advising college students with LDs.

Professionals in training should, if possible, have an opportunity to see how support groups are organized. Group sessions require careful planning and management. Students must be prepared for the wide range of reactions among the students with LDs. The fears, anxieties, and periodic episodes of depression among students with LDs require careful handling and support.

Special educators will need to help college students with LDs become their own advocates. They should assist them in requesting reasonable accommodations. Students in training should have opportunities to observe the approaches used by various professors on campus and become familiar with research on accommodations (Matthews, Anderson, & Skonick, 1987; Seidenberg & Koenigsberg, 1990).

Knowledge of Rules and Regulations

Professional preparation should include information regarding rules, regulations, and reasonable accommodations. A final seminar on the laws and rules with guest speakers is particularly effective. These sessions will introduce students in training to various model programs and procedures for accommodating students with disabilities. Our university and others have a course on Law and Special Education that is particularly helpful for doctoral students.

Evaluation of Progress and Programs

As yet, according to McGuire et al. (1990), Sergeant, Carter, Sedlaeck, and Scales (1988), and Vogel and Adelman (1990), there has been little systematic follow-up to indicate the most effective type of program for college students with learning disabilities. This, they say, may be related to the heterogeneity of the population. Because of the varied problems and levels of severity, follow-up investigations should be conducted. Future studies should include detailed descriptions of the students, the program, the institution, and all other factors that will allow replicability. Doctoral students in seminars can critique current studies to become more aware of variables that need to be described and controlled. Data regarding program effectiveness is particularly important to obtain further financial resources and administrative support.

Students in training should be familiar with procedures to measure progress and follow-up studies (Aaron & Phillips, 1986; Adelman & Vogel, 1991). As stated earlier, there are few data that compare intervention programs, but new studies of program effectiveness are emerging (Vogel, 1990; Chapter XIII by Pamela B. Adelman and Susan A. Vogel). Therefore, students should be taught how to keep careful records of goals, procedures, and progress. Records should include statements about what was and was not effective. In many instances, work samples and/or tape recordings of a student's performance, along with standardized tests, are important indicators of progress. If all new programs establish a good data base together with objectives, intervention procedures, and progress, the field as well as students with learning disabilities will profit. Doctoral students may elect to take courses in which they learn how to do single-subject design studies along with other procedures for studying change.

Transition

The special educator should be prepared to help students make transitions into the world of work whenever possible (Browyn, Halpern,

Hasazi, & Wehman, 1987). This does not mean that the educator is a vocational counselor. Rather, the educator helps students with the decision-making process. Rogan and Hartman (1990) found that college students from their program were in many walks of life, as did Adelman and Vogel (Chapter XIII, this volume) and Johnson and Blalock (1987). Other studies have been done to show the needs of adults with LDs, although some did not specifically focus on postsecondary students (Hoffmann et al., 1987). The choice of occupation depends on motivation, interest, overall intellectual capabilities, and achievement levels. The ultimate objective is to help the person with a learning disability become an independent, autonomous learner who is prepared for the world of work and for independent living.

References

Aaron, P.G., & Phillips, S. (1986). A decade of research with dyslexic college students. *Annals of Dyslexia, 36*, 44–68.

Ackerman, P.T., McGrew, J., & Dykman, R.A. (1987). A profile of male and female applicants for a special college program for learning disabled students. *Journal of Clinical Psychology, 34*(1), 67–78.

Browyn, L., Halpern, A.S., Hasazi, S.B., & Wehman, P. (1987). From school to adult living: a forum on issues and trends. *Exceptional Children, 53*(6), 546–554.

Bruininks, R.H., Woodcock, R.W., Weatherman, R.F., & Hill, B.K. (1985). *Scales of Independent Behavior.* Austin, TX: DLM Teaching Resources.

Collins, T.G., & Price, L. (1986). Micros for LD college writers: Rewriting documentation for word-processing programs. *Learning Disabilities Focus, 2*(1), 49–54.

Cordoni, B.K., & Goh, D. (1989). A comparison of the performance of college students with learning disabilities on the Stanford-Binet Intelligence Scale, fourth edition, and the Wechsler Adult Intelligence Scale-Revised. *Learning Disabilities, 1*(2), 35–39.

Cuenin, L.H. (1990). Use of the Woodcock-Johnson Psycho-Educational Battery with learning disabled adults. *Learning Disabilities Focus, 5*(2), 119–123.

Dalke, C. (1988). Woodcock-Johnson Psycho-Educational Test Battery profiles: A comparative study of college freshmen with and without learning disabilities. *Journal of Learning Disabilities, 21*, 567–570.

Dunn, L., & Dunn, L. (1981). *Peabody Picture Vocabulary Test-Revised.* Circle Pines, MN: American Guidance service.

Englert, C.S., Raphael, T.E., Anderson, L.M., Gregg, S.L., & Anthony, H.M. (1989). Exposition: Reading, writing, and the metacognitive knowledge of learning disabled students. *Learning Disabilities Research, 5*(1), 5–24.

Federal Register. (August 1977). *42*(163).

Fitts, W.H., & Roid, G.H. (1988). *Tennessee Self-Concept Scale-Revised Manual.* Los Angeles: Western Psychological Services.

Frith, U. (Ed.). (1980). *Cognitive processes in spelling.* New York: Academic Press.

Gajar, A., Salvia, J., Gajria, M., & Salvia, S. (1989). A comparison of intelligence achievement discrepancies between learning disabled and non-learning disabled college students. *Learning Disabilities Research, 4*(2), 119–124.

Gregg, N. (1983). College learning disabled writers: Error patterns and instructional awareness. *Journal of Learning Disabilities, 16*(6), 334–338.

Gregg, N., & Hoy, C. (1985). A comparison of the WAIS-R and the Woodcock-Johnson Tests of Cognitive Ability with learning disabled college students. *Journal of Psychoeducational Assessment, 3,* 267–274.

Hoffmann, F.J., Sheldon, K.L., Minskoff, E.H., Sautter, S.W., Steidle, E.F., Baker, D.P., Bailey, M.B., & Echols, L.D. (1987). Needs of learning disabled adults. *Journal of Learning Disabilities, 20*(1), 43–52.

Houck, C.K., Engelhard, J., & Geller, C. (1989). Self-assessment of learning disabled and nondisabled college students: A comparative study. *Learning Disabilities Research, 5*(1), 59–67.

Hoy, C., & Gregg, N. (1986). The usefulness of Woodcock-Johnson Psycho-Educational Battery cognitive cluster scores for learning disabled college students. *Journal of Learning Disabilities, 19*(8), 489–491.

Jastak, S., & Wilkinson, G.S. (1984). *Wide Range Achievement Tests-Revised* Wilmington, DC: Jastak Associates, Inc.

Johnson, D.J. (1987). Assessment issues in learning disabilities research. In S. Vaughn & C.S. Bos (Eds.), *Research in learning disabilities: Issues and future directions* (pp. 141–151). Boston, MA: College-Hill Press.

Johnson, D.J., & Blalock, J.W. (1987). *Adults with learning disabilities.* Orlando, FL: Grune & Stratton.

Kavanagh, J.F., & Truss, T.J. (1989). *Learning disabilities: Proceedings of the National Conference.* Parkton, MD: York Press.

Leonard, F.C. (1991). Using Wechsler data to predict success for learning disabled college students. *Learning Disabilities Research and Practice, 6,* 17–24.

Leuenberger, J., & Morris, M. (1990). Analysis of spelling errors by learning disabled and normal college students. *Learning Disabilities Focus, 5*(2), 103–118.

Litowitz, B. (1987). Problems of conceptualization and language: Evidence from definitions. In D.J. Johnson & J.W. Blalock (Eds.), *Adults with learning disabilities: Clinical studies* (pp. 131–143). Orlando, FL: Grune & Stratton.

Lyon, G.R. (1983). Learning-disabled readers: Identification of subgroups. In H.R. Myklebust (Ed.), *Progress in learning disabilities,* Vol. V (pp. 103–134). New York: Grune & Stratton.

McGuire, J.M., Norlander, K.A., & Shaw, S.F. (1990). Postsecondary education for students with learning disabilities: Forecasting challenges for the future. *Learning Disabilities Focus, 5*(2), 69–74.

Mangrum C.T., II, & Strichart, S.S. (1984). *College and the learning disabled student.* New York: Grune & Stratton.

Matthews, P.R., Anderson, D.W., & Skonick, B.D. (1987). Faculty attitude toward accommodations for college students with learning disabilities. *Learning Disabilities Focus, 3*(1), 46–52.

Mellard, D.F. (1990). The eligibility process: Identifying students with learning disabilities in California's community colleges. *Learning Disabilities Focus, 5*(2), 75–90.

Rogan, L.L., & Hartman, L.D. (1990). Adult outcome of learning disabled students 10 years after initial follow-up. *Learning Disabilities Focus, 5*(2), 91–102.

Saracoglu, B., Minden, H., & Wilchesky, M. (1989). The adjustment of students with learning disabilities to university and its relationship to self-esteem and self-efficacy. *Journal of Learning Disabilities*, *22*, 590–592.

Seidenberg, P.L., & Koenigsberg, E. (1990). A survey of regular and special education high school teachers and college faculty: Implications for program development for secondary learning disabled students. *Learning Disabilities Research*, *5*(2), 110–117.

Sergeant, M.T., Carter, R.T.G., Sedlaeck, W.E., & Scales, W.R. (1988). A five-year analysis of disabled student services in higher education. *Journal of Post-secondary Education and Disability*, *6*, 21–27.

Shaughnessey, M. (1977). *Errors and expectations: A guide for the teacher of basic writing*. New York: Oxford University Press.

Stone, C.A. (1987). Abstract reasoning and problem solving. In D.J. Johnson & J.W. Blalock (Eds.), *Adults with learning disabilities* (pp. 67–80). Orlando, FL: Grune & Stratton.

Strichart, S.S. (1990). College opportunities for students with learning disabilities: Issues and practices. *Learning Disabilities*, *1*(3), 119–127.

Vogel, S.A. (1986). Levels and patterns of intellectual functioning among LD college students: Clinical and educational implications. *Journal of Learning Disabilities*, *19*(2), 71–79.

Vogel, S.A. (1987a). Eligibility and identification considerations in postsecondary education: A new but old dilemma. In S. Vaughn & C. Bos (Eds.), *Research in learning disabilities: Issues and future directions* (pp. 121–132). Boston: Little, Brown.

Vogel, S.A. (1987b). Issues and concerns in LD college programming. In D.J. Johnson & J.W. Blalock (Eds.), *Adults with learning disabilities* (pp. 239–275). Orlando, FL: Grune & Stratton.

Vogel, S.A. (1989). Special considerations in the development of models for diagnosis of adults with learning disabilities. In L.B. Silver (Ed.), *The assessment of learning disabilities: Preschool through adulthood* (pp. 111–134). Boston: College-Hill Publication.

Vogel, S.A. (1990). An overview of the special topical issue on adults with learning disabilities. *Learning Disabilities Focus*, *5*(2), 67–68.

Vogel, S.A., & Adelman, P.B. (1990). Intervention effectiveness at the post-secondary level for the learning disabled. In T. Scruggs & B. Wong (Eds.), *Intervention research in learning disabilities* (pp. 329–344). New York: Springer-Verlag.

Wechsler, D. (1981). *Wechsler Adult Intelligence Scale-Revised*. San Antonio, TX: Psychological Corp.

Woodcock, R.W., & Johnson, B. (1989). *Woodcock-Johnson Psycho-Educational Battery—Revised*. Allen, TX: DLM Teaching Resources.

VII
Faculty Development: Changing Attitudes and Enhancing Knowledge About Learning Disabilities

ERNEST ROSE

During the 1980s, there was a dramatic increase in the number of students with learning disabilities (LDs) enrolling in postsecondary education programs (Bursuck, Rose, Cowen, & Yahaya, 1989; Decker, Polloway, & Decker, 1985; Edgar, 1988; Garnett & LaParta, 1984; Mangrum & Strichart, 1989). This meant a greater demand on colleges and universities to provide reasonable accommodations for admission to programs and in academic coursework. The response to this demand was to establish an array of services for students with LD including the hiring of LD specialists within the framework of Disabled Student Services (Adelman & Vogel, 1990; Barbaro, Christman, Holzinger, & Rosenberg, 1985; Dalke & Schmitt, 1987; Mangrum & Strichart, 1989; Vogel, 1982). Despite this response, one of the greatest ongoing challenges faced by college students with learning disabilities and their service providers is gaining and maintaining the acceptance and cooperation of academic faculty (Amsel & Fichten, 1990; Morris, Leuenberger, & Aksamit, 1987; Rose & Bursuck, 1989). Research cited in the following section indicates that this challenge exists because there is a considerable lack of understanding as to what learning disabilities are and are not. The purpose of this chapter, then, is to explore the topic of faculty development with regard to changing attitudes and enhancing knowledge about learning disabilities.

Research on Faculty Attitudes Toward Students with Learning Disabilities

As the need for LD services has increased on college campuses, investigators have studied the attitudes of faculty toward students with learning disabilities. These studies have usually focused on faculty attitudes either across disabilities or in comparison with other college personnel. For example, Leyser (1989) conducted a study on the attitudes of 124 faculty in education and professional studies at a midwestern university. His findings suggested that these faculty members had a positive view towards academic accommodations for students with sensory and physical disabilities but were less supportive of accommodations for students with learning disabilities. According to Leyser, faculty questioned the ability of persons with LDs to pursue a college degree. In fact, only 57% strongly supported the admission of students with LDs to the university. These conclusions were similar to those of Minner and Prater (1984), who found that college faculty had negative expectations of students with LDs.

Comparisons of attitudes toward students with LDs on college campuses have suggested that significantly more positive attitudes are expressed by student services personnel than by faculty (Aksamit, Morris, & Leuenberger, 1987; Farrell & Harckham, 1988). This is not surprising given that one would expect student services staff to be more aware of the nature of learning disabilities and understand the potential of students with LDs to succeed in college programs. In fact, awareness or level of information about disabilities has been found to promote more favorable attitudes among college personnel (Aksamit et al., 1987; Farrell & Harckham, 1988; Leyser, 1989; Lundeberg & Svien, 1988). In addition, those faculty with previous experience and contact with students who have learning disabilities and other disabilities hold more positive attitudes toward them than faculty with no or very limited contact (Amsel & Fichten, 1990; Fichten, Amsel, Bourdon, & Creti, 1988; Fichten, Bourdon, Creti, Amsel, & Martos, 1986; Fonosch & Schwab, 1981; Morris et al., 1987). Although these investigations are restricted in their findings due to single-campus sampling, they do establish a framework of agreement: The more faculty tend to know about learning disabilities, the more they tend to support education and services for students with LDs.

Promoting Awareness of Learning Disabilities on College Campuses

The studies cited above are unanimous in suggesting that in-service programs for college faculty and staff on the topic of learning disabilities make a significant difference in promoting positive attitudes and in encouraging faculty to adapt course activities for students with LDs. With this evidence in mind, Lundeberg and Svien (1988) have proposed a four-step model for developing faculty understanding of students with learning disabilities. Their model incorporates a number of suggestions from other authors who have provided in-service or staff development workshops (Rose & Bursuck, 1989; Rose, Bursuck, Cowen & Burke, 1989; Vogel, 1982; Vogel, 1990).

The first step is to assess campus needs and concerns. This can be accomplished through individual interviews, campuswide assessment surveys, or open meetings. The choice will probably depend on the size of the campus, time, cost, and other factors. Whatever method is used, it is important to capture as much information as needed from as many faculty and staff as possible. In this step, the process is as important as the product. Thus, it is good practice to involve faculty in determining what information is needed and how it will be gathered. By including faculty in this process, they see themselves as stakeholders in potential outcomes down the line.

Lundeberg and Svien (1988) have reported on the successful use of open meetings to determine needs for in-service programs, whereas other authors (Gajar, 1986; Matthews, Anderson, & Skolnick, 1987; Rose & Bursuck, 1989) have described the success of using service advisory committees (SAC) to develop and distribute needs assessment and attitudinal surveys. Service advisory committees should include an administrator, two or three faculty from different colleges or divisions, a student with a learning disability, and a LD service specialist. The duty of a SAC is to integrate their perspectives on the current status of LD services and the roles faculty play in the service-provision scheme (Gajar, 1986; Mangrum & Strichart, 1989; Rose & Bursuck, 1989). The committee should identify objectives and uses for their survey information and methods for obtaining the greatest amount of faculty participation.

Within the current topic, one use is to determine issues to be addressed in in-service workshops. A survey on faculty attitudes toward providing accommodations in their courses is included in Appendix 7.1. This survey contains items covering both general and specific accommodations. Responses to these items will help the SAC in setting an agenda for in-service workshops. Whatever means are used to determine LD service needs, it is important to use the information in a way that will facilitate productive in-service meetings and establish ongoing communication between faculty, students, and student service providers.

The second step in the Lundeberg and Svien (1988) model is using needs assessment data for in-service design. Based upon the information gathered from step one, an in-service (or series) can be designed that integrates the needs of faculty and staff with those of students and LD service providers. Often, this design includes presentations on the (1) definition and characteristics of learning disabilities; (2) students' concerns and perspectives; (3) faculty's concerns and perspectives; and (4) methods for faculty, students, and service specialists to work together to implement reasonable accommodations. Depending on the attitudinal climate and resources of the college, it may be helpful to bring in a speaker to address points (1) and (4). Professionals from off campus can often establish or reinforce the credibility of students and service specialists with faculty, staff, and administrators who may be reluctant to cooperate. These points are covered in more detail later in this chapter.

In-service program developers have found that concerns and perspectives of students are best presented by a panel of students with LDs who are succeeding in their college programs because of their abilities, motivation, and the services and accommodations provided (Lundeberg & Svien, 1988; Rose & Bursuck, 1989). These presentations are often powerful and convincing descriptions of how students from different program majors have learned to cope with their learning disabilities and progress toward their educational goals. Faculty frequently consider student presentations as the most helpful part of an in-service and may change their negative or indifferent attitudes toward accommodating students with LDs (Rose & Bursuck, 1989).

Just as students are effective in discussing their concerns and perspectives, faculty can also be helpful in presenting these same topics (point 4). Whenever possible, in-service planners should attempt to employ faculty from a variety of disciplines to discuss their experiences in providing course modifications for students with LDs. Their colleagues in the audience are often surprised to learn that the presenters have agreed to accommodations and have occasionally developed specific accommodations on their own (Rose & Bursuck, 1989).

Step three is to include activities to make the in-service as interactive as possible. These activities are in addition to the suggested speakers identified in step two. Lundeberg and Svien (1988) have described activities that facilitate discussions among faculty and staff regarding the feelings and frustrations of students with learning disabilities, their own feelings, and the pros and cons about providing accommodations in course requirements. Some examples of activities are presented in the next section. Of course, the number and extent of activities in relation to the number of speakers will depend upon time allotted for the in-service.

The final step of the model (Lundeberg & Svien, 1988) is to evaluate the in-service to gather additional data and generate further interest. Unfortunately, this step is often overlooked when planning an in-service workshop, but it is a critical step to determine whether or not the identified outcomes were accomplished and to what degree. By having this information, one can determine the kind of follow-up needed to build on the original outcomes and design future in-service presentations based upon newly identified outcomes. In addition, some unanticipated outcomes (positive and/or negative) may have occurred that need immediate attention.

Common Questions Among Faculty

Over the past several years, the author has conducted a number of in-service workshops for college faculties and staff on the topic of learning disabilities. During this time, four common questions seem to have come up over and over again: What are learning disabilities? What are my responsibilities under the law? What can I do for these students in the classroom? Do reasonable accommodations mean lower standards for students with learning disabilities? Although this does not represent an inclusive set of questions, these must be answered in order to develop faculty support for learning disabilities services.

What are learning disabilities?

The importance of the answer to this question lies in helping faculty to understand that (1) learning disabilities are *real* and constitute a life-long condition; (2) they are different from other disabilities that affect learning in that individuals with LDs have at least average intellectual potential, and the learning problems caused by a learning disability are not the result of other disabilities such as mental retardation, emotional disturbance, or sensory impairment; and (3) learning disabilities affect individuals in different ways, which helps explain why a student with LDs may perform adequately in some courses and poorly in others. You must remember that the question: "What is a learning disability?" is not the same for all faculty. Some want to know what causes the disability whereas others may be more interested in whether or not persons with learning disabilities should be taking college courses. Certainly, there are notable examples to give in the latter case. Nelson Rockefeller, a prominent political figure, openly discussed his dyslexia, and biographical data suggest a learning disabilities profile for scientists Thomas Edison and Albert Einstein, the French sculptor Auguste Rodin, and President Woodrow Wilson, who was also a noted scholar (Lerner, 1989).

In addition to the definition of learning disabilities, it is often helpful to use simulation exercises so that faculty can "experience" a learning disability. The purpose here is to take a group of selected individuals who do not question their own ability to learn, and to demonstrate to them how a learning disability impedes academic skill performance in areas such as reading, writing, and speaking. These simulations can be provided with inexpensive materials such as overhead transparencies, pocket mirrors, and cassette recorders and tapes. Exercises that tend to be powerful examples are selecting professors to (1) read a page of text projected on a screen as it would appear to someone with dyslexia (Figure 7.1); (2) write a short dictation while looking into a pocket mirror held at a 45° angle to their notebooks (an example of dysgraphia or poor fine-motor control); (3) take notes from a lecture recorded at one-and-a-half times normal speed (demonstrating an auditory processing problem); and (4) give a two-minute speech on a specific topic using words that have three syllables, no more, no less (an example of a verbal expression problem). The point of using simulations is to create the awareness that students with learning disabilities must work through difficulties and frustrations not faced by students who have no disability. Furthermore, the point must be stressed that learning disabilities make many academic tasks more time-consuming.

How Is Your Visual Perception?

Please decode the following:

E ach ad ut mitha ie ar mimp bisadility is am iubiubnal, het someg ene ral charact eristic s ho exist

He or sve has aver ape or adove averape iwtellipence; so me of thw wore quenalvet sywgto ws appear to de—bis or hers of wotor ac tivity; bisorder sof ewotionalith; bisorbeRs of berceb tiou; bisorb era of coucegtion; d. sorner s of attentiow; bisorders of wewory.

NOM let, s biscus s sowe of your "percegtual brodlews."

1. Lis t swe o f tye things tyat wabe yonr reabinp tash wor e biff i cnlt.

2. Li st sowe oft he tying s yon bib th at enadled yon to reab tyis gaper.

Wyat mere so we of you r jeelings or tho ug ts mylie a ttemgting tor ea b tyis?

FIGURE 7.1 Adapted from McGinnis, L. R., & Miller, R. (1985). *What is a learning disability?* River Grove, IL: Triton College.

For example, those individuals whose learning disability affects reading comprehension must read material several times over to understand textual meaning and concepts that non-learning disabled students may comprehend in one reading. Thus, learning disabilities do not impair the potential to learn; rather, they impair the process of learning.

What are my responsibilities under the law?

Once faculty have been introduced to a definition of learning disabilities, the next step is to make them aware of certain obligations that postsecondary educational institutions have under federal law (Public Law 93–112, Section 504, Subpart E). There are a number of aspects that could be discussed, but faculty must be clear on the meaning of "qualified handicapped individual." The term "handicapped individual" includes students with learning disabilities, and the term "qualified" refers to persons with handicaps who *meet the academic and technical standards* for admission to college or university programs. The second point is particularly salient so that faculty understand that there is no "open-door" policy solely for students with learning disabilities. They must meet whatever entrance criteria are set by the college or university. In some cases colleges will have special admissions policies for underrepresented groups that may include students with disabilities, but such policies are not established for their benefit alone. Consequently, faculty must realize that providing accommodations for students with any disability is not voluntary or an act of charity, but an obligation by the fact that these students did meet the admissions criteria of the institution and, hence, are protected by the law. (See Chapter II by Laura Rothstein and Chapter V by Susan A. Vogel for in-depth discussions.)

The most critical concept for faculty to grasp is that of *reasonable accommodations*. As with many federal laws, the reasonable accommodations concept has been defined by a set of rules and regulations and continues to be defined further by occasional litigation (Federal Programs Advisory Service, 1989). The spirit of the law directs administrators and faculty to provide accommodations that enable persons with learning disabilities access to programs and activities on their campuses. Vogel (1990) has identified two types of accommodations that are generally provided in postsecondary education: (1) teaching methods employed by faculty and (2) the means by which faculty measure or evaluate learning in their students. (See Chapter I by Susan A. Vogel for a discussion on this subject.) These two types of accommodation form the foundation for answering the third common question.

What can I do for these students in the classroom?

When this question arises it often enables the service provider to determine those faculty members who are eager to cooperate and those who may be reluctant. Herum (1982) has written about his reluctance in accepting the existence of learning disabilities and his responsibility in working with these students through the educative process. In overcoming his reluctance, Herum came to three conclusions. The first was that professors do not appreciate confronting reluctant learners in their classrooms, and thus, should not be reluctant themselves to learn about the impact of learning disabilities on students. Second, professors must become aware of the fact that not all students learn the same way in the same amount of time; that individuals have different styles of learning, and can benefit from teaching that complements their learning style. Third, making general coursework adaptations that are helpful to students with learning disabilities are typically beneficial to all students.

Suggestions have been given for promoting the awareness of learning disabilities and for overcoming the reluctance of faculty to acknowledge the existence of this condition. Here, attention is on teaching and class activities that tend to be helpful for all students including those with learning disabilities. This is often a key issue when working with college professors. If they understand that a few changes will benefit all their students and not cost them a lot of extra time, or necessitate a total overhaul of their courses, many are very willing to cooperate. Chapter I provides an in-depth discussion of general and specific suggestions that college faculty will find helpful for their students.

Faculty should consider their own teaching styles since this can lay the groundwork for them to work with students and specialists in developing more specific accommodations. Rose (1989) has developed the Instructional Style Survey to facilitate this process (see Appendix 7.2). The survey is organized into seven areas of interest to students and LD service providers: (1) materials and equipment; (2) lectures; (3) student involvement and feedback; (4) assignments; (5) examinations; (6) examination schedules; and (7) accommodations for students with disabilities. These areas were selected based on consultation with LD specialists who participated in a three-year U.S. Department of Education demonstration grant, the Northern Illinois Postsecondary Education Project-(NIPEP) (Rose & Bursuck, 1989). NIPEP was developed to assist college and university disability service providers to enhance their support services for students with learning disabilities.

One of the needs LD specialists identified was to find a method for assessing the instructional style of faculty, and then to assist students to develop course survival strategies. Faculty who have students with learning disabilities enrolled in their courses are requested to fill out the survey for those courses and for all courses they teach if their style differs from one course to another (e.g., seminar vs. lab). Once this has been done, the LD specialist can meet with the target student(s) and discuss strategies for success in the classroom, on assignments, and on exams. For example, if the instructor marks that he or she often uses an overhead projector in class, the student would be advised to sit near the front of room to ensure a good view of the material presented on transparencies. Another example can be selected from section E., Examinations. If the instructor marks that he or she always uses a multiple-choice format for tests, the student is advised to concentrate on strategies for reading and answering those types of questions, with particular emphasis on the subject matter of the course.

Finally, section G., Accommodations for Students with Disabilities, can serve as a spot check on an instructor's attitude toward providing reasonable accommodations for students with LDs or other disabilities. The Instructional Style Survey is used by LD specialists at several community colleges in Illinois. In fact, the author and some of his colleagues have found the survey to be a useful way of informing all students in their courses about their particular instructional styles.

Do reasonable accommodations mean lower standards for students with learning disabilities?

In the course of answering the first three questions it is easy to assume the present question has been answered, but this is often a false assumption. An effective presentation, whether it is in a classroom of students or an in-service for faculty and staff, follows the same principles. One of them is to repeat and summarize important points. When the question is asked, it means someone or a group within the audience has not understood the given answer. Be reassuring and direct: Standards are *not* to be lowered; rather, accommodations are designed to enable students with LDs to meet the existing standards. Reasonable accommodations are implemented so that students with learning disabilities do not have to face additional handicaps and so that they have a learning experience more like that of other students. Whenever possible, offer the audience some practical examples. For instance, some professors do not like the idea of extended time on testing even though they realize it takes students with LDs longer to read questions and write responses. In this case it is often helpful to offer an example from the world of work. Many people in business, industry, and education simply have too much work to finish within a given workday or work period. The solution to this problem is to work overtime, that is, come to work early, stay late, take work home. If this accommodation is acceptable to employers, why not to educators? Of course, there will always be exceptions. In some cases, it is as important for students to be graded on the rate as well as the quality of their work. For example, nursing majors must learn to perform certain critical life-saving tasks with speed and accuracy prior to graduation. In such a case, extended-time is not a reasonable accommodation, and other means may have to be considered. This is often a good opportunity to engage the audience in some solution sharing and brainstorming. However, it is always important to have prepared examples to fit the diversity of faculty being addressed.

Maintaining and Extending Faculty Support

The previous discussion dealt with providing presentations and activities for promoting an awareness of learning disabilities and some of the basic accommodations faculty can make in their courses for students with LDs. Although a single in-service is usually insufficient to educate faculty and maintain their support over time, it is also probable that they will tire of continued workshops. So, if multiple in-service programs are necessary they should be scheduled to touch upon all the necessary topics within an academic year. Beyond that, workshops should be conducted for new faculty and staff and for continuing faculty when assessments indicate the need for them.

It is necessary, of course, to maintain contact with faculty and continue to work with them in ways that will provide appropriate accommodations for students. This is best achieved through methods that make it easy for faculty to communicate with service specialists. Although contact may be easily achieved by face-to-face meetings in smaller colleges, written communication and telephone calls tend to be the most efficient means at larger colleges and universities. Whatever the means of communication, there is a number of practical considerations.

First, make sure that faculty are able to contact service specialists when they feel the need. Print and distribute labels with names, campus addresses, and telephone numbers that can be stuck to rolodex cards or put in address books. Make sure faculty know the name of the person to contact for questions regarding services for students with learning disabilities.

Second, for those students who are willing to give their permission, it may be useful to give professors a list of students with LDs in their courses and the kinds of services they receive outside the classroom.

Third, although it is not the responsibility of faculty to identify students with potential learning disabilities, some faculty are particularly sensitive to students who are having problems in their courses. In these cases, faculty should have a means to refer a student (with the student's knowledge) to the disabilities service office. Appendix 7.3 provides an example of a faculty referral checklist that has been used for just this purpose.

To encourage the use of such checklists, faculty need to be informed of the disposition of their referrals. This should be done in a timely fashion, so that the referring faculty member knows the service system can react to referrals in an efficient manner.

Fourth, keep faculty informed about interesting facts and activities related to learning disabilities and LD service specialists on campus. This can be done through a newsletter sent out each semester that includes short articles by service specialists, students, and faculty. Another idea is to use monthly "For your information (FYI)" memos. These memos can let faculty know about data on retention and graduation rates of students with learning disabilities and about workshops and conferences that provided additional skill training to service staff who attended. The purpose of these communication strategies is to keep reminding faculty that there is assistance for students with LDs and for them in devising accommodations when necessary. Remember also that there is no substitute for thoughtfulness in thanking cooperative faculty with a note or a telephone call. These ideas and more can be generated by the continuing work of a SAC.

Summary

With increasing numbers of students with learning disabilities entering colleges and universities, there will be a corresponding need to increase the awareness of faculty about the learning characteristics of these students and about the instructional accommodations they need. Clearly, it will fall upon service specialists at each postsecondary institution to provide awareness and education of faculty about their roles and responsibilities in teaching students with LDs and to keep and improve faculty support on a day-to-day basis.

References

Adelman, P., & Vogel, S.A. (1990). College graduates with learning disabilities—Employment attainment and career patterns. *Learning Disability Quarterly*, *13*, 154–166.

Aksamit, D., Morris, M., & Leuenberger, J. (1987). Preparation of student services professionals and faculty for servicing learning disabled college students. *Journal of College Student Personnel, 28*, 53–59.

Amsel, R., & Fichten, C.S. (1990). Interaction between disabled and nondisabled college students and their professors: A comparison. *Journal of Postsecondary Education and Disability, 8*, 125–140.

Barbaro, F., Christman, D., Holzinger, S.M., & Rosenberg, E. (1985). Support services for the learning disabled college student. *Journal of the National Association of Social Workers, 30*, 12–18.

Bursuck, W.D., Rose, E., Cowen, S., & Yahaya, M.A. (1989). Nationwide survey of postsecondary education services for students with learning disabilities. *Exceptional Children, 56*(3), 236–245.

Dalke, C., & Schmitt, S. (1987). Meeting the transition needs of college-bound students with learning disabilities. *Journal of Learning Disabilities, 20*(5), 176–180.

Decker, T., Polloway, E., & Decker, B. (1985). Help for the LD college student. *Academic Therapy, 20*, 339–345.

Edgar, E. (1988). A longitudinal study of graduates of special education. *Interchange: The Secondary Transition Intervention Effectiveness Institute, 8*, 3–5.

Farrell, M.L., & Harckham, L.D. (1988). Attitude of college personnel toward learning disabled college students. *Journal of Postsecondary Education and Disability, 6*, 7–13.

Federal Programs Advisory Service. (1989). *Handicapped requirements handbook*. Washington, DC: Thompson Publishing Group.

Fichten, C.S., Amsel, R., Bourdon, C.V., & Creti, L. (1988). Interaction between college students with a physical disability and their professors. *Journal of Applied Rehabilitation Counseling, 19*, 13–21.

Fichten, C.S., Bourdon, C.V., Creti, L., Amsel, R., & Martos, J.G. (1986). Professor-physically disabled college student interaction: Scoring manual. Abstracted in *Resources in Education, 21*, 81. (ERIC Document Reproduction Service No. 268–709).

Fonosch, G.G., & Schwab, L.O. (1981). Attitudes of selected university faculty members toward disabled students. *Journal of College Student Personnel, 22*, 229–235.

Gajar, A. (1986). *Assisting the learning disabled—A program development and service delivery guide for university service providers, diagnosticians, tutors, counselors, and learning disabled students*. University Park, PA: The Pennsylvania State University.

Garnett, K., & LaParta, S. (1984). *College students with learning disabilities*. New York: Hunter College.

Herum, J. (1982). *A college professor as a reluctant learner: Facing up to the learning disabled*. Ellensburg, WA: Central Washington University.

Lerner, J. (1989). *Learning disabilities: Theories, diagnosis, and teaching strategies* (5th ed.). Boston: Houghton Mifflin.

Leyser, Y. (1989). A survey of faculty attitudes and accommodations for students with disabilities. *Journal of Postsecondary Education and Disability, 7*, 97–108.

Lundeberg, M., & Svien, K. (1988). Developing faculty understanding of college students with learning disabilities. *Journal of Learning Disabilities, 21*(5), 299–300; 306.

Mangrum, C.T., & Strichart, S.S. (1989). *College and the learning disabled student: Program development, implementation, and selection* (2nd ed.). Orlando, FL: Grune & Stratton.

Matthews, P.R., Anderson, D.W., & Skolnick, B.D. (1987). Faculty attitudes toward accommodations for college students with learning disabilities. *Learning Disabilities Focus*, *3*, 46–52.

Minner, S., & Prater, G. (1984). College teachers' expectations of LD students. *Academic Therapy*, *20*, 225–229.

Morris, M., Leuenberger, J., & Aksamit, D. (1987). Faculty inservice training: Impact on the postsecondary climate for learning disabled students. *Journal of Postsecondary Education and Disability*, *5*, 57–66.

Rose, E. (1989). *Instructional style survey*. DeKalb, IL: Northern Illinois University.

Rose, E., & Bursuck, W.D. (1989). *The Northern Illinois postsecondary education project: Final report*. DeKalb, IL: Northern Illinois University.

Rose, E., Bursuck, W.D., Cowen, S., & Burke, L. (1989). *Project TAPE: Technical assistance for postsecondary education: Final report*. DeKalb, IL: Northern Illinois University.

Vogel, S.A. (1982). On developing LD college programs. *Journal of Learning Disabilities*, *15*, 518–528.

Vogel, S.A. (1990). *College students with learning disabilities: A handbook for college LD students, admissions officers, faculty, and administrators* (3rd ed.). Pittsburgh: National Learning Disabilities Association.

Appendix 7.1

Accommodations for Students with Learning Disabilities

This questionnaire is an attempt to ascertain how the faculty feel about making accommodations in their classes for students with learning disabilities. Consider how you would respond to a student in your class with a documented learning disability, if he/she requested any of the following. Please check (×) the first column if you *would* make the accommodation, the second column if you *would not*, and the third column if you *do not know* if you would make the accommodation.

	Would	**Would Not**	**Do Not Know**
1. Extend deadlines for completion of class projects, papers, etc.	____	____	____
2. Analyze the process as well as the final solution. (For example, give the student partial credit if the correct mathematical computation was used even though the final answer was wrong.)	____	____	____
3. Allow the student to complete alternative assignments.	____	____	____
4. Allow the student to do an extra credit assignment when this option is not available to other students.	____	____	____
5. Allow the student to give oral presentations or tape-recorded assignments rather than produce written projects.	____	____	____
6. Allow the use of proofreaders to assist in the correction of spelling, grammar, and punctuation.	____	____	____
7. Allow the use of proofreaders to assist in the reconstruction of the student's first draft of a written assignment.	____	____	____
8. Allow the use of a proofreader to assist the student in the substitution of a higher level vocabulary for the original wording.	____	____	____
9. Allow the student to take an alternative form of your exams. (For example, some students with learning disabilities have trouble taking tests using computer-scored answer sheets. Others might do better on multiple-choice tests than essay tests.)	____	____	____
10. Allow a proctor to rephrase test questions that are not clear to the			

student. (For example, a double
negative may need to be clarified.)   _____   _____   _____
11. Allow the student extra time to
    complete tests.   _____   _____   _____
12. Allow the student to dictate answers to
    a proctor.   _____   _____   _____
13. Allow the student to respond orally to
    essay questions.   _____   _____   _____
14. Allow exams to be proctored in a
    separate room to reduce distractions. _____   _____   _____
15. Allow the student to use calculators
    during tests and in-class assignments. _____   _____   _____
16. Allow misspellings, incorrect
    punctuation, and poor grammar
    without penalizing the student.   _____   _____   _____
17. Allow the student to substitute a course
    for a required course. (For example,
    substitute for a foreign language
    requirement.)   _____   _____   _____
18. Provide the student with an early
    syllabus to give ample time to complete
    reading and writing assignments.   _____   _____   _____
19. Allow the student to tape record
    classroom lectures.   _____   _____   _____
20. Provide the student with copies of
    instructor's lecture notes after he/she
    attends the lecture.   _____   _____   _____
21. Allow the student to withdraw from a
    course after the usual cutoff date.   _____   _____   _____
22. Allow the student to take advantage of
    priority registration. (For example, be
    among the first to register.)   _____   _____   _____
23. Protect the student against undue
    anxiety by relaxing academic probation
    and suspension procedures.   _____   _____   _____

Comments:

Adapted from Matthews, P.R., Anderson, D.W., & Skolnick, B.D. (1987). Faculty attitudes toward accommodations for college students with learning disabilities. *Learning Disabilities Focus*, *3*, 46–52.

Appendix 7.2

Instructional Style Survey

Instructor _____   Semester/Quarter _____
Course Number and Title _____

In order to assist our students in meeting the demands of college level courses it is important to teach them study skills. As support service personnel, the more we know about an instructor's specific instructional style, the better we can prepare students to develop strategies to meet the requirements of the course. We would appreciate your assistance in filling out this survey. Thank you for your time and effort.

Please respond to each item as it best describes your style:

A. Materials and Equipment	Never	Sometimes	Often	Always
1.0 I provide students with a detailed course syllabus.	____	____	____	____
1.1 I use the visua! aids listed below:				
1.1.0 Overhead projector	____	____	____	____
1.1.1 Films	____	____	____	____
1.1.2 Filmstrips	____	____	____	____
1.1.3 Handouts	____	____	____	____
1.1.4 Chalkboard	____	____	____	____
1.1.5 VCR	____	____	____	____
1.1.6 Charts	____	____	____	____
1.1.7 Computer-assisted instruction	____	____	____	____
1.1.8 Models	____	____	____	____
1.1.9 Other _____	____	____	____	____
1.2 I use auditory aids (e.g., tapes, records, etc.).	____	____	____	____
1.3. I use amplification equipment.	____	____	____	____
1.4 Other _____	____	____	____	____
1.5 I present an outline of the lecture on:				
1.5.1 Handouts	____	____	____	____
1.5.2 Transparency	____	____	____	____

1.6 The textbook I use is:
   Name of text _____
   Publisher _____

1.7 I assign readings in addition to, or in substitution for, a text.
   Number of articles _____
   How do students obtain them? _____

Comments:

	Never	Sometimes	Often	Always

B. Lecture

2.0 I use demonstrations to support my lecture through:

	Never	Sometimes	Often	Always
2.0.1 Examples	___	___	___	___
2.0.2 Simulations	___	___	___	___
2.0.3 Role Playing	___	___	___	___
2.1 I summarize important points of the lecture at the end of the class, throughout the class, or at the beginning of next day's lessons.	___	___	___	___
2.2 I pause to give students time to think, write, reply.	___	___	___	___
2.3 I verbally stress and/or repeat key words, phrases, and ideas.	___	___	___	___
2.4 I stress key issues and words by writing them on the board or on transparencies.	___	___	___	___
2.5 I stress material mainly from the textbook and/or readings.	___	___	___	___

Comments:

	Never	Sometimes	Often	Always

C. Student Involvement and Feedback

	Never	Sometimes	Often	Always
3.0 I encourage student participation during lecture.	___	___	___	___
3.1 I incorporate small group activities into lecture (2–6 people).	___	___	___	___
3.2 I incorporate large group activities into lecture (7–12 people).	___	___	___	___
3.3 I give assignments to be done in class.	___	___	___	___
3.4 I call on students only when they raise their hands.	___	___	___	___
3.5 I call on students at random to solicit their comments or questions.	___	___	___	___

Comments:

	Never	Sometimes	Often	Always

D. Assignments

	Never	Sometimes	Often	Always
4.0 I assign group oral presentations (No. ___).	___	___	___	___
4.1 I assign individual oral presentations (No. ___).	___	___	___	___

	Never	Sometimes	Often	Always
4.2 I assign short papers of 3–5 pages (No. ____).	____	____	____	____
4.3 I assign term papers of 6–15 pages or more (No. ____).	____	____	____	____
4.4 I assign group term papers (No. ____).	____	____	____	____

Comments:

E. Examinations

	Never	Sometimes	Often	Always
5.0 I use the test formats listed below:				
5.0.1 Multiple choice	____	____	____	____
5.0.2 True/False	____	____	____	____
5.0.3 Fill-in-the-blank	____	____	____	____
5.0.4 Essay	____	____	____	____
5.0.5 Oral	____	____	____	____
5.0.6 Pop quizzes	____	____	____	____
5.1 I typically stress:				
5.1.1 Application	____	____	____	____
5.1.2 Definitions	____	____	____	____
5.1.3 Understanding of concepts	____	____	____	____
5.1.4 Material from assigned readings	____	____	____	____
5.1.5 Material from lectures/class discussion	____	____	____	____
5.1.6 Material from readings and class meetings equally	____	____	____	____
5.2 Math-Related Examinations				
5.2.1 I provide students with formulas to complete computation.	____	____	____	____
5.2.2 I allow students to use calculators on exams without penalty.	____	____	____	____
5.2.3 I stress formula memorization.	____	____	____	____

Comments:

F. Evaluation Schedule

	Never	Sometimes	Often	Always
6.0 I give:				
6.0.1 Weekly quizzes	____	____	____	____
6.0.2 Midterm and final examinations	____	____	____	____
6.0.3 I provide students with a quiz/test schedule	____	____	____	____

Comments:

	Never	Sometimes	Often	Always
G. Accommodations for Students with Disabilities				
7.0 I will allow students to tape record lectures.	___	___	___	___
7.1 I will allow students to have a notetaker in class.	___	___	___	___
7.2 I will allow students to arrange for extended time on exams without penalty.	___	___	___	___
7.3 I will allow students to have an interpreter in class.	___	___	___	___
7.4 I will allow students to substitute oral exams for written exams, or vice versa.	___	___	___	___
7.5 I will allow students to have an approved proctor read exam questions to them.	___	___	___	___
7.6 I will allow students to arrange to take exams in a quiet, distraction-free room.	___	___	___	___
7.7 I will allow students to use a dictionary or word book to check spelling on written exams.	___	___	___	___

Comments:

The Instructional Style Survey was developed by Ernest Rose, Ph.D., as part of Grant No. GOO 8630230, The Northern Illinois Postsecondary Education Project (NIPEP).

Appendix 7.3

Faculty Checklist

Student's Name —————————— Class ————————————
Instructor's Name —————————— Date ————————————

Directions: This checklist is designed to help you, the college instructor, identify those students who need assistance because they are having difficulties in your class. You can use this checklist to determine in which teaching situations or skill areas the student is having the most difficulty. You may find it helpful to observe these characteristics over the course of several class periods.

Use the key to indicate the frequency of the problem(s) as compared to typical students in your class.

N = Never   R = Rarely   O = Occasionally   F = Frequently
DNA = Does Not Apply

General Observations

Requires assistance	N	R	O	F	DNA
Difficulty in interacting with classmates	N	R	O	F	DNA
Belittles or overrates abilities	N	R	O	F	DNA
Copies work inaccurately	N	R	O	F	DNA
Misses class	N	R	O	F	DNA
Comes late for class	N	R	O	F	DNA
Comes unprepared for class	N	R	O	F	DNA

Lecture

Difficulty following oral directions	N	R	O	F	DNA
Difficulty keeping place in text or on handouts	N	R	O	F	DNA
Fidgety or restless in class	N	R	O	F	DNA
Difficulty taking lecture notes	N	R	O	F	DNA
Difficulty understanding jokes or sarcasm	N	R	O	F	DNA
Difficulty following classroom and/or laboratory procedures	N	R	O	F	DNA

Discussion

Fails to participate in class discussion	N	R	O	F	DNA
Spoken ideas are incomplete or poorly organized	N	R	O	F	DNA
Difficult to understand speech	N	R	O	F	DNA
Difficulty recalling what was just heard	N	R	O	F	DNA
Impulsive in verbal responses or decisions	N	R	O	F	DNA

Assignments

Difficulty in organizing or sequencing content	N	R	O	F	DNA
Ideas expressed in writing are poorly developed	N	R	O	F	DNA
Difficulty in abstract reasoning	N	R	O	F	DNA
Work looks disorganized, spatial arrangements poor	N	R	O	F	DNA
Reverses numbers, letters, words	N	R	O	F	DNA

Poor quality handwriting	N	R	O	F	DNA
Spelling and/or grammar inaccurate	N	R	O	F	DNA
Difficulty with math skills and application	N	R	O	F	DNA
Assignments late	N	R	O	F	DNA
Doesn't follow assignment direction	N	R	O	F	DNA

Test Taking

Difficulty in selecting main points	N	R	O	F	DNA
Difficulty in recalling a sequence of events	N	R	O	F	DNA
Completes test sooner or later than other students	N	R	O	F	DNA
Exhibits much test anxiety	N	R	O	F	DNA
Test scores fail to reflect competence shown in other class work	N	R	O	F	DNA
Difficulty in recalling specific facts	N	R	O	F	DNA

Additional Comments:

The Faculty Checklist was developed by Linda Burke, Ed.D., as part of Grant No. 600 8630230, The Northern Illinois Postsecondary Education Project (NIPEP).

VIII
Assessing and Developing Metacognitive Attributes in College Students with Learning Disabilities

MARGARET M. POLICASTRO

Introduction

In 1981, Roosevelt University established the Learning and Support Services Program (LSSP) to help college students with learning disabilities undertake their education. Typically, many of these students lack the active strategies and skills that are necessary to complete tasks in college courses. Moreover, they do not possess the self-regulating skills or awareness levels involved in thinking and knowledge processes that are essential for survival in college. In short, these students do not have strong metacognitive skills.

In the past decade, due to the wealth of support programs, many college students with learning disabilities (LDs) have made progress in most academic areas. A critical question in the study of these students centers around how they can assume a more active role in their learning process (Fischer, 1984). Of particular concern is how these students can develop a strong metacognitive awareness base and become responsible for their own learning. In essence, when students are empowered with some metacognitive strategies, they can take control of their own learning and also be responsible for it (Kuhrt & Farris, 1990). For example, Newton (1991) used response journals as a metacognitive strategy with non-learning disabled college students. She found that when students record and evaluate their interaction with text, they begin to understand how the reader negotiates meaning from a text and establishes specific sources of his or her own meaning making. Consequently, this knowledge is empowering because it invites the students to be in charge of their own learning. Moreover, when individuals take responsibility for their own actions, they are allowed to have choices in their lives. Too often, students with learning disabilities have not had much experience with choices and decision-making processes for the events that occur in their lives. At Roosevelt University, we have observed students whose choice range has been limited. Parents, teachers, siblings, and others have been the primary decision maker for choices about what to learn, when to learn, how to learn, and so on. Consequently, this has left the student with learning disabilities quite disempowered for the actions and thoughts in his or her life. Calkins (1991), in her recent book titled *Living Between the Lines* which focuses on writing instruction, refers to stepping backward in our lives, reflecting on our thoughts, and letting our insights take root and grow as much more than the revision process in writing, but much more like thought itself. Students with learning disabilities have a difficult time letting their insights take root and grow. This is unfortunate because through self-reflection and insight we become wide awake to our world rich and full of experiences and possibilities.

The purpose of this chapter will be to examine the LSSP at Roosevelt University. Specifically, we will investigate how metacognitive skills are assessed and strategies implemented within a program for college students. This chapter will therefore highlight the following: (1) a description of Roosevelt University; (2) a description of the LSSP, including entry-level characteristics and history of students served; (3) the definition and background of metacognition, including a questionnaire to assess metacognitive attributes; (4) a case study highlighting the implementation of metacognitive strategies; and lastly (5) summary and implications.

Introduction to Roosevelt University

Roosevelt University was founded in 1945 as a private, nonsectarian, coeducational institution of higher learning. Roosevelt was one of the first institutions of higher learning in America to provide equal educational opportunities for students of all backgrounds. It was (and continues to be) a pioneer in the education of adults and nontraditional students. Roosevelt University has two campuses. The main campus is in the Auditorium Building, a National Historic Landmark, in the South Loop of downtown Chicago. The Albert A. Robin campus is in the northwest suburb of Arlington Heights. The student enrollment at Roosevelt University is approximately 6,100, of which one-third are pursuing graduate studies. There are 75 major and professional programs leading to a Bachelor's degree. The Graduate division grants a Doctorate in Education and 10 Master's degrees in 35 programs and departments.

Admission requirements for freshman applicants are as follows:

1) Top half of high-school class or GED with an average score of 55;
2) Minimum ACT composite of 18, or minimum SAT scores of 475 verbal and 410 mathematics.

The Learning and Support Services Program

Historically, Roosevelt University has been a pioneer in the education of adults and nontraditional students. The inception of a program for college students with learning disabilities was a natural outgrowth of the ongoing mission of the university. The LSSP began with an initial grant for a pilot project. The program, gradually increasing in number, initially served seven students. It currently serves approximately 25 students per semester. The students are charged an additional fee for this program.

Services Provided

The LSSP provides services to students on an individual basis. Emphasis is placed on advising, with the intent of providing an individualized program and the proper match of instructor and student. All tutoring is done on a one-to-one basis and is course-related, focusing specifically on the course goals and assignments while implementing study skills. The University does not have special courses designed for students enrolled in the LSSP (all courses are for credit towards a degree). Auxiliary aids, including tape recorders and computers, are available for student use. When necessary, arrangements are made with faculty for modification of course pace and examination type. Career counseling is encouraged for all students through the University counseling center.

Enrollment Procedures

Enrollment into the LSSP is a dual process with admission to the University. The student applies to the University and follows the LSSP application process: (1) interested students must first write a letter to the director requesting services; (2) they then have an interview with LSSP staff; (3) their academic reports, including transcripts of all schools attended, test results (with achievement, individual intelligence quotient (IQ), and other measures of academic performance), the latest Individual Education Plan (IEP), and medical history are forwarded; and (4) an admission meeting is conducted to evaluate eligibility and possible enrollment.

Staff Characteristics

The staff of the LSSP includes a director with faculty status. This position is half administration and half professor in education. Additionally, two associate directors are each half-time, and there are two tutors, one who works one-fourth of the time, and one, a math/science and writing tutor, who works on an hourly basis. The salary for each staff member is paid from the LSSP, derived directly from the special fee assessed for the program. Essentially, the program is totally self-supporting from the fees generated.

History of Students Served

Since 1981 the LSSP has served 88 students and currently serves 26. To date, 13 students have graduated with degrees. Of the 13 students, 10 have graduated with a major in Arts and Sciences, 2 in Continuing Education, and 1 in Business Administration. The majors within Arts and Sciences consisted of Speech Communications, Sociology, Journalism, Psychology, and Biology. Continuing Education majors consisted of Public Policy and Education. Within the area of Business, the major consisted of Management. Of the 88 students served, 8 have transferred to other institutions. In most instances, the goal of transferring to a campus school away from home was established early on. The students who transfer are from the Chicago area and want to have a foundation of successful college experiences before moving on. Nine students have been mainstreamed into the University and are no longer receiving LSSP services. These students have proven that they can function and survive independently. Three students have returned to Roosevelt after leaving for a period of time. Thirty-five students, of the eighty-eight, have left the University due to other attrition reasons (grades, financial pressure, lack of goals, etc.)

Entry-level Characteristics

The entry-level age of a student enrolling into the LSSP program is typically several years older than that of the traditional college student. The mean age for the 1990–1991 year was 25.9 years old, with a range from 19 to 39.

The Socioeconomic status (SES) of the students enrolled in the LSSP ranges from lower to upper level, as inferred from high-school income (community income). In order to determine SES, the parents' occupation must be known. Roosevelt University's application process does not ask for this information; therefore the parents' occupation is typically not known. For the 1990–1991 academic year, the number of students living at home with their parents is 20, 4 live in the dorm, and 2 live independently off campus. A major factor to consider when students are applying to the program is whether they should live in the dormitory or, if possible, commute from home. If students commute, services are provided at both campuses. Students are encouraged to use both sites to gain the experience of commuting into the city as well as taking classes at the Arlington Heights campus. Initially, commuting presents a problem for many students. In most cases, they have never travelled into the city alone. Practice sessions are encouraged along with modeling of appropriate behaviors. Living in the dormitory is also a necessary option for the students. It is important that, at the right time, the option be provided to live independently. This presents a unique situation, since the dormitory is located as a part of the University, in the South Loop of Chicago. Living in an urban dormitory allows students to gain first-hand experience of both a cultural and business community. Unlike students at a regular college campus, those at Roosevelt are immersed in a community setting demanding appropriate and mature behavior at all times.

The predominant social characteristic that many of the LSSP students have at entry level is immaturity. This is documented by our observations in both academic and social settings. When students first enter the program, we seem to devote a lot of time to observing and then discussing at staff meetings the collection of events we watch. The time spent discussing our observations is valuable because it allows us to explore what underlies these behaviors. In addition, we are often able to gain and find new insights through these observations. The events that we observe are not necessarily big events; rather they are the day-by-day moments of first-time college students. What makes this special for our team is that these students with learning disabilities often have difficulty going through ordinary events. In going through the actions and scenes, we observe behaviors that are not always appropriate. For example, during registration, parents will want to give the staff checks for tuition. They feel that their child is "not mature or responsible" enough to handle money. Bart, a twenty-year-old student, met a young woman during his first semester while commuting home. He would wait for her every evening in the train station while commuters passed him. When he finally spotted her one day, he asked for her phone number and she declined. During another student's first semester, we received a call from a professor whose office was down the hall from the LSSP office. She reported that one of the LSSP students was sitting outside kissing a young woman. Another student, during the interview process, laughed and made inappropriate comments about women. One student announced during his first semester that he would not be in the next day for class or tutoring, because it was his birthday. As we continue to watch the events of starting college unfold, we are observing valuable first-time experiences. These experiences become another chapter in their lifeline as learners.

Another area which our observations and discussions center on is the decision-making process. We observe students who generally are not empowered to make decisions for themselves. In many cases parents have dominated a large part of their decision-making process, leaving little room for the student. For example, during an interview with a student I asked him, "Why are you at Roosevelt?" and he responded by saying, "Everybody thinks I should be here." As we continued our discussion, it was evident that his parents and counselor had urged him to attend Roosevelt, clearly not his first choice. As we worked over the first semester, his true hidden life goal unfolded, going to Purdue University. We worked on this goal as his choice and, after two years at Roosevelt, he was accepted to Purdue and will graduate in May of 1991. Lack of experiences in choices is evident on a daily basis with these students. We observe students who cannot make decisions about what to study, read, write, or talk about. Often times their schema for making decisions is at best weak. This lack of decision making reveals important information about self-reflection as well. Through self-reflection, choices we make about our life are revised over and over. When students have not been encouraged to have this kind of reflection, they have been denied options and possibilities. This translates into dilemmas over what courses they should take, how many semester hours, what days and times to come to school, and eventually what they should major in.

It is no surprise that these students enter college with a lowered self-concept. A history of unsuccessful schooling has also not helped develop a positive image of themselves. During the interview process, we ask students to discuss and reflect on how school has been for them. In most instances, they either recall how hard first grade was, not passing first grade, being in the lowest reading groups, not being able to spell, and having poor writing skills.

In order to cope with the many personal issues these students encounter, the majority are involved in private counseling when they enter; continuation is strongly encouraged.

Definition and Background on Metacognition

The last 20 years of reserach on metacognition, cognition, and strategy instruction has provided a new era in thinking, teaching, and learning for the entire education community. Moreover, the impact of this research for college students with learning disabilities has opened up new possibilities for their future success as active learners (Wong, 1987). This section will first highlight the historical development of metacognition and explain how the terms evolved into current practices. Second, research on differences between skilled and less skilled and the learning disabled's use of metacognitive behaviors will be examined. Finally, a Metacognitive Attribute Questionnaire will be presented.

Metacognition: A Definition

Little did we realize in the early 1970s that the emergence of meta-cognition would play such an important role in learners' self-knowledge and regulation of their thought processes. Flavell's (1971) pioneer work in memory studies referred to knowledge about one's own memory as metamemory. Flavell (1976; 1978) further introduced the theoretical construct of metacognition to explain one's knowledge or self-awareness concerning one's own cognitive processes, strengths, and weaknesses.

In addition, the term refers to controlling one's own learning, or self-regulation, and monitoring of these behaviors (Baker & Brown, 1984; Brown, 1980).

Brown (1980) further extended the theoretical construct of meta-cognition to include the reading process, highlighting the strategies that efficient readers utilize. Flavell (1981) developed a global model of cognitive monitoring to include metacognitive knowledge, experience, and strategy use. Metacognitive knowledge concerns ourselves, the tasks we face, and the strategies we employ (Garner, 1987). A metacognitive experience could take place as a reader stops and wonders if a selection needs to be reread for complete comprehension. Strategy use entails utilization of an appropriate strategy to reread the information. Wade and Reynolds (1989) have defined and applied three subcomponents of metacognitive awareness—task, strategy, and performance—to academically strong and weak high-school and college students. They define task awareness as knowing what information to study in a learning situation, strategy awareness as how best to learn it, and performance awareness as whether and to what extent the information has been learned. This research has provided valuable information about the overlapping subcomponent processes that often take place simultaneously; this allows for the metacognitive processes to be broken down for instructional purposes.

Most recently, Wang and Palinscar (1989) have termed metacognitive behaviors as the students' ability to assume an active role in their learning as self-instructive. Specifically, students need to know when and where to seek assistance for learning and problem solving, not just for the moment, but for future tasks as well. Furthermore, they point out that not all students acquire these skills on their own and can therefore benefit from instruction about methods on learning. This is a critical breakthrough for college students with learning disabilities who traditionally have been perceived as passive learners. This allows the student to be viewed, and subsequently to view herself or himself, as a self-instructive learner; the student will also take an active role in the learning process and will manage these behaviors not just for the immediate task but for future tasks as well.

Metacognitive Differences in Students with Learning Disabilities

Research on metacognition reveals how skilled readers (Garner, 1987; Paris & Myers, 1981; Wong, 1987) and writers (Graham & Harris, 1987; Wallace & Bott, 1989; Wong, 1987) differ from less skilled students and students with LDs in metacognitive behaviors. Furthermore, strategy implementation, including study time allocation between skilled, less skilled, and students with LDs is also distinguished (Billingsley & Wildman, 1988; Bireley & Manley, 1980; Griffey, 1988; Rueda & Mehan,

1986; Wiens 1983). Lastly, a distinction is made between social and emotional behaviors in the learning disabled and non-learning disabled persons (Axelrod, 1982; Barbaro, 1982; Labercane & Battle, 1987; Larson & Gerber, 1987; Vaughn, 1985).

Reading Differences

Skilled readers differ from students with LDs in the way they read (Wong, 1987). Good readers make use of superior cognitive and meta-cognitive skills to construct meaning from what is read (Bingman, 1989), are generally aware of the meaningful purpose for reading, and are knowledgeable about which strategies to employ when they read (Forrest & Waller, 1980; Weisberg, 1988). This stands in sharp contrast to poor readers and students with learning disabilities who lack awareness for higher order metacognitive skills, put emphasis on decoding (Wong & Wong, 1986), tend to view reading as a decoding process (Gambrell & Heathington, 1981; Garner & Kraus, 1982; Paris & Myers, 1981), and are considered to be passive readers (Elrod, 1987). Furthermore, poor readers and students with learning disabilities are less sophisticated in their strategy use; they tend not to know when to use comprehension monitoring (Graves, 1986) and self-questioning techniques as they read (Billingsley & Wildman, 1988; Griffey, 1988).

Writing Differences

Similar metacognitive behaviors have been differentiated among learners in the writing process as well. Wong, Wong, and Blenkinsop (1989) found that adolescents with learning disabilities have a developmental delay in metacognitive aspects of writing. Normal writers display a mature conceptual understanding of what writing involves and can predict what might pose problems for them as they compose. They view writing as both purposeful and as a tool for self-expression. Furthermore, they are able to explain about their own writing process and can visualize the content and revision of their writing prior to the task. For students with learning disabilities, this study (Wong, et al., 1989) found that they were not able to articulate their ideas for writing and what it involves. In addition their conception of writing was centered on low-level processes such as mechanics. In interviewing intermediate-grade students, Englert, Raphael, Fear, & Anderson (1988) found that students with learning disabilities were less aware than high-achieving students of modeled writing strategies and stages in the writing process.

Social Emotional Differences

According to Paris and Oka (1989), when students with learning disabilities have difficulty learning effective strategies for reading, they develop negative self-perceptions, lose enthusiasm, and jeopardize future achievement. Often, students with learning disabilities describe themselves as low in motivation, distractible, having self-concept problems, and lacking organizational skills (Buchanan & Wolf, 1986). Barbaro (1982) states that college students with learning disabilities have psychological deficits independent of failure and frustration. What makes these behaviors metacognitive in nature is that students with learning disabilities are generally poor at problem solving (Kronick, 1984) and tend to have inaccurate perceptions of their learning disability and how it affects their lives (Buchanan & Wolf, 1986).

Students with learning disabilities have been described as lacking an awareness of social impact on others, having poor social judgment, being demanding of others (Alley & Deshler, 1979), immature (Smith, 1981), and inefficient at monitoring their social behavior and judging their acceptability (Kronick, 1984). Vaughn (1985) describes students with learning disabilities as having difficulty interacting with others, including teachers and peers. Furthermore, she states that peers and adults perceive these students as socially unappealing. Clary (1984) discusses the need for college students with learning disabilities to be aware of how they relate to others, including authority figures. She points out that attention must be given to define their social needs and to provide assessment through self-monitoring techniques.

Assessing Metacognitive Behaviors

Now that we have defined metacognition and differences among learners, we will focus specifically on the metacognitive behaviors that have been observed in our college students over the years. The learning community and student rapport that is established to assess students are described. Three behavior attributes (educational, psychological, and social) are discussed to help those students with learning disabilities establish where they stand as far as their metacognitive abilities are concerned. More specifically, this assessment model helps allow the individual with a learning disability to self-assess how they perceive themselves. This assessment also allows for an in-depth investigation and exploration of the entire educational environment from which the students' experiences are derived.

Establishing Student Rapport Through the Community of Learning

In order to assess our LSSP students and to help them self-assess their own learning, a commitment to a safe and caring environment must be established. Many directors of programs and tutors working in programs such as the LSSP have the opportunity to work with students for many years beyond the traditional four. This long-term investment with students allows us to get a view of their lives through different lenses. This begins with the interviewing process, wherein we read, listen, and see the histories of their lives as struggling learners unfold. When putting together the events and experiences surrounding their college life and their life before college, we in essence are establishing their lifelines as learners and appraising their metacognitive craftsmanship. We observe on a day-to-day basis their encounters with all the aspects and experiences that surround college and their life. Often they will share with us what happened at home before school, coming to school, and other pertinent information affecting their lives. It is this rich type of relationship that we establish with our students that takes them through the lifeline of learning. Through this commitment with students, a relationship is established that can allow us to get to know the individual and the lives they lead. At Roosevelt, we have observed over the years a sense of community with the LSSP environment. It is a special place for students to visit and express their frustrations, joys, struggles, and successes. We celebrate when students have earned a good grade; we also are saddened when a student has failed. Somewhere in between all these feelings commitment and intimacy are established, a relationship about the life that surrounds learning in a college setting.

Assessment of Attributes: Questionnaire

Tables 8.1–8.3 are lists of behaviors and questions to help the tutor or student assess a student's strengths and weaknesses as a learner in a particular area. The behaviors are distinguished by three main attribute areas (educational, social, and psychological), and three main categories of investigation for each (awareness to each of the following: strengths, weaknesses, and strategies,) question are provided to help the tutor and student explore their own behaviors. In the next section, a case study is presented with results of the student completing the questions in a self-assessment manner.

Case Study

This section will focus on one student who has been at Roosevelt University since 1989. First, background information on the student will be presented. The information provided comes from a variety of sources including learning evaluations completed in 1986 and 1988. Other data were obtained from interviews, observations, and results of the student completing the Metacognitive Attribute Questionnaire. The second part of this case study will focus on how specific metacognitive strategies have been implemented on a daily basis.

TABLE 8.1. Educational attributes.

Study Skills	*Awareness of strengths and weaknesses*
	Can the student identify areas of specific strengths and weaknesses in study habits? Examples?
	Awareness of strategy use
	Can the students identify specific strategies that they use? Examples? Can they discuss how and when to change strategies as they study?
Organization	*Awareness of strengths and weaknesses*
	Can the students identify areas of strengths and weaknesses in their organization for school? Can they give examples?
	Awareness of strategy use
	Can the students identify specific organization strategies that they use? Examples?
Reading	*Awareness of strengths and weaknesses*
	Can the students identify specific strengths and weaknesses in their reading? Can they give examples?
	Awareness of strategy use
	Can the students identify specific strategies they use as they read or strategies used to become better readers? Can the students discuss changing strategies as they read? Examples?
Writing	*Awareness of strengths and weaknesses*
	Can they identify their strengths and weaknesses as writers? Can they give examples?
	Awareness of strategy use
	Can the students identify specific strategies they use as they write or strategies used to become better writers? Examples?
Speaking	*Awareness of strengths and weaknesses*
	Can the students identify strengths and weaknesses as speakers? Can they give examples?
	Awareness of strategy use
	Can the students identify specific strategies they use as they speak or strategies they use to become better speakers? Examples?

Background Information

Suzanne is a 21-year-old, attractive female who transferred to Roosevelt after attending a small, private, liberal arts college in Iowa for one year. Currently she is enrolled as a second-year college student, attending both the downtown campus and the Robin campus in Arlington Heights. Suzanne lives with her parents in an upper middle-class suburban area where she graduated from high school, in 1987. Suzanne's mother is employed as a dietician at a hospital; her father is retired. Suzanne is the youngest of two children.

During the initial interview with Suzanne, her mother stated that there was no known history of learning disabilities in the family. However, she did mention that learning problems seem to prevail in the family. Suzanne's older sibling had difficulty getting through school. The mother admitted that school was not always easy for her either.

TABLE 8.2. Social attributes.

Relating to Others	*Awareness of strengths and weaknesses*
	Can the students identify where they have strengths and weaknesses in relating to others in an educational setting? Examples?
	Awareness of strategy use
	Can the students identify strategies to use in educational situations to relate to others? Examples?
Perception of Self in Social Settings	*Awareness of strengths and weaknesses*
	Can the students identify strengths and weaknesses in how they perceive themselves in educational settings? Examples?
	Awareness of strategy use
	Can the students identify strategies for self-perception (reflection)? Examples?
Age-Appropriate Behavior	*Awareness of strengths and weaknesses*
	Can the students identify their strengths and weaknesses in age-appropriate behavior in an educational setting? Examples?
	Awareness of strategy use
	Can the students identify strategies for acting their age? Examples?
Group Interaction	*Awareness of strengths and weaknesses*
	Can the students identify strengths and weaknesses of group interaction in educational settings? Examples?
	Awareness of strategy use
	Can the students identify the strategies they use during group interaction? Examples?
Authority Figure Interaction	*Awareness of strengths and weaknesses*
	Can the students identify strengths and weaknesses in interactions with authority figures such as parents and teachers? Examples?
	Awareness of strategy use
	Can the students identify strategies for working with authority figures? Examples?

Suzanne was born with pneumonia and required an extended stay in the hospital. After her birth, she had a seizure. At the age of four, Suzanne was identified as having a prolapsed mitral valve. To this date, Suzanne reports that due to her heart problem she tires easily and must restrict her physical activity to some extent. Over the course of the year, Suzanne on many occasions would appear fatigued and have a bad cold. She would frequently mention that it was related to her heart problem. In 1986, Suzanne was diagnosed as having a mild conductive hearing loss for the right ear and a moderate conductive loss for the left ear. Suzanne was fitted with a hearing aid in late January of 1986. Up until this time, her mother reported that she was followed audiologically through school screenings and by her pediatrician, with no reports indicating a hearing problem.

Suzanne was formally evaluated in 1986 to assess both expressive and receptive language skills. The results indicated that both receptive and expressive language skills were equally delayed and somewhat attributable to the hearing loss.

TABLE 8.3. Psychological attributes.

Problem Solving (school, self, career)	*Awareness of strengths and weaknesses* Can the students identify strengths and weaknesses in the area of problem solving for school, self, and career? Examples? *Awareness of strategy use* Can the students identify strategies used to solve problems? Examples?
Self-Concept	*Awareness of strengths and weaknesses* Can the students identify strengths and weaknesses in their self-concept? Examples? *Awareness of strategy use* Can the students identify strategies used to build or maintain self-concept? Examples?
Attitude Toward School	*Awareness of strengths and weaknesses* Can the students identify strengths and weaknesses in their attitude toward school? Examples? *Awareness of strategy use* Can the students identify strategies used to build and maintain their attitude toward school? Examples?
Academic Stress	*Awareness of strengths and weaknesses* Can the students identify strengths and weaknesses in dealing with stress related to school? Examples? *Awareness of strategy use* Can the students identify strategies used to cope with stress? Examples?
Dependency on Others	*Awareness of strengths and weaknesses* Can the students identify strengths and weaknesses for their dependency on others for school-related tasks? Examples? *Awareness of strategy use* Can the students identify strategies for how they depend on others in school?

Educational History and Diagnostic Information

During the interview process, Suzanne remembered being diagnosed with a learning disability in the second grade. During that grade, she received help from a resource teacher. Her mother reported that she was placed in a self-contained learning disabilities class for grades 3 through 6. From seventh grade through high school, Suzanne received resource help and worked with a special reading teacher. Suzanne remained in the basic track throughout her high-school experience: In 1986 Suzanne had a learning evaluation done to assess receptive and expressive vocabulary skills as well as auditory and visual perceptual skills. During this formal evaluation the Peabody Picture Vocabulary Tests (PPVT), Expressive One-Word Picture Vocabulary test (EOWPV), and the Detroit Tests of Learning Aptitude (DTLA-2) were administered. Suzanne achieved an age equivalent score of 10-8 on the PPVT. This placed her at the third percentile and demonstrated a significant delay in receptive vocabulary skills. During conversations with her, the examiner noted that at times she had difficulty with understanding the examiner's utterances. When the examiner rephrased things for her using simpler vocabulary, Suzanne's comprehension improved. Expressive vocabulary skills were assessed using the EOWPV-Upper Extension. On this assessment, Suzanne received an age equivalent of 11-1. This score was fairly commensurate with her receptive vocabulary score. Suzanne was observed to give associative or categorical responses but had difficulty with single lexical items. This may indicate that Suzanne has some difficulty with word retrieval skills.

The DTLA-2 was given to assess auditory and visual learning skills. In general, Suzanne had much more difficulty with the auditory subtests than the visual subtests. Using a standard score of 10 as the mean, Suzanne's scores on the subtests were as follows:

Word Opposites: 6
Sentence Imitation: 4
Oral Directions: 10
Word Sequences: 2

It appeared that Suzanne had greater success in the Oral Directions subtest because it employed visual cues. Suzanne's performance on the visual subtests was generally higher and appeared to be a relative strength for her. On the Visual subtests, Suzanne received the following standard scores:

Design Reproduction: 12
Object Sequences: 8
Symbolic Relations: 8
Conceptual Matching: 10
Word Fragments: 8

Suzanne appeared to be a stronger visual learner, and her weaker skills may have reflected a perceptual deficit that could somewhat be attributed to an inability to process auditory information effectively because of her hearing acuity problems.

In 1988 Suzanne was referred for a learning evaluation and diagnosis of her language and literacy skills. This assessment would provide entrance level information for the college she wished to attend. The results of her formal assessments are presented in Table 8.4.

On the Lindamood Auditory Conceptualization Test (LACT) Suzanne indicated she had no difficulty discriminating and sequencing isolated sounds. When these sounds were combined into phoneme monosyllables (e.g., "pi" is a single syllable composed of two phonemes) Suzanne was unable to discriminate or sequence the sounds composing the syllables; in a change from "vaps" to "aps" Suzanne noticed something had changed. She indicated that there were still four sounds and that it was the final "s" sound that had changed. The number and order of sounds in single and

TABLE 8.4. Test results.

Lindamood Auditory Conceptualization		
Test	79 + 1	(raw score)
WAIS	94	Verbal
	96	Performance
	94	Full Scale
Peabody Picture Vocabulary Test (Form M)	13–8	Mental
Woodcock Reading Mastery Tests	3.7	Grade level
Slosson Oral Reading	5.9	Grade level
Gray Oral Reading	5.0	Grade level

multisyllable words is difficult for her to identify, leading to difficulty in the orthographic requirements of English.

Suzanne's performance on the Wechsler Adult Intelligence Scale (WAIS) indicates that she is functioning at the average level. However, her receptive vocabulary, as measured by the PPVT, put her five years below her age level, a result consistent with earlier assessments. Overall reading performance ranges from the end of third grade to the end of fifth grade.

Observed Behaviors

Upon first meeting Suzanne, one is struck by her beauty and meticulous appearance. She appears socially appropriate for college in her dress. It is obvious that she spends a lot of time taking care of herself; she also knows how to present herself in a well-groomed manner. Suzanne has a positive attitude about herself and her self-confidence appears to be high. Although Suzanne is quiet, she responds to peers and adults with guarded behavior. This has become more apparent due to her lack of ability in establishing friendships at Roosevelt. Also, she finds it extremely difficult to talk to professors and ask questions about her coursework when in doubt. Whenever we discuss this, she gets very apprehensive and says, "I am working on it and trying not to be so shy." Suzanne often discusses her weekend plans that include a wide realm of activities. Not only are many family activities common but she also includes activities with her boyfriend who attends another university. Last, Suzanne works part time while attending school. She started as a cashier and has now moved up to a vault cashier. It appears that Suzanne is able to aptly balance work, school, and friends.

Results of Suzanne's Metacognitive Attribute Questionnaire

With assistance, Suzanne responded to the questions with examples about each attribute area. We reviewed these for two one-hour sessions. The results of her self-assessment are below in Tables 8.5–8.7.

TABLE 8.5. Educational attributes results.

Study Skills	*Strengths*: time management, not giving up until I know the material, staying positive *Weaknesses*: not understanding the teacher, getting all the information from lecture down, not going to the teacher for help, afraid to go to the teacher *Strategy use*: tape recorder, read material and take notes, go to tutors for help
Organization	*Strengths*: color-code notebooks to match textbooks, make a list of things that need to be done during the week, use a computer *Weaknesses*: too frustrated that I am so organized, keep doing things over and over to get them neat, keep doing rough drafts to get them perfect *Strategy use*: color-code, list making, tell myself to do the list, do the things the way I think they should be done
Reading	*Strengths*: take all the time I need, not giving up, keep struggling *Weaknesses*: not understanding what I am reading *Strategy use*: ask someone to explain it to me
Writing	*Strengths*: feel that I write well and can do a pretty good paper, very emotional when I write *Weaknesses*: spelling, don't write enough information, cut it short *Strategy use*: getting a topic that I know about or feel comfortable with, use grammar and spell check on the computer, depend on the computer; boyfriend helps me write, pulls information from me
Speaking	*Strengths*: I speak pretty well, don't use big vocabulary but I do fine *Weaknesses*: hard for me to talk to others, they use big words and I don't understand them, quiet and shy; *Strategy use*: write down words I don't know and ask my dad to explain them to me

TABLE 8.6. Social attributes results.

Relate to Others	*Strengths*: good listener and always able to help others *Weaknesses*: not easy, I fell very shy around others, I have been shot down by others and so I close up and keep everything to myself, feel that I am behind other people my age, "slow" and don't know as much as everybody else *Strategy use*: try to understand and fit in the situation
Perception of Self	*Strengths*: no response *Weaknesses*: I sometimes feel out of place, haven't made any friend, seems students know each other from high school *Strategy use*: really put an effort into talking to others in my classes
Age-Appropriate Behavior	*Strengths*: fell that I have to act older than my age; when I got a hearing aid, surgery made my whole body change and feel older *Weaknesses*: no response *Strategy use*: acting older than my age
Group Interaction	*Strengths*: using group interaction to find answers to questions *Weaknesses*: don't talk, don't input to group discussion, afraid to give wrong answer *Strategy use*: same as strengths
Anthority Figure	*Strengths*: very close family ties, talk to my dad a lot, he help me with everything *Weaknesses*: afraid of teachers *Strategy use*: no response

TABLE 8.7. Psychological attributes results.

Problem Solving (school, self, career)	*Strengths*: I try to solve problems on my own and stay strong *Weaknesses*: keeping to myself *Strategy use*: when I seek out help from other people, I usually let all my feelings out
Self-Concept	*Strengths*: feel that I have a good positive attitude *Weaknesses*: no response *Strategy use*: I exercise and try to eat well to keep my self-concept good
Attitude Toward School	*Strengths*: I try to stay positive and not let things get me down *Weaknesses*: when things don't go well for me in school, I can get a bad attitude *Strategy use*: my family and boyfriend help me to keep a good attitude
Academic Stress	*Strengths*: I try not to let it build up *Weaknesses* *Strategy use*: no response
Dependency on Others	*Strengths*: both a strength and a *weakness* is that I rely on my family too much *Strategy use*: try to work things out on my own

Implementing Metacognitive Strategy Instruction with Suzanne

Research on strategy instruction has given valuable insight into the types of instruction we can implement with students (Groller, Kender, & Honeyman, 1991; Pressley & Levin, 1983; Pressley & Harris, 1990; Wang & Palincsar, 1989). Wang and Palincsar (1989) state that some students can acquire metacognitive or self-instructive strategies on their own. However, others can benefit from instruction about methods of learning as well. Wiens (1983) argues that adolescents with learning disabilities may become more active learners by being taught a system of strategies for learning. Bireley and Manley (1980) state that students with learning disabilities can develop the ability to regulate and realistically monitor their performance and learn to effectively use these skills. Not only is this information important to the future of students but it also has direct implications for teachers and those working specifically with students with LDs. Moreover, the instruction being carried on with students is regulated and guided by the teacher. Therefore, teacher preparation must include both an understanding and knowledge of cognitive intervention strategies (Wang & Palincsar, 1989).

This section will highlight how metacognitive strategy instruction was implemented with Suzanne as well as a detailed description of how task, strategy, and performance instruction were demonstrated, modeled, and taught directly to her in one course. The course, Physical Geography, is used as the primary example. Other courses are discussed in light of how these strategies can transfer across the curriculum.

There are questions that both the learning disabilities tutor and the student must ask when approaching the work involved in a course. These center around the three awareness levels (task, strategy, and performance) that Wade and Reynolds (1989) have defined. The three main questions are: What to study in a particular course? What study methods to use or How best to learn the information in a particular course? Have I learned the information? In assisting Suzanne during her Physical Geography course, I was amazed at how unaware she was of the global tasks ahead of her. For instance, during an initial encounter with her, she had no notion of where to begin in introducing herself to the materials; she lacked strategies in how to acquaint or familiarize herself with the course information and assignments. I decided to break down the course into task, strategy, and performance, being very specific about each area and making the content relate directly to Physical Geography.

Task Awareness: What to study in Physical Geography

At this level, Suzanne did not know where to begin; she was not overwhelmed with the material; rather, she lacked prior experience on how to proceed. We examined the syllabus to obtain an overview and a preview of what the course was about (see Requirements below). We reviewed the major requirements, the textbooks, and how points were distributed for grades.

Requirements

The first requirement consisted of workbook exercises, primarily short answer, and fill-in-the-blank types of task (see sample of workbook exercise in Table 8.8).

The second requirement consisted of map exercises that entailed shading different types of landforms as well as identifying certain points on the map. With the other requirements, Suzanne was able to verbalize some of the details of specific assignments that the instructor had discussed in class (see Table 8.9). For example, she was able to talk about what places you could tour for a field trip or about appropriate topics for an oral report.

TABLE 8.8. Sample workbook exercise.

Exercises:
   1. Write a short paragraph explaining what geography is.
   2. Write a short statement on the development of
      geography in each of these time periods:
      A. Ancient Greece and Rome
      B. Geography in the Middle East
      C. Geography during the Renaissance

TABLE 8.9. Course requirements for physical geography.

1. Workbook Exercises 1-2-14-15-16-17-18-19-20-21-22-23-24
2. Map exercises: 4 maps and locations
3. One field trip of your choice
4. Complete one oral report in class
5. Complete working with maps and models
6. Complete one final and three unit exams

Points given:

4 Maps	20
1 Field trip	25
1 Oral report	20
Workbook exercises	50
3 Unit exams	90
1 Final exam	50
Models maps	20
Class participation	25

It was clear that Suzanne was unsure about what to focus on first. In other words, should she work on the textbook readings and workbook exercises or on the maps? We used the requirement list on the syllabus as a guide each time we would meet. I reviewed each expected assignment, and I asked questions about each, trying to model the questions that would focus on the same topic each time. The syllabus for this course represents task awareness through the list of requirements. In addition to the textbook reading and the requirements on the syllabus, the instructor provided chapter summaries of the textbook readings (see example of Chapter 13 in Table 8.10). The explanation, which I provided, of this task was directly related to the unit exams and final exams.

Once the tasks were identified and discussed, we worked on prioritizing the tasks on a weekly basis, that is, on identifying the important tasks and on ranking them from most to least important. This was accomplished when assignments were due and in planning ahead for both written assignments and exams.

TABLE 8.10. Chapter 13: Introduction to landform study.

Chapter key concepts and terms
  Nature of the earth
    1. crust
    2. mantle
    3. mohorovococ discontinuity
  Composition of the earth
    1. minerals
    2. rocks
    3. magma
  Terms and concepts
    1. topography
    2. landforms
    3. geomorphology

A basic task for survival in a college course, although not usually written on the course requirement, is taking notes in class from lectures and discussions. As part of the task awareness for this course, we reviewed the process of taking notes using a tape recorder.

Strategy Awareness: How Best to Learn Information From Tasks in Physical Geography?

Once the tasks have been identified in a particular course and their relative importance established, the next step is to decide how best to use the information. In Suzanne's Physical Geography course, we needed to decide what study methods or strategies she should utilize when she studied. Prior to beginning such course requirements as the workbook exercises, we needed to discuss how to read the textbook. Typical of a college textbook, its text was filled with technical terms, subheadings, maps, pictures, diagrams, and chapter summaries. Without prior experience in dealing with such textbooks, it is often difficult for students to know where to begin reading. Since the instructor had provided the chapter summaries to accompany the readings, I suggested that they be used together. Suzanne had no notion how to begin reading the chapters. In my experience with similar students, they do not use "underlining" or "highlighting" as a study strategy. They are aware of the technique, but they do not know what information is most important to emphasize. I recommended that Suzanne use her chapter summaries as a guide with her reading; she could then highlight in the text any information listed in the chapter summary. I further suggested that each term, concept, and so on that she encountered in the chapter summary be written on an index card. In the beginning, I asked Suzanne how she would proceed to learn about the concepts and vocabulary in the chapter summaries. She responded by saying that, "the definitions are in the back of the book." It became apparent to me that she was not up to the task ahead; this response indicated her lack of experience in this task. It seemed that the only way to move ahead was to provide a step-by-step demonstration. She needed a clear understanding on how to obtain information specifically outlined in the chapter summaries. After a session where we studied the chapter and found pertinent information to transfer to index cards, I felt that Suzanne could perform the task on her own. After several sessions, Suzanne found that the workbook exercises were really not that difficult, primarily because she could refer to the note cards previously prepared. The strategies used to complete the map exercises consisted of examining the textbook for maps which were already completed and contained the needed information and of finding an atlas that also had the information. As the course progressed, Suzanne became more comfortable with these processes, both for completing the workbooks and the map exercises. It was evident that these strategies for learning information were becoming more routine for her. My role as a demonstrator evolved to the point where she would report to me each week on how she had accomplished her tasks. Occasionally, she would require an explanation of a term; this generally occurred when she did not understand an issue in the chapter summary. After several weeks, I realized that Suzanne had stored much information in her lecture notes. I recommended that she begin tape recording the lecture and rewriting the notes after each class. I was very impressed with Suzanne's initiative in dealing with the task requirements for the field trip and the oral report. Suzanne's field trip consisted of a visit to the city on a Saturday to tour the Museum of Natural History; she freely answered questions on her own about the visit. The oral report she presented pertained to a trip to Hawaii. Suzanne provided pictures to supplement the talk. In both instances, she was able to relate the task to her prior experience (i.e., knowledge of the museum and the previous trip she had taken). The last tasks, and probably the most important, were how to study for the unit and final exams. The instructor provided a study guide for the exams; it was identical to the chapter summary. He mentioned that if the students knew the contents of the summary, the exam would be relatively easy for them. In fact, the exam consisted of defining and answering questions pertaining to the exact chapter summaries provided in class. In preparation for the exams, we reviewed each term on the index cards (her stack had grown to five inches), and she would orally explain the information to me. We generated questions that we thought might appear on the exam in conjunction with the chapter summaries. Since Suzanne had maintained the index-card system, she was well prepared for the exams.

The following chart summarizes the tasks and strategies used in the Geography course (see Table 8.11).

Performance Awareness: Have I Learned the Information in Physical Geography?

After strategies have been implemented in a course, students must then go on and continue to self-monitor whether or not they have learned the information. Often, students will say that they have used a strategy, but

TABLE 8.11. Task and strategy summary.

Task	Strategy
Reading text	Highlight information
Chapter summary	Write information on index cards; have terms explained
Workbook exercise	Find information on index cards, books, and class notes
Map exercise	Reread/skim text for maps; utilize atlas
Field trip	Prior experience of museum
Oral report	Relate experience of prior trip to Hawaii
Lecture notes	Tape-record, listen, rewrite
Exams	Memorize index cards; self-question; reread text, lecture notes; listen to tape

they have not learned the information. In working with Suzanne, her confidence level increased gradually with the feedback she received from the professor. When her workbook exercises were returned early in the semester, with a B, she was sure she had used the correct strategy to accomplish the task. When she realized that she did not know something, she would at least feel comfortable enough to ask me for help. Because of the nature of this course and of all the work we did on task awareness, Suzanne was able to predict ahead and self-assess her confidence in learning. With each exam, Suzannes's strategies were reinforced. Her final grade for the course was also a B.

During Suzannes's second semester, she enrolled in Physical Geography II with the same instructor. She was able to transfer all the information concerning tasks, strategies, and performance awareness to the course. The format remained the same; consequently she had no difficulty adjusting to the tasks. She again finished the course with a B. During this semester, Suzanne also enrolled in an Early Childhood course. What we found in this course was that, unlike a Physical Geography course, she had to conceptualize and think at a different level. For example, she was required to interview an Early Childhood teacher and ask specific as well as open-ended questions. She had a difficult time summarizing the interview, making hypotheses, and reflecting on the experience in general. The task itself had been well organized and structured by the instructor; however, Suzanne was not able to adjust her strategies to have a successful experience. From the start, she had a difficult time thinking about whom she would actually interview and where. It appeared to be the kind of task Suzanne was not comfortable with. Many social parameters came in: She had to make a contact with a school, present herself as a future teacher, and ask informative questions. What was brought to my attention in this course was how lacking Suzanne was in problem-solving strategies and in social interaction with authority figures. Many of the assignments (tasks) were open ended. For example, she had to develop a lesson plan to teach a kindergarten class. The lesson had to revolve around a theme and contain goals, objectives, and all other parts of a lesson plan. It was difficult for Suzanne to break down a lesson plan into a task analysis and to see how all the parts fit together. Moreover, I tried to explain how a theme-related topic would cover more than one lesson, but Suzanne's knowledge base lacked prior experience in a classroom. Although she had observed classroom situations during clinical experiences, she was not able to reflect on previous experiences and relate them to the present task. It was evident that she could not generalize, reflect, or predict about the Early Childhood profession. Another element that entered into the problem with the course related to participating in class discussion about her experiences, again suggesting that her social interaction skills were weak. The instructor felt that Suzanne was not at the same level as the other students and that she was intimidated by her peers. This of course was right on target with Suzanne's own social attribute assessments. For example, another task was to find, in a journal article, activities that would be appropriate for Early Childhood experiences. The students were to share these in class. Suzanne, however, was timid about sharing and responding. When analyzing the tasks and strategies for the course (see Table 8.12), it was clear that the strategies demanded higher level thinking, and much more social interaction and problem solving than Physical Geography.

Suzanne's performance awareness level for this class was at a lower level than I had expected. She did not seem to be aware of what she was *not* learning. Furthermore, her self-confidence was greatly reduced due to the teacher's questioning her ability as a future teacher. The professor related her concerns to me, and I then related them to Suzanne. Her failure to comprehend the task and strategy level was evident all along in the course. Even though I demonstrated and tried to adjust and change strategies, it did not work. In this situation, what seemed to be lacking most from Suzanne's ability to adopt and use new strategies was her lack of experience in a classroom. Perhaps with guided clinical observations where tasks and strategies were gradually increased to a higher level of thinking and problem solving, she could have achieved a better level of performance. In short, although she had the ability to succeed in higher level thinking tasks, dealing with these must be a gradual, guided, and monitored process, spread over more than a semester.

Suzanne was advised not to take anymore Early Childhood courses until she completes her Liberal Arts courses. During the first semester of her second year (Fall 1990), Suzanne took History, English, and Math. Suzanne was able to transfer all the strategies that she had learned from Physical Geography to History. With both English and Math, Suzanne was able to more readily identify tasks for the course. As she progressed, strategies for completing writing and math assignments were developed in a similar format to Physical Geography. With each semester, Suzanne seems to acquire new strategies for learning. She is beginning to recognize when and where to use strategies, ask how to develop new strategies, and knows when things are not going well. She seems to be constantly self-assessing her ability to progress through each task within each course. She now is able to break down the course into component tasks and find the

TABLE 8.12. Task and strategy summary.

Task	Strategy
Interview	School contact; ask questions, tape-record; social skills; analysis of information; relate to ECE experiences; summarize
Lesson plan	Plan goals; objectives; relate to theme; reflective of experience
Journal activity	Write out activity; share in class
Class participation	Discuss, reflect, relate to experiences

right strategies to continue. The larger issue of gaining first-hand experience within an early childhood setting still remains. However, in the meantime, she is well on her way to advancing and completing the courses she needs for a Liberal Arts degree.

Summary and Implications

Since 1981, Roosevelt University has successfully provided services to college students with learning disabilities. The success that these students have experienced has been due, in part, to implementing metacognitive skills. Research on metacognition and strategy instruction has brought forth a new era in the future for college students with learning disabilities. Often traditionally viewed as passive learners, they can now look to brighter horizons as active, self-instructive learners. A future goal will be for students not merely to be going through the motions of learning but to be actively involved. This new kind of thought, thinking about thinking, requires a deeper type of self-reflection. This kind of reflection and self-questioning, thinking about a new kind of thought, takes time to germinate. These nontraditional changes will not be easy to make, but, because we all stand a chance of attaining enormous progress, the effort of change is dutifully worth it. In the process of all these encounters, we are helping students take hold of their life, take charge of their own thinking, and become lifelong active learners.

Finally, a new viewpoint, strategy instruction, about how the instruction teachers and tutors provide for students with LDs takes on a new role is emerging. The implications of strategy instruction take on critical dimensions for those working with students who have learning disabilities, and those preparing teachers to work with this population.

References

Alley, G.R., & Deshler, D.D. (1979). *Teaching learning disabled adolescents: Strategies and methods.* Love Publications.

Axelrod, L. (1982). Social perception in learning disabled adolescents. *Journal of Learning Disabilities*, *15*(10), 610–613.

Baker, L., & Brown, A.L. (1984). Cognitive monitoring in reading. In J. Flood (Ed.), *Understanding reading comprehension: Cognition, language, and the structure of prose* (21–24). Newark, DE: International Reading Association.

Barbaro, F. (1982). The learning disabled college student: Some consideration in setting objectives. *Journal of Learning Disabilities*, *15*(10), 599–603.

Billingsley, B.S., & Wildman, T.M. (1988). The effects of prereading activities on the comprehension monitoring of learning disabled adolescents. *Learning Disabilities Research*, *4*(1), 36–44.

Bingman, M.B. (1989). Learning differently: Meeting the needs of adults with learning disabilities. (ERIC Document Reproduction Service No. ED 312 479).

Bireley, M., & Manley, E. (1980). The learning disabled student in a college environment: A report of Wright State University's Program. *Journal of Learning Disabilities*, *13*(1), 12–15.

Brown, A.L. (1980). Metacognitive development and reading. In R.J. Spiro, B.C. Bruce, & W.F. Brewer (Eds.), *Theoretical issues in reading comprehension* (453–481). Hillsdale, NJ: Erlbaum.

Buchanan, M., & Wolf, J.S. (1986). A comprehensive study of learning disabled adults. *Journal of Learning Disabilities*, *19*(1), 34–38.

Calkins, L. (1991). *Living between the lines*. Portsmouth, N.H: Heinemann.

Clary, L. (1984). Identifying metacognitive social skills in young adults. (ERIC Document Reproduction Service NO. ED 170 806).

Elrod, G. (1987). Turning passive readers into active readers in content area subjects. *Reading Horizons*, *27*(3), 197–201.

Englert, C., Raphael, T., Fear, L., & Anderson, L. (1988). Metacognitive knowledge about how to write informational texts. *Learning Disability Quarterly*, *11*(1), 18–46.

Fischer, L. (1984). A new approach to learning disability programs in post-secondary education. (ERIC Document Reproduction Service No. ED 249 702).

Flavell, J.H. (1971). First discussant's comments: What is memory development the development of? *Human Development*, *14*, 272–278.

Flavell, J.H. (1976). Metacognitive aspects of problem-solving. In L.B. Resnick (Ed.), *The nature of intelligence* (231–235). Hillsdale, NJ: Erlbaum.

Flavell, J.H. (1978). Comments. In R.S. Siegler (Ed.), *Children's thinking: What develops?* (97–105). Hillsdale, NJ: Erlbaum.

Flavell, J.H. (1981). Cognitive monitoring. In W.P. Dickson (Ed.), *Children's oral communication skills* (35–60). New York: Academic Press.

Forrest, D.L., & Waller, T.G. (1980). What do children know about their reading and study skills? Paper presented at the annual meeting of the American Education Research Association, Boston.

Gambrell, L., & Heathington, B. (1981). Adult disabled readers metacognitive awareness about reading tasks and strategies. *Journal of Reading Behavior*, *13*, 215–222.

Garner, R. (1987). *Metacognition and reading comprehension*. Norwood, NJ: Ablex.

Garner, R., & Kraus, C. (1982). Good and poor comprehender differences in knowing and regulating reading behaviors. *Educational Research Quarterly*, *6*, 5–12.

Graham, S., & Harris, K. (1987). Improving composition skills of inefficient learners with self-instructional strategy training. *Topics in Language Disorders*, *7*, 66–77.

Graves, A.W. (1986). Effects of direct instruction and metacomprehension on finding main ideas. *Learning Disabilities Research*, *1*, 90–100.

Griffey, Q.L. (1988). The effects of self-questioning and story structure training on the reading comprehension of poor readers. *Learning Disabilities Research*, *4*(1), 45–51.

Groller, K., Kender, J., & Honeyman. (1991). Does instruction on metacognitive strategies help high school students use advance organizers? *Journal of Reading*, *34*(6), 470–475.

Kronick, D. (1984). The learning disabled adult. *Association for Citizers with Learning Disabilities Newsbriefs*, 6.

Kuhrt, B.L., & Farris, P.J. (1990). Empowering students through reading, writing, and reasoning. *Journal of Reading*, *33*, 436–441.

Labercane, G., & Battle, J. (1987). Cognitive Processing strategies, self-esteem, and reading comprehension of learning disabled students. *British Columbia Journal of Special Education*, *11*(2), 167–185.

Larson, K.A., & Gerber, M.M. (1987). Effects of social metacognitive training for enhancing overt behavior in learning disabled and low achieving delinquents. *Exceptional Children*, *54*(3), 201–211.

Newton, E. (1991). Developing metacognitive awareness: The response journal on College Composition. *Journal of Reading*, *34*(6), 476–478.

Paris, S.G., & Myers, M. (1981). Comprehension monitoring, memory, and study strategies of good and poor readers. *Journal of Reading Behavior*, *13*, 5–22.

Paris, S.G., & Oka, E.R. (1989). Strategies for comprehending text and coping with reading difficulties. *Learning Disability Quarterly*, *12*(1), 32–42.

Pressley, M., & Levin, J.R. (1983). *Cognitive strategy research: Educational applications*. New York: Springer-Verlag.

Pressley, M., & Harris, K.R. (1990). What we really know about strategy instruction. *Educational Leadership*, *48*, 31–34.

Rueda, R., & Mehan, H. (1986). Metacognition and passing: Strategic interactions in the lives of students with learning disabilities. *Anthropology and Education Quarterly*, *17*, 145–165.

Smith, S. (1981). *No easy answers: The learning disabled child at home and school*. New York: Bantam Books.

Vaughn, S. (1985). Why teach social skills to learning disabled students? *Journal of Learning Disabilities*, *18*(10), 588–591.

Wade S.E., & Reynolds, R.E. (1989). Developing students' metacognitive awareness may be essential to effective strategy instruction. *Journal of Reading*, *33*, 6–15.

Wallace, G., & Bott, D. (1989). Statement—Pie: A strategy to improve the paragraph writing skills of adolescents with learning disabilities. *Journal of Learning Disabilities*, *22*(9), 541–543.

Wang, M.C., & Palinscar, A.S. (1989). Teaching students to assume an active role in their learning. In M.C. Reynolds (Ed.), *Knowledge base for the beginning teacher*. Elmsford, NY: Pergamon.

Wiens, J.W. (1983). Metacognition and the adolescent passive learner. *Journal of Learning Disabilities*, *16*(3), 144–149.

Weisberg R. (1988). 1980's: A change in focus of reading comprehension research: A review of reading-learning disabilities research based on an interactive model of reading. *Learning Disability Quarterly*, *11*(2), 149–159.

Wong, B.Y.L. (1987). How do the results of metacognitive research impact on the learning disabled individual? *Learning Disability Quarterly*, *10*, 189–195.

Wong, B.Y.L., & Wong, R. (1986). Study behavior as a function of metacognitive knowledge about critical task variables: An investigation of above average, average and learning disabled readers. *Learning Disabilities Research*, *1*, 101–111.

Wong B.Y.L., Wong, R., & Blenkinsop, J. (1989). Cognitive and metacognitive aspects of learning disabled adolescents' composing problems. *Learning Disability Quarterly*, *12*(4), 300–325.

IX
Strategy Instruction: Programming for Independent Study Skill Usage

WILLIAM D. BURSUCK AND MADHAVI JAYANTHI

As persons with learning disabilities (LDs) are enrolling in postsecondary education in ever-increasing numbers, there is disturbing evidence that many of these students are having difficulty staying in and completing these programs (Sitlington & Frank, 1990). One contributing factor to this problem is the fact that postsecondary classrooms require an extensive repertoire of independent learning skills. As Dalke and Schmitt (1987) pointed out, the demands of college environments are quite different from those of high school. Indeed, they are characterized by a significant decrease in student–teacher contacts, by greater academic competition, and, in general, by a less protective environment. Furthermore, college courses appear to require a much higher level of reading, writing, listening, and verbal interactive skills, areas in which students with learning disabilities have been shown to have a deficit (Houck, Engelhard, & Geller, 1989; Mangrum & Strichart, 1988). Certainly, postsecondary service providers will need to teach their students with learning disabilities these most important independent learning skills.

A critical goal in our work with students with LDs is to help them become more independent learners. For the purposes of this chapter, an independent learner is one who knows his or her strengths and weaknesses, who knows how these strengths and weaknesses may interact with course demands (potential successes and problems), who recognizes the need for and applies a range of learning strategies to meet demands that may be problematic, who monitors the effectiveness of these strategies (adjusting usage as necessary), and who is motivated to persist in task completion, even in the face of initial failure. Of particular concern to service providers at the postsecondary level is the fact that there is considerable research indicating that students with learning disabilities are likely to have serious problems in one or more of these areas.

With respect to knowledge of strengths and weaknesses and their impact on meeting environmental demands, Aune (1991), as part of an investigation of the self-advocacy skills of 29 high school seniors with learning disabilities who were enrolled in a college transition program, found that only 19% of the students could explain their learning disability and that only 44% could verbalize needed accommodations. Not one student in the sample could describe personal strengths, a finding consistent with other research indicating that university students with LDs often have poor self-esteem (Saracoglu, Minden, & Wilchesky, 1990). McWhirter and McWhirter (1990), in a recent description of a program for students with LDs at Arizona State University, reported that knowledge of strengths and weaknesses was lacking in many of their students and thus formed an important part of their program of support. Clearly, this key component of independent learning needs to be considered as we provide learning strategies instruction for college students with learning disabilities.

There is also considerable research indicating that college students with learning disabilities do not have access to a repertoire of independent learning strategies. A number of studies have indicated that college students with LDs lack strategies for problem solving (Johnson & Blalock, 1987; Stone, 1987), time management (Bursuck & Jayanthi, 1991a; Johnson & Blalock, 1987; Vogel, 1985; 1987; Aune, 1991), note taking (Mangrum & Strichart, 1988; Rose & Sloan, 1990; Vogel, 1985; 1987), test taking (Mangrum & Strichart, 1988; Vogel, 1985; 1987), organization of written language (Johnson, 1987; Mangrum & Strichart, 1988; Vogel, 1985; 1987), and textbook reading (Mangrum & Strichart, 1988; Vogel, 1985; 1987). Certainly, the direct instruction of these skills could comprise the core of study skills courses for college students with LDs.

As mentioned previously, the ability to monitor strategy usage is also a critical component of independent learning (Pressley, Symons, Snyder, & Cariglia-Bull, 1989; Swanson, 1989). Once again, there is evidence to suggest that college students with LDs are deficient in this area (Mangrum & Strichart, 1988, Johnson & Blalock, 1987). The latter reported that, "Those who came in for remediation were encouraged to ask themselves, 'Does this make sense?' or 'Is it right?.' Whether the task involved reading, mathematics, or social skills, they had to be activated to think about meaning" (p. 165).

A final component critical for independent learning is task persistence. Certainly, students need to be motivated to pursue tasks to completion, regardless of their difficulty, or of any short-term setbacks. Unfortunately, for many students with learning disabilities, past failures can lead to self-doubt of abilities, which in turn can lead pupils to believe that their efforts are futile (Tollefson et al., 1980; Torgesen, 1980). It also appears that the ability to set long-term goals for oneself may also influence task performance (Tollefson et al., 1980). There is some evidence to suggest that college students with LDs may experience serious difficulty in areas of both self-efficacy (Sarcoglu et al., 1990; Schunk, 1989) and goal setting (Mangrum & Strichart, 1988). Such problems could seriously undermine efforts to teach these students to be independent and will need to be considered carefully in designing instructional interventions for them.

Traditionally, independent learning skills have been taught at the college level through what are commonly construed as study skills courses. In the study skills approach, students are taught to perform particular skills in the areas of textbook reading, written expression, test taking, note taking, and time management. Although the performance of specific skills in these areas is a necessary component of independent learning, Ellis (1990) cautions that we must concentrate on more than just discrete skills or how to teach them. He suggests that instructors must also create "strategic environments." In strategic environments, teachers interact with students in ways that promote strategic thinking and behavior, the primary components of independent action. Ellis (1990) further cautions that a failure to provide strategic environments for students can seriously undermine independence by supporting behaviors with which it is incompatible.

One particularly promising approach to fostering independent learning that emerged during the 1980s was the learning strategies approach. Deshler, Warner, Schumaker, and Alley (1983) have defined a learning strategy as an individual's approach to a task; it includes how the person thinks and acts when planning, executing, and evaluating performance on a task and its outcomes. Thus, the learning strategies model is more comprehensive than study skills programs in that, in addition to learning how to perform particular skills, students also learn why and when to use these skills as well as how to monitor their implementation. In the learning strategies approach, the accent is on independent skill application as well as acquisition. This is critical for students with learning disabilities for whom skill transfer or application may be a serious problem (Ellis, 1990; Ellis, Deshler, & Schumaker, 1989). It is also important to note that, although the learning strategies approach has traditionally been defined as including common study skills areas such as note taking, test taking, textbook usage, and time management, its principles also apply to many other areas within the basic skill domains of math, reading, and writing. Indeed, if they are to learn to apply basic skills, students with LDs will need to know why they are important, when to use them, and, most importantly, how to monitor their implementation.

The purpose of this chapter is to present a technology for teaching study skills that draws from the learning strategies literature and maximizes the probability of independent skill application. We believe that the application of such a technology will enable college students with learning disabilities to achieve levels of independence necessary for success in college. Training for independence will be presented within the context of four major aspects of the instructional process: assessment, curriculum design, skill acquisition and fluency, and skill generalization.

Assessment Practices

Although assessment practices with college students with LDs have been covered elsewhere in this book (see Chapter VI by Doris Johnson and Chapter X by Pamela Adelman and colleagues), aspects of the assessment process that have a significant impact on skill independence will be discussed here.

Student Strengths and Learning Needs

As stated previously, knowledge of academic strengths and learning needs is an important precursor to being an independent learner. Students who are aware of their strong and weak areas can learn to both capitalize on their strengths and apply selected strategies to bypass or overcome weak areas. Unfortunately, as also mentioned earlier, there is evidence to suggest that college students with learning disabilities are not aware of their learning strengths and needs (Mangrum & Strichart, 1988; McWhirter & McWhirter, 1990). In fact, repeated research in the area of self-image indicates that these students tend to magnify their weaknesses and downplay or ignore their strengths entirely (Aune, 1991). The resulting lack of confidence can seriously erode the high level of task commitment needed to acquire and apply independent learning skills. Instructors and tutors are thus advised to assess students' knowledge of self prior to beginning study skills instruction and to teach students their learning profiles if necessary.

Assessing Learning Environments

A key variable in study skills application concerns how well the instructor prepares students to meet the specific demands they encounter daily in their own particular classrooms. Thus, these demands must be systematically assessed and incorporated into a study skills regime. As mentioned previously, college students with LDs may be unaware of the important relationships between their disability, course demands, and needed strategies and accommodations (Aune, 1991). Rose and Bursuck (1989) have developed an instrument to assess systematically college learning environments called The Instructional Style Survey. This instrument assesses college classroom demands in the following areas: materials and equipment (e.g., syllabus, visual aids, textbook and other readings); lectures (e.g., summaries, examples, key points); student involvement and feedback (e.g., groupings, in-class assignments, student participation); assignments (e.g., papers, projects); examinations (test formats, test content); evaluation schedule (test or assignment frequency); and accommodations for students with disabilities (e.g., tape recorders, extended time, etc.). The Instructional Style Survey can be completed by either the instructor or the student. Once the information is obtained, the student and the instructor analyze it in view of the student's diagnostic information, and a list of potential successful and problem situations is developed. In this way, the instructor is assured that the study skills taught are relevant and meaningful to the student, an important ingredient in motivating adult learners.

For example, Tom is a college student with LDs who is strong in verbal ability and basic knowledge but weak in visual processing skills and written language. He is enrolled in Dr. Brown's history class. Dr. Brown stresses information that he presents in lectures, offers all-essay test formats, and is receptive to allowing accommodations for students with disabilities. Tom and his study skills instructor decide that the emphasis on lectures will benefit Tom because of his good oral language skills and extensive background knowledge. Furthermore, they decide to begin work on strategies to improve Tom's essay-writing skills. In the meantime, they will seek oral testing as an accommodation until Tom acquires more competence in writing essay questions. In this manner, Tom's strategy instruction is geared to his particular abilities and classes. Furthermore, a process of arriving at an individual accommodation has been modeled for Tom and will, it is hoped, lead to his pursuing future accommodations on a more independent basis.

Although this process is effective in adapting strategy programs to individual needs, a word of caution is in order, particularly for persons offering large-group study skills instruction. Obviously, in these situations the instructor will be unable to individualize for all students. It is suggested that areas in which most students have difficulty be selected.

Goal Setting

A key aspect of independence is that students are motivated to first acquire and then apply strategies to a range of potential problem situations. This requires a long-term commitment that persists even in the presence of short-term failures; a commitment that, as indicated earlier, college students with LDs may lack due to a history of failure. As cited in Ellis, Lenz, and Sabornie (1987), de Charms (1976) has suggested that such a commitment can be fostered by making sure the students are clear about their own reasons for learning a skill and then by helping them set realistic goals based on these reasons. As discussed previously, students who are aware of their strengths and weaknesses, as well as how these interact with the demands of their courses, should have a clear idea of their study-skills needs. Thus, they will be in a good position to set relevant goals for themselves. For example, Tom, in the case described above, selected essay-test writing as an area of instruction based on an awareness of his problems in written language as well as of the fact that his history teacher stressed essay-question formats. This should ensure a greater long-term commitment than if essay-question writing were selected because it was included in the first chapter of the study-skills text.

Monitoring Student Independence

By now it should be clear to the reader that for college students with LDs the goal of independent learning is not something we can ordinarily expect to emerge out of study-skills instruction but is a matter that must be actively programmed by the teacher into all aspects of instruction. An important part of that programming process is to assess carefully whether students are indeed becoming more independent learners. Three options that will be discussed here are self-evaluations, teacher evaluations, and grades. Self-evaluations, which will be covered in greater depth later in this chapter, involve having students evaluate themselves regarding skill application. For example, after completing a multiple-choice test in one of her classes, Sara checked off all of the steps in the test-taking strategy that she followed. She then shared the results with her study-skills instructor during their next session. This approach is valuable not only because it allows the instructor to monitor independent strategy usage but also because it simultaneously teaches students a critical metacognitive skill that is important for skill independence. Recent research has shown that college students with LDs often lack and will need to be encouraged to use these most critical skills (Johnson & Blalock, 1987; Chapter VIII by Margaret M. Policastro).

Despite the importance of self-evaluation, the use of other measures of skill usage is desirable to provide external validation of one's teaching procedures. Teacher evaluations involve having the student's course instructors measure student behaviors in areas relevant to the particular study skill taught. For example, in our implementation of a time-management program for students with learning disabilities at a community college, we requested that the student's teachers report to us valuable information such as student attendance, tardiness, and work-completion rates, outcome areas directly related to our time-management curriculum (see Figure 9.1 for a sample form). Finally, instructors and tutors will want to monitor student grades, as these should ultimately reflect whether or not a given program is successful. Grades can be collected at the end of the semester or, if teachers are willing, at pre-designated points throughout the semester.

Curriculum Design

Another aspect of study-skills instruction that can enhance the likelihood of independent learning is the curriculum design. Eight components of curriculum design taken from Ellis et al. (1987) and Carnine, Silbert, and Kameenui (1990) will be discussed.

Attendance and Assignment Sheet

Student Name: _____   Class: _____
Instructor: _____
AS = assignment
Attendance   + = came to class and was not on time
          ++ = came to class and was on time
           − = did not come to class

Data	Attendance	Number of AS due	Number of AS submitted on time	% accuracy on AS	GPA to date

FIGURE 9.1. *Source*: Bursuck, W., & Jayanthi, M. (1991a). Teaching time-management skills to college students with LD. Manuscript in preparation.

Determine Preskills Necessary for Strategy Performance

Carnine et al. (1990) define preskills as components of a strategy that need to be taught before the strategy itself. For example, COPS (Schumaker et al., 1981) is a self-questioning strategy designed to help students proofread their written work. The specific questions asked are as follows:

C Have I capitalized the first word and proper names?
O How is the overall appearance (spacing, legibility, etc.)?
P Have I put in commas and end punctuation?
S Have I spelled all the words right?

In order to perform this strategy students need to have mastered rudimentary writing mechanics such as capitalization and punctuation rules and their applications as well as the ability to recognize words that are misspelled. Students who are lacking in these preskills will find implementation of the strategy difficult if not impossible. Thus, prior to introducing the COPS strategy, instructors need to assess students on the preskills and preteach them if necessary. This may be particularly important for college students with learning disabilities, who are likely to be deficient in one or more basic-skills areas (Johnson & Blalock, 1987;

Vogel, 1985). This will increase the likelihood of successful skill acquisition, and, ultimately, independent skill application.

Strategies Should Be Task-Specific

Ellis et al. (1987) have defined a *task-specific strategy* as one that can be employed with a variety of different or similar tasks and can be used across content areas. For example, the COPS strategy discussed above can be used across many situations and content areas as long as they involve writing. Strategies that are not task-specific would relate to highly specialized situations or content (e.g., how to proof Dr. Smith's highly specialized biology lab reports), and would not be likely to result in independent usage in other areas. Teaching task-specific strategies to college students with LDs would seem to make sense from a number of standpoints. First, given the fact that college students with LDs often need to spend more time studying outside of class, there is simply not enough time available to learn strategies for each individual class. In addition, both study skills and individual tutorial formats have built-in time constraints. Thus, the potential efficacy of a task-specific approach is appealing. Finally, as college students with LDs may have difficulty acquiring, storing, and retrieving strategies, study-skills instructors and tutors will be more effective, and students will be less burdened, if efficient, generalizable strategies are emphasized.

Strategies Should Include No More Than Seven Steps, Should Begin with a Verb and a Word Directly Related to the Strategy, and Be Encased in a Mnemonic Device

These aspects of curriculum design, also suggested by Ellis et al. (1987), are critical for independent skill application that requires that the strategy be readily memorized and then retrieved from memory when it is applied. Research indicates that college students with LDs have difficulty in both areas (Johnson & Blalock, 1987; Mangrum & Strichart, 1988; Vogel, 1985). While not an absolute necessity, encasing the strategy in a mnemonic can facilitate the memory and retrieval process for students with LDs (Scruggs & Mastropieri, 1990). The following word identification strategy, DISSECT, developed by Lenz, Schumaker, Deshler, and Beals (1984) and recently validated with college students with LDs by Bursuck and Jayanthi (1991b), meets all of these guidelines.

D *D*iscover the context.
I *I*solate the prefix.
S *S*eparate the suffix.
S *S*ay the stem.

E *E*xamine the stem.
C *C*heck with someone.
T *T*ry the dictionary.

Include Self-Instructional Cues to Use Cognitive or Metacognitive Strategies

A key aspect of independence is self-instruction, or being able to give oneself instructions while performing a particular task. These instructions can involve evaluating a situation to see what strategy is called for, rehearsing the steps necessary to carry out that strategy, and monitoring strategy performance to see if any changes in performance are necessary. These areas of metacognition may be problematic for college students with LDs (Vogel, 1987; Mangrum & Strichart, 1988; Johnson & Blalock, 1987). Thus the issue of whether or not the strategy cues the student to engage in metacognitive behaviors is an important one. An example of this curriculum-design feature is shown in the following test-taking strategy (SCORER) developed by Carman and Adams (1972) and validated with students with learning disabilities by Idol-Maestas and Ritter (1986).

S *S*chedule your time.
C Look for *c*lue words.
O *O*mit difficult questions.
R *R*ead carefully.
E *E*stimate your answer.
R *R*eview your work.

In the SCORER strategy students are cued to carry out the specific steps of the strategy (e.g., Look for cue words; Omit difficult questions) as well as to monitor strategy performance (e.g., Review your work).

Use a Broad Range of Examples to Present the Strategy

An important aspect of independent performance is being able to recognize situations that call for use of the strategy. Although data validating this characteristic for college students with LDs are not available, research with younger students with learning disabilities indicates that they may have difficulty making this important application (Hallahan, Kauffman, & Lloyd, 1985; Lovitt, 1989). Carnine et al. (1990) have suggested that the selection of examples one uses to teach a strategy can facilitate strategy application. They suggest presenting a broad range of situations that call for usage of the strategy. For example, in teaching the SCORER strategy to college students with LDs, examples of its usage in answering both objective and essay questions in the classes they are currently taking would increase the eventual likelihood of independent skill application. Similarly, in teaching the DISSECT strategy, explicit reference to its application to a range of college textbooks would be important.

Use Nonexamples to Clarify Appropriate Strategy Usage

As mentioned previously, independent skill usage requires students to monitor themselves to make certain they are correctly performing the strategy. Thus, students must recognize when their behavior does not conform to the requirements of a given strategy. The presentation of nonexamples of strategy usage can facilitate this recognition. For example, a nonexample of using the DISSECT strategy would involve showing students someone who proceeds directly to analyze the stem of every difficult multisyllabic word, instead of initially doing a context, prefix, and/or suffix analysis. Students would then be asked to indicate whether they felt this was appropriate or inappropriate strategy usage and why. Similarly, in presenting SCORER, the nonexample of someone answering every test item in order and not looking for clue words could be shown and discussed.

Summary

A carefully designed curriculum can increase the likelihood of the occurrence of independent learning by not only facilitating rapid acquisition of skills with very few errors but also by promoting generalization and maintenance of skills learned. Another factor that accentuates the probability of students attaining mastery-level performance is the manner in which the skills are taught. Effective instructional techniques that help ensure accurate and fluent skill usage are explained in the next section.

Instructional Techniques to Build Skill Accuracy and Fluency

As previously discussed, independent usage of learning strategies is dependent on a number of factors. One particular factor is whether or not study skills have been taught to mastery levels of performance. Again, although research data in this area with college students with LDs are scant, research on younger students with LDs shows that these students are usually unable to generalize the strategy to other nontrained situations until they perform the strategy at the specified mastery levels (Beals, 1984; cited in Lovitt, 1989; Borkowski, Estrada, Milstead, & Hale, 1989).

Mastery-level performance incorporates two components: (1) accuracy and (2) fluency (Kameenui & Simmons, 1990). Students initially learn to perform the strategy routines correctly. However, once strategy skills are performed with accuracy, the instructional emphasis shifts to encompass fluent performance of the strategy at mastery levels. Thus, the early stage of strategy instruction emphasizes the need for students to acquire and perform the strategy correctly and fluently at mastery levels.

The results of at least two decades of effective teaching research indicate that the probability of students attaining mastery levels of a skill is greatly influenced by the manner in which the skills are taught to students (Evertson, Anderson, Anderson, & Brophy, 1980; Rosenshine, 1986). It is also clear that this research applies to students with learning disabilities in general (Leinhardt, Zigmond, & Cooley, 1981; Lloyd, Cullinan, Heins, & Epstein, 1980; Reith, Polsgrove, & Semmel, 1982) and to college students with learning disabilities in particular (Vogel, 1987). According to Vogel (1987), research in education has shown that "one of the most critical factors, if not the most critical factor, in a student's learning is the individual teacher. In the case of the battle-scarred and insecure LD adult, this is even a more critical factor" (p. 262). Cowen, Bursuck, and Rose (1989), in a synthesis of the effective research literature, have characterized effective teaching practices as they relate to college students with learning disabilities as follows:

1) Instructional goals are based on assessment information.
2) Instructional goals are based on learner's needs. The learner helps decide goals.
3) Instructional activities are consistent with goals.
4) Teacher provides explicit explanation of the steps necessary to perform academic tasks.
5) Instruction is introduced in small segments and at a slow pace.
6) Teacher provides guided practice with sufficient examples and review until mastery is reached.
7) Teacher provides positive and corrective feedback during the learning process.
8) Teacher addresses the adult's affective needs during instruction. The teacher is aware of potential emotional or psychological blocks to learning and provides genuine encouragement.
9) Instruction includes a self-monitoring component. Learner should be an integral part of lesson evaluation.

It is important that study-skills instruction incorporate these principles of effective instruction. The following steps, adapted from the learning strategy instructional model (Schumaker, Denton, & Deshler, 1984), are consistent with the effective teaching research and are suggested for use during the acquisition and fluency stage.

A) Determine student's current level of strategy competence.
B) Clarify teaching and learning expectations.
C) Demonstrate strategy use.

D) Provide rote drill on strategy steps.
E) Provide guided and independent practice in controlled situations.
F) Provide guided and independent practice in real-life situations.
G) Post-test the student.

A. Determine Student's Current Level of Strategy Competence

1. Assess Current Strategy Usage

In a previous section, assessment was discussed in terms of an overall framework tying together students' learning profiles and the specific demands of their college courses. The purpose of assessment in this phase is to determine students' current level of competence on particular strategies that have been targeted for instruction. For college students with learning disabilities, this is an important first step towards an awareness of their current skill levels and their goals for future performance. As mentioned previously, college students with LDs often experience difficulties with these metacognitive functions (Seidenberg, 1987). Information regarding current strategy competence can be obtained from various sources.

a. Direct Observation

Using the SCORER test-taking strategy described previously as an example, the teacher would first develop a checklist of the observable steps in the strategy. Then, the teacher would watch while the student is taking a test and record the observable steps that the student performed correctly. A sample checklist for SCORER is shown in Figure 9.2.

b. Student Self-Report

In this form of assessment, students are asked to perform a task such as taking a test, are given a checklist of strategy steps, and are then asked to indicate which of these steps they used or did not use. In addition to providing useful information regarding strategy behaviors that cannot be directly observed, student self-evaluations also form a foundation for self-monitoring, a behavior critical for independent strategy usage. Self-report measures can also include interview questions to clarify strategy usage further. For example, while assessing SCORER, a teacher asked, "What was the first thing you did when you received your test?" A sample checklist student self-report for SCORER is included in Figure 9.3.

c. Faculty Report

Teachers can also be a good source of information regarding student strategy competence, particularly in the area of independent strategy usage. If willing, instructors can measure students' strategy competence

Test-Taking Skills: Assessment Form for Teacher

Student's Name: _____   Date: _____
Teacher's Name: _____   Class: _____

Directions: Please observe the student and respond to the following statements by circling YES or NO.

The student

1. Is aware of how much time he/she has to take tests.		Y	N
2. Answers questions that he/she knows first.		Y	N
3. Goes back to answer more difficult, time-consuming questions.		Y	N
4. Checks answers after finishing the test to avoid careless mistakes.		Y	N
5. Knows what type of questions to answer.		Y	N
6. Looks for clue words to determine what information is given and what information is needed to answer the questions.		Y	N
7. Spends less time on known questions, thus saving time for unsure questions.		Y	N
8. Reads all the directions before beginning the test.		Y	N
9. Asks for help when directions are not understood.		Y	N
10. Reads the entire questions and answers when they are given.		Y	N
11. Reads over the answers.		Y	N
12. Asks himself/herself if the answers make sense.		Y	N
13. Guesses only after honestly attempting to answer.		Y	N
14. Uses information given to help estimate the answer.		Y	N
15. Checks over the answers before handing in the tests.		Y	N
16. Presents work that is neat and legible on the tests.		Y	N
17. Checks to make sure all questions are answered before handing in the tests.		Y	N
18. Always makes sure own name is on the tests.		Y	N

FIGURE 9.2. Adapted from Beansoleil, B., Galen, L., Himmel, C., Holly, W., Myszka, K. (1989). *A testtaking strategy assessment tool for students with learning disabilities*. Unpublished manuscript, Northern Illinois University, Faculty of Special Education, DeKalb, Illinois.

by engaging in activities such as checking and evaluating students' notes and observing students' test-taking behaviors. An example of a checklist (Burke, Cowen, Rose, & Bursuck, 1988) designed to evaluate students' test-taking behaviors is shown in Figure 9.4.

2. Target Preskills

Effective strategy instruction emphasizes the need to teach preskills prior to teaching the actual study strategy skills (Carnine et al., 1990; Kameenui & Simmons, 1990). For example, an important prerequisite to

Test-Taking Skills: Self-Assessment Form

Student's Name: _____   Date: _____
Teacher's Name: _____   Class: _____

Directions: Please read each statement and circle YES or NO according to your own test-taking behaviors. Be sure to mark every item.

1. I am aware of how much time I have to take tests.	Y	N
2. I answer questions that I know first.	Y	N
3. I go back to more difficult, time-consuming questions.	Y	N
4. I check my answers after I finish my test to avoid careless mistakes.	Y	N
5. I know what type of question to answer.	Y	N
6. I look for clue words to determine what information is given and what information I need to answer myself.	Y	N
7. I spend less time on questions I know, saving my time for those that I am unsure of.	Y	N
8. I read all the directions before beginning the test.	Y	N
9. When I don't understand directions, I ask for help.	Y	N
10. I read the entire questions and answers when they're given.	Y	N
11. I read over my answers.	Y	N
12. I ask myself if my answers make sense.	Y	N
13. I guess only after honestly attempting to answer.	Y	N
14. I use information given to help estimate my answer.	Y	N
15. I check over my answers before handing in my tests.	Y	N
16. My work is neat and legible on tests.	Y	N
17. I check to make sure all questions are answered before handing in my tests.	Y	N
18. I always make sure my name is on my test.	Y	N

FIGURE 9.3. Adapted from Beausoleil, B., Galen, L., Himmel, C., Holly, W., Myszka, K. (1989). *A testtaking strategy assessment tool for students with learning disabilities*. Unpublished manuscript, Northern Illinois University, Faculty of Special Education, DeKalb, Illinois.

the DISSECT strategy is basic decoding skills. Students who are unable to perform these skills will have great difficulty acquiring the strategy. Along with this difficulty is the additional risk of motivational problems developing if initial efforts of strategy instruction are not successful. This is critical, as both the acquisition and eventual independent application of study skills will depend largely on a high level of student motivation. Therefore, it may be essential to teach preskills in isolation before introducing actual strategy instruction. As mentioned previously, this may be an important consideration for college student with LDs who may be deficient in a number of strategy preskills (Johnson & Blalock, 1987; Vogel, 1985).

The Faculty Checklist

Student's Name: _____   Date: _____
Teacher's Name: _____   Class: _____

Directions: Use the key to indicate the frequency of the problem as compared to typical students in your class.

Test Taking

1. Difficulty in selecting main points.	N R S F DNA
2. Difficulty in recalling material presented in lecture rather than text.	N R S F DNA
3. Difficulty in recalling specific terminology.	N R S F DNA
4. Difficulty in recalling specific facts.	N R S F DNA
5. Completes test sooner or later than other students.	N R S F DNA
6. Exhibits much test anxiety.	N R S F DNA
7. Difficulty with essay questions.	N R S F DNA
8. Test scores fail to reflect competence shown in other classwork.	N R S F DNA

FIGURE 9.4. N = never; R = rarely; S = sometimes; F = frequently; DNA = does not apply.
Source: Burke, L., Cowen, S., Rose, E., & Bursuck, W. (1988). The faculty checklist. In S. Cowen & L. Burke (Eds.), *Assessment: A training manual for community college personnel*. DeKalb: Northern Illinois University.

B. Clarify Teaching and Learning Expectations

1. Describe the New Strategy

In this step the strategy steps are shown and explained briefly to the students. For example The word identification strategy is called DISSECT and it can be explained as follows:

D *D*iscover the context.
I *I*solate the prefix.
S *S*eparate the suffix.
S *S*ay the stem.
E *E*xamine the stem.
C *C*heck with someone.
T *T*ry the dictionary.

2. Give Rationale for Why the Strategy Is Important

The purpose of this phase is to provide the students with a reason for learning the strategy. Seidenberg (1986) has stressed the importance of this step for college students with LDs as a necessary step in moving from teacher control to student self-control of learning. The students are initially provided with information (regarding their current performance) that was obtained from the assessments described in the previous section. The relationship between current performance and course demands, potential benefits of the learning strategy, and future personal gains is also explained to the students at this time. For example, the teacher can explain this relationship by saying, "DISSECT will help you identify unknown words in psychology class. You know how important it is to read and comprehend the textbook in Haskin's class." Knowledge of this relationship will enhance student motivation to learn and become independent over time.

3. Explain the Instructional Objectives

For this step, the results expected from strategy usage are explained by presenting the instructional objectives established in the goal-setting phase. For example, Mike will read his psychology textbook using the DISSECT strategy with 100% accuracy for three consecutive sessions. Involving students in the development of instructional objectives is one way of fostering responsibility and independence. Also, knowledge of such a projected instructional outcome can be a powerful motivator for college students with LDs, many of whom may view study skills as just another remedial service that, like many others, will not make much difference in their lives.

4. Develop Timeline for Meeting Objectives

Here, the approximate number of days or sessions it will take to master the strategy is explained to the students. For example, the teacher can post a timeline and carefully explain each step in the instructional process (e.g., demonstrating the strategy, independent practice, etc.), indicating approximately how long it will take to master the strategy. The advantage of presenting this information on a chart is that steps can be checked off or crossed out as they are completed. Students are generally motivated to learn and perform skillfully when they are aware that with the appropriate effort success can be achieved in a short period of time.

It is important to note that the emphasis here is on mastery learning as opposed to content coverage. Traditionally, study skills classes have been geared towards the latter, providing students with an information base on a range of learning strategies, with limited concern for the explicit instruction of these strategies. There is some evidence to suggest that this approach is not effective for college students with learning disabilities (Cowen, 1988). We believe that a more structured, mastery-oriented approach will increase the likelihood of skill acquisition as well as of independent skill usage.

5. Avoid Competitive Goal Structures

Competitive goal structures tend to be detrimental to the process of acquiring and generalizing study skills (Ellis, 1986; Ellis et al., 1987). Competitive goal structures result in a student's success being negatively correlated to the success of his or her peers in the classroom (Licht & Kistner, 1986). As a result, students are less attentive to the demands of the task and to the role effort plays in succeeding at the task (Ames, 1984). Certainly the fragile sense of self ascribed to many college students with learning disabilities has resulted in part from being consistently at the bottom of the normal curve. While competition in regular college classrooms is quite institutionalized and therefore largely unavoidable, study-skills classes, even if they are for credit, should be more mastery-oriented, with a "cooperative" rather than a "competitive" orientation. Students who are encouraged and allowed to work towards their goal, at their own pace, within established guidelines, are generally more motivated to learn and be independent. Furthermore, students who are working to acquire study skills in concert with their peers may be more likely to apply these skills to their college courses (Kerr, Nelson, & Lambert, 1987).

C. Demonstrate Strategy Use

1. Perform Study Skill While Thinking Out Loud

After the strategy objectives and timelines have been explained, the next step in acquisition and fluency is to demonstrate how the skill is used. Researchers have suggested that for college students with learning disabilities, the "process" one goes through in performing a task or solving a problem should be as carefully analyzed and explained as the final product (Vogel, 1987). Thus it is important that skill demonstration involve a careful delineation of both "thinking" and "doing" behaviors. Teachers should talk aloud to themselves while performing a skill, thus emphasizing the critical cognitive and behavioral components that may not be obvious to persons with learning disabilities (Johnson & Blalock, 1987). For example for step D (Discover the context) of DISSECT, the teacher could say, "I don't know how to say this word. I will use DISSECT. For step D, I will have to 'discover the context.' I will skip the word and read the remaining sentence. Maybe I will be able to figure out the word from the context." An understanding as well as mastery of the covert cognitive processes involved in study-skill usage is critical for future independent performance.

2. Present Examples and Nonexamples

In this phase, the teacher presents examples and nonexamples of the new strategy, carefully explaining why they are either examples or nonexamples. As discussed in the curriculum development section, the examples and nonexamples serve two purposes. First, they help the student discriminate between appropriate and inappropriate strategy usage. For example, the step E (Examine the stem) of DISSECT requires the students to initially divide the word into small segments using certain rules called "rules of twos and threes." However, while demonstrating, the teacher could say "I have to examine the stem. I think I have to use some rules. But, I don't remember them. I think I will divide the word exactly in half and try to pronounce it. I think I will be able to figure out the word." The teacher can then discuss whether that was appropriate or inappropriate strategy performance and why, thus helping students to identify the critical features of correct strategy usage that, again, may not be obvious to college students with LDs (Johnson & Blalock, 1987).

Second, examples and nonexamples help students understand the conditions under which the strategy may be applicable. For example, the correct mix of examples can help students realize that utilizing the DISSECT strategy in history and psychology classes is appropriate while the utilization of the same strategy in a math class may be inappropriate and thus not worth trying.

3. Ask Questions Frequently to Test Understanding

Throughout the acquisition and fluency process the teacher needs to test the student's understanding of appropriate and inappropriate strategy use. Careful monitoring of student performance will be helpful for college students with LDs, many of whom may have attentional or listening problems (Johnson & Blalock, 1987; Vogel, 1987). For example, the teacher should ask questions such as, "What does D of DISSECT mean? Is it okay if I did . . .?" Questions enable the teacher to test for student understanding, and monitor student progress, providing additional practice and instruction as necessary.

Researchers have suggested avoiding a large number of open-ended questions as they are negatively related to learning gains (Stallings & Kaskowitz, 1974, cited in Stevens & Rosenshine, 1981). In addition, while asking questions, teachers should provide a sufficient wait time or thinking time before allowing the students to respond (Carnine et al., 1990), a key concern for college students with LDs who may need more time to process auditory, visual, or conceptual information (Johnson & Blalock, 1987). The more difficult the question, the longer the wait time should be. However, too long of a wait time may result in off-task behavior, while a too short wait time may result in a high rate of errors.

D. *Provide Rote Drill on Strategy Steps*

In this step students are encouraged to memorize the strategy steps. Class sessions should be targeted to provide intensive verbal rehearsal of strategy steps. For example, at the beginning or ending of every class, the teacher could ask the students what the acronym DISSECT means. Students must be able to say the steps both accurately and fluently.

The purpose of rote drill is to integrate the strategy steps into students' repertoires at an automatic level (Pressley, Johnson, & Symons, 1987), thus ensuring that the students will not have to spend a great deal of time recalling them. This approach is consistent with research indicating that limited retrieval time facilitates independent strategy usage (Carnine et al., 1990).

Whereas automatic recall of the strategy is important, researchers suggest not spending too much time memorizing strategy steps, particularly for students with short-term memory problems (Ellis et al., 1987). This is an important consideration in working with college students with learning disabilities who may indeed have short-term memory problems (Vogel, 1985; Johnson & Blalock, 1987). An inability to memorize the steps may result in frustration and decreased motivation to work toward mastering the strategy. Under such circumstances, it may be prudent to provide the student with prompts such as cue cards to facilitate recall of the study skill.

E. Provide Guided and Independent Practice in Controlled Situations

Controlled materials are (1) generally at the student's reading level; (2) usually of high interest; and (3) relatively free of complex vocabulary and concepts. As controlled materials do not place any additional content demands on the students, they are conducive to initial learning of the strategy (Deshler, Alley, Warner, & Schumaker, 1981). Furthermore, these materials allow for initial success in the program, a factor important to student motivation.

1. Provide Ample Practice

Students will need regularly scheduled, intensive practice in controlled situations if they are to learn to perform study skills accurately and fluently. When dealing with study-skills classes that stress group rather than one-to-one instruction, extra practice will need to be scheduled for those students who are unable to keep pace with the group. One rule of thumb is to move to the next step when 80% of the group has mastered the previous step. It is important that mastery-level performance not be compromised in an attempt to cover course content. We believe that it is more beneficial for students to learn one or two skills well than to be merely introduced to a series of skills without mastering any of them, a method that does not appear to be effective for college students with learning disabilities (Cowen, 1988).

2. Use Systematic Error-Correction Procedures

Provisions will need to be made for the sustained use of error-correction procedures as long as incorrect responses occur (Larrivee, 1986). Initially, error correction is done directly by the teacher. Later on in the instructional process, the teacher should provide prompts (e.g., questions) or models rather than telling the answer or calling on another student. For example, the teacher could ask the question, "What do we do next? . . . Remember your rules of twos and threes." Prompts and cues stimulate student thinking, encourage self-corrections, and shift control from the teacher to the student, thus paving the way toward independence. This is important in working with students with learning disabilities who may be prone to becoming too dependent on the teacher (Hallahan, Kauffman, & Lloyd, 1985).

3. Use Praise Judiciously

The nature of the feedback teachers provide to students can have an important impact on strategy acquisition and ultimately on independent strategy usage. Feedback and praise should be task-directed, specific, positive, constructive, and justified (Carnine et al., 1990; Larrivee, 1986). In addition, praise should be directed at difficult rather than easy tasks (Licht & Kistner, 1986). Praise statements with many superlatives (e.g., this is the best performance I have ever seen) tend to reduce the credibility of the teacher (Ellis, 1986; Ellis, 1990).

It is important to note, however, that the overuse of teacher-controlled praise and feedback can result in the development of dependency behaviors, attitudes, and other learning characteristics that are detrimental to the development of independence in students (Ellis et al., 1987). Ellis et al. (1987) suggest asking students how well they think they performed (e.g., "How do you think you did?") instead of actually stating their performance (e.g., "You did a good job."). Such a line of questioning encourages self-evaluation, a critical component of independent learning and, again, a must for college students with learning disabilities who may be lacking in these important metacognitive skills (Johnson & Blalock, 1987).

Students should also be encouraged to engage in self-reinforcing behaviors. For example, after performing well on a particular task, the students can be encouraged to say, "I did a good job. I need to do the same the next time." By attributing their difficulties and successes to factors under their own control, students are able to build a positive self-image (Paris & Oka, 1989), an area that may be a problem for college students with LDs (McWhirter & McWhirter, 1990). Such self-reinforcing behaviors and the resulting positive attitudes help motivate students to become more independent users of strategies.

4. Maintain a Brisk Pace During the Lesson

A brisk pace needs to be maintained during instruction, with active student questions to keep the students interested and actively engaged in the task at hand. A high rate of teacher presentation with frequent opportunities for students to respond produces high levels of student attention and correct responding as well as increased learning rates (Carnine et al., 1990). It is important to note that attending to task may be problematic for college students with learning disabilities (Vogel, 1987). As a 26-year-old man with LDs related, "I feel overloaded a lot, and get easily distracted from a task. I lose my train of thought. I guess I just need a lot of structure and consistency" (Johnson, 1987, p. 281). While *just* going faster is not recomended, the use of frequent unambiguous questions along with a brisk pace can provide that needed structure and consistency.

Provide Guided and Independent Practice in Real-Life Situations

To maximize the probability of independent learning, students with LDs should be taught under conditions that, to the greatest extent possible, approximate their college classes. This is particularly important in view of research indicating that persons with learning disabilities are likely to have trouble generalizing across settings (Smith, 1991; Lovitt, 1989; Ellis et al., 1987). Such activities are also more likely to motivate college students with learning disabilities because they represent a direct application that will be highly relevant and of immediate potential utility. Therefore, teachers should repeat practice, feedback, and drill procedures using materials from current coursework until students are performing skills accurately and fluently under these conditions. Instruction should proceed gradually from easier applications to more difficult applications. For example, an instructor teaching the word-identification strategy, DISSECT, would start with a textbook that has limited content and processing demands and then move to textbooks where multisyllabic word-identification demands are more exacting and rigorous.

G. Post-Test the Student

Before moving to the maintenance and generalization phase of instruction the teacher should measure students' performance to ensure that they are able to apply the strategy accurately and fluently to tasks comparable to those encountered in their coursework.

Summary

Accurate and fluent use of study skills to mastery levels is an essential prerequisite for independent learning. For college students with learning disabilities, such levels of learning are facilitated by providing systematic and methodical teacher-directed instruction. These include: (1) determining a student's current level of strategy competence; (2) clarifying teaching and learning expectations; (3) demonstrating strategy use; (4) providing rote drill on strategy steps; (5) providing guided and independent practice in controlled situations; (6) providing guided and independent practice in real-life situations; and (7) post-testing the student.

Maintenance and Generalization

The independent usage of study skills will depend in large part on two key areas. First, once strategies are acquired, students will need to maintain their mastery levels over time. Skill maintenance is an area that may be problematic for college students with LDs, many of whom may have underlying memory (Dalke, 1988) or motivational (Schunk, 1989; Seidenberg, 1987) problems. Second, students must be able to generalize the skills from the study-skills class or tutorial sessions to their courses. Generalization involves the ability to recognize when a particular skill is needed, to retrieve and apply that strategy, to monitor strategy performances, and to make changes when necessary. Such a high level of organization may be quite problematic and will thus need to be carefully programmed for college students with LDs (Johnson & Blalock, 1987; Kahn, 1980). In this section, key instructional strategies that facilitate skill maintenance and generalization will be discussed.

Maintenance

In order to facilitate independence, it is essential that students maintain their newly acquired skills for extended periods of time. Maintenance is facilitated by two factors: (1) mastery-level performance and (2) continued usage of the skill. The various techniques used to promote mastery-level learning during instruction were discussed in the previous section. Once students have acquired skills the teacher should periodically test the student to monitor skill maintenance and also provide periodic opportunities for strategy usage. Coordination between study-skills instructors, tutors, and teachers from content-area classrooms may be necessary for effective administration of periodic maintenance checks.

Nevertheless, while these practices are necessary, if the ultimate goal is for students to maintain their skills independently, then such practices should be faded out as soon as possible. Indeed, students are more likely to maintain their skills if they have a need for them in real-life settings (e.g., taking notes in various classes) and are able to apply them successfully.

Generalization

Long-term independent usage of a strategy is dependent to a large extent on the ability of the students to generalize skills from study-skills or tutorial sessions to their classes (Ellis et al., 1989). We have previously discussed ways that study-skills teachers can facilitate generalization in the assessment and teaching stages of learning-strategy instruction. In this section, tactics for facilitating generalization *after* learning strategies have been acquired will be described.

1. Teach Generalization Directly

After acquiring skills at the mastery level, college students with LDs must be actively or directly taught to generalize these skills to other settings (Seidenberg, 1986). Ellis et al. (1987) suggest three steps for teaching generalization directly. These include orientation, activation, and implementation.

Orientation

In this step, students must be oriented or made aware of the fact that they need to generalize the skill to other settings. They should also be encouraged to ask questions such as, "In which classes do I need to use this strategy?" An analysis of the instructional demands in the various classrooms employing the Instructional Style Survey (Rose & Bursuck, 1989; see also Chapter VII by Ernest Rose) would provide students with the necessary information to determine where they need to apply their newly learned strategies.

Activation

Here, students are made aware of their need to work actively for generalization to occur (e.g., set priorities, monitor their performance, engage in extra practice directed toward mastery). Students are required to apply the strategy in their courses and then report back to the instructor for feedback. In addition, students should be provided with self-monitoring forms that will help them regulate their performance. This is particularly important as students with learning disabilities may have difficulty with self-monitoring (Hallahan, Kauffman, & Lloyd, 1985; Smith, 1991). A form used by Bursuck and Jayanthi (1991a) to help students self-monitor the implementation of a time-management strategy is shown in Figure 9.5.

Time Management: Self-Monitoring Form

Student's Name: _____
Class: _____
Directions: Answer the checklist everyday after reviewing your schedule book at the end of the day. If you completed an activity put a (+) in the box; if you did not complete the activity put a (−) in the box.

Date	
Did you cross out completed activities?	☐
Did you circle activities not completed?	☐
Did you reschedule activities not completed?	☐
Did you enter due dates for assignments?	☐
Did you schedule study time?	☐

FIGURE 9.5. *Scource*: Bursuck, W., & Jayanthi, M. (1991a). Teaching time-management skills to college students with LD. (Manuscript in preparation).

Implementation

In this step, the student makes a commitment to remember and use the strategy, when necessary, in new settings. This final step is critical, as motivation, commitment, and the desire to master and use the strategy pave the way for long-term use of the strategy in applied settings.

2. Involve Course Instructors

Generalization from the training setting (study-skills classroom or tutorial setting) to a student's classes can be facilitated by their course instructors or tutors (Deshler et al., 1981). For example, instructors can be provided with the steps in a particular strategy, and, if willing, can periodically provide cues (e.g., Be sure to use your SCORER test-taking strategy) and feedback. As indicated previously, course instructors can also be a good source of information regarding whether or not the study skills are being applied, and, if so, how well they are being used. However, it is important to note that regular in-services and administrative support may be necessary to convince course instructors of the need for their assistance (Rose, 1991; see Chapter VII by Ernest Rose).

3. Use Peer-Mediated Techniques

Students' classmates can be very helpful in getting them to apply study skills to their courses (Kerr, Nelson, & Lambert, 1987). Ellis et al. (1987)

have suggested pairing students who have attained mastery-level performance with those who still need some assistance to perform accurately. Such peer pairs can cue each other to use the strategy and also provide each other with valuable feedback regarding the quality of skill performance. Instructors can support this process further by encouraging students to report their activities back to the class.

4. Use Self-Mediated Stimuli

Stokes and Baer (1977) recommend this technique. Very often in study-skills classes the teacher takes control of student performance by means of questions, prompts, cues, corrections, and feedback. Although such instructional behaviors are necessary during initial skill development, continued use of these techniques after skills have been acquired may be detrimental to generalization and independence (Ellis et al., 1989; Ellis, 1990). In order to facilitate generalization, researchers have suggested encouraging student behaviors such as self-correcting, self-questioning, self-reinforcement, and self-monitoring (Ellis, 1990). By using these self-mediated stimuli, the behavior is brought under the control of the student, and this control can be exercised regardless of the setting. The spontaneous use of self-mediated stimuli, often referred to as metacognition (see Chapter VIII by Margaret Policastro), can be problematic for college student with LDs (Johnson & Blalock, 1987; Seidenberg, 1986) and is an essential part of ensuring that study skills become part of a student's independent learning repertoire.

5. Use Indiscriminable Contingencies

Deshler et al. (1981) and Stokes and Baer (1977) recommend using indiscriminable contingencies. During the initial acquisition stage teachers generally provide reinforcement on a regular basis. This is appropriate given the fact that more teacher support is needed when skills are first learned. However, the use of continuous reinforcement schedules can lead to a situation where students fail to exhibit the behaviors in course settings that are characterized by less reinforcement, and continuous reinforcement may ultimately be responsible for the dependency patterns of students with learning disabilities, including those in college settings. Thus, to facilitate generalization and independence, it is suggested that the predictability and quantity of the reinforcers in study-skills classes and tutorial settings be gradually faded to a variable rate such as, praise every now and then without a pattern (Deshler et al., 1981) and that it be specifically geared toward other strategic behaviors such as self-monitoring and skill application across settings (Ellis, 1990).

Another way of reducing the predictability of reinforcers is by means of delayed reinforcement (Stokes & Baer, 1977). According to this procedure, reinforcement is not provided immediately following the target behavior but at a later point in time. For example, if a student performs

well in the study-skills class, instead of providing reinforcement immediately, the teacher waits and reinforces outside the class, after the class is
over.

Summary

The independent usage of learning strategies depends to a large extent on
the ability of the students to maintain and generalize their skills. As
college students with learning disabilities may have difficulty in both
areas, study-skills instructors and tutors will need to apply teaching techniques that encourage maintenance and generalization. Maintenance of
skills is facilitated by two factors: (1) mastery-level performance and (2)
continued usage of the skill; students are more likely to maintain their
skills if they have a need for them in their real-life settings.

In order to promote generalization of skills, generalization should be
actively programmed during the instructional phase, instead of being
viewed as a passive outcome of the learning process (Stokes & Baer,
1977). Researchers have suggested including a number of tactics to
promote generalization. These include (1) teaching generalization directly;
(2) involving course instructors; (3) using peer-mediated techniques; (4)
using self-mediated stimuli; and (5) using indiscriminable contingencies.

References

Ames, C. (1984). Achievement attributions and self-instruction under competitive
and individualistic goal structures. *Journal of Educational Psychology*, *76*,
478–487.

Aune, E. (1991). A transition model for postsecondary bound students with
learning disabilities. *Learning Disabilities Research and Practice*, *6*, 177–187.

Beals, V.L. (1984). The effects of large-group instruction on the acquisition of
specific learning strategies by LD adolescents. *Unpublished doctoral dissertation*,
University of Washington, Seattle.

Borkowski, J.G., Estrada, M.T., Milstead, M., & Hale, C. (1989). General
problem-solving skills: Relations between metacognition and strategic processing. *Learning Disability Quarterly*, *12*(1), 57–70.

Burke, L., Cowen, S., Rose, E., & Bursuck, W. (1988). The faculty checklist. In
S. Cowen & L. Burke, *Assessment: A training manual for community college
personnel*. DeKalb: Northern Illinois University.

Bursuck, W., & Jayanthi, M. (1991a). *Teaching time management skills to college
students with LD*. Manuscript in preparation.

Bursuck, W., & Jayanthi, M. (1991b). *Teaching word-identification skills to
college students with LD*. Manuscript in preparation.

Carman, R.A., & Adams, W.R. (1972). *Study skills: A student's guide for
survival*. New York: Wiley.

Carnine, D., Silbert, J., & Kameenui, E.J. (1990). *Direct Instruction Reading*
(2nd ed.). Columbus, OH: Merrill.

Cowen, S.E. (1988). Coping strategies of university students with learning disabilities. *Journal of Learning Disabilities*, *21*(3), 161–164.

Cowen, S., Bursuck, W., & Rose, E. (1989). Efficient Strategies. In W.D. Bursuck (Ed.), *Specific intervention strategies, participants' manual, Project TAPE*. DeKalb: Northern Illinois University.

Dalke, C. (1988). Woodcock-Johnson Psycho-Educational Test Battery Profiles: A comparative study of college freshman with and without learning disabilities. *Journal of Learning Disabilities*, *21*(9), 521–584.

Dalke, C., & Schmitt, S. (1987). Meeting the transition needs of college-bound students with learning disabilities. *Journal of Learning Disabilities*, *20*(3), 176–180.

de Charms, R. (1976). *Enhancing motivation*. NY: Irvington.

Deshler, D.D., Alley, G.R., Warner, M.M., & Schumaker, J.B. (1981). Instructional practices for promoting skill acquisition and generalization in severely learning disabled adolescents. *Learning Disability Quarterly*, *4*(4), 415–421.

Deshler, D., Warner, M.M., Schumaker, J.B., & Alley, G.R. (1983). Learning strategies intervention model: Key components and current status. In J.D. McKinney & L. Feagons (Eds.), *Current topics in learning disabilities* (pp. 245–283). Norwood, N.J.: Ablex.

Ellis, E.S. (1986). The role of motivation and pedagogy on the generalization of cognitive strategy training. *Journal of Learning Disabilities*, *19*(2), 66–70.

Ellis, E.S. (1990). What's so strategic about teaching teachers to teach strategies? *Teacher Education and Special Education*, *13*(2), 56–62.

Ellis, E.S., Deshler, D.D., & Schumaker, J.B. (1989). Teaching adolescents with learning disabilities to generate and use task-specific strategies. *Journal of Learning Disabilities*, *22*(2), 108–119.

Ellis, E.S., Lenz, B.K., & Sabornie, E.J. (1987). Generalization and adaptation of learning strategies to natural environments: Part 2: Research into practice. *Remedial and Special Education*, *8*(2), 6–23.

Evertson, C., Anderson, C., Anderson, L., & Brophy, J. (1980). Relationships between classroom behaviors and student outcomes in junior high mathematics and English classes. *American Educational Research Journal*, *17*, 43–64.

Hallahan, D.P., Kauffman, J.M., & Lloyd, J.W. (1985). *Introduction to learning disabilities* (2nd ed.). Englewood Cliffs, NJ: Prentice-Hall.

Houck, C.K., Engelhard, J., & Geller, C. (1989). Self-assessment of learning disabled and non-disabled college students: A comparative study. *Learning Disabilities Research*, *5*(1), 61–67.

Idol-Maestas, L., & Ritter, S. (1986). Teaching middle school students to use a test-taking strategy. *Journal of Educational Research*, *79*(6), 350–357.

Johnson, D.J. (1987). Disorders of written language. In D.J. Johnson & J.W. Blalock (Eds.), *Adults with learning disabilities: Clinical studies* (pp. 145–172). Orlando, FL: Grune & Stratton.

Johnson, D.J., & Blalock, J.W. (Eds.). (1987). *Adults with learning disabilities: Clinical studies*. Orlando, FL: Grune & Stratton.

Kahn, M.S. (1980). Learning problems of the secondary and junior college learning disabled student: Suggested remedies. *Journal of Learning Disabilities*, *13*(8), 445–449.

Kameenui, E.J., & Simmons, D.C. (1990). *Designing instructional strategies: The prevention of academic learning problems*. Columbus, OH: Merrill.

Kerr, M.M., Nelson, C.M., & Lambert, D.L. (1987). *Helping adolescents with learning and behavior problems*. Columbus, OH: Merrill.

Larrivee, B. (1986). Effective teaching for mainstreamed students is effective teaching for all students. *Teacher Education and Special Education*, 9(4), 173–179.

Leinhardt, G., Zigmond, N., & Cooley, W. (1981). Reading instruction and its effects. *American Educational Research Journal*, 18, 343–361.

Lenz, B.K., Schumaker, J.B., Deshler, D.D., & Beals, V.L. (1984). *Learning strategies curriculum: The word identification strategy*. Lawrence: The University of Kansas.

Lovitt, T.C. (1989). *Introduction to Learning Disabilities*. Needham Heights, MA: Allyn & Bacon.

Licht, B.K., & Kistner, J.A. (1986). Motivational problems of learning disabled children: Individual differences and their implications for treatment. In J.K. Torgesen & B.Y.K. Wong (Eds.), *Psychological and educational perspectives on learning disabilities*. New York: Academic Press.

Lloyd, J., Cullinan, D., Heins, E.D., & Epstein, M.H. (1980). Direct instruction: Effects on oral and written language comprehension: *Learning Disability Quarterly*, 3(4), 70–76.

McWhirter, B.T., McWhirter, J.J. (1990). University survival strategies and the learning disabled college student. *Academic Therapy*, 25(3), 345–357.

Mangrum, C.T. II, & Strichart, S.S. (Eds.). (1988). *College and the learning disabled student: Program development implementation and selection* (2nd ed.). Orlando, FL: Grune & Stratton.

Paris, S.G., & Oka, E.R. (1989). Strategies for comprehending text and coping with reading difficulties. *Learning Disability Quarterly*, 12(1), 32–42.

Pressley, M., Johnson, C.J., & Symons, S. (1987). Elaborating to learn and learning to elaborate. *Journal of Learning Disabilities*, 20(2), 76–91.

Pressley, M., Symons, S., Snyder, B.L., & Cariglia-Bull, T. (1989). Strategy instruction research comes of age. *Learning Disability Quarterly*, 12(1), 16–30.

Reith, H.J., Polsgrove, L., & Semmel, H.I. (1982). Instructional variables that make a difference: Attention to task and beyond. *Exceptional Education Quarterly*, 2(3), 61–71.

Rose, E. (1991). Project TAPE: A model of technical assistance for service providers of college students with learning disabilities. *Learning Disabilities Research and Practice*, 6, 25–33.

Rose, E., & Bursuck, W. (1989). The Instructional Style Survey. In E. Rose, W.D. Bursuck & S. Cowen. *Northern Illinois postsecondary education project: Final Report*. Northern Illinois University, DeKalb.

Rose, E., & Sloan, L. (1990). *Teaching note-taking strategies to adults with learning disabilities*. Unpublished manuscript, Northern Illinois University, DeKalb.

Rosenshine, B.V. (1986). Synthesis of research on explicit teaching. *Educational Leadership*, 4, 60–69.

Saracoglu, B., Minden, H., & Wilchesky, M. (1990). The adjustment of students with learning disabilities to university and its relationship to self-esteem and self-efficacy. *Journal of Learning Disabilities*, 22(9), 590–592.

Schumaker, J.B., Denton, P., & Deshler, D.D. (1984). *The learning strategies curriculum: The paraphrasing strategy*. Lawrence: The University of Kansas.

Schumaker, J.B., Deshler, D.D., Nolan, S., Clark, F.L., Alley, G.R., & Warner, M.M. (1981). *Error monitoring: A learning strategy for improving academic performance of LD adolescents* (Research Report No. 32). Lawrence: University of Kansas Institute for Research in Learning Disabilities.

Schunk, D. (1989). Self-efficacy and cognitive achievement: Implications for students with learning disabilities. *Journal of Learning Disabilities*, *22*(1), 14–22.

Scruggs, T.E., & Mastropieri, M.A. (1990). Mnemonic instruction for students with learning disabilities: What it is and what it does. *Learning Disability Quarterly*, *13*(3), 271–282.

Seidenberg, P.L. (1986). Direct instruction of learning study strategies. *Learning Disabilities News*, *1*(2), 1–4.

Seidenberg, P.L. (1987). *Social and personal characteristics of the learning disabled: Limitations and implications for the adolescent and young adult.* Brooklyn. N.Y.: Long Island Transition Project. Position paper series: Document 9.

Sitlington, P.L., & Frank, A.R. (1990). Are adolescents with learning disabilities successfully crossing the bridge into adult life? *Learning Disability Quarterly*, *13*(2): 97–111.

Smith, C.R. (1991). *Learning disabilities. The interaction of learner, task and setting* (2nd ed.). Needham, MA: Allyn and Bacon.

Stallings, J., & Kaskowitz, D. (1974). *Follow through classroom observation evaluation, 1972–73*. Menlo Park, CA: Stanford Research Institute.

Stevens, R., & Rosenshine, B. (1981). Advances in research on teaching. *Exceptional Education Quarterly*, *2*, 1–10.

Stokes, T.F., & Baer, D.M. (1977). An implicit technology of generalization. *Journal of Applied Behavior Analysis*, *10*(2), 349–367.

Stone, A.C. (1987). Abstract reasoning and problem solving. In D.J. Johnson & J.W. Blalock (Eds.), *Adults with learning disabilities: Clinical studies*, (pp. 67–80). Orlando, FL: Grune & Stratton.

Swanson, H.L. (1989). Strategy instruction: Overview of principles and procedures for effective use. *Learning Disability Quarterly*, *12*(1), 3–16.

Tollefson, N., Tracy, D., Johnson, E., Borgers, S., Buenning, M., Farmer, A., & Barke, C. (1980). *An application of attribution theory to developing self-esteem in learning disabled adolescents* (Research Report No. 23). Lawrence: The University of Kansas Institute for Research in Learning Disabilities.

Torgesen, J. (1980). Conceptual and educational implications of the use of efficient task strategies by LD children. *Journal of Learning Disabilities*, *13*(7), 364–371.

Vogel, S.A. (1985). Learning disabled college students: Identification, assessment, and outcomes. In D.D. Duane & C.K. Leong (Eds.), *Understanding learning disabilities: International and multidisciplinary views* (pp. 179–203). New York: Plenum.

Vogel, S.A. (1987). Issues and concerns in LD college programming. In D.J. Johnson & J.W. Blalock (Eds.), *Adults with learning disabilities: Clinical studies* (pp. 67–80). Orlando, FL: Grune & Stratton.

X

The Integration of Remediation and Subject-Matter Tutoring: Support at the College Level

Pamela B. Adelman, Jody O'Connell, Dee Konrad, and Susan A. Vogel

The increased awareness of the chronicity of learning disabilities (LDs) emphasizes the need for ongoing assistance for students with LDs at the postsecondary level. Even among students capable of attending college, their persistent processing difficulties and resulting underachievement have affected academic progress in reading, written language, and mathematics (Vogel, 1986; Vogel & Adelman, 1990). Nationwide, colleges and universities have recognized the needs of college students with learning disabilities and have developed services and programs to help them succeed in spite of their deficits.

Services commonly provided to college students with learning disabilities include reasonable accommodations (e.g., extended time for taking exams) and auxiliary aids and assistance that enable them to circumvent their learning disability (Adelman & Olufs, 1986; Vogel, 1982, 1990a). These bypass strategies typically include (1) listening to textbooks either on tape or using machines that read the text; (2) using computerized grammar and spelling programs to correct written language; (3) relying on calculators for math computation; and (4) using note takers in lectures and readers for help with reading exams. Chapter XI of this book is a comprehensive review of assistive technology that has enabled students with LDs in postsecondary settings to develop bypass strategies.

The use of bypass strategies has helped many students with LDs not only to graduate from college but also to achieve success in the workplace (Adelman & Vogel, 1990; Vogel & Adelman, 1990). In addition to encouraging students to use these strategies when appropriate, comprehensive programs for students with learning disabilities integrate remediation of basic skills with subject-matter tutoring. Remediation of basic skills can help students become less dependent on auxiliary aids and/or assistance from other people (Adelman, 1985).

The goal of remediation is to help students improve skills through self-knowledge of their individual strengths, deficits, and learning styles and through direct instruction. This remediation might include teaching mnemonic devices to compensate for their difficulty with remembering math facts or using a multisensory approach to teach word-attack skills.

For some students with LDs, college may be the most appropriate time in their education to receive remediation. The impact of the challenge of college courses and the motivation to succeed, combined with increased emotional, social, and cognitive growth, may result in a more receptive attitude (Adelman & Vogel, 1991). If students no longer have to worry about being embarrassed by the stigma of going to the LD specialist or resource room, they may be more willing to work on improving their skills. Furthermore, students who were first diagnosed in college have never received appropriate remediation, and college may be the first opportunity for them to be taught basic skills by specialists who understand how learning disabilities affect students' progress in developing reading, written language, and math skills.

This chapter will focus on the integration of remediation and subject-matter tutoring as the primary type of support for college students with learning disabilities by (1) reviewing the research on cognitive abilities and achievement levels of college students with LDs; (2) identifying the key components for developing an individual educational plan that integrates remediation and subject-matter tutoring; (3) describing an instructional approach that integrates remediation and subject-matter tutoring; and (4) presenting a case study of a student who received ongoing remedial help while in college.

Cognitive Abilities and Achievement Levels

Several research studies have been conducted to determine the characteristic cognitive abilities and achievement levels of college students with learning disabilities. These studies identify the ongoing processing difficulties that affect academic progress.

Cognitive Abilities

Adelman & Vogel (1990) reported the cognitive abilities of 36 college graduates with learning disabilities and found that the mean Verbal, Performance, and Full Scale intelligence quotients (IQs) were average and quite even ($\bar{X}$ = approximately 103) with Similarities and Comprehension the two highest mean scaled scores (11.23 and 12.45 respectively). The pattern of subtests grouped according to the Bannatyne categories was similar to other samples of LD and non-LD college students in the average IQ range with Verbal Conceptualization (Similarities, Comprehension, and Vocabulary) the highest or next to highest and "ACID" (Arithmetic, Digit Symbol, Information, and Digit Span) the next to lowest (Cordoni, O'Donnell, Ramaniah, Kurtz, & Rosenshein, 1981; Vogel, 1986).

After reviewing several studies that assessed intellectual functioning by administering the Wechsler scales and the revised versions—Wechsler Intelligence Scale for Children (WISC), Wechsler Intelligence Scale for Children-Revised (WISC-R), Wechsler Adult Intelligence Scale (WAIS), Wechsler Adult Intelligence Scale-Revised (WAIS-R)—Salvia, Gajar, Gajria, and Salvia (1988) concluded that "like children with learning disabilities, adults with learning disabilities may show VIQ-PIQ differences, considerable scatter on subtests, Bannatyne's hierarchy of category scores, and lower performance on the ACID cluster" (p. 633). Bannatyne's hierarchy is a regrouping of WISC and WISC-R subtests into four composites: spatial (Object Assembly, Picture Completion, and Block Design), verbal conceptualization (Comprehension, Similarities, and Vocabulary), sequential (Digit Span, Arithmetic, and Coding), and acquired knowledge (Information, Arithmetic, and Coding). The hierarchy is spatial, verbal conceptualization, sequential, with the placement of acquired knowledge varying within the sequence. Although no characteristic cognitive profile that can be used to diagnose learning disabilities such as VIQ-PIQ discrepancy has emerged from studies using the Wechsler scales, significant variability in the subtest scores has been a pervasive finding (Blalock, 1987a; Buchanan & Wolf, 1986; Salvia et al., 1988; Vogel, 1986).

Further evidence of the variability of cognitive profiles among college students with LDs was noted by Cowen (1988). She administered the Woodcock-Johnson Psycho-Educational Battery (WJPEB) (Woodcock & Johnson, 1977) to 25 college students previously identified as learning disabled. She found that 22 of the 25 students had 1 of 3 profiles associated with learning disabilities; 6 subjects had low verbal ability and high reasoning ability; 5 subjects had high verbal ability and low reasoning ability; and 11 subjects had high verbal ability and reasoning and low perceptual speed and memory.

Although there is considerable evidence that Verbal-Performance IQ discrepancy should not be used for diagnosing learning disabilities in adults, this information contributes to understanding the manifestations of the learning disability and in planning remedial and support services (Vogel, 1986). Whereas individuals with nonverbal deficits may have difficulty developing social maturity and independence and may require extensive psychotherapy (Blalock, 1981; 1982; Johnson, 1987; Vogel, 1986), those with verbal deficits may have underlying problems in oral language (Blalock, 1981; 1982; 1987b; Vogel, 1986) and may require long-term remediation in order to improve basic skills.

Achievement Levels

There is evidence of continuing deficits in reading, mathematics, spelling, and written composition among college students with learning disabilities (Adelman, 1985; Adelman & Vogel, 1990; Cordoni, 1979; Cowen, 1988; Dalke, 1988; Vogel, 1985; Vogel & Moran, 1982; Vogel & Konrad, 1988). Table 10.1 presents several studies that assessed reading, mathematics, and spelling achievement of college students with learning disabilities. Included in the table are size of the sample, IQ, the age at evaluation, the dependent measures, and a summary of the results.

A major residual effect of having a learning disability, even for highly accomplished adults with learning disabilities, is poor spelling. After reviewing 18 follow-up studies, Schonhaut and Satz (1983) concluded that even educationally and occupationally successful adults who were diagnosed as having a reading disability during childhood have life-long problems with using language, particularly with spelling. Underlying language deficits were often evident from analyses of spelling errors that reveal problems with sound discrimination, memory, and understanding of linguistic patterns.

There are other important aspects of written language in addition to spelling; although less easily quantified, these deficits are often significant. A learning disability may also affect development of basic writing skills, and these difficulties often persist in students with learning disabilities who enter postsecondary institutions.

Vogel and Moran (1982) examined written language abilities of college students with learning disabilities. They compared writing samples of college students with LDs with those of their nondisabled peers. Their essays were compared on frequency, type, and accuracy of punctuation and capitalization marks, spelling accuracy, and usage. Not only did the writers with learning disabilities use significantly fewer punctuation marks, but they used only 69% correctly, while their nondisabled peers used 85% correctly. In regard to spelling accuracy, the students with learning disabilities made significantly more spelling errors than their nondisabled peers ($p < .008$). This difference occurred despite the fact that writers of essays may avoid words they do not know how to spell. Cordoni (1979) also reported that the lowest subtest score on the Peabody Individual Achievement Test (PIAT) for a group of college students with learning disabilities was the spelling subtest (see Table 10.1).

Correct usage, another aspect of basic writing skills, was also found to discriminate between students with and without learning disabilities (Vogel & Konrad, 1988). Characteristic usage and sentence construction errors in college students with learning disabilities included sentence fragments, run-on sentences or comma-splice errors, lack of subject and predicate agreement, and inappropriate coordination and/or subordination (Vogel & Konrad, 1988).

TABLE 10.1. Results of studies assessing achievement of college students with learning disabilities.

Study	Size of sample	IQ $\bar{X}$(SD)	Age at evaluation	Dependent measures	Results GE or SS
Adelman & Vogel (1990)	36	WAIS FS IQ 103.97 (9.81)	$\bar{X}$ = 22 18–44 years	*Reading Comprehension*	
				Stanford	9.7
				PIAT	10.7
				W-J Passage	
				Comprehension	11.0
				Spelling	
				TOWL	8.4
				WRAT	8.3
				PIAT	10.4
				Math	
				PIAT	9.6
				WRAT	6.9
				W-J	
				Quantitative Concepts	10.0
				Calculation	9.0
				Applied Problems	9.0
Cordoni (1979)	NR	NR	NR	*Spelling*	
				PIAT	10.5

Study	n	Ability Measure		Achievement Measure	
Cordoni & Snyder (1981)	16	NR	19–4	*Reading Recognition*	
				PIAT	9.8
				WRAT-1978 NORMS	8.4
				Arithmetic	
				PIAT	12.0
				WRAT-1978 NORMS	7.2
Cowen (1988)	25	Woodcock-Johnson Psycho-Educational Battery: Tests of Cognitive Ability $\bar{X} = 101.24$	NR	W-J Clusters	
				Reading Achievement	94.76
				Math Achievement	102.80
Dalke (1988)	36	Woodcock-Johnson Psycho-Educational Battery: Tests of Cognitive Ability $\bar{X} = 89.69$	NR	W-J Clusters	
				Reading Achievement	88.06
				Math Achievement	89.81
				Written Language Achievement	86.08

Note: NR = Not reported

Dalke (1988) also studied written language abilities in college students with learning disabilities. She compared the performance of college freshmen with and without learning disabilities on the WJPEB. Although significant differences existed between the two groups on all the cognitive and achievement tests, the lowest mean standard score for the group with learning disabilities was on the Written Language cluster, a measure of basic writing skills.

The Remedial Plan

Remedial services are generally found in comprehensive programs for college students with learning disabilities and are provided by LD specialists. Chapter V of this book discusses the continuum of services offered by colleges and universities. Several factors enter into developing a remedial plan for a college student with learning disabilities. These factors include (1) using information from psychoeducational diagnostic testing for developing goals to improve basic and daily living skills and to identify the appropriate major in college; (2) involving faculty through ongoing communication and education about learning disabilities in general as well as individual abilities and needs of students in their classes; and (3) careful advising of students into developmental and regular classes that meet their academic needs and interests.

Assessment

A remedial plan for college students begins with obtaining information about their cognitive and academic strengths and weaknesses (Adelman, 1988; Vogel, 1982; 1986). In addition to this information, Polloway, Smith, and Patton (1984) note the importance of considering those factors that will help with successful adjustment once a student is no longer in school. Thus, career goals and daily living skills should also be included in developing the remedial plan.

Psychoeducational diagnostic testing provides the information to understand the students' individual strengths and weaknesses. Assessment of adults with learning disabilities is discussed in Chapter VI of this book. Information gained from testing can be used to identify long-term goals (e.g., to improve spelling) and to recommend effective learning strategies (Adelman & Olufs, 1986; Vogel, 1990a). Figure 10.1 is an example of a diagnostic report prepared in a format students have found easy to follow.

Diagnostic information is also used to prepare a plan for remediating basic skills that will enhance the students' academic progress and, if necessary, improve skills needed to become independent adults. Figure 10.2 is an example of an Individual Education Plan (IEP). In order to

BARAT COLLEGE: Learning Opportunities Program

NAME: _____L.M. 2951_____

DATE: _____Sept. 17, 1984_____

L.D. Specialist: _____J.N._____

Academic Areas Involved:
  Reading Comprehension
  Written Language
  Mathematics
  Study Habits

Strengths	Areas for Improvement
Auditory Receptive/Expressive Language – Ability to abstract and label the essential characteristics of objects in the environment. – Ability to understand a variety of vocabulary words. – Knowledge and use of the rules for adding endings to words to form plurals, possessives, past tense, etc.	*Auditory Receptive/Expressive Language* – Ability to recall specific words. – Recognition of correct use of grammar in sentences presented orally. – Ability to identify synonyms of words.
Auditory Processing – Ability to recall verbal presentations with a visual stimulus.	*Auditory Processing* – Ability to discriminate between similar sounding words. – Ability to break words down into and build up from their component syllables and sounds (auditory analysis and synthesis). – Short-term memory for words and sentences.
Written Language – Ideation in written language. The ability to address a specific topic in an organized manner.	*Written Language* – Recognition of appropriate sentence structure in written language. – Knowledge of appropriate capitalization, punctuation, and usage. – Knowledge of phonetic spelling rules, letter-sound correspondences, and memory

FIGURE 10.1. *Continued*

Strengths	Areas for Improvement
	for phonetically irregular words.
	– Remembering and writing main concepts of a paragraph presented orally.

Strengths	Areas for Improvement
Reading	*Reading*
– Knowledge of the meanings of common prefixes, suffixes, and root words.	– Reading comprehension.
– Reading comprehension of single words.	– Ability to scan and skim an article for specific information.
– Ability to locate words with similar meanings.	– Decoding—word-attack and phonics skills.
	– Ability to identify sight vocabulary.
Math	*Math*
– Knowledge of basic math concepts—numeration, place value.	– Knowledge of fractions, decimals, percentages, and ratios.
– Calculation of basic math processes.	– Application of math concepts in verbal problems.
	– Monitoring of errors in calculation.
Visual Processing	*Visual Processing*
– Ability to interpret visual details in drawings.	– Spatial relationships.
– Ability to place pictures according to a logical sequence.	– Short-term visual memory for letters.
	– Ability to rapidly associate names with visual objects (visual to auditory processing).
Study Habits and Work Methods	*Study Habits and Work Methods*
– Completion of assignments.	– Test anxiety.
– Organization of materials and study area.	– Monitoring for errors.
– Willingness to maintain open lines of communication with teachers.	– Test-taking strategies.
	– Time management.

Long-Term Goals

– Improve study habits and work methods.
– Improve reading comprehension.
– Improve written language.
– Improve math skills.

FIGURE 10.1. *Continued*

Effective Learning Strategies

To Improve Study Habits and Work Methods
- Develop a system of time management with your LD specialist utilizing a calendar for course requirements and study and free time.
- Develop and practice rehearsal techniques for test taking.
- Work with your LD specialist to develop test-taking strategies.
- Break down long assignments into short, manageable steps.
- Tape record class lectures. Listen to tape later and add to your class notes.

To Improve Reading Comprehension
- Use books on tape for difficult sections.
- Use highlighting and color-coding for important ideas and information.
- Pause after each section you read to state the main idea to yourself.
- Use outlining and summarizing when reading. Note important details, facts, and terms on notecards.
- Develop questions to ask yourself before reading to relate ideas.

To Improve Written Language
- Outline essay questions and papers before you write.
- Maintain a personal checklist of common errors in mechanics for monitoring.
- Utilize resources such as *Write Right!* for accuracy.
- Work with your LD specialist to improve punctuation skills and your understanding of sentence structure.
- Maintain a personal glossary of difficult spelling words. Refer to a spelling aid such as *Misspeller's Dictionary*.

To Improve Math Skills
- Develop a basic checklist to monitor math work for computational and process errors.
- In applied math problems, list the steps to follow and determine essential information.
- Work with your LD specialist to increase your understanding of fractions, decimals, and ratios.
- Utilize a calculator when allowed for quick, accurate computation.

FIGURE 10.1.

develop this IEP, specific errors made by the student both on formal tests and in writing samples were analyzed to determine the remedial plan. The IEP specifies both the long-term goal to improve written language skills and the way the goal is to be accomplished by setting short-term objectives and identifying the teaching strategies, materials, measurement procedures, and the amount of tutoring required.

Diagnostic information is also important in helping students identify career goals. This step may be accomplished through joint meetings with

Short-Term Instructional Objectives

Student: L.

Learning Disabilities Specialist: Jody O'Connell

Long-Term Goal: To improve written language skills

Short-term objectives	Teaching strategy/materials	Measurement procedures	Tutoring (hours weekly)	Date instruction begun
L. will differentiate between run-ons, fragments, and complete sentences.	*Warriner's*, pps. 200–287	Improvement in written assignments	2 hours	9/86
L. will use coordination and subordination correctly in sentences.	*Write Right!*	Post-test		
L. will utilize sentence combining.	Coursework papers and essays			
L. will develop a personal checklist for monitoring of errors in punctuation and grammar.	Error analysis *Write Right!*	Improvement in independent written assignments	2 hours	9/86
L. will use personal spelling reference book of choice to monitor spelling errors.	*Misspeller's Dictionary* and *Webster's Spelling Dictionary*			
L. will develop a personal spelling list and learn five new words per week.	Course text reading *3140 Important Spellbound Words*	Post-test Improvement in written assignments	2 hours	9/86

FIGURE 10.2.

the student, career counselor, and LD Specialist (Adelman & Wren, 1990). Maglione (1989) developed a Personal Employability Profile designed to assist students in choosing an appropriate and realistic career direction that considers the effect their learning disability may have upon their career. The plan considers the students' academic skills, the type of learning disability, including modality strengths and weaknesses, and cognitive abilities.

Faculty Involvement

Ongoing communication with faculty is necessary for several reasons. Most common is the need to explain the specific learning disabilities of students enrolled in the course and the reasonable accommodations they may require. Contact with faculty is sometimes necessary to clarify course objectives and requirements of the course for the student. LD specialists/faculty often provide additional insight into the students' specific learning skills and needs and offer valuable suggestions of ways to achieve success in the course. Staffings with faculty who teach courses that are specifically designed to improve reading, written language, and math skills can be very helpful to the LD specialists (Adelman, 1988; Adelman & Olufs, 1986; Vogel, 1982).

Communication with faculty may be initiated by the student, the LD specialist, or the LD specialist and the student. Some students prefer to advocate for themselves, whereas others ask their LD specialist to advocate for them. Students are always encouraged to become self-advocates and learn advocacy skills. In some cases, the LD specialist and student meet with the individual faculty members at the beginning of the year. As the year progresses, students are encouraged to meet with the faculty on their own (Adelman, 1988; Adelman & Olufs, 1986; Vogel, 1982; 1990a).

In order to establish open lines of communication, it is important for faculty to have a knowledge base about learning disabilities that will eliminate misconceptions about the abilities and needs of college students with learning disabilities. Colleges and universities have won support from faculty by offering in-services that include such activities as workshops, speakers who are experts on learning disabilities, and films (see Chapter VII by Ernest Rose). Possibly the most effective in-services present panels of successful college students and graduates who explain how their learning disabilities affected their academic progress and the motivation and perseverance they needed to succeed (Adelman, 1988; Vogel, 1982; 1990a). Ongoing in-service is important to maintain a positive attitude among faculty about students with LDs. One way of maintaining faculty support is asking them to serve on advisory councils that involve them in program evaluation and policy decisions (Adelman, 1988; Vogel, 1982; 1990a). Additional information about developing faculty awareness and education is in Chapter VII of this book.

Advisement

Careful advisement contributes significantly to the success of college students with learning disabilities (Vogel & Adelman, 1990). Vogel and Adelman conducted an eight-year follow-up study on four-year degree completion and academic failure rate of 110 students with LDs. The students were compared to a random stratified sample of 153 peers attending the same college for at least one semester. They reported that the students with LDs graduated at the same rate and within the same time frame as their non-disabled peers. Moreover, their academic failure rate was no higher than that of the non-disabled students. Vogel and Adelman identified special academic advising as a key factor contributing to these positive outcomes.

Special academic advising involves guiding students in the development of a schedule that considers their individual strengths, weaknesses, and interests. For example, a student with reading deficits would be encouraged to limit the number of courses with heavy reading. When appropriate, special academic advising also involves placing students in (1) developmental courses specifically designed to improve reading, written language, and math skills and (2) regular college-level courses that contain the type of content and requirements easily integrated with remediation of basic skills (e.g., introductory courses and composition courses).

Reading Courses

Students with learning disabilities may have difficulty with reading for several reasons. Diagnostic testing identifies the specific needs of the student by assessing such skills as phonemic analysis and synthesis; structural analysis; and comprehension of single words, sentences, and passages. The rate of reading and the reading skills of skimming and scanning are also measured. This information may then be used to place students in the appropriate reading course. For example, at Barat College, Reading Strategies I and II are offered. Reading Strategies I is designed to meet the specific needs of students with poor word-attack skills and inadequate knowledge of vocabulary. The focus of this course is on phonology, morphology, and vocabulary development. Reading Strategies II focuses on reading comprehension (Adelman, 1985).

Adelman (1985) found that an effective way to improve reading skills is to coordinate assignments in the reading course with reading required in the students' other courses. Reading assignments required students to apply strategies learned in the reading course directly to their reading assignments. For example, a reading exercise in Reading Strategies II directed the students to identify different types of sentences in several paragraphs (e.g., topic sentences, explanatory sentences) in textbooks they were reading in their other classes. Post-testing results indicated that those students in classes with considerable reading (e.g., psychology, business, or sociology), compared with students in classes with minimal reading (e.g., rhetoric, studio arts, or performing arts), made the most progress. These results emphasized the importance of applying skills learned in the reading course.

Writing Lab Courses

Writing lab courses, established as supplements to a Freshman Writing Program or supported by a writing center, can be advantageous for the college student with learning disabilities who seeks assistance with writing. These supplements are useful because they provide extra time both for processing material and additional work on language problems that result in deficits in written language. (See Figure 10.1 on p. 213) Labs also offer less standardized and more personalized approaches to writing. Overall, they provide obvious reinforcement of the freshman writing courses and become an important factor in alleviating students' writing anxiety.

In these lab courses, only limited adjustments, well within "reasonable accommodations," are necessary. For example, some students can be given extended time, allowed to test in a private room, or given oral tests. Some students can be given special tasks and objectives (always in consultation with the LD faculty). The taping of required spelling lists that students can use at their convenience is another possible modification. It is important, however, to have sustained communication between the lab programmers and the LD faculty (Konrad, 1984).

Vocabulary/Spelling

A developmental course in vocabulary expansion can focus on roots of words, prefixes, and suffixes. This specialized approach offers an often unexplored and underutilized way to acquire "spelling sense." Exercises involving different usages of words and simple repetitive spelling tasks can increase spelling accuracy. For some students who have profound problems with spelling, shorter lists of words and extended, varied exercises can prove productive.

Working with fewer words seems less intimidating to many insecure spellers. Instead of studying 20 words at a time, for example, working with only a few new or old words they find difficult to spell seems more manageable and promotes a feeling of success. Students can use their imagination by incorporating target words in their own sentences or by completing fill-in sentence exercises given by the instructor. Students can work on paragraphs requiring the insertion of words being studied, or they might proofread a paragraph and circle those same words when they are correctly spelled. Progress may be slow, but it can be achieved.

Proofreading

A course in proofreading and editing can provide another focus for developing written language skills and can serve well as an auxiliary to a composition course. A proofreading course frequently includes both learning disabled and non-learning disabled students. This class composition often eases the concern of students with LDs when they become aware that many of their peers have the same needs.

Students are asked to present writing problems that have surfaced in past writing. The content of the course is then tailored to those problems within a standard structure of activities. As much as possible, grammar and punctuation rules are simplified. Exercises in a variety of printed and student-generated materials can be used on a regular basis. Sentences and paragraphs requiring correction or fill-in items can focus on grammar rules being taught or reviewed for specific students. If feasible for the class, students can work in teams and write sentences or paragraphs that require correction by the other students. Punctuation rules might be numbered, for example, Comma Rule #1: Use a comma before *and* separating two independent thoughts. Then exercises can be developed to apply Comma Rule #1. Most of the work is done in the classroom; limited home work assignments remove a degree of pressure.

As students review their most common errors, they can be encouraged to develop a checklist to be used in proofreading and editing their written work. The isolation of these specific items can be another step forward in the development of written language skills and achieving independence and self-confidence (See Figure 10.3).

As students gain proficiency in identifying and correcting one type of error, they can move on to another specific problem, which can then also be added to the list. Proofreading a paragraph or a page for just one error at a time (such as possessive apostrophes or vowel transpositions) will be helpful.

Overall, this approach to proofreading and editing provides good strategies for students to use in the revision process.

Sentence-Construction Lab

A sentence-construction lab is either a helpful auxiliary to a composition course or a useful follow-up to one. In the lab, students can review grammar rules and deepen their understanding of correct usage through concentration on the sentence and the paragraph. This focus on shorter pieces of writing can be much more comfortable for the student with LDs than a focus on longer assignments such as an essay or a research paper.

Personal Proofreading Checklist
(prepared from five regular assignments of one student)

Punctuation
Missed commas:
    Intro phrases and clauses   _____
    Examples: In addition ($\checkmark$) the facts . . .
              As Uncle John remarked ($\checkmark$) "We . . .

Omitted Semicolons:
    With independent clauses—no conjunction   _____
    Example: The dinner party was planned for seven o'clock ($\checkmark$)
              no one came until three hours later.

Apostrophes:
    Contractions   _____
    Example: that($\checkmark$)s
    Possession   _____
    Examples: Laurie($\checkmark$)s; Charles($\checkmark$)s

Grammar
Verb endings:
    Tense   _____
    Example: spoked ($\checkmark$)
    Dropped endings   _____
    Example: The Colonel retain ($\checkmark$) his . . .
    Fragments: _____
    Example: When John brought in the mail for us.

Spelling
Confusing words: _____
    Examples: its   it's
                bare   bear   _____
                your   you're
                trial   trail
Missed vowels:
    Examples: pomp($\checkmark$)us
              activit($\checkmark$)es
              be($\checkmark$)n

FIGURE 10.3.

Attention to writing phrases and clauses, writing different kinds of sentences, avoiding dangling or misplaced modifiers, and using appropriate coordination and subordination helps writers with LDs (as well as others) develop a sense of style and then experience a degree of pleasure in writing because of their growing ability.

The extended use of sentence-combining demonstrates the variety of ways in which writers express themselves. Students often begin with short simple sentences that they combine in different ways to explore alternative meanings. Other steps that involve transitional words and phrases construct examples of subordination, coordination, and coherence. Embedding ideas promotes conciseness. Students observe that writing is flexible and personal; they learn to value their own expression and to improve it.

Math Courses

Students in college who continue to have difficulty with computation, mathematical reasoning, and application of quantitative concepts would benefit from developmental math courses. A course in math skills could provide a concentrated review of fractions, decimals, percentages, ratios and proportions, and signed numbers, with emphasis on solving word problems. A course in introductory algebra could focus on the development of basic concepts of algebra, including signed numbers; on solving first-degree equations; on operations with polynomials; and on inequalities. Emphasis should be on reasoning and applications (solving word problems) since by using a calculator the student can readily bypass difficulties with computation.

College-Level Courses

The content and requirements of some courses are better designed than others for addressing the remedial needs of a student. For example, a course with several short papers offers the opportunity to work on written language skills. Rather than spending a lot of time doing research, students can address specific problem areas, such as organization, development, and mechanics. If reading has been identified as the area needing remediation, a course with more concrete information such as Introduction to Business might be a good choice for the student. Rather than struggling with understanding of more abstract concepts, this type of course content permits students to concentrate on developing their reading skills (e.g., understanding main ideas, supporting details, and graphs and charts).

Either limiting the number of credits or taking courses with a minimal amount of reading and writing in the freshman year can provide more time for remediation. For example, if students enroll in studio and performing arts courses or physical education or dance courses, they may be able to spend more time on direct remediation of reading, written language, and math skills.

Instructional Approach

The goal of integrating remediation and subject-matter tutoring is to use students' coursework to help them acquire skills that they can both maintain and generalize to new learning situations. By helping students gain self-knowledge of their individual strengths, deficits, and learning styles, the LD specialist teaches students to capitalize on learning strengths and to compensate for individual learning deficits. For example, the LD specialist teaches a student with strong visual processing skills (and weak auditory memory skills) to use the strategy of color-coding notes, which helps the student recall ideas by associating them with colors.

For college students with learning disabilities, integration of remediation and subject-matter tutoring is an effective approach both for achieving success in courses and improving learning skills. Students are most concerned with successfully completing class assignments; therefore, they are more motivated to work on material that is directly related to their coursework. By using the students' coursework, the LD Specialist can identify the specific way in which the student's learning disability is affecting academic progress. For example, while working on an outline for a paper, the LD specialist spends time teaching the student how to group or categorize ideas, a strategy the student with weak organizational abilities lacks.

Specific learning strategies can be taught that assist college students with LDs with acquiring skills and mastering course work. The case history that follows describes how the needs of a college student with a learning disability are met by an instructional approach that integrates remediation and subject-matter tutoring.

Case Study

Background Information

Student:	Lori M.	Sex:	Female
Birth Date:	3/19/66	Marital Status:	Single
High School Graduation:	6/12/84	Home:	Ohio
Entered College:	9/15/84		
College Graduation:	6/10/89		

Family Background

Lori is the younger of two children in a divorced family. Her home residence is with her natural mother and step-father in the same community as her natural father. Lori communicates and visits regularly with her father and step-mother.

Medical History

General health is good. Screening results indicated hearing within normal limits, and vision is 20/20 with corrective lenses. As a young child, Lori suffered from ear infections with resulting ear drainage and tube insertion. A history of frequent sinus trouble, coughs, and headaches was reported. Lori has allergies that are currently being treated through shots, medication, and diet.

Developmental History

Conditions during pregnancy and Lori's birth were reported as being uncomplicated, with no unusual occurrences noted. Developmental milestones in the motor area were age-appropriate. Lori is left-handed, and it was noted that she had some difficulty learning to use scissors. Language development was delayed, and problems with speech production were noted. She was described as being quiet and not talking a lot.

Educational History

Lori attended private schools for pre-school and kindergarten. She then attended one public elementary school for grades 1–6, middle school for grades 7–8, and high school for grades 9–12 with no retentions. Academic records indicated early learning problems in the areas of reading and math. Remedial support was provided during grades 1 and 2.

Lori was first referred for special education services in the third grade. As a result of the evaluation, Lori received the services of the learning disabilities resource program for remediation in reading, spelling, and math. The results of this and future evaluations indicated that Lori was functioning within the average range in intelligence, with deficits in auditory memory and intersensory integration. Achievement in reading comprehension, spelling, and math was not commensurate with ability. Continued resource services were recommended throughout elementary, middle, and high school.

Reports from elementary and high-school special education teachers indicated that her primary deficit areas were vocabulary and comprehension. Auditory processing difficulties affected her speech and spelling. Slow processing speed affected Lori's reading, writing, study, and test-taking abilities. In-class behavior was described as being cooperative and attentive. Lori was well liked by adults and peers and was described as having a generally positive disposition with a good sense of humor. Hobbies and outside interests included photography and art.

For a one-year period during high school, Lori attended sessions with a psychologist in order to help her resolve conflicts at home involving communication with her mother.

In high school Lori's cumulative grade point average was 1.939 on a 4.0 scale. She performed well in developmental and art courses. Significant difficulties were experienced in history, math, and science. Lori self-reports that she was not committed to the special services during her first two years of high school. A desire to appear "normal" in the eyes of her peers caused Lori to reject special help until her last two years. At that time, she utilized the resource services and sessions with a private LD specialist. Improvements were noted in specific skills, attitude, study habits, and class performance.

Lori applied to Barat College during her senior year in high school and was accepted by the college and the support program for students with LDs. On a standard administration of the SAT, Lori achieved a verbal score of 320 and a Math score of 310. As part of the application procedure, the WAIS-R was required (See Figure 10.4).

Psychoeducational Diagnostic Battery

A comprehensive diagnostic battery was administered prior to Lori's first semester of college. Following is a summary of the results.

Language

Relative strengths were found in the ability to abstract and label the essential characteristics of objects in the environment, the ability to

---

WAIS-R Results (8/15/84; C.A. 17–11)

V: 96   P: 98   FS: 95

Verbal Subtests	Scaled Score	Performance Subtests	Scaled Score
Information	6	Picture Completion	10
Digit Span	6	Picture Arrangement	12
Vocabulary	7	Block Design	7
Arithmetic	7	Object Assembly	10
Comprehenson	8	Digit Symbol	7
Similarities	13		

FIGURE 10.4.

understand a variety of vocabulary words, and the knowledge and use of the rules for adding morphological endings. Specific deficits were found in the ability to recognize meaning through intonation, the ability to recognize correct use of grammar in sentences, and the ability to rapidly and accurately reproduce the sequence of sounds within multisyllabic words.

Processing

Auditory processing deficits were found in the areas of analysis of sounds and syllables, discrimination, short-term memory, and synthesis of word parts. A relative strength in auditory attention and processing was noted when a visual component was provided immediately following the verbal presentation.

Visual perceptual deficits were in the area of spatial relations, the ability to abstract visual information to form concepts, and short-term memory for letters. Lori exhibited strengths in the ability to understand pictures and arrange them in a logical sequence, to recall essential details of objects from the environment, and to analyze visual patterns and utilize feedback to synthesize the patterns into subsets.

Achievement

Reading

Lori exhibited average ability in reading comprehension of single words and the ability to locate words with similar meanings. Her knowledge of word parts was also within the average range. Lori's word-attack skills were significantly below average, as was the ability to identify sight vocabulary. Reading comprehension, both literal and inferential, of sentences and paragraphs and the ability to skim and scan a selection for details and meaning were below average.

Mathematics

Lori exhibited the ability to do computations involving addition, subtraction, division, and multiplication. She was able to compute some elementary problems involving addition and subtraction of fractions. Test results indicated a good knowledge of basic math concepts such as numerical reasoning, exponential notation, and place value. Areas of weakness were found in knowledge of fractions, decimals, percentages, ratios, and problem solving. Frequent computation errors were noted because of problems with monitoring for errors.

Written Language

Lori's essay indicated good ability to address a specific topic. However, difficulty in organization and development impaired written language production. Weaknesses were noted in her knowledge and application of appropriate sentence structure and in the knowledge and use of the rules of mechanics. Specific difficulties were found in spelling and grammar usage and in the ability to monitor written work.

Study Habits and Attitudes

Lori's major strength was her determination to succeed, which was evident from her expressed desire to improve her basic skills. Study habits targeted for improvement were test anxiety, monitoring for written language errors, organization, and the development of a time-management system.

Clinical Observations

During the testing sessions, Lori was friendly, motivated, and conscientious. Verbal interaction was appropriate; Lori responded well to the examiner and initiated conversation when appropriate. Throughout the testing, Lori exhibited a lack of confidence in her abilities and frequently questioned her performance. She was not visibly reactive to praise or encouragement but remained serious and intent throughout. Lori put forth effort on both easy and hard tasks. On more difficult tasks, she exhibited fatigue and anxiety, was very conscious of errors, and extended her time to respond. She frequently asked for repetition or verification of directions. Lori's testing behavior showed great desire to succeed and indicated a willingness to persevere when faced with a challenge.

Summary

Lori's diagnostic report describes the specific strengths and areas for improvement, identifies academic goals, and recommends effective learning strategies (see Figure 10.1 on p. 213).

Integration of Skill Building and Course Content

Freshman Year

Course Enrollment

Course enrollment for Lori's freshman year (as in subsequent years) was limited to a maximum of 25 hours (rather than 30). Lori was prepared to attend summer school or to spend a fifth year in college in order to complete major requirements and to allow herself the time for optimum performance. Developmental courses were selected that addressed Lori's specific remedial needs (see Figure 10.5).

The remainder of Lori's courseload was comprised of academic courses that fulfilled general education requirements. Theatre Participation and

Lori's Coursework.

Freshman Year

Fall semester	Grade	Spring Semester	Grade
Theatre Participation	P	Rhetoric I	B−
English Fundamentals	A	Proofreading	P
Math Skills	A	Reading Strategies II	P
Reading Strategies I	P	Assertiveness Management	P
English Fundamentals Lab	P	Introduction to Algebra	B+
Beginning Photography	A−	Sentence Construction	P
GPA: 3.533			

Sophomore Year

Fall Semester	Grade	Spring Semester	Grade
Teaching as a Profession I	A	Psycho-Ed Prob of Except.	A
Introduction to Field Experience	P	Rhetoric II	A−
Culture and Values/West. Civ.	A	Business Math	A
Inter Comm/Group Dynamics	A	Chicago Theatre Experience	A
GPA: 3.778			

Summer	Grade
Fundamentals of Psych.	B

Junior Year

Fall Semester	Grade	Spring Semester	Grade
Introduction to LD	A	Foundations of Science	A
Field Experience	P	Science Methods: El	A
Art Education	A	Teaching as a Profession II	P
Descriptive Statistics	B	LD Methods and Materials	A
Child Psychology	A	Field Experience-LD	P
		Field Experience-Math	P
		Math for Teachers	B

GPA: 3.759

Senior Year

Fall Semester	Grade	Spring Semester	Grade
Health Education	B	Methods of Language	
Field Experience	P	Learning	A
Psycho-Educational Diagnosis	A−	Methods/Materials SED	A
Psycho-Ed. Diag. Practicum	A−	Field Experience-Lang. Arts	P

FIGURE 10.5. *Continued*

Lori's Coursework.

Person. Prob.: Beh. Dis. Chld.	B	Field Experience-Spec. Ed.	P
		Field Experience-SED	P
		Music Education Methods	B+
GPA: 3.698			

Summer	Grade
Intro. to Sociology	B
Biology	C

Fifth Year

Fall Semester:	Grade	Spring Semester	Grade
El. Sch. Mthds & Materials	A−	Student Teaching: Elemen.	A
American Government	A	Student Teaching Seminar	A
Juvenile Delinquency	A−	Student Teaching: LD	A
		Student Teaching Seminar	A
GPA: 3.754			

FIGURE 10.5.

Beginning Photography were chosen because of Lori's interests and because success in these courses was not as dependent upon reading and written language skills. The selection of these courses for Lori's first year gave her the opportunity to pursue particular interests, to concentrate on the improvement of skills necessary in further coursework, and to gain confidence through academic success.

Instructional Techniques

Lori was placed in developmental courses to focus on improving basic skills in reading, mathematics, and written language. Individual Educational Plans were developed and updated to meet Lori's remedial needs. An example of an IEP in written language is found in Figure 10.2 (see p. 216). Other instructional objectives included time management and organizational skills.

All remedial activities were integrated with coursework. For example, in the area of written language, emphasis was placed on organization, style, and mechanics using sentence writing assignments from the skill-building courses and short essay assignments for Freshman Rhetoric I. To compensate for memory deficits, Lori developed a checklist of common errors in written language for use when proofreading her papers.

Practice and review of specific reading strategies were incorporated into all reading assignments. After modeling by the LD specialist, Lori read course reading assignments using the SQ4R method of text reading (Survey, Question, Read, Recite, Reflect, Review). Word-attack skills were addressed from a multisensory approach. For example, text vocabulary words were analyzed structurally, with simultaneous pronunciation of each syllable. Lori pronounced each syllable and wrote the target sounds on cards. The sounds were then blended to form the word. This process was repeated until Lori could visually analyze the word and pronounce it correctly. Words with similar sounds and phonetic rules were then presented for generalization with repeated visual analysis and auditory analysis, writing, and blending as necessary.

Outcomes

Lori's performance in coursework as reflected by her grades (see Figure 10.5) indicated good progress in improving her basic skills, time-management, and study habits. Results of post-testing (see Table 10.2) indicated excellent progress in developing word attack-skills, with the need for continued concentration on reading comprehension. Lori made excellent progress in her ability to recognize correct sentence structure in written language. However, analysis of her written language indicated the need for continued work on the use of sentence combining to write more complex and varied sentences. She made good progress in improving her knowledge and use of capitalization and punctuation; she needed improvement in monitoring papers for correct grammar and punctuation. Spelling skills improved but continued to be an area where remediation was needed. Work in math computation, application, and monitoring of errors progressed well.

Sophomore Year

Course Enrollment

In her sophomore year, Lori took courses that fulfilled general education requirements, continued to address needs in written language and math, and was introduced to courses in her major, Psychology/Education. Teaching as a Profession I, Psycho-Educational Problems of the Exceptional Child, and Culture and Values in Western Civilization required text and related readings, exams, and written assignments. She enrolled in courses in interpersonal relationships and group dynamics and in The Chicago Theatre Experience because they interested her, because they did not require a lot of reading, and because they centered around individual and group participation. Work in Freshman Rhetoric II and Business Math continued the focus on effective writing and math applications.

TABLE 10.2. Case Study: Pre-Testing and Post-Testing.

Test / Date	Pre 8/84	Fall 12/84	Spring 5/85	Fall 12/85	Spring 5/86	Fall 12/86	Spring 5/87	Fall 12/87	Spring 5/88	Fall 12/88
Stanford Reading										
Comprehension	29/60 7.8 G.E. 11%ile		31/60 8.3 G.E. 13%ile		37/60 9.9 G.E. 24%ile		48/60 H.S. Grad. 55%ile			50/60 H.S. Grad. 63%ile
Word Meaning	21/30 12.0 37%ile	27/30 H.S. Grad. 81%ile	20/30 11.4 G.E. 32%ile							
Word Parts	23/30 H.S. Grad. 70%ile	23/30 H.S. Grad. 70%ile								
Phonetic Analysis	20/30 7.6 G.E. 43%ile							27/30 H.S. Grad. 80%ile		
Structural Analysis	16/24 9.4 G.E. 35%ile							21/24 H.S. Grad. 73%ile		
Scan/Skim	14/32 9.3 G.E. 33%ile								20/32 10.4 G.E. 47%ile	
Fast Reading	8/30 7.9 G.E. 10%ile								14/30 G.E. Grad. 68%ile	
PIAT Reading Comprehension	69/84 12.8 G.E. 54%ile		70/84 12.8 G.E. 57%ile							
W.J. Word Attack	8/26 2%ile	23/26 55%ile					23/26 41%ile			
DTLS Sentence Structure:	19/35 26%ile		28/35 50%ile		29/35 58%ile					23/35 45%ile

Table 10.2. *Continued*

Table 10.2. *Continued*

Test Date	Pre 8/84	Fall 12/84	Spring 5/85	Fall 12/85	Spring 5/86	Fall 12/86	Spring 5/87	Fall 12/87	Spring 5/88	Fall 12/88
TOWL Style	17/25 16%ile			23/25 75%ile						
TOWL Usage	20/25 37%ile									24/25 91%ile
W.J. Proofing	20/29 46%ile			22/29 58%ile						
W.J. Dictation	29/40 35%ile		30/40 84%ile						31/40 76%ile	
WRAT Spelling	29/51 8.3 G.E.		36/51 9.7 G.E.							
WRAT-R Spelling				29/51 9 G.E.	35/51 12 G.E.					
PIAT Spelling	63/84 10.4 G.E.				79/84 12.9+ G.E.					
DTMS Arithmetic	24/35 39%ile	27/35 56%ile	30/35 70%ile		30/35 70%ile					
DTMS Algebra			26/35 45%ile							
W.J. Quantitative Concepts	31/46 32%ile		37/46 76%ile			34/46 36%ile				
W.J. Applied Problem	34/49 21%ile					35/49 14%ile				
PPVT	152 20-5 58%ile									168 33-8 93%ile

Instructional Techniques

In written language, the focus was on application of correct sentence structure, punctuation, and capitalization. Because Lori was now taking traditional college-level courses such as Culture and Values in Western Civilization, an emphasis was placed on developing note-taking and test-taking skills.

Considerable time was spent on improving Lori's reading comprehension. Lori read her texts using color-coded highlighting to aid her in identifying and recalling main ideas, details, and so on, and to coordinate with highlighted sections of class notes. For example, chapter headings were highlighted in red, main ideas in blue, and key terms/vocabulary in green. After discussing the reading with the specialist, Lori wrote out the key concepts, terms, details, and so forth on separate color-coded index cards for study and reference and then wrote and verbalized summaries of the content.

Outcomes

Performance in coursework (see Figure 10.5) indicated Lori's increased ability to improve comprehension of reading materials and to retain information through review and practice. Post-testing (see Table 10.2) indicated improvement in reading comprehension. In written language, Lori made progress in her ability to recognize and formulate accurate and varied sentences. Spelling skills improved in both recognition of correctly spelled words and in written spelling.

Junior Year

Course Enrollment

In her junior year, Lori took required courses for her major in psychology/education and certification in elementary education and learning disabilities. Education and psychology courses required text reading, written assignments, and exams. In addition, courses in teaching methods required the development of lesson plans. All of these courses contained research components for selected written assignments. Field experiences were completed in clinical school sites and required written journals.

Instructional Techniques

In written language and reading, an emphasis was placed on the maintenance of strategies for comprehension, monitoring of errors, test-taking, and note-taking skills. Because of the heavy demands for research and written work, the focus of remediation was on the organization and production of written essays and papers. Using library reference materials, Lori outlined information for papers and wrote note cards for each reference. The use of color-coding on note cards, reading materials, and resources was expanded to include coordination with the numbering system used on Lori's outline for the organization of each paper.

For example, all facts, ideas, and citations applying to a particular part of her outline for the paper were color-coded and assigned the same number designation as that on the outline. Lori used these numerical references to aid her in accurately sequencing her information for development into paragraphs and sections in her papers. Because of Lori's difficulties in spatial relations, charts and diagrams were enlarged, highlighted, and/or interpreted using color coding, numerical ordering, and directional arrows.

Outcomes

Performance in coursework (see Figure 10.5) indicated continued improvement in organization and development of ideas in written language. Lori exhibited excellent ability to internalize strategies for review and study, and independently expanded on some strategies (verbal rehearsal, personal checklists, index study cards).

Post-testing (see Table 10.2) indicated continued improvement in reading comprehension. Good maintenance of skills was seen in word attack. Performance on the measure of math concepts was weaker than on the previous administration; however, performance in math-related coursework indicated good maintenance of skills in math concepts and monitoring skills. Monitoring of errors in written language improved, and Lori continued to utilize resources to aid in accuracy.

Senior Year

Course Enrollment

Lori continued to take courses that fulfilled the requirements for her major and for teacher certification. The education methods courses required text reading, research, and the development of written lesson plans. Coursework in Health Education, Personality Problems, and Psycho-Educational Diagnosis included text and related readings, written assignments, and exams. In addition, the research component of the diagnosis class required Lori to become proficient in the administration and interpretation of various diagnostic tests. Lori completed field experiences in clinical settings and completed a written journal.

Instructional Techniques

Because Lori had become adept at using the selected instructional techniques introduced in the past years, an emphasis was placed on maintenance of strategies and on fostering independence. For example, Lori verbally rehearsed concepts, theories, and terms from textbooks and notes immediately prior to taking an exam. For her diagnosis course, the administration of the tests was modeled by her specialist, and Lori developed checklists of procedures for accurate administration and monitoring of accuracy in scoring.

To improve organization and development of ideas in written language, Lori orally read her papers by sections into a tape recorder. She then listened to and edited her work for appropriate sequence, sentence structure, paragraph transition, and so on, using her note cards for reference.

Outcomes

Performance in coursework as reflected by Lori's grades (see Figure 10.5) indicated excellent progress in reading comprehension, written language, and maintenance of effective strategies. Post-testing (see Table 10.2) indicated improvement in Lori's ability to scan reading materials for pertinent information and in her rate of reading. Improvement was evident in organization and development of ideas in written language as well as in the monitoring of papers for grammar, spelling, and punctuation. Lori continued to utilize learned strategies effectively and to generalize these strategies to other related assignments and tasks.

Fifth Year

Course Enrollment

Lori completed her final (fifth) year in college with three required courses during the fall semester and student teaching to certify in Elementary and Special Education during the spring semester. All her coursework required reading, written assignments, and exams. In addition, American Government included the passing of the required tests on the federal and state constitutions.

Instructional Techniques

An emphasis was placed on the continued practice and maintenance of learned strategies. Because Lori was required to pass basic skills and competency tests for teacher certification, time was spent on reviewing and preparing for these tests. Lori outlined information, made note cards for study, and practiced through verbal rehearsal. To enhance recall and integration of concepts, hypothetical classroom situations were presented to Lori, and she applied specific concepts, theories, practices, and so on from her education courses to answer specific questions or to solve problems regarding the situations. For review of basic skills in writing, Lori wrote sample paragraphs and proofread them using her checklists of common errors.

Outcomes

Lori's performance in coursework (see Figure 10.5) and her excellent evaluations during student teaching indicated excellent growth in the areas targeted for improvement. Lori became proficient at determining and using appropriate strategies for assignments and tasks. She was able to approach reading assignments with confidence and to direct her attention immediately to read, comprehend, and prepare materials for study effectively. Furthermore, she was able to begin research independently and to prepare papers that were well organized and well developed. Time needed to complete tests and exams was reduced, although Lori continued to pace herself and to be aware of time constraints. She used resources well (dictionary, thesaurus, writing manual), and maintained her checklists for monitoring spelling and errors in mechanics in written language.

Post-testing indicated excellent gains in reading comprehension and receptive vocabulary. In written language, Lori again exhibited some difficulty in identifying correct sentence structure; however, her independent written work reflected a good improvement in constructing varied and accurate sentences. Because Lori had completed coursework including the administration of various diagnostic tests, she was not evaluated by these tests. Lori passed the state competency tests in basic skills, elementary education, and learning disabilities.

Lori graduated from college with a cumulative GPA of 3.754. She earned certification in elementary education and learning disabilities and is currently teaching in a learning disabilities classroom in Ohio.

Bibliography

Adelman, P.B. (1985). Developing a reading program for dyslexic college students. *Bulletin of the Association on Handicapped Student Service Programs in Post-Secondary Education*, *3*, 87–92.

Adelman, P.B. (1988). An approach to meeting the needs of the learning disabled students in a four-year college setting. In C.T. Mangrum, II & S.S. Strichart (Eds.), *College and the learning disabled student: Program development, implementation and selection* (2nd ed., pp. 237–249). Orlando, FL: Grune & Stratton.

Adelman, P.B., & Olufs, D. (1986). Assisting college students with learning disabilities: A manual written for the Association on Handicapped Student Service Programs in Post-Secondary Education. Columbus, OH.

Adelman, P.B., & Vogel, S.A. (1990). College graduates with learning disabilities—Employment, attainment, and career patterns. *Learning Disability Quarterly*, *13*(3), 154–166.

Adelman, P.B., & Vogel, S.A. (1991). The learning disabled adult. In B. Wong (Ed.), *Learning about Learning Disabilities* (pp. 563–594). New York: Academic Press.

Adelman, P.B., & Wren, C.T. (1990). *Learning disabilities, graduate school, and careers: The student's perspective*. Lake Forest, IL: Barat College.

Blalock, J.W. (1981). Persistent problems and concerns of young adults with learning disabilities. In W. Cruickshank & A. Silver (Eds.), *Bridges to tomorrow* (Vol. 2, The best of ACLD, pp. 35–55). Syracuse: Syracuse University Press.

Blalock, J.W. (1982). Residual learning disabilities in young adults: Implications for rehabilitation. *Journal of Applied Rehabilitation Counseling, 13*(2), 9–13.

Blalock, J.W. (1987a). Intellectual levels and patterns. In D. Johnson & J. Blalock (Eds.), *Young adults with learning disabilities: Clinical studies* (pp. 47–65). Orlando, FL: Grune & Stratton.

Blalock, J.W. (1987b). Auditory language disorders. In D. Johnson & J. Blalock (Eds.), *Young adults with learning disabilities: Clinical studies* (pp. 81–105). Orlando, FL: Grune & Stratton.

Buchanan, M., & Wolf, J. (1986). A comprehensive study of learning disabled adults. *Journal of Learning Disabilities, 19*(1), 34–38.

Bursuck, W.D., Rose, E., Cowen, S., & Yahaya, M.A. (1989). Nationwide Survey of postsecondary education services for students with learning disabilities. *Exceptional Children, 56*(3), 236–245.

Cordoni, B. (1979). Assisting dyslexic college students: An experimental program design at a university. *Bulletin of the Orton Dyslexia Society, 29,* 263–268.

Cordoni, B., O'Donnell, J., Ramaniah, N., Kurtz, J., & Rosenshein, K. (1981). Wechsler Adult Intelligence score patterns for learning disabled young adults. *Journal of Learning Disabilities, 14*(7), 404–407.

Cordoni, B.K., & Snyder, M.K. (1981). A comparison of learning disabled college students' achievement from WRAT and PIAT grade, standard, and subtest scores. *Psychology in the Schools, 18,* 28–34.

Cowen, S.E. (1988). Coping strategies of university students with learning disabilities. *Journal of Learning Disabilities, 21*(3), 161–164.

Dalke, C. (1988). Woodcock-Johnson Psycho-Educational Test Battery profiles: A comparative study of college freshmen with and without learning disabilities. *Journal of Learning Disabilities, 21*(9), 567–570.

Deshler, D.D., Schumaker, J.B., Lenz, B.K., & Ellis, E. (1984a). Academic and cognitive interventions for LD adolescents: Part I. *Journal of Learning Disabilities, 17*(2), 108–117.

Deshler, D.D., Schumaker, J.B., Lenz, B.K., & Ellis, E. (1984b). Academic and cognitive interventions for LD adolescents: Part II. *Journal of Learning Disabilities, 17*(3), 170–179.

Dunn, L., & Markwardt, F. (1970). *Peabody Individual Achievement Test.* Circle Pines, MN: American Guidance Service.

Educational Testing Service. (1977). *Sentence structure test, college board descriptive tests of language skills.* Princeton, NJ: Author.

Hammill, D., & Larsen, S. (1978). *Test of written language.* Austin, TX: Pro-ed.

Haring, K.A., Lovett, D.L., & Smith, D.D. (1990). A follow-up study of recent special education graduates of learning disabilities programs. *Journal of Learning Disabilities, 23*(2), 108–113.

Jastak, J., & Jastak, S. (1978). *The Wide Range Achievement Test.* Wilmington, DE: Jastak Associates, Inc.

Johnson, D. (1987). Nonverbal disorders and related learning. In D. Johnson & J. Blalock (Eds.), *Young adults with learning disabilities: Clinical studies* (pp. 219–232). Orlando, FL: Grune & Stratton.

Karlsen, B., Madden, R., & Gardner, E. (1977). *Stanford Diagnostic Reading Test* (Blue Level). Chicago: Harcourt, Brace, Jovanovich.

Konrad, D. (1984). The Barat college writing lab. In W. Cruickshank & J. Klebhan (Eds.), *Early adolescence to early adulthood: The best of ACLD* (Vol. V, pp. 177–182). Syracuse: Syracuse University Press.

Maglione, L.P. (1989). *Assisting college students with learning disabilities prepare for employment*. The Ramapo College Project for Students with Learning Disabilities, Ramapo College of New Jersy.

Polloway, E.A., Smith, J.D., & Patton, J.R. (1984). Learning disabilities: An adult development perspective. *Learning Disability Quarterly, 7*, 179–187.

Salvia, J., Gajar, A., Gajria, M., & Salvia, S. (1988). A comparison of WAIS-R profiles of nondisabled college freshmen and college students with learning disabilities. *Journal of Learning Disabilities, 21*(10), 632–641.

Schonhaut, S., & Satz, P. (1983). Prognosis for children with learning disabilities: A review of follow-up studies. In M. Rutter (Ed.), *Developmental Neuropsychiatry* (pp. 542–563). New York: Guilford Press.

Vogel, S.A. (1982). On developing LD college programs. *Journal of Learning Disabilities, 15*(9), 518–528.

Vogel, S.A. (1985). Syntactic complexity in written expression of college writers. *Annals of Dyslexia, 35*, 137–157.

Vogel, S.A. (1986). Levels and patterns of intellectual functioning among LD college students: Clinical and educational implications. *Journal of Learning Disabilities, 19*(2), 71–79.

Vogel, S.A. (1990a). *The college student with a learning disability: A handbook for college LD students, admissions officers, faculty, and administrators*. DeKalb, IL: Author.

Vogel, S.A. (1990b). Gender differences in intelligence, language, visual-motor abilities, and academic achievement in students with learning disabilities: A review of the literature. *Journal of Learning Disabilities, 23*(1), 44–52.

Vogel, S.A., & Adelman, P.B. (1981). Personnel development: College and university programs designed for learning disabled adults. *Illinois Council for Exceptional Children Quarterly, 1*, 12–18.

Vogel, S.A., & Adelman, P.B. (1990). Intervention effectiveness at the postsecondary level for the learning disabled. In T. Scruggs & B. Wong (Eds.), *Intervention research in learning disabilities*. New York: Springer-Verlag.

Vogel, S.A., & Konrad, D. (1988). Characteristic written expressive language deficits of the learning disabled: Some general and specific intervention strategies. *Journal of Reading, Writing, and Learning Disabilities International, 4*, 88–99.

Vogel, S., & Moran, M. (1982). Written language disorders in learning disabled college students. A preliminary report. In W. Cruickshank & J. Lerner (Eds.), *Coming of age: The best of ACLD 1982* (Vol. 3, pp. 211–225). Syracuse: Syracuse University Press.

Vogel, S.A., & Walsh, P. (1987). Gender differences in cognitive abilities in learning disabled females and males. *Annals of Dyslexia, 37*, 142–165.

Wechsler, D. (1949). Wechsler intelligence scale for children. New York: Psychological Corp.

Wechsler, D. (1955). Wechsler adult intelligence scale. New York: Psychological Corp.

Wechsler, D. (1974). Wechsler intelligence scale for children-Revised. New York: Psychological Corp.

Wechsler, D. (1981). Wechsler adult intelligence scale-Revised. New York: Psychological Corp.

Woodcock, R., & Johnson, M.B. (1977). *The Woodcock-Johnson Psycho-Educational Battery*. Allen, TX: DLM Teaching Resources.

Woodcock, R., & Johnson, M.B. (1989). *The Woodcock-Johnson Psycho-Educational Battery-Revised*. Allen, TX: DLM Teaching Resources.

XI
Technology for Postsecondary Students with Learning Disabilities

MARSHALL H. RASKIND AND NEIL G. SCOTT

According to Aldous Huxley (1956), technological progress has merely provided mankind with a more efficient means of going backward. Evidently, Mr. Huxley did not have persons with disabilities in mind when he made this statement, for technology has enabled many persons with disabilities to take great strides forward in realizing their optimal potential and to become fully functioning and integrated members of our society. Technology has helped the visually impaired to read by means of optical character recognition, the hearing impaired to hear with hearing aids, the paralyzed to gain mobility through electronically controlled wheel chairs, and the nonspeaking to talk through speech synthesizers. This technology, when utilized to help persons with disabilities compensate for their difficulties, is referred to as "assistive technology."

Assistive technology can be used to help persons with learning disabilities (LDs) as well, including those attending postsecondary institutions. In fact, the majority of work in assistive technology and learning disabilities has resulted primarily from the efforts of those concerned with the provision of educational support services to meet the demands of the increasing number of students with learning disabilities attending postsecondary institutions. Although a number of authorities in the field (Brown, 1987; Collins, 1990; Mangrum & Strichart, 1988; Scheiber & Talpers, 1985; Vogel, 1987) have addressed the benefits of using assistive technology to enhance the academic success of postsecondary students with LDs, their discussions are limited in scope and depth. To fill the void, this chapter will (1) examine the various technologies available to help postsecondary students with LDs achieve academic success; (2) provide criteria for selecting and evaluating technology for postsecondary students with LDs; and (3) offer guidelines for instructing postsecondary students with LDs in the use of technology. In addition, sources for the purchase of this technology will be provided.

This chapter is based upon six years of work with postsecondary students with LDs in the Learning Disability Program and Computer Access Lab of the Office of Disabled Student Services at California State

University, Northridge. To date, approximately 100 of the 300 students with LDs registered with the program have been trained to use technology to compensate for their disabilities and help ensure academic retention and success as well as successful transition to the workplace. Although results of this training can only be reported as "clinical observations," students have been able to compensate successfully for difficulties in the areas of reading, writing, spelling, oral language, math, organization, attention, and memory. In addition, many students have shown decreased anxiety toward academic tasks and increased self-confidence. These observations are soon to be investigated through controlled experimental designs with the expectation of similar findings.

Compensation Versus Remediation

Before we discuss the available technology, it is important to distinguish between two basic approaches to alleviating the difficulties of post-secondary students with LDs—*remedial* and *compensatory*. Each approach has a different intent and generally necessitates different technologies and methods. The purpose of a *remedial* approach is to improve areas of deficiency. In contrast, a *compensatory* approach is directed toward the development of coping strategies that allow a task (within an area of difficulty) to be performed in a different manner. For example, a remedial approach to a reading disability would attempt to teach the student phonics to improve the deficit skill whereas a compensatory approach would take the reading disability as a "given" and arrange to have a student's text put on audiotape.

The discussion of technology in this chapter will be based on a compensatory approach. In some instances, technologies will be discussed in regard to how they may assist, augment, or supplement task performance within a given area of disability. In others, technologies may be examined in regard to their attempt to circumvent or "work around" the disability entirely. Strategies of this nature have been referred to as "bypass strategies" (Vogel, 1987).

A compensatory approach is taken for several reasons. First of all, many postsecondary students with LDs suffer from what might be termed "remedial burnout." Remedial burnout is characterized by an extremely negative attitude toward the use of remedial techniques. Considering that many postsecondary students with LDs have spent a number of years receiving remedial services that often resulted in little or no improvement, it is no wonder that as adults, they are resistant to continuing such an approach.

Another consideration is the fact that remedial approaches (even if they do work) often take much longer to alleviate difficulties. The post-secondary student with a reading disability who must cover 400 pages of text in three weeks does not have time to receive the "phonic training" that might in turn enhance reading abilities so that he or she can read the assigned text in time for the mid-term examination! In contrast, using a compensatory approach (such as having the text put on audiotape so the student can listen to the material rather than read it) can offer a far more expeditious solution than remedial training. Learning disabled post-secondary students often require an immediate solution with immediate results, and generally, they do not have the "luxury of time" to receive remedial training.

This is not to say that remedial approaches should not be utilized but rather that, within a postsecondary setting, it does not povide the most efficient means of enhancing academic success. Often, a dual approach of remediation and compensation is the most efficient method of alleviating difficulties. It should also be emphasized that remediation and compensation are not necessarily mutually exclusive. For example, Kerchner and Kistenger (1984) found that students with LDs who used word processors as a compensatory writing strategy also became better writers when using pencil and paper. In other words, a compensatory strategy can have remedial results. However, for the purposes of this chapter, technology will be addressed from a compensatory rather than remedial perspective.

Technology for Postsecondary Students with Learning Disabilities

This section will discuss some of the most significant technologies for assisting postsecondary students with learning disabilities. However, it should be stressed that not all the technologies discussed will be appropriate for all students with LDs. Postsecondary students with learning disabilities are comprised of a heterogeneous group, each student having a unique profile of strengths, weaknesses, interests, and experiences. Therefore, a technology that might be a "godsend" for one student could mean disaster for another. The importance of matching each student to the appropriate technology will be explored later in the chapter.

What then, are the technologies available to help postsecondary students with LDs compensate for their disabilities? The following section will examine these technologies and discuss them in relation to the dif-ficulties experienced by postsecondary students with LDs. Technologies will be grouped together into basic product categories. Immediately following each category heading is an indication of the area(s) of dis-ability addressed by the technology. A matrix of the technologies accord-ing to disability area appears in Figure 11.1. A list of specific product recommendations appears in Appendix 11.1.

Technology	Written Language	Reading	Organization	Memory	Listening	Math
Word Processing	X					
Spell Checking	X					
Proofreading Programs	X					
Outlining/Brainstorming	X					
Abbreviation Expanders	X					
Speech Recognition	X					
Speech Synthesis/Screen Review	X	X				
Optical Character Recognition Systems		X				
Personal Data Managers			X	X		
Free-Form Databases			X	X		
Variable Speech Control Recorders		X		X	X	
Listening Aids					X	
Talking Calculators						X

FIGURE 11.1. Technologies by area of disability.

Word Processing—Written Language

The written language difficulties of postsecondary students with learning disabilities have been well documented (Gregg & Hoy, 1989; Hughes & Smith, 1990; Morris & Leuenberger, 1990; Vogel, 1985; Vogel & Moran, 1982). In fact, Blalock (1981) asserts that between 80% and 90% of adults with LDs exhibit written language disorders. Such adults have been found to have difficulty with grammar, punctuation, spelling, organization, and coherency. Several researchers (Collins, 1990; Primus, 1990) have found word processors valuable in helping students with LDs compensate for written language difficulties. Unlike the conventional methods of writing with "pencil and paper" or typewriter, word processors (whether they are "stand-alone" devices or personal computer

[PC] systems) allow students with LDs to write without having to be overly concerned with making errors since the text first appears on the computer screen before it is printed out and thus, can be easily corrected. Omitted words may be added, inappropriate words or blocks of text deleted, sentences or paragraphs moved, and spelling and punctuation corrected. In addition, specified text is easily "bolded" (highlighted), underlined, or centered.

When not preoccupied with the "mechanical" aspects of writing, students with LDs are then free to focus on the "meaning" of their written communication. This is particularly important for students who have developed a fear of translating their thoughts to text as a result of making frequent errors and of having those errors pointed out to them over a period of many years. Knowing that they can simply "generate" language and correct errors later reduces their anxiety and is often enough to "liberate" their writing abilities. As a result, many students with LDs are better able to express themselves at a level commensurate with their intelligence.

Furthermore, since errors are easily corrected on the computer monitor before printing, students end up with a neat and organized document. This serves to help students develop a sense of pride in their work and may also enhance the self-image they have of themselves as writers. In turn, students may end up in a more positive frame of mind from which to approach writing tasks. (The psychological benefits associated with word processing and postsecondary students with learning disabilities have been documented by Collins [1990]).

As the result of fine-motor or visual-spatial difficulties some students with LDs might have difficulty developing proficient keyboarding skills. However, in most instances the benefits of using a word processor far outweigh any problems they might encounter typing on a keyboard. There are several "typing tutorial" software programs that can help students improve their keyboarding skills without inducing stress. Furthermore, a number of different technologies (e.g., key repeat inhibitors, mouse interface, abbreviation expansion), when used in conjunction with a word processor, can assist keyboarding efforts or circumvent the keyboard entirely (e.g., speech recognition). Several of these technologies will be discussed later in the chapter.

Although the level of complexity of word-processing programs varies considerably, most postsecondary students with LDs should be able to learn basic operational procedures within three to four hours. The cost of word processors also varies to a large degree. Stand-alone word processors (which do word processing only) range from approximately $250 to $700. Word-processing software programs used on an existing PC system range in price from approximately $50 to $300. If a PC is not already available, a complete system (computer, keyboard, monitor, printer, start-up software) of sufficient quality necessary to meet the needs of a postsecondary student with LDs can be purchased for around $1,000 to $2,000.

Spell Checking—Written Language

Many postsecondary students with LDs have written language disorders that often include difficulty with spelling. The use of spell checkers, which are included in the majority of word-processing programs, can compensate for such problems. Spell checkers permit students to check for misspelled words within a document before a final copy is made.

Spell checkers match the words in a document against words in the spell checker's dictionary. If a match is not found, the user is alerted by a visual or auditory cue (e.g., the word might be highlighted). Generally, when spell checkers find a misspelled word, they present the user with a list of words from which to choose the correctly spelled word. The user selects the correct word and the computer automatically corrects the misspelled word in the text.

Selecting the "correct" word from a list of options can be a difficult task for many postsecondary students with LDs. Cross-checking the words for synonyms in the word processor's thesaurus (if one is available) can assist in the selection process. If the particular word processor has a dictionary (in some cases dictionary programs can be added), then looking up the meaning of the word can also aid in selecting the correct word from the list. It should be kept in mind that only misspelled words will be picked up with a spell checker. Therefore, the incorrect use of homonyms (e.g., there and their), which plagues many writers with LDs, will not be "red-flagged."

Spell checkers may not contain all words, especially in the case of highly technical language. However, spell-check programs usually allow the student to add words to the spell-check list. There are also special programs that can be added to existing spell checkers to increase the number of words available for checking.

It should be noted that some spell checkers alert the user to spelling errors when typing, rather than checking for spelling mistakes after the document has been completed. However, for many students these programs tend to "interrupt" the writing process and in some cases end up doing more harm than good. Individual preferences will have to be considered in this regard. For a comparative analysis of spell-check programs for use with postsecondary students with LDs, refer to Cutler (1990).

In addition to spell checkers that are part of word processing programs, there are also battery-operated stand-alone spell checkers that are available in desktop and pocket sizes. In order to use these spell checkers, students simply enter a word (via a small keyboard) the way they think it is spelled. The more basic units will simply verify and correct spelling on an LCD display. There are more sophisticated devices that also include a dictionary for access to word definitions and a thesaurus for synonyms. Many of these spell checkers are equipped with speech synthesizers, so the word in question can be heard as well as seen. There are a wide variety of such spell checkers now on the market with a range of capabilities, and the most appropriate one will depend on the specific needs of each student. Prices range from approximately $30 for the more basic checkers to $350 for more sophisticated units. These products are relatively simple to use and generally require no more than 15 minutes to 1 hour to learn to operate.

Proofreading Programs—Written Language

Postsecondary students with written language problems can also benefit from the use of proofreading programs. These software packages can scan documents and alert users to probable errors in punctuation (e.g., missing question marks), grammar (subject–verb agreement), word usage (homonyms), structure (transition words), spelling, style (trite words), capitatlization ("i"). These programs understand the relationship different words have to each other in a sentence. They use a technique called "parsing:" each word in a sentence is compared to a dictionary file listing the parts of speech (noun, verb, adjective, etc.) that 50,000 to 120,000 of the most common English words can "legally" assume (Frankel, 1990). The dictionary also includes plurals and irregular conjunctions. After the potential function of each word has been analyzed, the parser examines the order in which each word is placed, determines main grammatical components of a sentence, "diagrams" it, and subjects it to a complex set of language rules embodied in the program.

Most of these programs can be used to either mark probable errors, or mark the error along with a commentary (e.g., "Be sure you are using 'is' with a singular subject."). Many programs include on-line tutorials that allow the user to study the language rules checked by the program. Once probable errors have been flagged, the document may be edited from within the proofreading program.

In many cases, a student may not want to check for errors in all categories. The majority of these programs enable the user to turn off various rule options in order to focus on specific areas of difficulty. For example, a student who has difficulty in the area of subject–verb agreement can tell the program to ignore errors in other categories (e.g., capitalization) and check only for subject–verb agreement. Similarly, a student who confuses homonyms can tell the program to search for errors only in this area. Many of the programs also provide a statistical summary feature for such items as total number of words, number of problems detected, and average word length.

Although at first glance, proofreading programs may appear to be "miracle workers" for postsecondary students with written language difficulties, they do have limitations. First of all, proofreading programs are not completely accurate and, on the average, pick up only about 25% of the grammatical errors and 80% of the "objectionable phrases" in a document (Frankel, 1990). These programs may also make incorrect suggestions. Prompting the student with a learning disability to correct parts of his writing that are not really incorrect can be quite confusing. Even if a program is correct in its flagging of probable errors, in many cases the student may not understand the program's suggestions.

In addition, some students may find these programs demeaning and demoralizing. Possible errors flagged by these programs are seen as merely a criticism of their writing—interpreted as the same "negative feedback" the student has received for so many years. This reaffirmation of incompetence by an "electronic teacher" marking up the paper may add fuel to student's already poor self-image as a writer, and may be so intimidating that the generation of written language is inhibited rather than fostered. Each student's response to proofreading programs should be closely monitored.

Commercially available proofreading programs can usually be purchased for under $100 and require about two hours of training before they can be used reasonably well.

Outlining/Brainstorming—Written Language

Although students with LDs may have great ideas in their "heads," getting them down on paper may be quite another story. Writing that first word or sentence can be an insurmountable task; even if they can get started, they may not know where to go from there. Many students with LDs may have difficulty organizing a paper with regard to topics, categories, and sequence.

Such difficulties are often addressed by encouraging the student with LDs to begin with an outline. Unfortunately, an outline can be counterproductive because it requires the student to mentally "sequentialize" (place topics in linear order) and to categorize before writing—processes that are problematic for the student to begin with. This can lead to even greater inhibition.

A more appropriate method for many postsecondary students with LDs is to allow them to "dump" any ideas or thoughts on paper without regard to organization. This frees them from having to predetermine the sequence and categories of the material to be covered. Once the ideas are down, they can be categorized and placed in the order deemed most appropriate. Scheiber and Talpers (1985) have recommended such methods for postsecondary students with learning disabilities.

Outlining programs for use on personal or laptop computers can enable the user to dump information in an unstructured manner, information that can subsequently be placed in appropriate categories and order more easily. Such programs work in the following manner. The student types in any idea or thought on a specified topic without regard to overall organization. By using a few simple key strokes, the outlining program will automatically create the Roman numerals for the "major headings" and letters and numbers for "subordinate headings." The student need not be concerned with order, levels of importance, or categories since text can be easily moved at a later time. Once the student's basic ideas have been written down, those ideas or thoughts that are related or "seem to go together" provide the basis for major headings or categories. Ideas that fall under any major heading can be easily reduced to any level of subordinate heading. There is no problem even if the student determines later on that an idea does not belong under a certain heading. Any piece of text can easily be moved within the outline as many times as may be necessary. When a particular heading is moved, all of the subordinate headings and information is moved along with it. This reduces the possibility of losing information at a subordinate level. The program will automatically reorganize the Roman numerals, letters, and numbers designated for specific headings.

Outlining programs also enable students with LDs to limit what they view on the computer screen to only the major headings. Consequently, students can get an overview of what they are writing without being distracted by details. Similarly, it is possible to select only one heading and view all information under it for a detailed analysis. In other words, outlining programs allow the user to "collapse" all subordinate headings under the major headings or to "expand" any particular heading in order to display all subordinate headings and details. In this way, the student has the option of either seeing the "forest" or the "trees." This feature is especially useful for both students with LDs who appear to get so hung up on the detail that they can never express the big picture and those students whose writing is excessively skeletal and lacking in detail. It also enables the student to reduce screen clutter—some students with LDs become quite disturbed if there is too much information displayed on the screen.

Outlining programs usually require about two to four hours of practice before they can be used with any degree of proficiency. Some word-processing programs now include an outlining feature as part of the total package. If an "add-on" outliner has to be purchased, it is available for between approximately $75 and $150.

Abbreviation Expanders—Written Language

Abbreviation expansion programs may be used in conjunction with word-processing programs to permit students with LDs to create their own abbreviations for frequently used words, phrases, or standard pieces of text. For example, a student in a U.S. history class who frequently has to write out "Civil War" in completing written assignments might create the abbreviation "cv." Similarly, a student studying psychology might use the abbreviation "sf" for "Sigmund Freud" or "cj" for "Carl Jung." In order to expand an abbreviation, the student simply types in the abbreviation (e.g., "cv"), presses the spacebar on the keyboard, and the abbreviation is expanded (e.g., "civil war").

Abbreviation expansion programs are "memory resident," operating simultaneously with the word-processing program. Abbreviations are easily recorded by pressing a predetermined "hot key" and executing a few simple commands. These abbreviations may be saved from one writing session to another.

The use of abbreviation expansion programs by postsecondary students with learning disabilities is helpful for several reasons. First of all, abbreviations reduce the number of keystrokes and consequently the length of time required to prepare a written document. Consider the example "sf" for "Sigmund Freud." Thirteen keystrokes are needed to type out "Sigmund Freud." In contrast, only three keystrokes are needed if the abbreviation is used. The reduction in keystrokes is even greater if a student is using abbreviations for standard passages or phrases (e.g., "fe" for "for example"). Considering that postsecondary students with learning disabilities spend considerably more time on their studies than their nondisabled peers (Vogel, 1987), any procedure that can reduce the amount of time spent on academic tasks is bound to be beneficial.

Abbreviation expansion programs are also helpful for students with spelling difficulties. By creating abbreviations for commonly misspelled words (and using those abbreviations rather than trying to spell the entire word), students can have their spelling corrected automatically as they write. For instance, if a student has difficulty with the word "appreciate," he or she might use the abbreviation "ap" in its place. The abbreviation "cy" might be used in place of the word "conscientiously." Similarly, students can substitute abbreviations for parts of words (e.g., "tn" for "tion") as well as words they misspell in a consistent pattern (e.g., "porshun" instead of "portion"). This feature enables the student to focus more on what he or she is trying to communicate rather than on the mechanics of communicating it.

The choice of abbreviations should be left entirely to the student. In this way, abbreviations will based upon what is most meaningful. This will serve to facilitate recall of the abbreviations and allow for their easier integration into the writing process. For example, whereas one student may choose the abbreviation "la" for "Los Angeles," another may find "smog" a more meaningful abbreviation.

Abbreviation expanders run about $100 and require only about one or two hours of training before they can be used efficiently.

Speech Recognition—Written Language

One of the most exciting and important breakthroughs in technology available to postsecondary students with learning disabilities is speech (or voice) recognition. Simply put, speech recognition allows the user to operate the computer by speaking to it. The ability to talk to a computer and to have it write out what a person has said has long been a dream of computer scientists as well as of professionals in the field of learning disabilities. This dream has now become a reality and has tremendous implications for postsecondary students with LDs, particularly those students whose oral language exceeds their written language abilities.

At the writing of this chapter, there is only one commercially marketed system that is sophisticated, yet simple enough, to use with postsecondary students with learning disabilities, the DragonDictate[tm] by Dragon Systems, Inc. of Newton, Massachusetts (see Appendix 11.1).

This system enables the user to dictate to the computer at 40 to 70 words per minute (depending on the speed of the particular computer in which the system is installed). DragonDictate automatically learns the phonetic characteristics of each person's voice as that person dictates to the system. The more the system is used, the better able it is to understand what the user is saying. The system has phonetic models built for 25,000 words, which means that these words can be used without any need to train the program. There is also room for 5,000 words defined by the user. Another 80,000 words are available from a copy of the Random House Unabridged Dictionary® held on the system's hard disk.

When used with word-processing software, this system is an excellent compensatory aid for the student with a learning disability who is better able to communicate through oral rather than written language. Whether the student is writing a term paper or answering an essay question on an exam, the system will allow him or her to "play" to a strength rather than a weakness. In order to use the system, the student simply dictates through a microphone. A calculated pause at least 1/10 of a second is required between words. DragonDictate places a menu on the screen containing three or four words. The word the system "thinks" the student has spoken is placed on the screen within the word-processing text. Simultaneously, the word appears as the first word in an on-screen menu and is typically followed by two or three "similar sounding" words. If the word is correct (and in most instances it is), the student speaks the next word he or she wants to write. If the word is incorrect, the student can choose from the list of remaining words by saying for example, "choose 2" or "choose 3." If the word is not one of the other words listed, then the user says, "Begin spell mode," starts spelling the correct word, and DragonDictate will automatically recognize the correct word. It should be noted that all keyboard editing and control commands (e.g., "delete word") can be done through voice recognition.

It takes approximately fifteen hours to train a student to work independently with the system. Training has two components: (1) instruction in the basic operational procedures; and (2) training the system to recognize the user's voice. The cost of DragonDictate is approximately

$9,000. Moreover, a 386 computer is required to operate the system at an additional cost of approximately $2,000. As more companies introduce speech recognition systems into the marketplace over the next several years, prices should drop dramatically.

Speech Synthesis/Screen Review— Written Language, Reading

Several authors have suggested that speech synthesis be used as an assistive technology for postsecondary students with learning disabilities (Brown, 1987; Norris & Graef, 1990). Speech synthesis refers to a "synthetic" or computerized voice output system usually consisting of an internal board or external hardware device. In conjunction with "screen-reading" software, a speech synthesizer will read back text displayed on the computer screen so that the user can hear as well as see what is displayed. Text can be read back a letter, word, line, sentence, paragraph, or "screen" at a time. In most cases, the speed, pitch, and tone of voice can be set to accommodate individual preferences. The voice quality of speech synthesizers varies considerably from more "human" to more "mechanical" sounding. In some instances, more mechanical sounding voices may actually be more intelligible. There are also synthesizers available that provide the user with the opportunity to select a number of different voices (e.g., male, female, young, old).

Speech synthesis/screen review technology, when combined with a word-processing program, can be a very powerful writing tool for postsecondary students with learning disabilities. This is particularly true for students who possess oral language skills that are superior to their written language abilities. For these students, the ability to hear what they have written (in some cases in addition to seeing it, and in others in lieu of seeing it) enables them to catch errors in grammar, spelling, and punctuation that might otherwise go unrecognized. Having the auditory feedback may also help alert students with LDs to problems regarding the coherency and semantic integrity of the document. Students will tend to read a document the way they think it should be, rather than the way it actually appears. A speech synthesis program will help alleviate this problem, since it "tells" it the way it is.

The use of a speech synthesis system can also be of great value when using the spell-check mode on word processors. Some students may have difficulty utilizing spell checkers effectively, since they may not be able to recognize and choose the correct word from the list of correctly spelled options. If students use a speech synthesizer to listen to—as well as read—each word, they are often in a better position to make the correct choice.

The benefits of speech synthesis systems are not limited solely to use with word processors. They may also be used to review materials written by others, including software tutorials, on-line help systems, letters, and reports. Some companies are now producing "books on disk" that make it possible for the student to listen to textbooks and popular titles by means of a speech synthesis system.

Speech synthesis systems used by students with learning disabilities have been adapted from systems designed for the blind. Such systems are sometimes difficult for students with LDs to use since command sequences are not "intuitive" and lack the associative meaning between command and function for sighted persons. Since a blind person often needs continual auditory feedback to monitor keystrokes, these programs can actually provide too much auditory feedback for students with LDs and result in "stimulus overload." However, Norris and Graef (1990) pointed out that such problems can be avoided by using screen reading programs that allow for the creation of user-defined commands and command sequences and that can be set up specifically for students with LDs. A new screen-reading program designed specifically for persons with learning disabilities was recently released by HumanWare, Inc.

The cost of commercially available speech synthesizers varies greatly, ranging from approximately $100 to $7,000. However, a synthesizer of sufficiently high quality can be purchased from between $700 and $1,600. Screen-reading programs appropriate for use with postsecondary students with LDs generally run between $400 and $600. The amount of time needed to learn screen-reading programs also varies from product to product. However, most students should be able to operate the program adequately within one hour.

Optical Character Recognition Systems/Speech Synthesis—Reading

An optical character recognition (OCR) system might be thought of as a "reading machine." Such systems provide a means by which to directly input text or printed material (e.g., a page in a book, a letter) into a computer. Text is input by using either a hand-held scanner that the student moves across (or down depending on the particular system) a page of text or a full-page scanner in which a page of text is placed face down on the device. Once the text has been scanned into the computer, it can then be read back to the user by means of a speech synthesizer. Considering that many postsecondary students with learning disabilities have difficulty reading print (Hughes & Smith, 1990) and that many are better able to comprehend what they hear (Spadafore, 1983), the use of an OCR system to help compensate for reading difficulties can be quite effective.

OCR systems are of two basic types, stand-alone or PC-based systems. Stand-alone (or "self-contained") systems have all components built into one device including the scanner OCR software/hardware and the speech synthesizer. Some stand-alone systems are portable; others are desktop units. The PC-based systems consist of a number of components hooked up to a PC. These components consist of a full-page (desktop) or hand-held scanner, an OCR board and/or software, and a speech synthesizer. Some units now provide automatic document feeders.

The quality and capabilities of OCR systems vary considerably including the rate at which text can be entered into the computer, the accuracy of the entry, the font size and typestyles the system is able to recognize, whether text can be spoken during scanning, the rate at which the text can be read back, and the quality of the speech synthesizer. The cost of OCR systems also varies widely, ranging in price from $1,200 to $12,000 (excluding the computer on the PC-based systems). Unlike some of the systems marketed several years ago, which required as much as 15 hours of training, many newer systems can be used quite effectively after only a couple of hours of instruction.

Personal Data Managers—Organization and Memory

Postsecondary students with learning disabilities often have difficulty remembering, organizing, and managing personal information (Mangrum & Strichart, 1988; Vogel, 1987). It may be a question of scheduling classes and appointments, prioritizing activities and assignments, remembering important dates/deadlines, or recording and accessing names, addresses, and phone numbers. The use of personal data managers can be quite helpful to students in compensating for difficulties in this area.

Personal data managers are available as software programs for use in personal and laptop computers, as well as self-contained hand-held units. These technologies allow the user to store and retrieve vast amounts of personal information easily. Data are input and retrieved via a keyboard/keypad and are shown on a computer monitor or LCD display. The programs have numerous capabilities and offer a number of diverse combinations of functions. Typical features include monthly calendars, daily schedules/planners/appointments, clock/alarms, memo files, "to do lists," name/address books, telephone directories (some with electronic dialers), and bankbooks/check registers. These products range on the average from about $20 to $150 and require only from 15 minutes to 2 hours to learn.

Free-Form Data Bases

Like personal data managers, free-form data bases can provide an excellent tool for helping postsecondary students with LDs compensate for organizational and memory problems. Free-form data bases are software programs that work with personal and laptop computers and might be thought of as "computerized Post-Its™" note systems.

Like abbreviation expanders, they are memory resident and can be activated while in a word processor or other programs by simply pressing a "hot key." The user can create his or her own notes, of any length, on any subject, in much the same way a person uses Post-It^{TM} notes, a notepad, or scraps of paper to jot down important information. For the student with a learning disability, it may be a question of writing down the author of a book, the phone number and address of a friend, the guidelines for writing a term paper, or the date of a final examination. Unlike a manual system, free-form data bases enable the user to store the notes in the computer's memory electronically rather than on tiny pieces of paper that can be easily misplaced.

Although the ability to store information electronically is quite useful to the postsecondary student with a learning disability, the real advantage of such programs lies in the way the stored information is retrieved. A note can be retrieved by typing in any piece of information contained in the note. The following example will help clarify this process. A student has written an electronic note on a prospective job contact:

Mr. Steve Green, President
United Ecological Services
7854 Valley View Blvd.
Northridge, California 91330
(818) 973-6284

This note would pop up on the screen if the student were to input any of the following information, including, but not limited to, "Steve," "President," "Ecological," "View," "Northridge," or "818." Even if only a fragment of a piece of information is recalled by the user (e.g., "Eco," "North"), the note will be pulled up and displayed on the screen. In cases where there are several notes that contain "overlapping" information (for example, more than one note containing the word "Northridge"), all the notes with this common information will appear. Through a simple cursor movement that highlights each note, students can browse through all the notes within the data base until they find the one they are looking for. However, the more information a student recalls regarding a particular note, the greater the likelihood that the specific note will come to the "top of the pile." In the event that the student cannot remember any specific information on the note, he or she may browse through the entire pile. If there are too many notes to be displayed on the screen simultaneously, continued browsing will uncover notes "hidden" toward the bottom of the pile. The ability to retrieve information by only remembering a fragment or piece of information contained within a note can be quite beneficial for postsecondary students with memory and organizational difficulties.

The basic functions of a free-form data base are relatively simple to learn and can be mastered in about two hours. Programs can be purchased for about $100.

Variable Speech Control Tape Recorders—Listening, Memory, and Reading

Portable audio-cassette recorders have been recommended by a number of authorities as a compensatory aid for postsecondary students with learning disabilities (Mangrum & Strichart, 1988; Scheiber & Talpers, 1985). Tape recorders can be utilized to tape-record classroom lectures as either an alternative or supplement to taking notes. This is particularly helpful to students who have listening difficulties (either because of difficulty processing oral language or attentional disorders) since they can review lectures at a later date and listen to tapes as many times as is needed to understand the material. The ability to commit a lecture to a permanent record is also helpful to students with other types of learning disabilities. This includes students who find it troublesome to take notes and listen simultaneously, students with fine-motor dysfunctions, and those with auditory memory problems.

Tape recorders can also be used as playback units for listening to books on tape. Students with reading difficulties can circumvent their disability by listening to prerecorded texts (books, journals, newspapers). Prerecorded text is available from a number of sources including The Library of Congress and Recordings for the Blind (see Appendix 11.1) and a number of private companies. Volunteer groups and student aids can also be used to record materials. Organizations that offer such services require professional verification of a student's learning disability.

It is important to keep in mind that not all audiotapes will work on all tape recorders, since they may have varying speeds (1⅞ ips, 15⁄16 ips) and formats (two-track, four-track). Care should be taken to ensure that there is a match between the play-back unit and the tapes. The reader is referred to Mangrum and Strichart (1988) for a more detailed discussion of tape recording as a compensatory strategy for students with LDs.

Although tape recorders are excellent compensatory aids, they do present special problems for some postsecondary students with LDs. First of all, since some persons with learning disabilities process auditory information at significantly slower rates than nondisabled counterparts (McCroskey & Thompson, 1973), they may have difficulty comprehending taped material (e.g., lecture, book on tape) played back at standard rates. Second, even if a student does not have difficulty processing speech at standard rates, it takes a considerable amount of time to listen to taped material. For example, a student enrolled in 12 semester units would have to devote an additional 12 hours per week of time to review lectures that had been recorded during the week. The increased amount of time necessary to use tape recorders contributes to an already existing problem—the majority of postsecondary students with LDs already spend far more time studying than their nondisabled peers.

These problems can be resolved by using variable speech control (VSC) tape recorders. VSC recorders enable the user to play back audiotaped material at rates that are slower or faster than those at which it was initially recorded. They key factor here is that the rate can be changed without the loss of intelligibility (e.g., "chipmunk"-like speech at faster speeds). Intelligible speech at varying rates is easily achieved by simply adjusting speed and pitch control levers (VSC recorders are not to be confused with the numerous recorders that allow for different recording and play-back speeds but require play back at the same speed as recording, and therefore will not permit rate adjustments without the loss of intelligibility).

The ability to adjust speech rates means that students who have difficulty comprehending recorded speech at standard rates can reduce the speed of play back to more comprehensible levels without the loss of voice quality. Similarly, VSC tape recorders enable the student to increase the speech rate in order to reduce the amount of time it takes to relisten to class lectures or prerecorded text. Most of these recorders can reduce the speech rate by approximately 25%, and increase play-back speed up to 100% without loss of intelligibility.

VSC tape recorders range from approximately $100 to $200 and usually require no more than 30 minutes of training.

Listening Aids—Listening

Research has indicated that some students with learning disabilities have difficulty focusing auditorily on a speaker (Hasbrouck, 1980). Students with such difficulties are likely to have a very hard time attending to lectures and may leave the classroom missing or misunderstanding material covered by the professor.

One device that can help students focus on a speaker is a personal FM listening system. This technological aid consists of two basic components, a wireless transmitter with a microphone and a receiver with a headset or earphone. The speaker (e.g., professor) "wears" the transmitter unit, which is only about 2″ × 3″, while the student wears the receiver unit (also about 2″ × 3″). The transmitter or receiver is easily clipped to a belt or shirt pocket. The microphone is only about 1½″-long and can also be easily clipped to clothing (e.g., tie). Essentially, these systems carry the speaker's voice directly from the speaker's mouth to the listener's ear, helping to make the speaker's voice more salient. Volume is easily controlled by a dial on the receiver. These devices run on AA-size rechargeable or disposable batteries.

The cost of such devices ranges from \$300 to \$600. It takes only a matter of minutes for a student to learn to use the system.

Talking Calculators—Math

In the same way as a speech synthesizer and screen review program can assist some students with LDs to catch errors in their writing by providing auditory feedback, a talking calculator can alert students to mistakes in mathematical calculations. A talking calculator is simply a calculator with a speech synthesizer. When number, symbol, or operation keys are pressed, they are vocalized, or spoken, by a built-in speech synthesizer. In this way, the student receives simultaneous auditory feedback in order to check the accuracy of visual-motor operations. Once a calculation has been made the number can be read back via the synthesizer. This feature is particular helpful if students are transferring their answers from calculator to paper, since it enables them to "double-check" the answers they have written down. This is of great value to students who make transpositions, reversals, omissions, additions, or inversions when they write numbers.

There are several drawbacks to using talking calculators, though. First of all, the speed at which calculations are performed may be problematic since it takes longer to have operations spoken than displayed. Secondly, some students with LDs experience "stimulus overload" by having to contend with both visual and auditory feedback. As with all technologies, individual profiles and preferences will have to be considered.

Talking calculators take only about fifteen minutes to learn how to use. They can be purchased for between \$50 and \$100.

Selection and Evaluation of Technology

As a result of the plethora of technology that has now reached the consumer market and of the number of new technologies being introduced virtually on a daily basis, choosing correct hardware and software to assist postsecondary students with LDs can seem to be an insurmountable task. The following section is intended to help postsecondary students with LDs, as well as the persons serving them, wade through the mire of technology by providing guidelines for selecting and evaluating current and emerging technologies.

Functions to be Performed

The first consideration in selecting assistive technology is to determine which particular functions need to be performed. This requires careful analysis of the student's difficulties as well as the ways in which these difficulties can be circumvented in order to accomplish specific tasks. For instance, does the student have a written language disorder and need a technology (e.g., word processor) that can assist in writing term papers, or does he or she have an auditory memory problem that requires a device (e.g., tape recorder) to help retain information from class lectures? Is assistive technology (e.g., OCR) needed to help a student with a reading deficit keep up with reading assignments? Implicit in the selection of a technology that will circumvent a specific deficit is the understanding that it will also simultaneously "play" to the student's strengths. For example, a student with a reading and writing disorder, yet who has superior oral language ability, will benefit from a speech synthesizer not only because it circumvents the area of deficiency (written language) but also because it encourages the use of his or her area of strength (oral language).

Once a careful examination of the functions that need to be performed has been made, the search for a specific technology that will help compensate for the deficits and enable the student to accomplish what needs to be accomplished can begin. Right from the start, a determination must be made as to whether a specific technology can indeed circumvent the disability and perform the necessary functions, before the technology is purchased.

There are a number of ways in which this can be accomplished. In some cases, a manufacturer or retailer will allow potential buyers to evaluate the technology for a trial period. Although some companies are reluctant to do so, there are many that will allow a potential buyer to evaluate a product for a specified amount of time. If this is not an option, then an attempt should be made to find an individual who currently uses the product and would let the student try it out. It also may be possible to try out equipment at an assistive technology center. Many disabled student service programs at postsecondary institutions now have assistive technology available. It is also important to question current and past users (as well as persons selling a particular product) to be sure the product does indeed match the needs of the intended user. These suggestions should help ensure that a technology will accomplish what it needs to accomplish, and it will help avoid the expense and aggravation of purchasing a product that will be inadequate to the student's needs.

Contexts of Use

Postsecondary students with learning disabilities do not experience difficulties solely within the school environment. They must also function within home, workplace, and social settings and thus require technology that is appropriate to each. Optimally, an assistive technology will be appropriate across contexts. However, this is not always the case, and what might be appropriate for one setting is not necessarily the best for another.

An OCR with a synthetic voice, for example, might be suitable for reading a technical manual at work, but a book on tape may be more appropriate for an American Literature class that requires the reading of *Moby Dick*. For a student employed as a sales representative who is required to write up orders in the field, a hand-held spell checker would be easier to use than a spell-checking program attached to a word processor. Some of the factors that need to be considered within specific contexts include the visual surroundings (e.g., lighting, reflectance) and auditory surroundings (acoustics, noise level), spatial configurations and constraints (e.g., size of work area, proximity of other people), temporal constraints (e.g., speed at which a task must be performed), portability, climate/temperature, and social factors (e.g., reaction of others), and psychological climate (e.g., stress level).

Compatibility

Not all software and hardware are compatible with one another. Incompatible technologies can be particularly frustrating for the postsecondary student with a learning disability. Consider, for example, the student with a learning disability who invests a substantial amount of time in learning an outlining program only to find that it does not work with a preferred word processor or the student who purchases an expensive speech recognition system and discovers that his or her existing computer does not have the required memory or speed to operate the system. This is a waste of time and money and can discourage the use of technology as a compensatory strategy.

Compatibility should also be considered relative to the various contexts of use. If at all possible, students should try to use technology that is compatible between the various environments in which they function. For example, if they are currently working in an office that is using IBM computer systems, they may want to select compatible (and in some cases even the same) hardware and software for use in the postsecondary setting. Having to learn a multitude of diverse technologies can be confusing. The more the technologies from the various contexts intersect, the greater the likelihood that the student will use the equipment efficiently and comfortably.

Attention should also be given to the future contexts in which the student will function. For example, if a student is going to be entering a profession (e.g., graphics) in which the Macintosh is the "industry standard," then she or he will need to consider the relative benefits and drawbacks of using a different system (e.g., IBM). This is not to say that the student should "match" technologies at all costs. Selecting a technology that does not effectively help a student compensate for difficulties within the postsecondary setting just because it is the same kind used at work is a waste. Consistency of technology between contexts must be made in light of numerous considerations.

Portability

The advent of laptop computers has made it possible to transport assistive technology easily from one setting to another. Twenty-five years ago, it took a small room to hold a computer that had only a fraction of the capabilities of many of today's laptops. When selecting a computer, it is important to consider once again the various contexts of use. Does work need to be performed only at home, or will technology be helpful in other settings? Does the student need, in addition to home use, a computer for use in the classroom (e.g., for taking notes), in the library for writing up research, as well as for writing documents at work?

Transporting a laptop computer from one location to another does not pose much difficulty. Laptops can do everything that a desktop computer can do, but they weigh only an average of 6 to 20 pounds. It is now possible for a student to set up a portable system that can be taken anywhere and that includes word processing with spell and grammar checking, outlining, abbreviation expansion, personal data management, speech recognition, speech synthesis, and OCR.

The only possible drawback to using a laptop is that most have a "battery life" of only three hours and have to recharged at an AC power source. This may be problematic when the system must be used for longer periods or when an AC power source is not readily available. However, the manufacturers of laptops are working diligently to find ways to increase the amount of time a system can operate without recharging. (In fact, a few laptops have recently been introduced that will run for up to 20 hours.)

In addition to laptop computers, there are a number of other assistive technologies that can be easily moved from one setting to another. These technologies were discussed above and include such devices as "hand-held" and "pocket-sized" spell checkers/thesauruses/dictionaries, talking calculators, personal data managers, and tape recorders.

Ease of Use

Technology should be intuitive and straightforward to learn and operate. If students have to spend an inordinate amount of time learning to use it, they may consider it a matter of diminishing returns and return to doing things in the "usual" way. There are several considerations in this regard.

Commands and operational procedures should be designed in such a way as to become easy for the student to make the connection between the command and the function it performs. For example, a screen review/speech synthesis program that reads a paragraph by pressing the letter

"P" (for paragraph) on the keyboard is more likely to make sense and to be easier to remember than an arbitrary command such as "Ctrl X." In addition, technology providing an option for using a mouse (which allows the user to "point and click" as well as use a keyboard) can also enhance the ease of operation for many students with LDs. However, such choices are a matter of individual preference, and they should be closely evaluated for each student.

The number of commands (keystrokes, operations) required to perform a particular function will also affect the ease of use. Technology that requires a long, complicated series of commands to perform certain tasks can be quite frustrating to the student with LDs. This is particularly true for the student who has difficult sequencing and following directions. If a product is difficult to learn or complicated to operate, it will not be long before the student concludes that a specific technology is not worth the effort. Postsecondary students with LDs who have experienced difficulty and frustration with learning over the years do not need to experience more of it, especially from something that is supposed to make things easier.

Programs that incorporate "on-line help" systems are particularly important for enhancing ease of use. On-line help systems provide critical information on the features and operational commands of a given technology while the technology is being used. They might be thought of as an electronic instructional manual (although they are usually not as detailed as the text-based documentation). The information is displayed on screen and is activated by pressing a designated "help command." If a student runs into difficulty (such as forgetting the command to retrieve a file), a quick and easy reference can be made to the help system to resolve the problem. This also helps to foster greater independence in the user.

Collins and Price (1986) have made several suggestions for evaluating technology for postsecondary students with learning disabilities. Although they focus specifically on word processors, their recommendations are applicable to other technologies. According to the authors, a program should offer "visible program logic" on screen. It should have a "step-by-step structure that is progressive, straightforward and clear" and should "move the student from mode to mode and task to task with as few disruptions as possible" (p. 4). The screen should be free of clutter and present choices in a clear and comprehensible manner.

Reliability

Assistive technology must also be reliable. A student who depends on a particular technology to compensate for specific difficulties, whether at school, at home, or in the workplace, must know that it will work when needed and in a consistent and predictable way. The last thing a student with a learning disability needs is to have her tape recorder break down during the week before finals when professors are reviewing and summarizing course material or to be unable to retrieve a term paper from a word processor a few days before it is due. Before the product is purchased, it may be helpful to talk with current and past users of the product to ascertain their opinion regarding the product's dependability. There are a multitude of computer magazines that frequently publish product reviews that can be used to obtain similar information.

Quality of Documentation

It has been said that the lowest point in the English language was reached with the writing of the first computer manuals. Although there have been dramatic improvements, it is unfortunate that much of the documentation currently accompanying assistive technology is still difficult to comprehend. The postsecondary student with a learning disability requires documentation that is clearly written and easy to understand. The material must be at a level commensurate with the student's reading level and must limit the use of technical jargon.

Minimally, documentation should provide instructions for setting up or installing the technology, basic operating instructions, advanced operating instructions, and guidance on what to do when things go wrong. Information should be presented in short, discrete sections that are clearly identified and easily referenced. Whereas documentation should be complete and comprehensive, it should be presented in such a manner that the student can easily discern the most pertinent information without being bombarded with a multitude of highly specialized features and details. Many companies now provide product documentation on disk. Such documentation, if used in conjunction with a speech synthesizer, can be an excellent supplement or alternative to conventional manuals. Documentation provided on audio cassette can also be quite helpful to students.

Technical Support

Closely related to the quality of documentation is the quality of technical support. Even when a specific product provides excellent documentation, there are times when it may be necessary to have direct contact with the manufacturer or product representative. Direct contact may have to be made due to product malfunctioning, problems operating the product in combination with other technology, or simply difficulty following or understanding information presented in the documentation. The manner in which a company can assist the user in resolving these problems is an important consideration in selecting a specific product.

Many companies now provide technical support hot lines (1–800 numbers) that provide the user with immediate help in resolving problems with the product. If problems cannot be solved in this way, the manufacturer or retailer may need to send field representatives to assist the user. In other situations, it may be necessary to return the product for repair or replacement. Attention should also be paid to product warranties. Typically, warranties on hardware run one year "parts and labor," with the buyer paying shipping charges to the repair destination. The manufacturer generally picks up the shipping to send the equipment back to the consumer. "On-site" repairs are not customary. Most software is guaranteed for a period of 90 days with the consumer covering the cost of shipping.

In addition to the technical support provided by the manufacturer or retailer, a student's personal resources should also be considered. For example, does the user have the technical background to support the product independently, or is there a friend or family member who can lend the necessary technical expertise? If the product is used within the postsecondary setting, does the institution have resources to support the product? Answers to such questions, as well as the technical support provided by the manufacturer or retailer, must be considered to ensure that a student is not going to be left out in the cold if any problems arise. If the proper resources to support a product are not available, then purchasing the product is inadvisable.

Ease of Installation/Setup

The ease of setup varies greatly with each technology. Whereas a tape recorder may simply require a few seconds to put in batteries, a PC-based OCR system may require several hours to install hardware and software components. However, the ease of installing or setting up a particular technology is not dependent on whether it is simple or requires only a few steps. The most critical element is whether setup procedures are clearly defined, logical, and follow a step-by-step progression. Even high sophisticated technology can get a high rating on this criterion, providing its setup procedures are clear and comprehensible. Many software programs include a setup program that automates installation.

Cost

It is difficult to put a dollar amount on the benefits of a particular technology. However, some consideration might be given to what is termed the benefit/cost ratio. Simply stated, how do the potential benefits of the technology compare to its cost? Such an answer is very subjective and must be considered on a case-by-case basis relative to the specific nature of the disability and the financial resources of the student. For example, should a student with a mild decoding problem who is living on a student loan and has few other financial resources be encouraged to purchase a $10,000 OCR system? In the case of postsecondary institutions, the number of students who will benefit from a sepcific technology as well as whether its purchase (especially in the case of expensive equipment) will inhibit the purchase of other necessary products should also be considered.

In regard to the cost of a specific technology, other sources of funding should also be considered. Many state departments of rehabilitation now provide funding to their clients for the purchase of assistive technology. This is usually handled on a case-by-case basis and is dependent on the training, experience, and "predisposition" of the state and local agencies toward technology.

Federal legislation might also help offset the cost of purchasing technology for postsecondary students with learning disabilities. First of all, Section 504 of the Rehabilitation Act of 1973 (29 U.S.C. 794) directs postsecondary institutions that are recipients of federal funding to provide academic adjustments for disabled students and includes the provision of "auxiliary aids." Specifically, the regulation implementing the law (found at 34 C.F.R. Part 14) states that postsecondary institutions that are recipients of federal funding

shall take such steps as are necessary to ensure that no handicapped student is denied the benefits of, excluded from participation in, or otherwise subjected to discrimination under the education program or activity operated by the recipient because of the absence of auxiliary aids. (see 34 C.F.R. Section 14.44[d])

If a given technology is the only effective, reliable, or practical compensatory strategy that can be used to resolve a particular problem that is inhibiting a student's full access to the postsecondary institution, then it is the school's obligation to provide it. However, such determinations are made on a case-by-case basis.

An increasing number of postsecondary institutions are recognizing the importance of assistive technology and have been making a variety of technologies available for student use. The California Community College system, for example, has initiated "Hi-Tech Centers" that provide assistive technology to students with disabilities, including those with learning disabilities. Some institutions (e.g., California State University, Northridge) have programs that loan technology to students. As the benefits of technology in helping postsecondary students with LDs become more widely recognized, more and more institutions are likely to follow suit.

If students with LDs are currently employed, the employer may be responsible for absorbing the cost of assistive technology. Sections 503 (directed toward federal contractors) and Section 504 (directed toward recipients of federal funds) require employers to make "reasonable accommodations" for their disabled employees. Assistive technology is becoming more widely accepted as a "reasonable accommodation" and is being used by an increasing number of employers to meet this mandate. With the recent passage of the Americans with Disabilities Act (ADA) in July of 1990, demands are now being placed on all employers (who have 25 or more employees during the first two years to the legislation, and 15 employees thereafter) to provide reasonable accommodations to disabled employees including the "acquisition and modification of equipment and devices" such as adaptive hardware and software for computers, talking calculators, and audio recordings (Americans with Disabilities Act of 1990). However, the law is not clear as to the extent of the employer's obligation to provide assistive technology, since certain accommodations may not be required if they present an "undue hardship" on the employer. Like Section 504, interpretation will probably take place on a case-by-case basis.

In some cases, manufacturers of technology can be contacted directly regarding donations or discounts for persons with disabilities. For example, the speech recognition system DragonDictate is sold at a discounted price to persons with disabilities. Many of the larger companies are aware that technology can help persons with disabilities, and they have established departments that are dedicated to the transfer of technology to the disabled community. For example, IBM has established a National Support Center for Persons with Disabilities and Apple Computer has its Office of Special Education and Rehabilitation.

Funds may also be sought from private foundations. Although at present this does not appear to be an option, it is hoped that in the future, LD organizations will be able to help persons with learning disabilities purchase assistive technology. Finally, reference guides can also be used to identify possible sources of funding. Although there are no guides specifically targeted at learning disabilities and assistive technology, these reference guides provide valuable information regarding funding strategies and identifying possible sources of funding. Some of these references are listed below:

Enders, A., & Hall, M. (1990). *Assistive technology resource book*. Washington, DC: RESNA Press.

Schlachter, G.A., & Weber, R.D. (1990). *Financial aid for the disabled and their families*. San Carlos, CA: Reference Service Press.

Hoffman, A.C. (1990). *The many faces of funding*. Mill Valley, CA: Phonic Ear Inc.

When considering the cost of a technology, intrigue and fascination with a product often obscure the answering of a very basic but often overlooked question, "Is there a less expensive method of compensating for the disability?" Could a student with a reading problem be helped just as much, and at a lesser cost, through the provision of a reader rather than an OCR system? Or, could a transcriber be used as effectively as a speech recognition system at a considerably lesser cost? Although technology can offer the postsecondary student with learning disabilities a multitude of excellent compensatory strategies, it does not necessarily mean that technology is always the best way to go—both in terms of cost or effectiveness. Similarly, it is not necessarily always the "highest" or most expensive technology that can offer the best solution. In some cases, a "low-tech" solution such as a taped text and recorder to help a student compensate for a reading disability can be just as effective, and less expensive, than using an OCR system.

Standard versus Specialized Technology

Whenever possible it is better to select *standard* as opposed to *specialized* technology. *Standard* technology refers to technology that is commercially available from a number of different sources, is widely used in a variety of settings, and was designed for the general rather than disabled population. The word-processing program WordPerfect® is an example of a standard technology, since it can be purchased in just about any store that carries computer software, is commonly used in numerous business and educational settings, and is marketed for the general public.

There are several reasons to use standard products. First of all, the cost of standard technologies is generally less than that of technologies developed for disabled populations. Simply, since there are more non-disabled persons than disabled persons, a manufacturer can hold costs down because of the potential for a greater volume of sales. Second, there is likely to be more support available for a standard technology (although this is not always the case). Manufacturers of widely used technologies will generally have support service telephone lines as well as authorized dealers and service representatives in a greater number of locales than a small company selling a specialized product to a limited market. Furthermore, if a product is widely used by a large number of persons, there is a greater chance that the user will be able to find assistance from other sources (e.g., friends, family members, co-workers) should they encounter difficulties using the product.

Finally, the use of standard technology can facilitate the transfer of compensatory technology strategies across the various contexts in which the student functions. If a student could benefit from the use of a word processor within the postsecondary setting then, for example, it might be advantageous to choose a standard program (e.g., WordPerfect®) that the student will also be likely to find in many employment settings. Spending many hours learning to use a highly specialized word-processing program for school that is unlikely to be found in the workplace is probably not the most efficacious use of the student's time. The "greatest mileage" can be achieved when the technology provides for transfer across various contexts. Bridging the gap between education and employment is an important consideration in preparing the student with a learning disability for the "real world." It is one thing to get a student through the postsecondary setting; it is another to enhance his or her chances for career satisfaction and success.

Guidelines for Instruction

Readiness

Before direct instruction in assistive technology is initiated, the student with a learning disability must be in a state of "readiness." Several components must be in place in order to achieve this state, and in some cases it may be necessary for the student to receive counseling or therapy to ensure that these components are present. First of all, students must understand the nature of their learning disability. They must be aware of their strengths and weaknesses and how these strengths and weaknesses are manifested in various contexts. In addition, they need to be aware of their own unique learning styles or preferences (e.g., visual, auditory, kinesthetic, multisensory) and of the learning strategies that they have found to be the most useful. This self-awareness needs to be articulated to the technology instructor to the greatest extent possible.

The instructor must also have a thorough understanding of the student's disability. This understanding can be enhanced through a comprehensive evaluation that includes history, interview, observation, and formal diagnostic testing. A thorough understanding of a student's learning disability will require not only a recognition of the areas of definciency but, equally important, an awareness of a student's strengths, interests, and experiences. Furthermore, as it was important for the student to communicate the understanding of the disability to the instructor, it is also necessary for the instructor to communicate understanding to the student. Communication between the student and instructor must be reciprocal in order to develop a mutual understanding.

It is one thing to understand the nature of the disability; it is another to accept it. If positive instructional outcomes are to be achieved, then students must be willing to accept as well as understand their disabilities. Those who cannot or will not admit to themselves that they are disabled will have little motivation to improve their situation. They may be asking themselves, "Why should I bother trying to change things, if there isn't anything wrong in the first place?" However, if students can learn to accept their disabilities, then they will be more likely to take the necessary actions to improve the situation (with the proper resources and support). The importance of understanding, acceptance, and actions in enhancing chances for success of adults with learning disabilities have been emphasized by Ginsberg and Gerber (1990).

Recognize the Intent

The point at which the student is willing to take action is also the point at which assistive technology can be introduced. However, the intent of using technology must be stated clearly at this time. In other words, is the technology being used as a remedial strategy to improve specific skill deficits, as an instructional aid to teach subject matter, or as a compensatory strategy designed to circumvent the disability? It is impossible to provide the correct technology and instruction if one is not clear as to the intent and expected outcomes. Once again, these approaches are not mutually exclusive and, in some instances, using technology from one approach (e.g., compensatory) may have beneficial results in another (e.g., remedial).

Address Immediate Needs

Right from the start, students must recognize that technology can help them compensate for their disabilities and ultimately aid them in attaining their educational and career goals. In order to ensure that they recognize the benefits of technology, the instructor must first introduce a technology that will help the student in meeting a specific and *immediate* need. This means that there must be a direct and obvious connection between the technology itself and the function the student needs to perform within a given context.

For example, the student may be spending an inordinate amount of time reviewing taped lectures from a U.S. history class. If the student can be introduced to a VSC recorder and recognize that the device can immediately help save study time, the likelihood is greater that he or she will be interested in the technology and be willing to spend the necessary time to learn to use it competently. Similarly, if a student is having difficulty comprehending a psychology textbook but can be shown how an OCR system with speech synthesis can increase comprehension, then the impetus to invest time and energy in this technological solution will be given. The sooner students can see the benefits, the greater the chance that they will be willing to invest the time in learning to use it as well as to explore other technological solutions. Although this approach appears self-evident, instructors are far too often led by what they think a student needs rather than responding directly to what students tell them they need. Considering the importance of responding to individual needs (as well as individual learning styles), instruction in assistive technology generally needs to be conducted on a one-to-one basis.

In order to ensure that the student will find a meaningful technological solution, the instructor may want to give a sampling of different technologies. However, indiscriminate introduction to numerous technologies could turn the student off rather than on. Although the instructor may recognize that a number of different technologies could be utilized effectively with a particular student, the most prudent approach is generally to introduce the student to only one. New learning situations can be overwhelming for postsecondary students with learning disabilities and the thought of one more thing to do or learn may be just too much to handle. It is also important to realize that some students may not "take" to technology, and may actually be more comfortable using nontechnological compensatory strategies. This is something the instructor may have to accept; although the potential benefits appear obvious, a student cannot be forced to use technology.

Introduce Features and Operations as Needed

Once students recognize how a technology can be used to help compensate for their difficulties, instruction in its operation can begin. However, the concept of "need" should still be emphasized. Specific features/functions of the technology should be taught only as they are needed to accomplish a specific task. The teaching of all the "bits and pieces" of a particular technology at once, before there is an actual need to use them, is bound to overwhelm the student with a learning disability.

Consider, for example, that many word processors have hundreds of features with commands numbering in the thousands. Many manuals are over 500 pages. Trying to teach too many operations before there is a need to use them reduces the "meaningfulness" of the instruction. As a result, students are more likely to forget the skill by the time they have a need to use it. In addition, if too much information is presented, the student might experience a state of "information overload" and become frustrated and overwhelmed. This can in turn result in the development of a negative attitude toward assistive technology and dissuade further use entirely. In contrast, an approach that unfolds operational procedures as the student needs to know them, and follows the students' natural learning cycle by keeping instruction meaningful, fosters further exploration of technology. Similarly, students should be allowed to progress at their own pace, and not be required to meet an arbitrary timeline imposed by the instructor.

In order to limit the amount of information presented to the student, the instructor may find it useful to develop "help sheets." Help sheets list the operational procedures and commands for the most commonly used features and functions of a given technology on one page. The number of items listed should be limited to no more than 10 to 12, and should be presented in a clean, uncluttered format. Help sheets should be readily available to the student at all times for quick and easy reference.

Foster Confidence

Years of frustration and failure have made many postsecondary students with LDs apprehensive about entering new learning situations. They may expect to fail, and they may withdraw from the learning environment at the first sign of difficulty in order to avoid further failure. Therefore, it is critical that the technology instructor instill confidence as early as possible.

Confidence can be fostered by introducing operational procedures that are manageable and easy to learn, thus giving the student a feeling of "instant success." This should be done in a warm and reassuring atmosphere, with the instructor providing positive feedback and encouragement. A "small success" can go a long way in fostering confidence. A "small failure," feeding into years of previous failures, can destroy the development of confidence in the use of technology and discourage future use.

The instructor may also want to provide some recreational or leisure technological experiences. Many technologies are quite exciting, intriguing, and pleasurable to use. The instructor should capitalize on this to the greatest extent possible. Technologies such as drawing, music, and game programs, although not necessarily aimed at assisting a student in compensating for a deficit, can still provide positive, relaxing, and enjoyable experiences that foster a positive attitude toward technology. In some cases, having an enjoyable experience may be the most immediate need of a student with a learning disability.

Consider the Physical Environment

In addition to creating the proper psychological setting for the teaching of assistive technology, attention should also be paid to constructing the optimal physical environment. There is no best environment, since individual preferences may vary from student to student. Furthermore, there are certain givens within the environment that may not be alterable (e.g., building location). Nevertheless, there are several elements within the environment that are controllable and should be considered. Glare, for example, either directly from a light source or reflected off another surface, can be quite distracting. Shadows (which are dependent on the angle and distance of the light source), appearing either directly on the technology or within the instructional area, may also be bothersome to the student. The effects of localized lighting should be considered as well. As a general rule, the technology being used should occupy a space of greater illumination than surrounding objects not intended as the primary focus of attention. This is easily accomplished through the use of supplemental localized or spot lighting. Distraction in the visual field is often created when unwanted objects receive greater illumination than those intended for focus.

The auditory surroundings must also be considered in developing an instructional setting conducive to the learning of assistive technology. Excessive noise levels can be quite distracting and can significantly affect the learner's mood. The type of noise should also be considered. For example, intelligible speech is more distracting than nonintelligible conversation, and mechanical sounds are more disturbing than natural ones (Fitzroy, 1963). If distracting auditory stimuli are present, then the use of "white noise" (e.g., background music) can be used to mask it.

In addition to controlling visual and auditory factors, an attempt should be made to ensure that the technology and the student are positioned so as to create the optimal height and distance for efficient and comfortable operation. Operating a technology from an improper position can be quite tiring. Although this may apparently be obvious, every effort should also be made to keep the temperature within the student's comfort zone as well as to provide adequate ventilation within the instructional area.

Keep Language Simple

When instructing the postsecondary student with a learning disability in the use of technology, language must be kept as simple as possible. This is not an easy task considering that the "technological world" has its own language of technical jargon. To the greatest extent possible, technical words and concepts should be kept to a minimum, with the instructor "translating" or substituting more comprehensible words as needed. Students should be encouraged to generate their own words (based on what is meaningful to them) to replace less comprehensible technical words or concepts. While technical jargon should be kept to a minimum, the reality is that the student is entering a new "culture" and to a certain extent will have to learn its language. As previously discussed, the student need not be introduced to everything at once. Students can learn the technological vernacular as they need to know it.

The instructor should avoid placing too much emphasis on the "inner workings" of assistive technology. While it might be helpful for students to have a basic idea of how a particular technology works, it is not necessary for them to become junior electronic engineers. Rather, emphasis should be placed on the fact that it does work and can assist them in compensating for their difficulties. As a case in point, one does not have to be a combustion engineer to derive benefits from driving a car. Overemphasizing the inner workings of a technology can overwhelm the student and discourage further use. For some students, it may be difficult enough to learn how to use a technology without the added burden of having to know how it works.

Be Aware of Nonverbal Communication

Considerable research (e.g., Axelrod, 1982; Bryan, 1977; Sisterhen & Gerber, 1989) has indicated that many persons with learning disabilities have difficulty interpreting nonverbal communication. This can inhibit communication between the student and the instructor since nonverbal signals have a profound affect upon the meaning of a communication. Consequently, the instructor should be aware of the kinesic (facial expressions, gestures, body orientation, posture, movement) and para-linguistic signals (speech rate, speech rhythm, pauses, vocal volume, intonation) and emphasize, de-emphasize, or alter signals to help ensure that the student will adequately comprehend communications. The instructor should be sensitive to the nonverbal cues sent by the student in order to monitor the student's understanding. In many cases a student may express understanding or lack of understanding far more profoundly with a nonverbal signal (e.g., frowning) rather than with a verbal comment.

Use Technology to Teach Technology

Technology can be used effectively to teach technology. This might mean using a tape recorder to listen to instructional tapes discussing an outlining program (some companies have audiotaped tutorials), using a speech synthesizer and screen reading program to listen to the on-screen tutorial for a word-processing program, or taking notes on a word processor to learn how to use a word processor. Such approaches are helpful for several reasons. First of all, since assistive technology enables students with LDs to circumvent their areas of deficiency, there is no reason why such an approach would not be just as beneficial in learning to use technology itself. Second, this approach provides immediate feedback to the student on the benefits of technology. Finally, using technology to teach technology provides the student with the opportunity to learn different technologies simultaneously and to develop a sense for how technologies can be integrated with one another. The instructor should be careful, however, not to overload the student with too many technologies at one time.

Learn by Doing

Learn by doing is certainly not a new educational concept. However, it is particularly applicable to the teaching of technology to postsecondary students with LDs. An instructor may tend to jump in and perform various operations for the student who encounters difficulty. Although this may make an instructional session go a little smoother, it is in fact "robbing" the student of the learning experience. The student needs the freedom to make mistakes (in a warm and reassuring atmosphere). Alternative approaches might include talking the students through the procedures or, if they have difficulty comprehending oral language, moving their hands (thereby providing the student with kinesthetic feedback) to perform the various commands needed to operate a specific technology.

Use Mnemonics

Several authors have suggested the use of mnemonic strategies to help postsecondary students with LDs retain information (Mangrum & Strichart, 1988; Scheiber & Talpers, 1985). Such strategies can be applied to teaching assistive technology as well. Mnemonic strategies include the use of acronyms, visualization, "linking," rhyme, and rhythm. In developing mnemonic strategies, it is best to have the students draw from their own repertoire of experiences and meaning rather than to have the instructor impose an experiential base.

Conclusion

The technologies discussed in this chapter have important implications for assisting postsecondary students with learning disabilities compensate for their difficulties in the areas of writing, reading, organization, memory, listening, and math. Many technologies, mere dreams in the minds of engineers and educators only a decade ago, are now readily available. Considering the many technological breakthroughs that occur on almost a daily basis, the possibilities for helping students with learning disabilities appear limitless.

Although the possibilities are profound, care must be taken not to view technology as a panacea. Technology, regardless of its level of sophistication, cannot alleviate a learning disability. Technology is only one part of the complex web of teaching, counseling, assessment, tutoring, remediation, compensatory strategy training, and program planning needed to assist students with learning disabilities in the postsecondary setting. It must be carefully woven into this web through discriminant selection and mindful instruction based on the needs of individual students as well as on their own unique profiles of strengths, weaknesses, interests, and experiences. When approached in this manner, technology will provide a critical component in ensuring that students with learning disabilities succeed in the postsecondary setting and beyond.

References

Americans with Disabilities Act of 1990, P.L. 101–336, 42 U.S.C.A. 12, 101–12, 213 (West Supp. 1991).

Axelrod, L. (1982). Social perception in learning disabled adults. *Journal of Learning Disabilities*, *15*(10), 610–613.

Blalock, J. (1981). Persistent problems and concerns of young adults with learning disabilities. In W. Cruickshank & A. Silvers (Eds.), *Bridges to tomorrow, Vol. 2: The best of ACLD*. Syracuse: Syracuse University Press.

Brown, C. (1987). *Computer access in higher education for students with disabilities*. Washington, DC: Fund for the Improvement of Postsecondary Education, U.S. Department of Education.

Bryan, T. (1977). Learning disabled children's comprehension of nonverbal communication. *Journal of Learning Disabilities*, *10*(8), 501–506.

Collins, T. (1990). The impact of microcomputer word processing on the performance of learning disabled students in a required first year writing course. *Computers and Composition*, *8*(1), 49–68.

Collins, T., & Price, L. (1986). *A guide to selecting word-processing software for learning disabled college writers*. Unpublished Manuscript, University of Minnesota—General College.

Cutler, E. (1990). Evaluating spell checkers, thesauruses, dictionaries, and grammar editors for the community college student with learning disabilities. In H.J. Murphy (Ed.), *Proceedings of the Fifth Annual Conference on Technology and Persons with Disabilities*, *5*, 163–175.

Enders, A., & Hall, M. (1990). *Assistive technology resource book*. Washington, DC: RESNA Press.

Fitzroy, D. (1963). *Acoustical environment of school buildings*. New York: Educational Facilities Laboratories.

Frankel, S. (1990, May 27). Write right. *The Sunday Oregonian*, pp. K1, B4.

Ginsberg R., & Gerber, P. (1990, April). *Conquering success: Patterns of highly successful learning disabled adults in the workplace*. Paper Presented at the Annual Meeting of the American Educational Research Association.

Gregg, N., & Hoy, C. (1989). Coherence: The comprehension and production abilities of college writers who are normally achieving, learning disabled, and underprepared. *Journal of Learning Disabilities*, *22*(6), 370–372.

Hasbrouck, J.M. (1980). Performance of students with auditory figure-ground disorders under conditions of unilateral and bilateral ear occlusion. *Journal of Learning Disabilities*, *13*, 548–551.

Hoffman, A.C. (1990). *The many faces of funding*. Mill Valley, CA: Phonic Ear Inc.

Hughes, C.A., & Smith, J.O. (1990). Cognitive and academic performance of college students with learning disabilities: A synthesis of the literature. *Learning Disability Quarterly*, *13*(1), 66–79.

Huxley, A. (1956). *Tomorrow and tomorrow and tomorrow*. New York: Harper & Brothers.

Kerchner, L.B., & Kistenger, B.J. (1984). Language processing/word processing: Written expression, computers, and learning disabled students. *Learning Disability Quarterly*, *7*(4), 329–335.

Mangrum C.T., II, & Strichart, S.S. (1988). *College and the learning disabled student*. Philadelphia: Grune & Stratton.

McCroskey, R., & Thompson, N. (1973). Comprehension of rate controlled speech by children with specific learning disabilities. *Journal of Learning Disabilities*, *6*(10), 29–35.

Morris, M., & Leuenberger, J. (1990). A report of cognitive, academic, and linguistic profiles for college students with and without learning disabilities. *Journal of Learning Disabilities*, *23*(6), 355–360.

Norris, M., & Graef, J. (1990). Screen reading programs for students with learning disabilities. In H.J. Murphy (Ed.), *Proceedings of the Fifth Annual Conference on Technology and Persons with Disabilities*, *5*, 491–499.

Primus, C. (1990). *Computer assistance model for learning disabled*. (Grant #GOO8630152-88). Washingrton, DC: Office of Special Education and Rehabilitation Services, U.S. Department of Education.

Rehabilitation Act of 1973, P.L. 92–112, 29 U.S.C. 794 (1980).

Scheiber, B., & Talpers, J. (1985). *Campus access for learning disabled students*. Washington, DC: Closer Look.

Schlachter, G.A., & Weber, R.D. (1990). *Financial aid for the disabled and their families*. San Carlos, CA: Reference Service Press.

Sisterhen, D.H., & Gerber, P. (1989). Auditory, visual, multisensory, nonverbal social perception in adolescents with and without learning disabilities. *Journal of Learning Disabilities*, 22(4), 245–249.

Spadafore, G.J. (1983). *Spadafore Diagnostic Reading Test Manual*. Novato, CA: Academic Therapy Publications.

Vogel, S.A. (1987). Issue and concerns in LD college programming. In D.J. Johnson & J.W. Blalock (Eds.), *Adults with learning disabilities: Clinical studies* (pp. 239–275). Orlando, FL: Grune & Stratton.

Vogel, S.A. (1985). Syntactic complexity in written expression of LD college writers. *Annals of Dyslexia*, 35, 137–157.

Vogel, S.A., & Moran, M.R. (1982). Written language disorders in learning disabled students: A preliminary report. In W.M. Cruickshank & J.W. Lerner (Eds.), *Coming of age, Vol. 3: The best of ACLD* (pp. 211–225). Syracuse: Syracuse University Press.

Appendix 11.1: Product Resource List

The following technology has been used successfully to assist students with learning disabilities at California State University, Northridge.

Technology Category	Product Name	Source
Word processing software	WordPerfect®	WordPerfect Corporation 1555 N. Technology Orem, UT 84057 (801) 225–5000
Mouse interface software	MousePerfect	MousePerfect Inc. P.O. Box 367 Clarkston, GA 30021
Key repeat inhibitor	Filch™	Kinetic Designs 14321 Anatevka Olalla, WA 98359 (206) 857–7943
Spell checkers, dictionaries, Thesauruses (stand alone)	Franklin® Learning Resources Product Line	Franklin Learning Resources 122 Burrs Road Mt. Holly, NJ 08060 (800) 525–9673
Add-on software dictionary	Franklin® Dictionary	Franklin Software 122 Burrs Road Mt. Holly, NJ 08060 (609) 261–4800
	Definitions Plus™	Word Science Corporation 1415 Oakland Blvd. Ste. 220 WalnutCreek, CA 94596 (510) 939–1190
Proofreading software	Grammatik™ IV	Reference Software 330 Townsend Street, Ste. 123 San Francisco, CA 94107 (415) 541–0222
	Correct Grammar®	Writing Tools Group 1 Harbor Drive Ste. 111 Sausalito, CA 94965 (415) 332–8692
Outliner	Grandview®	Symantec Corporation 10201 Torre Avenue Cupertino, CA 95014-2132 (408) 253–9600

Technology Category	Product Name	Source
Abbreviation expansion software	Keyworks™	Alpha Software Corporation 30 B Street Burlington, MA 01803 (617) 229–2924
Speech recognition	DragonDictate™	Dragon Systems, Inc. 320 Nevada Street Newton, MA 02160 (617) 965–5200
Speech synthesizer	DECtalk™ Product Line	Digital Equipment Corporation Digital Drive MK02-1/K06 Merrimack, NH 03054 (603) 884–4047
	Keynote Gold® Product Line	HumanWare, Inc. 6245 King Road Loomis, CA 95650 (800) 722–3393
	Synphonix™ Product Line	Artic Technologies 55 Park Street, Suite 2 Troy, MI 48083 (313) 588–7370
Screen review software	SoundProof®	HumanWare, Inc. 6245 King Road Loomis, CA 95650 (800) 722–3393
	OutSpoken™	Berkeley Systems, Inc. 2095 Rose Street Berkeley, CA 94709 (415) 540–5535
Optical character recognition	Xerox/Kurzweil Personal Reader® and PC/KPR Product Line	Kurzweil Computer Products 9 Centennial Drive Peabody, MA 01960 (800) 343–0311
	Arkenstone Reader™	Arkenstone, Inc 1185 Bordeaux Drive, Suite D Sunnyvale, CA 94089 (408) 752–2200
Personal data manager software	WordPerfect Library™	WordPerfect Corporation 1555 N. Technology Way Orem, UT 84057 (801) 225–5000

Technology Category	Product Name	Source
	Encore™	Artic Technologies 55 Park Street, Suite 2 Troy, MI 48083 (313) 588–7370
Personal data manager "stand alone"	Texas Instruments Pocket Solutions™ Data Banks	Texas Instruments P.O. Box 2500 Lubbock, TX 79408 (806) 747–1882
Free-form database	Info Select™	Micro Logic Corporation P.O. Box 174 Hackensack, NJ 07602 (201) 342–6518
Books on disk	Computerized Books	Computerized Books for the Blind 37 Corbin Hall University of Montana Missoula, MT 59812 (406) 243–5481
Books on tape	Recorded Books	Library of Congress National Library Service for the Blind and Physically Handicapped 1291 Taylor St., NW Washington, DC 20542 (202) 707–5100
	Recorded Books	Recording for the Blind, Inc. 20 Roszel Road Princeton, NJ 08540 (609) 452–0606
Variable speech control tape recorder	GE Fastrac™	General Electric P.O. Box 1976 Indianapolis, IN 46206 (800) 447–1700
	Handi-Cassette	American Printing House for the Blind, Inc. 1839 Frankfort Avenue P.O. Box 6085 Louisville, KY (502) 895-2405
Listening aids	Easy Listener™	Phonic Ear, Inc. 3880 Cypress Drive Petaluma, CA 94954 (800) 772–3374

Technology Category	Product Name	Source
Talking calculator	Sharp® Talking Calculator EL-640	Sharp Electronics Corp. Sharp Plaza 20600 South Alameda Street Carson, CA 90810 (213) 637–9488

Part IV
Research on the Cutting Edge

XII
"Foreign" Language Learning Disabilities: Issues, Research, and Teaching Implications

LEONORE GANSCHOW AND RICHARD SPARKS*

Introduction

For years high-school foreign language educators have observed bright students who simply could not master the skills being taught in foreign language classes. In the 1960s these students were referred to as "under-achievers" (Pimsleur, Sundland, & McIntyre, 1964). Only the brightest of them went on to college, and many either dropped out if they could not pass the foreign language requirement, attended universities that did not have a foreign language requirement, or pleaded with the university to waive the requirement. Occasionally, universities had policies that granted waivers or course substitutions. This appears to have been the case at Harvard University, where Kenneth Dinklage, who has been on Harvard's counseling staff for over 30 years, began advising waivers in the 1950s for a select few who showed clear indications of a disability that could not easily be attributed to lack of motivation or overriding anxiety.

With the appearance of the term "learning disabilities" (LDs) in the 1960s and a full implementation of LD services in public schools guaranteed by Public Law 94-142 in 1975 and in colleges and universities by Section 504 of the Vocational Rehabilitation Act of 1973, some of these students now are being diagnosed as learning disabled *because* of foreign language learning difficulties. The Case Study at the end of this chapter featuring Dennis, who was first diagnosed in his senior year of college as having a learning disability, is an example. Furthermore, increasing numbers of students with early identified learning disabilities are now entering our colleges and universities, and some of them are discovering that the foreign language requirement presents a formidable obstacle to college success. What is puzzling to both foreign language educators and special educators who work with the learning disabled is the reason why study of a foreign language poses problems for these students. In this chapter we attempt to answer this question.

---

* The authors contributed equally in the preparation of this chapter.

283

In the first part of the chapter we begin first by examining the nature of a foreign language learning disability (hereafter referred to as FLLD) and its relationship to learning disabilities in general. Since there is little research on this subject, we must rely mostly on what learning disabilities experts have said anecdotally about the problems students with LD have in foreign language classes. Several empirical studies on students with LDs and students who have filed petitions and been granted a waiver/substitution of the foreign language requirement shed some light on the nature of these problems. Second, in order to provide an historical perspective on the increase in awareness of this new disability area, we review for the reader the literature by foreign language educators on "underachievers" or students "at-risk" for difficulty in learning a foreign language. In the 1960s several foreign language educators (Carroll, 1962; Carroll & Sapon, 1959; Pimsleur, 1966b) identified factors that contribute to ease or difficulty of learning a foreign language, and they developed tests to assess foreign language learning aptitude. Foreign language studies on affective variables, the role of intelligence, and learning styles and strategies are also reviewed. Third, our review of the foreign language literature leads into a discussion of current research we are conducting on the language-based nature of a FLLD. Here we present evidence that a foreign language learning disability does not exist in isolation; rather, it exists concomitantly with native language problems. Fourth, we discuss factors related to native language learning that are likely to have an impact on foreign language learning and propose linguistic coding deficits as a possible cause of a FLLD.

In the latter part of the chapter we move into approaches to identify and accommodate students at-risk for learning a foreign language. Instruments for diagnosis of a FLLD and interpretation of diagnostic information are suggested. We then describe approaches for accommodating these students, both in terms of procedures for students to follow in requesting a waiver/substitution of the requirement and of classroom accommodations. Finally, we speculate on teaching methodologies that we believe might enable some students with FLLD to be successful in foreign language classes. At the end of the chapter we return to our initial "why" question with a speculative answer that provides food for thought for future research directions.

Nature of a "Foreign" Language Disability and Its Relationship to Learning Disabilities

Dinklage was the first to liken in writing the relationship of difficulties experienced by students with foreign language problems to a kind of learning disability, dyslexia (Dinklage, 1971). Dinklage described students he had counseled at Harvard, which began granting foreign language waivers over 30 years ago to students who demonstrated clear evidence of having "experienced an inordinate amount of trying and failing" with foreign languages (p. 187). In a paper presented at the Modern Language Association convention in Chicago in 1985, Dinklage reviewed the ideas he had initially presented in 1971 and suggested that these Harvard students "were found to have a disability (e.g., dyslexia) which had caused language learning difficulties in their native tongue" (Dinklage, 1985).

Prior to Dinklage's provocative chapter there were descriptions in the foreign language literature of variables related to success or failure in learning a foreign language (examined later in this chapter). However, the term learning disabilities had not come into vogue, and in all likelihood, foreign language and special educators had not joined forces to communicate about the foreign language problems of students with histories of dyslexia. By the mid-1980s, as students identified as LD in elementary school were entering high school and students identified as LD in high school were entering college, special educators began to recognize that foreign language study was posing particular problems for these students, especially the college-bound, for whom foreign language study was often a deterrent.

It should be noted that special educators teaching in *private* high schools for students with LDs appear to have been aware of the difficulty of foreign languages for their students. This point was revealed to us in 1985 through an informal survey about the foreign language instructional practices in 24 private high schools for students with LDs. Of the 10 responses that were returned, only 1 respondent said that their students take a foreign language. In follow-up calls to several of the schools, we received comments such as, "English is really a foreign language to them;" "our students are not ready to take on foreign language;" and "for the kids we have, English is it . . . they have enough trouble in English."

What, then, is this so-called "disability" for learning a foreign language and what is its relationship to learning disabilities in general? As was mentioned already, some foreign language and special educators suspect that students who have problems learning a foreign language are likely also to have other learning problems; a FLLD is not likely to occur in isolation (Freed, 1987; Ganschow, Sparks, Javorsky, Pohlman, & Bishop-Marbury, 1991; Sparks, Ganschow, & Pohlman, 1989). Special educators know that, for the most part, learning disabilities involve difficulties with one's native language. It would seem logical, then, that students with native language difficulties would be likely to experience problems learning a second language. Nevertheless, this speculation has only begun to be tested empirically. There are other perspectives on foreign language problems to be examined first such as, for example, an historical perspective from the point of view of foreign language educators.

An Historical Perspective on Foreign Language Learning Problems

Foreign language educators are still vigorously investigating the reasons for failure to learn a second language. The literature in the 1950s, 1960s, and early 1970s focused to a great extent on intelligence and aptitude for learning a foreign language. The 1970s and 1980s, however, saw a shift in emphasis from aptitude to affective variables. Most recently, the emphases have been on learning styles, learning strategies, and communication in "natural" contexts. As stated by Horwitz (1990), "The prevailing research issue has changed from 'What is the best method of language teaching?' to 'What is the best method for a particular type of student?'" (p. 15). We briefly review here what foreign language educators have written about the role intelligence, aptitude, affective variables—attitude, motivation, and anxiety—and learning styles and strategies play in students' abilities to learn a foreign language.

Studies attempting to delineate the role of intelligence in learning a foreign language have concluded that language aptitude is relatively independent of measures of general intelligence (Gardner & Lambert, 1965; 1972; Genesse, 1976). Carroll (1985), coauthor of the Modern Language Aptitude Test (MLAT), found only a moderate correlation between intelligence and scores on foreign language aptitude measures. In a large study conducted in Canada, Wesche, Edwards, and Wells (1982) found that intelligence tests measured abilities that were distinctly different from abilities measured on foreign language aptitude tests. A recent study found no significant differences in intelligence between a group of successful foreign language enrolled students and a group of students who had petitioned and received a waiver from the foreign language requirement because of course failure (Ganschow et al., 1991). Thus, foreign language learning problems do not appear to be a result of low intelligence.

Research on foreign language aptitude began with the work of John Carroll (1958; 1962; 1968; 1973; 1981; 1985) who, in conjunction with Stanley Sapon, developed the MLAT (Carroll & Sapon, 1959), a test of foreign language aptitude. Using tests and measurements of cognitive abilities as well as a "work-sample" method (designing of simple learning situations that resemble aspects of second language learning), Carroll found that the following four measures each made significant and independent contributions to the prediction of success in foreign language courses: (1) phonetic coding—the ability to learn, recognize, and remember correspondences between particular sounds of a language and the printed symbols of those sounds; (2) grammatical sensitivity—the ability to recognize the grammatical functions of words and other components of sentences as well as apply grammatical rules; (3) inductive language learning ability—the ability to infer linguistic rules, forms, and patterns from new linguistic content; and (4) rote learning ability—the capacity to quickly learn a large number of phonetic and grammatical associations.

Paul Pimsleur (1966a) also developed a test of foreign language aptitude, the Language Aptitude Battery (LAB). He and his colleagues conducted research with "underachievers," individuals who had significantly less success in foreign language study than in their other courses. Through his work on aptitude for learning a foreign language, Pimsleur identified three variables: (1) verbal intelligence—the familiarity with words in the individual's native language and the ability to manipulate verbal material; (2) motivation—for which a test of interest for foreign language learning was designed; and (3) auditory ability—measured by sound-symbol association items. This latter component, measured by "sound-discrimination" and "sound-symbol" tasks, was hypothesized to be the factor that accounted for differences in language learning ability that could not be explained by low intelligence or a lack of interest (Pimsleur, 1966b; 1968; Pimsleur, Sundland, & McIntyre, 1964).

Data on the predictive validity of aptitude tests, measured by success in foreign language courses, indicate that validity coefficients on the average were .51 but might vary from .20 to .80 depending on the type of sample, type of instruction, and other factors (Carroll, 1985).

Since the 1970s there has been a heavy emphasis in the foreign language literature on studies supporting relationships between affect and foreign language proficiency. Much attention in the foreign language literature has been given to learning styles and learning strategies as well as to affective factors influencing ability to learn a foreign language such as attitude, motivation, and anxiety. Oller and Richards's (1973) book, *Focus on the Learner*, ushered in the "era of the learner" and turned the attention of foreign language teachers and researchers to student learning characteristics that might have an impact on second language acquisition (Horwitz, 1990). The affective areas of particular interest to foreign language researchers have been attitude and motivation for second language learning and anxiety. Generally, the foreign language literature suggests that affective factors play a large part in determining success in foreign language classrooms.

In their book on *Attitude and Motivation in Second Language Learning*, Gardner and Lambert (1972) suggested that students with positive attitudes toward the target language and language group were more successful than students with negative or less positive attitudes. They hypothesized two types of motivation, *instrumental* and *integrative*, and speculated that integratively motivated students who were interested in getting to know members of the target language group were more likely to seek out native speakers, and thus develop better communicative skills than instrumentally motivated students, who, for example, might study a foreign language in order to move ahead in their occupation. In another publication, Gardner (1973) stated that, "it seems clear that attitudinal-motivational characteristics of the student are important in the acquisition of a second language" (p. 244). Another writer (Savignon, 1976) put it more succinctly by saying that, "attitude is the single most important factor in second-language learning" (p. 295).

Although other foreign language educators have not questioned the importance of attitude in learning a foreign language, they have suggested that the instruments used to measure attitude have questionable validity (Oller, 1981; Oller & Perkins, 1978a; 1978b). Another criticism of Gardner's attitudinal-motivational model is its failure to make a causal link between poor attitudes and low motivation and foreign language success or failure (Au, 1988).

Foreign language educators also have examined the role of anxiety on one's ability to learn a foreign language (Curran, 1976; Guiora, 1983; Horwitz, 1990; Horwitz & Young, 1991; Krashen, 1982; Scovel, 1978). Recent proponents have compared foreign language anxiety to anxieties associated with mathematics and test taking (Horwitz, Howitz, & Cope, 1986). Highly anxious foreign language learners are said to have difficulty communicating even the simplest ideas in the second language and report the bodily symptoms and behaviors commonly associated with anxiety. Horwitz and her colleagues, for example, described the subjective behavioral responses of anxious foreign language learners in the following manner: "They have difficulty concentrating, become forgetful, sweat, and have palpitations. They exhibit avoidance behavior such as missing class and postponing homework (p. 126)." However, Sparks and Ganschow (1991) have speculated that affective differences such as anxiety are the result of language learning problems, particularly the phonological (sounds, spelling) and syntactic (grammar, structure) aspects of a language. Other foreign language educators have pointed to the lack of a clearcut relationship between anxiety and foreign language performance (Scovel, 1978).

The role of learning styles and strategies has been given increasing attention in the 1980s as foreign language educators search for techniques to increase the proficiency of students in the classroom. For example, it has been hypothesized that one's language learning style and the strategies one uses to learn a second language have a major effect on a student's ability to learn a foreign language (Moody, 1988; Oxford, 1990). Oxford has suggested that the following "learning style" factors may have an effect on second language learning: field independence-dependence, analytic-global processing, brain hemisphericity, sensory modality preferences, tolerance for ambiguity, and Myers-Briggs dimensions. Although research suggests that language learning style has an influence on a language student's choice of learning strategies, Oxford reported that "causal linkages between strategies and proficiency have not been explored in detail" (p. 37) and that there is no consensus about specific categories of strategies. In addition, little is known about how to measure strategies, and many learning-style and learning-strategy instruments lack adequate validity and reliability. One aspect of learning style, sensory modality testing and teaching, has not been shown to be effective and has generated little empirical support (Arter & Jenkins, 1977; Kampwirth & Bates, 1980; Kavale & Forness, 1987, 1990; Stahl, 1988).

Review of Literature on Foreign Language and Learning Disabilities

A considerably smaller body of evidence exists on the relationship between learning disabilities and foreign language learning. Although Pimsleur and his colleagues did conduct research with "underachievers," they did not hypothesize that these students might possess some type of *disability* specific to learning a foreign language. It was not until Dinklage (1971) wrote a chapter in a book about Harvard students he had counseled for foreign language learning problems that such a suggestion was made. Dinklage reported advising three types of students with histories of foreign language failure: (1) individuals who exhibited poor reading and spelling skills, reversals, and left–right confusions; (2) students who had poor auditory discrimination skills; and (3) students who had poor memory for auditory symbolic materials, often accompanied by poor auditory discrimination. Dinklage, then, actually described cases of students with histories of native oral and written language problems, symptoms commonly associated with dyslexia.

In the 1980s recognition of the foreign language learning difficulties encountered by students with LDs began to appear anecdotally in the literature (see, for example, Cohen, 1983; Demuth & Smith, 1987; Fisher, 1986; Ganschow & Sparks, 1986; 1987; Ganschow, Myer, & Roeger, 1989; Geschwind, 1985; Keeney & Smith, 1984; Kenneweg, 1988; Lefebvre, 1984; Lerner, Ganschow, & Sparks, 1991; Levine, 1987; Myer & Ganschow, 1988; Myer, Ganschow, Sparks, & Kenneweg, 1989; Pompian, 1986; Sparks, Ganschow, & Pohlman, 1989; Sparks, Javorsky, & Ganschow, 1990; Vogel, 1988). These anecdotal references suggested that students with LD were encountering substantial difficulty in foreign language courses. In several articles there was mention of a number of college students being referred for learning disabilities evaluation after college entry primarily because of difficulties experienced in foreign language courses (Lefebvre, 1984; Pompian, 1986; Sparks, Ganschow, & Pohlman, 1989).

To date, few empirical studies have been conducted on the foreign language learning abilities of students with LDs. The first reported study on identified students with LDs in relation to foreign language aptitude was conducted by Gajar (1987), who compared the performance between a group of Penn State students with LDs and foreign language enrolled students on the MLAT. Her results showed that students with LDs exhibited significantly lower performance on all five of the MLAT subtests. Gajar reported that Subtest IV, which measures sensitivity to grammatical structure, and Subtest V, which measures the listening rote memory aspects of learning a foreign language, were perhaps the best predictors of foreign language aptitude.

A recent study conducted by the authors and colleagues (Ganschow et al., 1991) compared the performance of successful and unsuccessful foreign language learners on several variables including intelligence, foreign language aptitude, and native oral and written language skills. The students, 30 college-level juniors and seniors, consisted of two groups: Successful foreign language learners who had received an A or B in at least two semesters of a foreign language, and petition students, who had filed petitions and been granted permission from their university to substitute another course for the foreign language requirement because of previous course failures. Students were matched for sex and year in college. Results of IQ testing showed no differences between the groups, but the petition students scored significantly poorer on the MLAT Short and Long Forms and the five MLAT subtests, supporting Gajar's (1987) findings. Likewise, performance on written and oral native language tests showed significant differences on measures of word identification, phonology, spelling, and grammar. No differences were found on measures of reading comprehension or vocabulary. Results suggested that the petition students had a relative weakness in the phonological and syntactic components of their native language, whereas the semantic component, measured by tasks involving reading comprehension and vocabulary, appeared relatively intact. This finding supported earlier case study observations by the authors (Sparks et al., 1989) and were consistent with the findings of Vellutino and Scanlon (1986), who found that poor readers have particular difficulties with the phonological and syntactic components of language. The authors suggested that petition students appeared to have subtle native language difficulties similar to the language problems of students currently identified as LD. This finding reinforced other recent evidence supporting the language difficulties of college-age students with LD (Morris & Leuenberger, 1990).

In an attempt to investigate affective characteristics of foreign language learners with LDs, the authors and a colleague recently completed a study comparing the self-perceptions of students with and without LD about foreign language courses (Javorsky, Sparks, & Ganschow, 1992). The students with LDs ($N = 60$), attending nine different universities, were receiving services from their respective institutions and had taken at least one semester of foreign language prior to or during college. The comparison group ($N = 144$) was enrolled in introductory Spanish courses at a Midwestern University. Demographic data indicated little or no differences in self-reported GPA, SAT, or ACT scores. The mean Full Scale IQ of the LD group was 110 (range = 87–127). Both groups completed an author-designed questionnaire that measured students' perceptions about their foreign language learning history; their attitudes toward foreign language learning situations, foreign language academic and content mastery skills, and foreign language tests and testing situations; and their instructional practices and modifications in the foreign language course. Results indicated that the college students with LDs perceived themselves as less capable and possessing fewer skills to master the oral and written language demands of foreign language courses. No differences in motivation to learn a foreign language were found between the two groups, but students with LDs felt more anxious when asked to perform or study the second language. The findings provided preliminary support for our speculation that the foreign language learning problems experienced by students with LDs are not related to attitude and motivation. We also speculated that the oral and written language problems of students with LDs most likely affected their ability to learn a foreign language, which in turn caused undue anxiety. Anxiety, then, might not be the *cause* of foreign language failure but could be correlated negatively with performance in the second language because of the difficulty that students with LDs have with native oral and written language tasks (i.e., the higher the anxiety, the lower the performance).

In a recent study by the authors and colleagues (Sparks, Ganschow, Javorsky, Pohlman, & Patton, 1992a) a battery of native oral and written language measures and a foreign language aptitude test (MLAT) were administered to high-school students determined as "low-risk" and "high-risk" for learning a foreign language and students currently receiving LD services in school. All three groups were enrolled in first-year foreign language courses. "Low-risk" and "high-risk" students were identified by means of a questionnaire designed by the authors (Ganschow & Sparks, 1991; Sparks & Ganschow, 1992a), by first quarter grades in the foreign language course, and by teacher recommendation. Results indicated significant differences between the low-risk and high-risk groups and the low-risk and LD groups on native language measures of reading, spelling (phonology) and written grammar (syntax) and on all subtests (as well as the total test score) of the MLAT (Carroll & Sapon, 1959). However, no significant differences were found between these groups on measures of picture vocabulary, antonyms–synonyms, and reading comprehension (semantics). Significant differences were found between the high-risk and students with LDs only on measures of word recognition and spelling, but no significant differences were found on most phonological, as well as all syntactic, semantic, and rote memory tasks. Also, no significant differences between high-risk and LD groups were found on any of the MLAT subtests or the Short and Long Forms. These findings suggested that both high-risk (non-LD) students and students with LDs share deficits in the phonological, syntactic, and semantic "codes" of their native language, which are reflected in foreign language learning difficulties. The literature on foreign language and learning disabilities, then, supports the idea that basic *aptitude* for language may play an important role in the learning of a foreign language.

Linguistic Coding Deficit Hypothesis

Findings in the learning disabilities literature led us to hypothesize that there may be a connection between first and second language learning problems experienced by students with LDs (Sparks & Ganschow, 1991; Sparks, Ganschow, & Pohlman, 1989). We have called this the "linguistic coding deficit hypothesis," a term borrowed from Vellutino and Scanlon's (1986) work with children who have reading disabilities. The "linguistic coding deficit hypothesis" assumes that foreign language learning, an attempt to learn language, is enhanced or limited by the degree to which students have control over the phonological, syntactic, and semantic components of their native language. A deficiency in one or more of the components is likely to affect the student's ability to learn a foreign language. Memory differences may further hinder a student's ability to gain access to the codes. While many students with LDs, as well as other students with subtle language learning differences, have developed compensatory strategies to deal successfully with their native language, these strategies become less functional and, perhaps, inoperable when the students are confronted with a foreign language and its new and unfamiliar linguistic coding system. Thus, in our view, it is the inefficiency of the codes that causes individual differences in the acquisition of a foreign language. Low motivation, negative attitudes, or high levels of anxiety are probably side effects, the result of deficiencies in the linguistic codes of a student's native language. In turn, high motivation, positive attitudes, and lower levels of anxiety are the result of an efficient linguistic coding system. How, then, does one determine whether these students have linguistic coding deficits sufficient to warrant a waiver or substitution for the foreign language requirement?

Evaluation of Individuals with Foreign Language Learning Problems

Most college and university policies recommend or require the diagnosis of a learning disability in order for students to be allowed to substitute courses or receive a waiver of the foreign language requirement (Keeney & Smith, 1984; Ganschow et al., 1989; Philips, Ganschow, &

Anderson, 1991). Although the process of evaluation is *not* undertaken primarily for this purpose, such policies make it necessary to consider assessment tools other than self-reported questionnaires, GPAs, and a foreign language aptitude battery. The diagnostician must recognize that assessment and subsequent documentation may be difficult because these students usually have compensated for their learning problems, as indicated by their relative success in managing the rigors of a postsecondary education.

A comprehensive evaluation for diagnosis of a FLLD involves these components: (1) a review of the student's developmental and family learning history; (2) a review of the student's elementary and secondary school learning history and academic transcripts; (3) a review of the student's foreign language learning history; (4) administration of specific standardized measures of intelligence, language, and academic achievement; and (5) nonstandardized assessment instruments. In keeping with our hypothesis of a linguistic coding deficit, we recommend that the examiner(s) obtain information that has the potential to reveal subtle and/or overt oral and/or written language deficits. Because assessment for LD is covered elsewhere in this volume, we will focus here primarily on measures that are likely to be related to foreign language learning.

Students who exhibit subtle foreign language learning difficulties often have histories of delayed development of speech and subtle or overt language problems. These early speech and language problems are often a precursor to later reading, spelling, and writing difficulties (Catts & Kamhi, 1986; 1987) and can result in subtle, and often undetected, problems in reading comprehension, listening comprehension, and oral and written expression. The student's developmental and family learning history should be obtained through a direct interview with the student with information provided in addition by parents, if possible.

A review of the student's elementary, high-school, and college transcripts is helpful in detecting a FLLD. Usually the student will have received low grades in courses that involved large amounts of reading and writing (e.g., social studies) or in courses that directly involved oral and written language (English). Elementary school transcripts in the primary grades might reveal low or failing grades in reading and spelling. Teacher comments written on the report card might include "poor word attack," "weak in phonics," "needs to study spelling more," or "can't comprehend what is read."

Reviewing the student's previous grades in foreign language courses and interviewing the student about his or her difficulties in foreign language classes are essential. Often the student initially did not fail the foreign language course but, like Pimsleur's "underachievers," obtained a low grade (C or D) while earning As and Bs in most other courses. Some students relate that they can memorize enough vocabulary words and grammar rules to pass the first semester, especially if they had taken the same language previously in high school. When the amount of information begins to accumulate, however, students find that rote memorization is not sufficient and their grades decline. A few students continue to maintain at least average grades by rote memorization, combined with an extraordinary amount of studying, often at the expense of grades in other courses.

In assessing a student for a FLLD, we recommend that a thorough psychoeducational evaluation should include instruments that test oral and written native language skills as well as foreign language aptitude. We would caution examiners, though, that there are few standardized diagnostic oral language tests designed for young adults (Vogel, 1985). Examiners also should note that these students seldom have a global language deficit; rather, they are likely to have specific deficits in the phonological, syntactic, and/or semantic "codes" of language (Sparks et al., 1989; see also Sparks & Ganschow, 1992b for a discussion of "prototypes" of students with specific linguistic coding deficits). A thorough evaluation is one that will tap each of these components. In our view, then, four types of tests should be administered: (1) intelligence; (2) academic achievement; (3) language processing; and (4) foreign language aptitude. Because intelligence and academic achievement are discussed elsewhere in this book, we will focus our attention only on suggested tests to measure language processing and foreign language aptitude. A suggested comprehensive battery of tests for the identification of a foreign language learning disability is presented in Appendix 12.1 and Appendix 12.2. Appendix 12.1 describes the instruments and Appendix 12.2 shows the areas covered by each assessment measure and the corresponding linguistic codes (see also Sparks, Ganschow, & Javorsky).

Language Processing

Tests in which a student demonstrates abilities in the processing of phonological, syntactic, or semantic information can be very helpful in analyzing the efficiency of the linguistic codes. Because of recent findings that weak phonological skills affect achievement in the first or second semester of a foreign language course (Ganschow, Sparks, Javorsky, Pohlman, & Bishop-Marbury, 1991; Sparks, Ganschow, & Pohlman, 1989; Sparks, Ganschow, Javorsky, Pohlman, & Patton, 1992a,b), subtests from the Goldman-Fristoe-Woodcock (GFW) Sound-Symbol Tests (Sound Blending; Spelling of Sounds) (Goldman, Fristoe, & Woodcock, 1974) can be particularly helpful, especially when the results are compared with the Woodcock-Johnson Psycho-Educational Battery (WJPEB) (Woodcock & Johnson, 1977), the Woodcock Reading Mastery Test-Revised Word Attack subtests (WRMT-R) (Woodcock, 1987), and the Wide Range Achievement Test-Revised (WRAT-R) (Jastak &

Wilkinson, 1984) Spelling subtest. We have also experimented with a phoneme segmentation task (Sparks, Ganschow, Javorsky, Pohlman, & Patton, 1992a,b) in order to determine whether this skill, along with other phonological awareness tasks, might be helpful in isolating phonological problems. Instruments such as the Test of Written Language-2 (TOWL-2) (Hammill & Larsen, 1988), the Test of Language Competence-Expanded Edition (TLC-E) (Wiig & Secord, 1989), and the Test of Adolescent Language-2 (TOAL-2) (Hammill, Brown, Larsen, & Wiederholt, 1987) could be useful in pinpointing syntactic and/or semantic problems. (These three tests are not normed on young adults.) Vocabulary tests such as the Peabody Picture Vocabulary Test-R (PPVT-R) (Dunn & Dunn, 1981) or WJPEB Picture Vocabulary and Antonyms–Synonyms subtests give further information about semantic skills. Testing in short-term auditory memory (e.g., memory for words or sentences), using the WJPEB Memory Cluster, might be very useful in determining the efficiency of a student's rote memory ability, an important variable in foreign language learning identified by Carroll (1981; 1985).

Foreign Language Aptitude

A test of foreign language aptitude, such as the MLAT or the LAB, should be administered routinely as a component of a thorough evaluation for second language learning problems. Although the MLAT yields only a total test score for both the Long and Short forms, the diagnostician should be aware that each of the five subtests measures different aspects of second language learning abilities. Number Learning (Subtest I) and Paired Associates (Subtest V) appear to measure aspects of rote learning and rote memory. (Number Learning may also tap phonological ability.) Phonetic Script (Subtest II) seems to be a direct measure of phonetic coding ability. Spelling Clues (Subtest III) appears to measure phonetic coding ability but is also a "disguised" vocabulary test (Carroll, 1981; 1985). Words in Sentences (Subtest IV) is a test of grammatical sensitivity. The diagnostician who is knowledgeable about the nature of these subtests and the impact of language learning differences can compare a student's performance on the phonological, syntactic, and semantic components of the MLAT with performance in similar linguistic codes on the oral and written native language measures described above.

Implications for Services

Two kinds of accommodations are currently available for students with FLLD. The extreme option is waiver or substitution. The less extreme is within-class accommodations.

Foreign Language Course Waivers or Substitutions

Increasing numbers of colleges and universities are now beginning to grant waivers or course substitutions for the foreign language requirement for students with identified LD (Ganschow, et al., 1989; Ganschow & Myer, 1992; Keeney & Smith, 1984). Procedures for initiating this procedure are complicated (Freed, 1987; Philips, Ganschow, & Anderson, 1991), and it is difficult to say at this time who should and who should not seek this option (Ganschow & Sparks, 1987). Levine (1987), for example, made this observation on who should be exempt:

Some students indeed seem unable to learn a second language. Often, they spend numerous hours struggling in vain. Ultimately, the wasted time and anxiety begin to erode other subject areas as well. At some point, it seems appropriate to call a halt to such a losing effort. It is certainly not worth sacrificing a child's academic career for the sake of a foreign language. (p. 382)

For information on the petitioning process or on establishing policies for foreign language course waivers or substitutions, the reader is referred to Freed (1987), Ganschow & Sparks (1987), and Philips, et al. (1991), as this information is beyond the scope of this chapter.

Two surveys on foreign language petition policies and procedures at colleges and universities were conducted by Ganschow, Myer, and Roeger (1989) and by Ganschow and Myer (1992). There were several important findings from these surveys that have implications for students with FLLD. Respondents to the first survey were comprised primarily of institutions with identified LD support personnel. Of the responding institutions to this survey (1/3 response rate), 60% said that they required a foreign language in at least one program area and 18% in all areas (total = 78%). About 30% of the responding institutions said a foreign language was necessary prior to college. Seventy-four percent of the colleges and universities indicated that they had either a formal or informal policy or procedure for waiver/substitution of the foreign language requirement. However, the nature of this policy or procedure was not spelled out in the first survey.

In an attempt to obtain a more generalizable sample and to find out more about institutions' petition policies and procedures, in 1989 a second survey (Ganschow & Myer, 1992) was sent to the academic deans of 600 institutions of four-year colleges obtained through a statistically randomized sample. Two hundred and eighty-two responses were received, however, 75 respondents did not complete the survey because a FL was not required at their institution. Of the 207 who completed the survey, 40% said their institution had no policy or procedure; 37% said that petitions were part of the general petitioning process; only a small percent (13%) said they had a specific petitioning process designed primarily for foreign language course waivers or substitutions. An important implication of this finding is the fact that unless someone on campus makes the policy known to foreign language faculty, LD support staff, or the students themselves, it is not likely to be used. Lack of awareness of the availability of the petition process is a problem in some colleges and universities (Philips et al., 1991). Evidence of a specific handicap was required by 80% and desirable by an additional 15% in the 1987 survey; in the 1989 survey, evidence was required by 61% and found desirable by an additional 24%. Thirty-seven percent in the 1987 survey (23% in the 1989 survey) recommended that the MLAT be used to provide evidence regarding a foreign language deficit. For information about other types of proof that were deemed to be highly desirable to support a foreign language disability, the reader is referred to Ganschow, Myer, and Roeger (1989).

The findings of these surveys have some important implications for students with FLLD and for diagnostic service providers who work with these students.

Take a Foreign Language Early

Given the current lack of knowledge about who can and who cannot succeed in a foreign language, we recommend that the student study a foreign language in high school (or earlier). The LD teacher should provide assistance to the foreign language instructor on strategies to use with the student, and the student with LDs should inform the teacher as to what seems to work best and least well for learning. Only after a reasonable attempt should the student consider dropping the language.

Find out About the College's Foreign Language Requirements and Waiver or Substitution Policy

Should the student have discovered early that she or he cannot succeed in a foreign language, that student should examine the chosen university's foreign language requirements. Some will not require a second language (Agresto, 1985); others will require one year, and some, especially in Arts and Sciences related fields, will require two years. Once the requirement is determined, the student will want to find out whether the institution permits waivers or substitutions for identified disabilities and whether special support or accommodations for foreign language study are provided. For this information, the student should talk to the LD support person at the institution or inquire at the Academic Dean's office. As a last resort, the unsuccessful foreign language learner may have to apply to a college that either does not have a foreign language requirement or that has an appropriate support system and petition policies and procedures in place.

Repeat the Same Language in College

If the student has had some success with a foreign language in high school, we recommend repeating that language in college. Generally, a college-level semester foreign language course is about the equivalent of two semesters of that same language in high school. We find that for some students, the repetition enables them to succeed in the first semester, and although many flounder in the second semester of the language, they at least have had some exposure to the culture. Furthermore, successful completion of one semester of the foreign language will most likely result in one less make-up course if a course substitution is granted.

Gather Supportive Documentation

The student who might need to petition for a foreign language course waiver or substitution should work with the LD specialist at the time of foreign language failure (e.g., in high school) to document the history of difficulties. In general, the college will want a current (within two years) psychoeducational evaluation verifying the learning disability (though a few colleges, especially those with specialized LD programs, prefer to do their own testing).

Start the Petition Process Early

The student is cautioned not to wait until the junior or senior year to petition, as the process is time-consuming and the student may be required to take the same number of course substitutes as are required to complete the language requirement.

Foreign Language Classroom Accommodations

The following classroom accommodations should be considered for students with FLLD: (1) providing compensatory strategies; (2) modifying pace of instruction; (3) providing tutorial support; (4) presenting materials both visually and auditorily simultaneously; and (5) monitoring the choice of language to be learned. Since there is little research on the effectiveness of these classroom accommodations, we are basing them on our experiences to date with at-risk learners and our knowledge of the native language accommodations and strategies found in the literature to be helpful to students with identified LDs.

Compensatory Strategies

In terms of compensatory strategies, Dinklage (1971; 1985) speculated that students with audiolingual deficits, that is, difficulties "hearing" the language, were likely to experience some success in learning a foreign language if they were allowed to read the language rather than being required to participate in oral communication settings. In fact, Dinklage suggested that many of the problems experienced by the Harvard students he counseled were due to a change from a reading emphasis to an oral communication approach in foreign language instruction, a change that occurred after World War II and is emphasized today even more, with a recent focus on "natural" communication contexts (MLA Newsletter, 1989). In our experience, we have come across one or two students with phonological problems who managed to be successful in classes where they were allowed to be tested on their ability to read the language rather than speak and/or listen to it. One case, in particular, involved a student who was tested as having more than a 2 standard deviation discrepancy between cognitive functioning and performance on tests of rote memory, phonological tasks, and listening comprehension. Nevertheless, this student managed to complete four semesters of German. In interviewing the student about his success, he related the strategies he had used to be successful. These included his personal contact with a professor, with whom he remained close throughout the course of his foreign language study and who had permitted him to take his tests on the written aspects of the language.

Students with LDs themselves have reported compensatory strategies that may be useful in foreign language classes. In a recent inventory of student attitudes about foreign language and their learning needs (Javorsky et al., 1992, in press), some interesting differences between a group of foreign language enrolled students and identified students with LD who had taken a foreign language emerged. On a 5-point scale ($1 =$ strongly agree to $5 =$ strongly disagree), significant differences favoring students with LDs were reported on the following: (1) helpfulness of sitting in front of the room ($p = .0001$); (2) making the syllabus available before class ($p = .007$); (3) taking untimed tests ($p = .0001$); (4) taking exams in a separate room ($p = .0001$); and (5) taking exams orally ($p = .0001$). While taking oral exams may seem contradictory (in that the student has to listen and speak), this format can be valuable because it is usually done on a one-to-one basis with extra time allowances. Audiotapes were not found to be particularly helpful in learning the language by either group (Xs were in the average range), although foreign language enrolled students appeared to find audiotapes some-what more helpful than students with LDs ($p = .03$). Both groups saw some benefit in using visual aids, having assignments both orally and in writing, having one-to-one sessions with a tutor or instructor, and being provided with a study guide. Both groups indicated that living in a foreign country would be highly beneficial (X {combined groups} $= 1.65$).

Other accommodations frequently mentioned in the LD college literature (see, e.g., Mangrum & Strichart, 1988; Vogel, 1985; 1986) include allowances for misspellings and preferential scheduling with a professor known for being understanding of the problems of students with LDs and other learning difficulties.

Pace of Instruction

Some of the students we have observed say that they feel they could have passed the foreign language if it had been taught at a slower pace. Indeed, these students probably experienced some limited success in high-school foreign language classes, which generally move at a slower pace than the college-level classes. In fact, these students sometimes are able to complete successfully the first semester of the same language in college *because* it is a repetition of what they learned over several years in high school. Studies of students with LDs indicate clearly that these students benefit from a slower pace of instruction with more repetition (Mangrum & Strichart, 1988; Vogel, 1985; 1986). In the foreign language classes designed specifically for students with LDs we have visited, pace of learning, with time for drill and practice, has been an essential ingredient for success. Pacing of vocabulary learning (e.g., providing short drills over a few words rather than lengthy drills over many words) may lead to better long-term retention of foreign language vocabulary (Levine, 1987). The problem in varying the pace of instruction in the regular foreign language classroom is that this is difficult to do with a class of 30 to 35 students. Slowing the pace of instruction is best accomplished in situations where students needing a slower pace are grouped together for instruction. However, grouping of individuals according to ability remains controversial in almost any instructional situation, including foreign language classrooms (Wesche, 1981).

Tutorial Support

Surveys of types of foreign language instructional support in colleges and universities indicate that tutoring is the most frequent type of support (Ganschow et al., 1989). In the student attitude survey mentioned earlier, students with LDs (as well as foreign language enrolled students) indicated that one-to-one tutoring would be helpful to them ($X = 2.16$ on a 5-point scale). We recommend that at-risk students seek tutoring at the first sign of a problem in the language and that a concerted attempt be made to work with the tutor. Documentation should be kept of these tutoring sessions, as the tutor may be called upon later to support the student's effort, should a waiver of the requirement be sought. We suggest that the LD specialist in a school system work with the tutor to devise instructional approaches that are likely to be successful for that student.

Simultaneous Visual and Auditory Presentations

Another accommodation that could prove beneficial in regular foreign language classrooms is simultaneous auditory and visual presentation of materials (Bilyeu, 1982). Here the instructor makes a point of highlighting spoken words and phrases through their written representation. For example, students might be presented with simple written "scripts" to follow as the instructor verbalizes the language structures. Overhead projectors could be used so that students can see highlights of what is being said as the instructor points to the words as they are spoken. Repetition of common phrases, once learned through visual/auditory associations, can be phased out visually. The instructor also can highlight the word in speech by accentuating each separate word in a phrase or sentence and, when introducing new words, accentuating each syllable. Opportunities should be utilized to make students aware of the redundancy of language through conscious attention to the relationship of more familiar root words to less familar derivatives, a metacognitive skill that is frequently lacking in students with language difficulties (Leong, 1989; Henry, 1988). For example, in the German word *Fernsehen*—(television), students familiar with the meaning of the words *sehen* (to see) and *fern* (far) are more likely to associate *Fernsehen* with television if parts of the word are brought to their conscious attention.

Language of Instruction

It has been suggested that for students with pronounced phonological difficulties, a language that relies primarily upon a different rule system (e.g., logographic as in Chinese) or upon reading (rather than oral communication, e.g., Latin) might be considered (Fisher, 1986; Ganschow & Sparks, 1987). The regularity of the sound system in Spanish is said to make it an appropriate language for using systematic phonics instruction (Goyen, 1989). The study of Latin is said to improve spelling performance (for non-LD learners) because of its focus on derivatives (Carlisle & Liberman, 1989; Robinson & Hesse, 1981). Perhaps because of the number of English words derived from Latin, study of this language might be helpful in developing vocabulary and spelling skills for students with LDs. However, the study of Latin might be impossible for students who have great difficulty grasping patterns of roots, suffixes, and prefixes (Levine, 1987). Experimental Latin and Spanish classes for at-risk students are in progress at the University of Colorado at Boulder (Downey, Bever, & Hill, 1991), where faculty are working on differential identification procedures.

Teaching Methodologies

When surveying foreign language teaching methodologies, we found as many different approaches to teaching a second language as there are methodologies to teach students to read and write their native language. Elson (1983) and Daggett (1986) have reviewed the many and varied approaches to second language teaching, citing methods that range from *grammar translation*, or those that focus on the second language in its written form and teach the course in the student's native language, to the *direct* method, in which the learner is exposed to the second language in oral form with little or no teaching done in the student's native language. The *audiolingual* approach attempts to inculcate the foreign language through overlearning and extensive use of oral language with little or no use of the student's native language during instruction. The *communicative* approach utilizes authentic materials and situations and emphasizes the communicative needs of the learner. The *total physical response* approach purports to use "right-brain" learning and emphasizes listening comprehension combined with the physical act of doing what has been said to illustrate the connection between language and context. Another approach, *suggestopedia*, recommends learning in a relaxed environment to help the student overcome psychological barriers in order to enhance competence in the second language. *Community language learning* permits students to design the course syllabus based on their self-expressed needs. Listening and speaking are emphasized, and the student's feelings are a prime consideration of the instructor.

Traditionally, achievement in a foreign language has been viewed in terms of knowledge of the structure of the language, such as vocabulary, grammar, and pronunciation or proficiency in the four basic skills, that is, listening, speaking, reading, and writing (Gardner, 1985). Recently, however, newer goals have placed emphasis on communicative proficiency or communicative competence, rather than grammatical accuracy (Barnett, 1988; Brumfit & Johnson, 1979). Familiarity with the second language culture and the development of positive attitudes towards speakers of that language have also been goals of the newer methods (Gardner, 1985).

As learning disability specialists, we have been puzzled by the focus in the foreign language literature on affective, learning styles, and personality variables and the corresponding lack of attention to the native oral and written language skills that the learner *brings into* the foreign language classroom. Learning disabilities professionals are cognizant of the uneven developmental patterns between and within students' oral and written language skills. However, second language educators appear to assume that "it is common knowledge that everyone learns his first language with a fair degree of success" and are troubled when "this innate ability seem(s) to decline for some when second language learning is the task" (Rubin, 1975, p. 41). Neufeld (1974) has claimed that individual differences in various aspects of language development are "mere frills," but Gardner (1985) has acknowledged that "there are extensive individual differences (in native language) . . . and such differences have considerable implications for communication" (p. 24). In our view, teaching methodologies must take into account individual differences in accessibility of the phonological, syntactic, and semantic codes as well as possible difficulties in memory for language symbols.

When speculating on appropriate second language methodologies for students with LDs, then, what approaches might work best, especially if individualized instruction is not available? The foreign language learning difficulties of students who otherwise had few problems succeeding in school have led us to speculate that students may have native language skill difficulties. The great majority of students whom we have evaluated have in common subtle problems with the phonological aspects of their native language. These students apparently have developed strategies that allow them to compensate when dealing with the oral and written demands of the native language. These strategies become unworkable, however, when the students encounter a new and unfamiliar linguistic coding system such as a foreign language. In a sense, the students have reentered an environment similar to the one they experienced when learning to listen, speak, read, and write their native language—a language in which they still experience subtle difficulties.

Given the subtle and/or severe language problems experienced by students with LDs, is there a methodology that has been shown to work, or at least hold promise, when teaching students with LDs a second language? Cummins (1984) has discussed the success of immersion school settings for children with LDs in Canada. Immersion as a methodology in the United States, though, is not a viable option for most students, and we question whether it would work for some of our adults with severe learning disabilities (Sparks & Ganschow, 1991). A whole class approach tends to be the only realistic option in most secondary and postsecondary schools. This does not mean, however, that students must be grouped in such a way that some will be unduly hampered by a slow or fast pace. Although grouping of individuals according to foreign language learning ability or aptitude is controversial (Wesche, 1981), this approach has the potential to match foreign language instruction with students' strengths and weaknesses in the linguistic codes and might allow for previous content to be mastered before moving on to more difficult material.

To date, in our search for viable approaches to foreign language study of students with LDs, we have encountered only one method that takes into account their phonological deficits and need for direct systematic instruction in the linguistic codes. The Orton-Gillingham (O-G) method for teaching reading and spelling (Gillingham & Stillman, 1960) has been modified and applied by two teachers at private high schools in order to teach Spanish to students with LDs and others at-risk for learning a second language. The O-G method stresses decoding of the student's native language via a phonetic, structured language approach utilizing multi-sensory input, thereby allowing the learner to hear, see, and write the language simultaneously. The method, adapted for foreign language instruction by Silvia Kenneweg of Hathaway Brown School in Cleveland,

OH, and Karen Miller of St. Paul's School for Girls in Baltimore, MD, introduces the sounds (phonology) of the second language (Spanish) through a multisensory approach. The new sounds are immediately synthesized into words that contain other sounds that the students have previously learned. The words are then used to build sentences that the students hear spoken by the teacher. The students repeat, then write (on the board or on paper) the sentence, and say the words aloud simultaneously. The teaching of phonology is complemented by the careful sequencing of materials, controlled pacing of presentations, oral practice, board drills, flash cards, filmstrips, and the integration of reading, spelling, and writing (Myer et al., 1989; Sparks, Ganschow, Kenneweg, & Miller, 1991). Kenneweg (1988) described the process this way:

In order for a student to learn sounds and vocabularly, he or she must first hear and repeat; second, must see them in their written form: and third, write and pronounce them simultaneously. Thus, the auditory learning pathway is reinforced through visual and kinesthetic channels complementing and filling any gaps in the learning process. (p. 17)

If such an approach sounds familiar to LD specialists, it is because similar methodologies have been recommended to teach reading and spelling to students with LDs Williams (1987), for example, wrote that such programs subscribe to the "direct and explicit teaching of phonics in a systematic, step-by-step structured manner. Only a small amount of material is presented at any one time; learning to mastery is deemed important, which requires a great deal of practice and review; and a multisensory approach is taken" (p. 26). A similar program of classroom adjustments for individuals with "earlier school difficulties with reading and spelling" and lacking in Carroll's "phonetic coding" skills was advocated by another foreign language educator (Wesche, 1981) who suggested:

... slower pacing and frequent repetition of auditory material (including deemphasis of tape-recorded materials); ... highly structured, incremental presentation of new material; frequent review of previously learned material; attention at every stage of presentation to ensure that students have thoroughly understood; and multisensory (including written) presentation and reinforcement of material. (p. 131)

This approach appeals to us not only because of our experiences in teaching students with LDs to read and write their native language but also because it meshes well with our linguistic coding deficit hypothesis, which suggests that students with phonological deficits may require explicit teaching of the phonology of the second language.

Recently, research on precursors of reading disability has begun to converge upon a small set of skills that play a part in future reading performance, the ability to access the phonological code in oral language. The majority of students with LDs have reading problems, and the majority of those reading problems seem to be caused at least in part by deficiencies in phonology (and its written counterpart, orthography—or letter/sound correspondences) (Adams, 1990; Stanovich, 1982; 1986). While many college students with LDs have learned to compensate well enough to read and write their native language, they may not have mastered thoroughly all of the principles of the phonological/orthographic codes. We have proposed elsewhere that those problems that interfered with the learning of the students' native language will now interfere with the acquisition of a second language (Ganschow et al., 1991; Javorsky et al., 1992; Sparks & Ganschow, 1991; Sparks et al., 1989; Sparks et al., 1990). Students with difficulties in the syntactic and semantic codes are, most likely, a numerically smaller, albeit overlapping, group. Whereas some may not need direct teaching of the second language phonological code, we would speculate that a multisensory approach may also prove beneficial because of its emphasis on "seeing" the elements of language through writing and its focus on helping learners consciously attend to language elements (Bialystok & Ryan, 1985). In particular, we would argue, these students need systematic practice and review in storing orthographic images and mastering the morphological and syntactic rule structures of the foreign language.

Another alternative found in the foreign language literature is a program that has been used with a group of at-risk foreign language learners at Boston University (Demuth & Smith, 1987). Rather than teach the phonology and grammar of the foreign language per se, the Department of Modern Languages and Literature elected to provide these students with a native language learning course that offered instruction in the basic elements of linguistic structure, including English phonetics, the "phonological process," morphology, and syntax. In essence, the students were "learning about language without having the pressure to perform in it" (p. 74). One goal of the course was to allow students to develop a "metalinguistic awareness" of language structure and usage. Pre- and post-test MLAT scores indicated that some students made widespread and dramatic gains. The authors speculated that "students with a strong grounding in their native language will be more successful at transferring those skills to the learning of another language" (p. 77).

The two approaches presented here follow a basic premise: Students with foreign language learning difficulties are those who have native language learning problems. Furthermore, phonology and syntax must be taught directly and systematically. Although it will take more time and require explicit instruction for students with LDs and other at-risk language learners, these approaches hold promise for allowing at-risk learners to succeed in foreign language courses.

Future Research Directions

At the beginning of the chapter, we raised the question of why a foreign language poses problems for most students with LD, and we promised to provide a tentative answer that would provide food for thought for future research directions.

Perhaps we might answer this question by explaining to our readers why two special educators who work with students with LDs have spent the past half dozen years straying out of the "comfort zone" of the LD research and plunging into the unknown territory of the foreign language literature. Our explanation has to do with what the learning disabilities field has discovered about the "language-based" nature of learning disabilities, about how children acquire the rules of language in their oral and written forms, and how a language system breaks down. It makes sense to us to view foreign language learning in the context of language learning in general. It has been puzzling to us that few second language educators have considered the hypothesis that problems in understanding and using the rule systems governing the mother tongue may have an impact on the learning of a second language. Now, with much research in progress but many questions yet unanswered, we propose that the study of how individuals with native language difficulties acquire a second language will provide us with new insights into the understanding of learning disabilities.

We believe that there is a need for research on the nature of "foreign" language learning disabilities and on ways to accommodate these learners. Numerous questions present themselves, among them, the following:

1) What is the nature of a "foreign" language learning disability and indeed is there such a specific "disability"? If so, at what point does it become a disability and how does one decide this? We are reminded here of Stanovich's (1988) and Shaywitz et al.'s (1992) comparison of reading difficulties (dyslexia) to the concept of obesity. Everyone accepts obesity as a health problem, but because it exists on a continuum, the decision about when obesity becomes injurious to one's health is a medical one. Likewise, a person's facility in learning to read (or learning a foreign language) is not a discrete entity but exists on a graded continuum, and we must rely on experts who are familiar with the "norms" to assist us in determining when a reading difficulty becomes "disabling."

2) What specific accommodations might help students with foreign language learning difficulties to be successful in learning the language? Would some of the accommodations currently recommended, such as individualized instruction, a slower pace, alternative test formats, and so on help these students be successful in today's foreign language classrooms?

3) Would an instructional approach that begins with and incorporates the direct teaching of the phonome-grapheme correspondences provide the foundation for teaching a foreign language to students with phonological deficits? In this chapter we have suggested that specific training using a multisensory, structured language approach, similar to the Orton/Gillingham techniques used for students with dyslexia, might help students to "crack the foreign sound/symbol code" (Kenneweg, 1988; Myer et al., 1989; Sparks et al., 1991; Wesche, 1981). We have also suggested that direct language intervention in the codes of one's native language might help students make the transition to a second language (Demuth & Smith, 1987). There is evidence from a small cadre of teachers who are using this approach with identified students with learning disabilities that it does help them to work through the early stages of learning Spanish. However, further investigation is needed to demonstrate its success empirically.

4) It there an optimal age for learning a second language among students with LDs? We have focused on secondary and adult learning of a second language. Might it be easier for students if they started a second language in elementary school?

5) Would some languages be easier to learn than others? Would choice of language be related to the ease of learning the phonological (orthographic) and syntactic rules of a particular language? For example, might Spanish or Latin, with their regular sound/symbol correspondences, be easier for students than other languages? Would Latin, a language that is primarily read, be easier for these students than a language that is primarily spoken?

6) What is it that foreign language educators really want their learners to do? Attain linguistic competence? Communicative competence? Be exposed to the culture of the language? The structure of a foreign language? What should we reasonably expect students with "foreign" language learning disabilities to learn in a given period of time?

7) Are the "natural" communication approaches recently developed by foreign language educators successful for all students? What is the impact of methodologies that emphasize listening and speaking on students with LDs and nonidentified "at-risk" students who have deficiencies in their linguistic coding systems?

8) Are there alternative, perhaps unconventional, assessment techniques that would assist educators in determining whether students will have difficulties in a second language course? For example, foreign language educators themselves could identify students who are likely to be "unteachable" in typical classroom settings (Levine, 1987). They might personally instruct the at-risk student over several one-to-one sessions to determine whether or not the student has the potential to succeed. If not, the student then would be referred for a psychoeducational

evaluation for a suspected "foreign" language learning disability and appropriate modifications would be implemented.

9) Might there be benefits to grouping students with linguistic coding deficits according to their foreign (and native) language learning aptitude, thereby enabling them to attain some proficiency in a second language? Pilot projects (for example, Demuth & Smith, 1987; Kenneweg, 1988) suggest that this may be the case.

We believe that the study of how students with LDs learn a foreign language provides yet another "window" through which to observe the language skills these individuals use to learn new information. It give us an opportunity to examine language learning in a new context. Their basic native language disabilities have been well compensated for over the years by these bright, motivated students who are working their way through college preparatory programs in high school, college, and sometimes graduate school. Nevertheless, without opportunities to fall back on learned strategies, the native language weaknesses inherent in their mother tongue emerge when these students are faced with the task of learning a foreign language. For the LD specialist, it is back to the drawing board to discover how to help students with LDs conquer yet another stumbling block in their academic career. Until we have validated effective teaching methods for FLLD, some of the recommended modifications may prove effective. When these are not feasible, petition policies and procedures for foreign language waivers or substitutions may need to be available for those with identified FLLD.

Case Study of Student with a Disability for Learning a Foreign Language

Background Information

Dennis, a middle class white male from a small city in the Midwest, was referred for evaluation for a suspected learning disability because of inability to complete the two-year foreign language requirement at the university he was attending. At the time of referral he was a second semester senior (23 years old) majoring in public administration and had completed the first of four semesters of Spanish. Spanish 102, 201, and 202 were the only courses he needed to graduate. Dennis had an overall GPA of 2.1, with a 2.4 in his major, Public Administration. He had graduated in the middle of his high-school class of around 140 students and was attending a Midwestern University with a highly competitive enrollment (Barron's *Profile of American Colleges*, 1988) of about 16,000 students.

Family Background

Dennis came from an upper middle-class family. His father was an executive vice president of a company and had a PhD from a prestigious Eastern University. Dennis's mother had started college but did not finish. His sister and two brothers also had jobs in the business world, and two had graduated from college. Dennis reported that both his mother and father had experienced difficulties with foreign language. His father had received Cs in Latin and Spanish and his mother, Cs and Ds. One of his sisters had been a "whiz in Spanish." One of his two brothers was college educated but had not taken a foreign language. The other had had difficulties in school and had dropped out of college. According to Dennis, all of his siblings had experienced difficulties in math. Dennis indicated that there was no history of medical or developmental difficulties.

Educational History

Dennis's self-reports indicated that he first began having school-related problems in junior high school, where he experienced significant difficulty with French in grades 6–8, resulting in his not taking a foreign language in high school. Dennis began having difficulties with higher level math in high school, where most of his grades were Bs and Cs, but he received Ds in Algebra I, Algebra II, and Physics. In college, his math difficulties continued. He failed intermediate college algebra and calculus and then changed majors in order to avoid the math requirement. When questioned about the nature of his math difficulties, Dennis reported that he "couldn't remember or understand the formulas."

His foreign language difficulties also followed him into college, where he scraped through Spanish 101 with a grade of D because, he reported, it was "a gift from the teacher for extra-credit work." Despite extensive tutoring and working with the professor, he was unable to complete Spanish 102. When asked what it would take to enable him to succeed in learning a foreign language, Dennis replied that he did not think he could learn, even if "dropped in the culture," where he thought he would probably "just survive."

In terms of learning preferences, Dennis indicated that he had "more trouble in a large lecture room" and preferred classes that had discussion groups with "contact between each other . . . teacher involved . . . not just lecture." Dennis stated that he "can't just (learn) through straight lecture because "they're (the teachers) not illustrating . . . I get a picture in my mind." It also "helps me when teachers start writing on the board . . . get idea of what's important." He mentioned that he did all written work on a computer using a spell checker.

Psychometric Profile

Results of a psychological evaluation showed that Dennis had a Full Scale IQ of 121 with a Verbal IQ of 118 and a Performance IQ of 123, placing him in the Superior Range of intelligence. Significant strengths were noted in verbal reasoning and social judgment on the Verbal scales with strengths in nonverbal problem solving on the Performance subtests. A significant weakness was apparent in his fund of general information and a relative weakness was seen in verbal arithmetic.

Results of an educational evaluation showed that Dennis had severe discrepancies of 1.5 to over 2 standard deviations between his ability and achievement in almost all areas tested. On reading measures, Dennis had a Standard Score of 86 on the Wide Range Achievement Test and a 94 on the Reading Cluster of the Woodcock-Johnson Psycho-Educational Battery: Tests of Achievement, with a Standard Score of 83 on the Word Attack subtest. In spelling, Dennis had a Standard Score of 100 on the Wide Range Achievement Test and a 95 on the Goldman-Fristoe-Woodcock Spelling of Sounds subtest. In math, Dennis had a Standard Score of 94 on the Math Cluster of the Woodcock-Johnson Psycho-educational Battery: Tests of Achievement. On the Test of Written Language, Dennis's Written Language Quotient Standard Score was 85. On the Test of Adolescent Language, his Adolescent Language Quotient Standard Score was 95, with a particular weakness in Grammar (Standard Score = 77). (It should be noted that Dennis was above the age criterion for the TOWL and TOAL.) A memory test (Woodcock-Johnson Psycho-Educational Battery, Tests of Cognitive Ability) showed that memory for sentences was a particular problem for Dennis as he obtained a Standard Score of 80, in contrast to memory for numbers (Numbers Reversed), where he achieved a Standard Score of 110. Finally, on the Modern Language Aptitude Test, a test of aptitude for learning a foreign language, Dennis's overall score was at the 15th percentile.

Observed Behaviors

Dennis is a highly personable and attractive young man. His communication skills were well developed and he had considerable self-confidence, despite his academic failures. Particularly noticeable were the richness of his vocabulary and the ease with which he was able to reflect on his own learning. Dennis himself reported strengths in the areas of organization and personal communication. He felt that he has a "natural . . . public presence and enjoys people."

Outcome

Dennis was one of our first referrals for a suspected FLLD in 1984. At that time, relatively unknown to faculty and students, the university was just beginning to establish course substitution procedures. Dennis heard about the process only because we had initiated a research study with the Spanish faculty and one of the professors involved in the study referred him to us. The Spanish professor had been puzzled by Dennis because she had been working with him three to four hours a week, in addition to his receiving peer tutoring three times a week, all to no avail.

When Dennis was advised to be tested for a suspected learning disability, he disappeared, only to return to our office again in 1986 as a senior. (It should be mentioned that these disappearances are not uncommon among previously undiagnosed individuals who are highly motivated and feel that they can "do it" if they work hard enough. Conversations with Dennis had indicated clearly that lack of motivation was not the problem in his case.) Upon his return to our office in 1986, we found that Dennis had passed Spanish 101 with a D, tried and failed second semester Spanish at another university, tried and failed Spanish again in his Junior year, been placed on and removed from academic probation, and changed majors because he could not meet the math requirements for that major.

Dennis agreed to be tested and was evaluated by the second author in the spring of 1987. That spring he was recommended for and was granted a waiver of the foreign language requirement due to a specific learning disability. However, because he had successfully completed only one semester of Spanish, he was asked to make up the foreign language deficiencies with three culture course substitutes: Latin American Studies and history, geography, or anthropology/religion courses related to Spanish-speaking countries. Dennis completed one in the second semester of his senior year. Contrary to most of the students with whom we have come in contact who are granted foreign language petitions, Dennis left school without graduating. Having been presented with a job offer he "couldn't resist," Dennis became gainfully employed in a large business firm. He received three promotions in his first year on the job and is currently a Regional Sales Manager.

Bibliography

Adams, M. (1990). *Beginning to read: Thinking and learning about print*. Cambridge, MA: MIT Press.

Agresto, J. (1985, October 8). *In commemoration of the 20th anniversary of the National Endowment for the Humanities*. Unpublished manuscript. Washington, DC: National Endowment for the Humanities.

Arter, J., & Jenkins, J. (1977). Examining the benefits and prevalence of modality instruction. *Journal of Special Education, 11*, 282–298.

Au, S. (1988). A critical appraisal of Gardner's social-psychological theory of second language (L2) learning. *Language Learning, 38*, 75–100.

Barnett, H. (1988, January). Success with the "new" foreign language learner—dream or reality. *New York State Language Association Bulletin*, 2–4.

Bialystok, E., & Ryan, E. (1985). A metacognitive framework for the development of first and second language skills. In D.L. Forrest-Pressley, G.E. MacKinnon, & T.G. Waller (Eds.), *Metacognition, cognition, and human performance* (Vol. 1). New York: Academic Press.

Bilyeu, E. (1982). *Practice makes closer to perfect: Alternative techniques for teaching foreign languages to learning disabled students in the university*. Fund for the Improvement of Postsecondary Education. (Project #116CH10305). Ellensburg: Central Washington University.

Brumfit, C., & Johnson, K. (Eds.) (1979). *The communicative approach to language teaching*. Oxford: Oxford University Press.

Carlisle, J.F., & Liberman, I.Y. (1989). Does the study of Latin affect spelling proficiency? *Reading and Writing: An Interdisciplinary Journal, 2*, 179–191.

Carroll, J. (1958). A factor analysis of two foreign language aptitude batteries. *The Journal of General Psychology, 59*, 3–19.

Carroll, J. (1962). The prediction of success in intensive foreign language training. In R. Glaser (Ed.), *Training and research in education* (pp. 87–136). Pittsburgh, PA: University of Pittsburgh Press.

Carroll, J. (1968). The psychology of language testing. In A. Davies (Ed.), *Language testing symposium: A linguistic approach* (pp. 46–61) London: Oxford University Press.

Carroll, J. (1973). Implications of aptitude test research and psycholinguistic theory for foreign language teaching. *International Journal of Psycholinguistics, 2*, 5–14.

Carroll, J. (1981). Twenty-five years of research on foreign language aptitude. In K.C. Diller (Ed.), *Individual differences and universals in language learning aptitude* (pp. 83–117). Rowley, MA: Newbury House.

Carroll, J. (1985). Second language abilities. In R. Sternberg (Ed.), *Human abilities: An information processing approach*. (pp. 83–102). New York: Freeman.

Carroll, J., & Sapon, S. (1959). *Modern Language Aptitude Test*. New York: Psychological Corporation.

Catts, H., & Kamhi, A. (1986). The linguistic basis of reading disorders: Implications for the speech-language pathologist. *Language, Speech, and Hearing Services in the Schools, 17*, 329–341.

Catts, H., & Kamhi, A. (1987). The relationship between reading and language disorders: Implications for the speech-language pathologist. *Seminars in Speech and Language, 8*, 377–392.

Cohen, J. (1983). Learning disabilities and the college student: Identification and diagnosis. In M. Sugar (Ed.), *Adolescent psychiatry: Developmental and clinical studies*. (Vol. 2, pp. 177–179). Chicago: University of Chicago press.

Cummins, J. (1984). *Bilingualism and special education: Issues in assessment and pedagogy*. San Diego, CA: College-Hill Press.

Curran, C. (1976). *Counseling-learning in second language*. Apple River, IL: Apple River.

Daggett, G. (1986). Eight approaches to language teaching. *ERIC Clearinghouse on Language and Linguistics*, 3–7.

Demuth, K., & Smith, N. (1987). The foreign language requirement: An alternative program. *Foreign Language Annals*, *20*(1), 67–77.

Dinklage, K. (1971). Inability to learn a foreign language. In G. Blaine & C. McArthur (Eds.), *Emotional problems of the student*. New York: Appleton-Century-Crofts.

Dinklage, K. (1985, December). *Regarding college students' inability to learn a foreign language*. Paper presented at the Modern Language Association Convention, Chicago.

Downey, D.M., Bever, K., & Hill, B. (1991). Foreign language modification program. Presentation at the 42nd Annual Conference of the Orton Dyslexia Society, Portland, OR, Nov. 6–9.

Dunn, L., & Dunn, L. (1981). *Peabody Picture Vocabulary Test-Revised*. Circle Pines, MN: American Guidance Service.

Elson, N. (1983). Why we do what we *do . . . TESOL Talk*, *13* (1–2), 16–30.

Fisher, E. (1986). Learning disability specialist looks at foreign language instruction. *Hilltop Spectrum*, *4*(1), 1–3.

Freed, B.F. (1987). Exemptions from the foreign language requirement: A review of recent literature, problems, and policy. *ADFL Bulletin*, *18*(2), 13–17.

Gajar, A. (1987). Foreign language learning disabilities: The identification of predictive and diagnostic variables. *Journal of Learning Disabilities*, *20*(6), 327–330.

Ganschow, L., & Myer, B. (1992). Unpublished data.

Ganschow, L., Myer, B., & Roeger, K. (1989). Implications of foreign language policies and procedures for students with language learning disabilities. *Learning Disabilities Focus*, *5*, 50–58.

Ganschow, L., & Sparks, R. (1986). Learning disabilities and foreign language difficulties: Deficit in listening skills? *Journal of Reading, Writing, and Learning Disabilities International*, *2*, 305–319.

Ganschow, L., & Sparks, R. (1987). The foreign language requirement. *Learning Disabilities Focus*, *2*, 116–123.

Ganschow, L., & Sparks, R. (1991). A screening instrument for the identification of foreign language learning problems: *Foreign Language Annals*, *24*(5), 383–397.

Ganschow, L., Sparks, R., Javorsky, J., Pohlman, J., & Bishop-Marbury, A. (1991). Identifying native language difficulties among foreign language learners in college: A "foreign" language learning disability? *Journal of Learning Disabilities*, *24*(9), 530–541.

Gardner, R. (1973). Attitudes and motivation: Their role in second language acquisition. In J. Oller & J. Richards (Eds.), *Focus on the learner* (pp. 235–245). Rowley, MA: Newbury House.

Gardner, R. (1985). *Social psychology and second language learning: The role of attitudes and motivation*. London: Edward Arnold.

Gardner, R., & Lambert, W. (1965). Language aptitude, intelligence, and second language achievement. *Journal of Educational Psychology*, *56*, 191–199.

Gardner, R., & Lambert, W. (1972). *Attitude and motivation in second language learning*. Rowley, MA: Newbury House.

Genesse, F. (1976). The role of intelligence in second language learning. *Language Learning*, *26*, 267–280.

Geschwind, N. (1985). Biological foundations of reading. In F. Duffy & N. Geschwind (Eds.), *Dyslexia: A neuroscientific approach to clinical evaluation* (pp. 197–211). Boston: Little, Brown.

Gillingham, A., & Stillman, B. (1960). *Remedial training for children with specific disability in reading, spelling, and penmanship.* Cambridge, MA: Educators Publishing Service.

Goldman, R., Fristoe, M., & Woodcock, R. (1974). *Goldman-Fristoe-Woodcock Sound-Symbol Tests.* Circle Pines, MN: American Guidance Service.

Goyen, K.D. (1989, February). Reading methods in Spain: The effect of a regular orthography. *The Reading Teacher, 370–373.*

Guiora, A. (1983). The dialectic of language acquisition. In A.Z. Guiora (Ed.), An epistemology for the language sciences. *Language Learning, 33*(5, special issue), 3–12.

Hammill, D., Brown, V.L., Larsen, S.C., & Wiederholt, J.L. (1987). *Test of adolescent language (TOAL-2).* Austin, TX: Pro-Ed.

Hammill, D., & Larsen, S. (1988). *Test of written language-2.* Austin, TX: Pro-Ed.

Henry, M. (1988). Beyond phonics: Integrated decoding and spelling instruction based on word origin and structure. *Annals of Dyslexia, 38,* 258–275.

Horwitz, E. (1990). Attending to the affective domain in the foreign language classroom. In S. Magnan (Ed.), *Shifting the instructional focus to the learner* (pp. 15–33). Middlebury, VT: Northeast Conference on the Teaching of Foreign Languages.

Horwitz, E., Horwitz, M., & Cope, J. (1986). Foreign language classroom anxiety. *Modern Language Journal, 70,* 125–132.

Horwitz, E., & Young, D.J. (Eds.). (1991). *Language anxiety: From theory and research to classroom implications.* Englewood Cliffs, NJ: Prentice-Hall.

Jastak, S., & Wilkinson, G. (1984). *Wide Range Achievement Test-Revised.* Wilmington, DE: Jastak Associates.

Javorsky, J., Sparks, R., & Ganschow, L. (1992). Perceptions of college students with and without learning disabilities about foreign language courses. *Learning Disabilities: Research and Practice, 7,* 31–44.

Kampwirth, T., & Bates, M. (1980). Modality preference and teaching method: A review of the research. *Academic Therapy 15,* 597–605.

Kavale, K., & Forness, S. (1987). Substance over style: Assessing the efficacy of modality testing and teaching. *Exceptional Children, 54,* 228–239.

Kavale, K., & Forness, S. (1990). Substance over style: A response to Dunn's animadversions. *Exceptional Children, 56,* 357–361.

Keeney, L., & Smith, N. (1984). Foreign language modifications for disabled students—The campus response. *AHSSPPE Bulletin, 2*(1), 4–5.

Kenneweg, S. (1988). Meeting special learning needs in the Spanish curriculum of a college preparatory school. In B. Snyder (Ed.), *Get ready, get set, go! Action in the foreign language classroom* (pp. 16–18). Columbus, OH: Ohio Foreign Language Association.

Krashen, S. (1982). *Second language acquisition and second language learning.* Elmspord, NY: Pergamon Press.

Lefebvre, R. (1984). A psychological consultation program for learning disabled adults. *Journal of College Student Personnel, 25*(4), 361–362.

Leong, C.K. (1989). Productive knowledge of derivational rules in poor readers. *Annals of Dyslexia, 39*, 94–115.

Lerner, J., Ganschow, L., & Sparks, R. (1991). Critical issues in learning disabilities: Foreign language learning. *Learning Disabilities Research and Practice, 6*(1), 50–53.

Levine, M. (1987). *Developmental variation and learning disorders.* Cambridge, MA: Educators Publishing Service.

Mangrum, C., & Strichart, S. (1988). *College and the learning disabled student.* Orlando, FL: Grune & Stratton.

MLA Advisory Committee on Foreign Language Programs. (1989). Language study in the United States: A draft statement. *MLA Newsletter, 21*(3), 16.

Moody, R. (1988). Personality preferences and foreign language learning. *Modern Language Journal, 72*, 389–401.

Morris, M., & Leuenberger, J. (1990). A report of the cognitive, academic, and linguistic profiles for college students with and without learning disabilities. *Journal of Learning Disabilities, 23*(6), 355–360; 385.

Myer, B., & Ganschow, L. (1988). Profiles of frustration: Second language learners with specific learning disabilities. In J.E. Lalande, II (Ed.), *Shaping the future of foreign language education: FLES, articulation and proficiency* (pp. 32–53). Lincolnwood, IL: National Textbook Co.

Myer, B., Ganschow, L., Sparks, R., & Kenneweg, S. (1989). Cracking the code: Helping students with specific learning disabilities. In D. McAlpine (Ed.), *Defining the essentials for the foreign language classroom* (pp. 112–120). Lincolnwood, IL: National Textbook Co.

Neufeld, G. (1974). A theoretical perspective on the nature of linguistic aptitude. *Proceedings of the 5th Symposium of the Canadian Association of Applied Linguistics.*

Oller, J. (1981). Research on the measurement of affective variables: Some remaining questions. In R. Anderson (Ed.), *New dimensions in second language acquisition research* (pp 13–42). Rowley, MA: Newbury House.

Oller, J., & Perkins, K. (1978a). Intelligence and language proficiency as sources of variance in self-reported affective variables. *Language Learning, 28*, 85–97.

Oller, J., & Perkins, K. (1978b). A further comment on language proficiency as a source of variance in certain affective measures. *Language Learning, 28*, 417–423.

Oller, J., & Richards, J. (Eds.). (1973). *Focus on the learner: Pragmatic perspectives for the foreign language teacher.* Rowley, MA: Newbury House.

Oxford, R. (1990). Language learning strategies and beyond: A look at strategies in the context of styles. In S. Magnan (Ed.), *Shifting the instructional focus to the learner* (pp. 35–55). Middlebury, VT: Northeast Conference on the Teaching of Foreign Languages.

Philips, L., Ganschow, L., & Anderson, R. (1991). The college foreign language requirement: An action plan for alternatives. *NACADA (National Academic Advising Association) Journal, 11*(1), 51–56.

Pimsleur, P. (1966a). *Pimsleur Language Aptitude Battery and Manual.* New York: Harcourt, Brace, Jovanovich.

Pimsleur, P. (1966b). Testing foreign language learning. In A. Valdman (Ed.), *Trends in language teaching* (pp. 175–214). New York: McGraw-Hill.

Pimsleur, P. (1968). Language aptitude testing. In A. Davies (Ed.), *Language testing symposium: A linguistic approach* (pp. 98–106). London: Oxford University Press.

Pimlseur, P., Sundland, D., & McIntyre, R. (1964). Underachievement in foreign language learning. *International Review of Applied Linguistics, 3*, 43–50.

Pompian, N. (1986). Like a Volvo lifted off my chest. *The Undergraduate Bulletin* (Dartmouth College), *3*, 1–2.

Robinson, J.W., & Hesse, K.D. (1981). A morphemically based spelling program's effect on spelling skills and spelling performance of seventh grade students. *Journal of Educational Research, 75*, 56–62.

Rubin, J. (1975). What the "good" language learner can teach us. *TESOL Quarterly, 9*, 41–51.

Savignon, S. (1976). On the other side of the desk: A look at teacher attitudes and motivation in second-language learning. *Canadian Modern Language Review, 32*, 295–302.

Scovel, T. (1978). The effect of affect: a review of the anxiety literature. *Language Learning, 28*, 129–142.

Shaywitz, S.E., Escobar, M.D., Shaywitz, B.A., Fletcher, J.M., & Makuch, R. (1992). Evidence that dyslexia may represent the lower tail of a normal distribution of reading ability. *The New England Journal of Medicine, 326*(3), 145–150.

Sparks, R., & Ganschow, L. (1991). Foreign language learning differences: Affective or native language aptitude differences? *Modern Language Journal, 75*, 3–16.

Sparks, R., & Ganschow, L. (1992a). *Foreign Language Screening Instrument-High School* (FLSI-H). Unpublished raw data.

Sparks, R., & Ganschow, L. (1992b). The impact of native language learning problems on foreign language learning: Case study illustrations of the linguistic coding deficit hypothesis. *The Modern Language Journal* (in press).

Sparks, R., Ganschow, L., & Javorsky, J. (1992). Diagnosing and accommodating the foreign language learning difficulties of college students with learning disabilities. *Learning Disabilities: Research and Practice, 7*(3), 150–160.

Sparks, R., Ganschow, L., Javorsky, J., Pohlman, J., & Patton, J. (1992a). Identifying native language deficits in high and low risk foreign language learners in high school. *Foreign Language Annals* (in press).

Sparks, R. Ganschow, L. Javorsky, J., Pohlman, J., & Patton, J. (1992b). Test comparisons among students identified as high-risk, low-risk, and learning disabled in high school foreign language courses. *The Modern Language Journal, 76*, 142–159.

Sparks, R., Ganschow, L., Kenneweg, S., & Miller, K. (1991). Using Orton-Gillingham methodology to teach a foreign language to learning disabled/dyslexic students: Explicit teaching of phonology in a second language. *Annals of Dyslexia, 41*, 96–118.

Sparks, R., Ganschow, L., & Pohlman, J. (1989). Linguistic coding deficits in foreign language learners. *Annals of Dyslexia, 39*, 179–195.

Sparks, R., Javorsky, J., & Ganschow, L. (1990). Role of the service provider in helping students with learning disabilities with foreign language learning problems. In J. Vander Putten (Ed.), *Reaching new heights.* (pp. 87–91).

Proceedings of the 1989 AHSSPPE Conference. Columbus, OH: Association on Handicapped Student Service Programs in Postsecondary Education.

Stahl, S. (1988). Is there evidence to support matching reading styles and initial reading methods? *Phi Delta Kappan, 70*, 317–322.

Stanovich, K. (1982). Individual differences in the cognitive processes of reading: Word decoding. *Journal of Learning Disabilities, 15*(8), 485–493.

Stanovich, K. (1986). Explaining the variance in reading ability in terms of psychological processes: What have we learned? *Annals of Dyslexia, 36*, 67–96.

Stanovich, K. (1988, April). The right and wrong places to look for the cognitive locus of reading disability. *Annals of Dyslexia, 38*, 154–177.

Vellutino, F., & Scanlon, D. (1986). Linguistic coding and metalinguistic awareness: Their relationship to verbal memory and code acquisition in poor and normal readers. In D.B. Yaden & S. Templeton (Eds.), Metalinguistic awareness and beginning literacy (pp. 115–141). Portsmouth, NH: Heinemann.

Vogel, S. (1985). Learning disabled college students: Identification, assessment, and outcomes. In D.D. Duane & C.K. Leong (Eds.), *Understanding learning disabilities: International and multidisciplinary views*. (pp. 179–201). New York: Plenum Press.

Vogel, S. (1986) *The college student with a learning disability: A college faculty, administrator, and student handbook*. Lake Forest, IL: Association of Children and Adults with Learning Disabilities.

Vogel, S. (1988). Some preliminary findings on predicting success for LD college students. In D. Knapke & C. Lendman (Eds.), *Proceedings of the 1988 AHSSPPE Conference* (pp. 111–115). Columbus, OH: Association on Handicapped Student Service Programs in Postsecondary Education.

Wechsler, D. (1981). *Wechsler Adult Intelligence Scale-Revised*. San Antonio, TX: Psychological Corpation.

Wesche, M. (1981). Language aptitude measures in streaming, matching students with methods, and diagnosis of learning problems. In K.C. Diller (Ed.), *Individual differences and universals in language learning aptitude* (pp. 119–153). Rowley, MA: Newbury House.

Wesche, M., Edwards, H., & Wells, W. (1982). Foreign language aptitude and intelligence. *Applied Psycholinguistics, 3*, 127–140.

Wiig, E.H., & Secord, W. (1989). *Test of Language Competence-Expanded Edition*. New York: Psychological Corporation.

Williams, J. (1987). Educational treatments for dyslexia at the elementary and secondary levels. In W. Ellis (Ed.,) *Intimacy with language: A forgotten basic in teacher education* (pp. 24–32). Baltimore: Orton Dyslexia Society.

Woodcock, R. (1987). *Woodcock Reading Mastery Test-Revised*. Circle Pines, MN: American Guidance Service.

Woodcock, R., & Johnson, M.B. (1977). *Woodcock-Johnson Psycho-Educational Battery: Tests of Cognitive Ability; Tests of Achievement*. Allen, TX: DLM Teaching Resources.

Appendix 12.1: Description of Instruments Used for the Identification of Foreign Language Learning Disabilities

GFW: Goldman-Fristoe-Woodcock Sound-Symbol Tests (Goldman, Fristoe, & Woodcock, 1974:

Sound Blending Subtest: tests ability to synthesize isolated sounds into meaningful words

Spelling of Sounds Subtest: tests ability to make phoneme (sound) to grapheme (written) translations

MLAT: Modern Language Aptitude Test (Carroll & Sapon, 1959): tests foreign language aptitude using a simulated format to provide an indication of probable degree of success in learning a foreign language; includes five subtests:

Part I (Number Learning): tests memory component and auditory comprehension of a foreign language

Part II (Phonetic Script): tests sound-symbol association ability and memory for speech sounds

Part III (Spelling Clues): tests ability to unscramble letters to form a word and select a word similar in meaning in a multiple-choice format

Part IV (Words in Sentences): tests sensitivity to grammatical structure

Part V (Paired Associates): tests rote memory aspect of learning a foreign language

PPVT-R: Peabody Picture Vocabulary Test-Revised (Dunn & Dunn, 1981): tests student's receptive vocabulary for standard American English

TLC-E: Test of Language Competence-Expanded Edition (Wiig & Secord, 1989): tests metalinguistic competence in syntax, semantics, and pragmatics; includes 4 subtests:

Subtest 1: tests ability to give two interpretations for sentences with ambiguities arising from multiple-meaning words or phrases

Subtest 2: tests ability to give two plausible inferences regarding intervening events when connecting event has been eliminated

Subtest 3: tests ability to create intent-driven sentences

Subtest 4: tests ability to interpret figurative expressions

TOAL-2: Test of Adolescent Language-2 (Hammill, Brown, Larsen, & Wiederholt, 1987): tests ability to respond orally and in writing to vocabulary and grammar items; includes eight subtests:

Listening/Vocabulary: tests ability to select from four pictures the one that best matches the stimulus word

Listening/Grammar: tests ability to listen to three sentences read aloud and select the two sentences with nearly equivalent meanings

Speaking/Vocabulary: tests ability to listen to a word and use it correctly in a sentence

Speaking/Grammar: tests ability to listen to a sentence said aloud and repeat it verbatim

Reading/Vocabulary: tests ability to read three stimulus words and select from new list the two words that are most closely associated with the stimulus words

Reading/Grammar: tests ability to recognize meaningfully similar but syntactically different sentence structures

Writing/Vocabulary: tests ability to read a word and use it correctly in a sentence

Writing/Grammar: tests ability to combine a number of brief sentences into one grammatically correct written sentence

TOWL-2: Test of Written Language-2 (Hammill & Larsen, 1988): measures the ability to write in both contrived and spontaneous formats; includes 10 subtests:

Vocabulary: tests ability to write a sentence that incorporates stimulus word

Spelling: tests ability to write dictated sentences using proper spelling

Style: tests ability to write dictated sentences using proper capitalization and punctuation rules

Logical Sentences: tests ability to read an illogical sentence and rewrite the sentence so it makes sense

Sentence Combining: tests ability to integrate meaning of several short sentences into one grammatically correct written sentence

Thematic Maturity: tests ability to write a story in response to a stimulus picture; student earns points when a predetermined element in story's content is mentioned

Contextual Vocabulary: tests vocabulary level in a composition by counting number of different words having seven or more letters

Syntactic Maturity: tests grammar by counting number of grammatically correct words in a composition

Contextual Spelling: tests spelling by counting number of correctly spelled words in a story

Contextual Style: tests number of instances in which different punctuation and capitalization rules are used in a story

WAIS-R: Wechsler Adult Intelligence Scale-Revised (Wechsler, 1981): tests general intelligence; includes 11 subscales. The subtests are: Information; DigitSpan; Vocabulary; Arithmetic; Similarities; Picture Completion; Picture Arrangement; Block Design; Object Assembly; Digit Symbol.

WJPEB: Woodcock-Johnson Psycho-Educational Battery (Woodcock & Johnson, 1977); includes four clusters:

Cognitive (Brief Scale) Cluster:

Antonyms-Synonyms Subtest: tests knowledge of word meanings

Picture Vocabulary Subtest: tests ability to identify pictured objects or actions

Memory Cluster: tests memory by having student repeat material presented auditorily (sentences and digits reversed)

Reading Cluster:

Letter-Word Identification Subtest: tests ability to identify isolated words

Word Attack Subtest: tests ability to read pseudowords

Passage Comprehension: tests ability to determine a word that would be appropriate in the context of passage

Written Language Cluster:

Dictation Subtest: tests ability to respond in writing to a variety of questions requiring knowledge of punctuation and capitalizaiton (8% of subtest items), spelling (82% of items), and usage (10% of items)

Proofing Subtest: tests ability to read a short passage and identify punctuation and capitalization (41% of subtest items), spelling (24% of items), or usage (35% of items) errors in the passage

WRAT-R: Wide Range Achievement Test-Revised (Jastak & Wilkinson, 1984):
  Spelling Subtest: tests performance on writing single words from dictation

WRMT-R: Woodcock Reading Mastery Test-Revised (Woodcock, 1987);
  Word Identification: tests ability to read isolated words
  Word Attack: tests ability to read pseudowords
  Word Comprehension: tests knowledge of antonyms, synonyms, and analogies
  Passage Comprehension: tests ability to read a short passage and identify a key word missing from the passage (cloze test)

Appendix 12.2: Instruments to Use for the Identification of Foreign Language Learning Disabilities

Tests*	WI	KS	RC	SP	WG	LS	SPK	VC	ME	AP	IQ	Linguistic Codes		
												PHO	SYN	SEM
Academic														
WJPEB: Reading Cluster														
Letter-Word Identification	x	x										x		
Word Attack		x										x		
Passage Comprehension			x									x	x	x
WRMT-R														
Word Identification	x	x										x		
Word Attack		x										x		
Word Comprehension								x				x	x	x
Passage Comprehension			x									x	x	x
WJPEB: Writing Cluster														
Dictation				x	x							x	x	
Proofing				x	x							x	x	
Spelling				x								x		
Punctuation					x								x	
Usage					x								x	
WRAT-R Spelling				x								x		
TOWL-2†					x			x				x	x	x

(Appendix 12.2 Continued)

Test*	WI	KS	RC	SP	WG	LS	SPK	VC	ME	AP	IQ	Linguistic Codes		
												PHO	SYN	SEM
Oral Language														
GFW Sound-Symbol Test		x		x								x		
TLC-E†						x	x						x	x
TOAL-2†	x		x		x	x	x	x				x	x	x
PPVT-R								x						x
WJPEB Cognitive Cluster														
Picture Vocabulary								x						x
Antonyms/Synonyms								x						x
Memory Cluster									x					
Foreign Language Aptitude														
MLAT										x		x	x	x
Intelligence														
WAIS-R											x			

*WI = word identification; KS = knowledge of sounds; RC = reading comprehension; SP = spelling; WG = written language/grammar; LS = listening; SPK = speaking; VC = vocabulary; ME = memory; AP = FL aptitude; IQ = intelligence; PHO = phonology; SYN = syntax; SEM = semantics
†Not standardized on adults

XIII
Issues in Program Evaluation

Pamela B. Adelman and Susan A. Vogel

In the 1980s, numerous programs and services developed in colleges and universities to serve students with learning disabilities (LDs). Although there is evidence of the success of individual students served by these programs, there is very little information as yet about formal or systematic inquiry into their effectiveness (Bursuck, Rose, Cowen, & Yahaya, 1989), which is needed to improve the quality of programs and to ensure their continuation and expansion.

Among the varying perspectives on how evaluation should be carried out, two basic distinctions have been almost universally accepted: formative and summative evaluation (Worthen & Sanders, 1987). Whereas

formative evaluation is conducted during the operation of a program to provide program directors evaluative information useful in improving the program . . . summative evaluation is conducted at the end of a program to provide potential consumers with judgments about that program's worth or merit. (p. 34)

Potential consumers of LD programs are future students who will be enrolling in the programs and college administrators who would want evaluative information before starting or continuing their own programs.

Most LD programs are ongoing, so formative evaluation would be the appropriate approach. In some situations, for example, when a program funded by a grant is terminated, a summative evaluation is conducted. The results of an evaluation study may be used for both summative and formative evaluation purposes. For example, grade reports can be used to determine whether students with learning disabilities have the ability to do college-level work and would therefore be effective in a summative evaluation. Grade reports would also be useful in determining the effectiveness of intervention for each student and therefore be part of formative evaluation.

Among the various approaches to either formative or summative evaluation, two may be particularly suited for assessing the merit of college programs for students with learning disabilities. A common approach is the objective-oriented evaluation (Worthen & Sanders, 1987). In this approach, the purposes of the program are specified and evaluation focuses on the extent to which those purposes are achieved. The strength of this approach is that it produces information that is relevant. It causes reflection about intentions and clarifies formerly ambiguous generalities about goals and outcomes. Furthermore, the objective-oriented evaluation approach provides face validity because the program is being held accountable for what its designers said it was going to accomplish (Worthen & Sanders, 1987).

Major weaknesses of the objective-oriented evaluative approach include (1) ignoring important outcomes other than those covered by the objectives (the unintended outcomes); and (2) omitting evidence of program value not reflected in its own objectives (Worthen & Sanders, 1987). For example, if general program goals are only student-oriented, they might include (1) achieving success in college; (2) preparing for a responsible and independent life; and (3) functioning effectively in the classroom, a chosen profession, and personal lives.

If evaluation only measures outcomes covered by these objectives, other important results might be overlooked such as whether or not the program helped achieve the institution's mission, brought the institution into compliance with Section 504, or was very effective in helping faculty understand the needs of learning disabled students as well as of students with other handicaps. Other outcomes to be considered are an increase in enrollment, retention, and receipt of grants.

Another evaluative approach introduced in the 1970s and 1980s is the naturalistic and participant-oriented approach (Worthen & Sanders, 1987) that may compensate for the limitations of objective-oriented evaluation. This new approach emphasizes "the human element" (Worthen & Sanders, 1987, p. 128). By focusing on the concerns and issues raised by the participants, the naturalistic and participant-oriented approach may uncover outcomes missed through the objective-oriented approach such as the importance of the qualifications of the individuals delivering the services.

The first section of this chapter exemplifies the objective-oriented approach and describes alternative models of evaluation to assess accomplishment of the general program goals listed above. The second section focuses on the naturalistic and participant-oriented approach and assesses the various perspectives of program participants.

Measuring Outcomes

The success of the program goals can be measured by assessing students' academic performance, basic skills improvement, social and emotional adjustment, and career attainments. By using both formative and summative measures, students' progress in accomplishing the goals while they are in the program as well as after they completed it can be assessed.

Academic Performance

Short-term outcomes of academic performance can be measured in several ways. Grade reports can be prepared including the number of withdrawals, the number of incompletes, and the number of failing grades (see Figure 13.1). Another way to measure academic performance is to determine the number of students who were on the Dean's list and the number who received scholastic warnings. The reasons the students received scholastic notices can be analyzed. Was it due to poor attendance, poor performance on assignments and tests, or both? This is very valuable qualitative information. If attendance appeared to be the main problem, this behavior may indicate the need for counseling to discuss motivational problems or for further help with time management and organization. If the reason for poor scholastic progress was the students' difficulties with understanding the course content, there may be a need for subject-matter tutors.

Graduation and failure rates can be used to measure long-term academic or educational attainments. Vogel and Adelman (1990) compared 110 college students with LDs to a random stratified sample (RSS) of 153 peers attending the same college between 1980 and 1988. The students with LDs received comprehensive, highly coordinated support services for at least one semester. The groups were matched on gender, college experience, and semester and year of entry to the college. The LD and RSS groups were compared on high-school preparation and performance, American College Testing Program (ACT) and college performance, and graduation and academic failure rate. Although the LD students' high-school records, ACT scores, and college performance were inferior to that of the RSS group, they graduated at the same rate and within the same time frame.

Vogel and Adelman identified three factors that contributed to these positive outcomes: (1) the students with learning disabilities self-referred at admissions; (2) they were screened for intellectual abilities, type and severity of LD, and motivation and attitude toward the teaching-learning process; and (3) they requested and used comprehensive, highly coordinated support services and special academic advisors.

Improvement of Basic Skills

Improvement in basic skills can be determined by post-testing at the end of each semester. However, in order to measure improvement in basic skills, there must be some baseline information. For example, at Barat College, all students who were accepted by both the Learning Opportunities Program and the college participated in two days of

Spring, 1990	Cumulative
3.606	3.625
3.583	3.606
3.500	3.139
3.400	2.958
3.262	2.952
3.167	2.933
3.083	2.923
3.077	2.875
3.000	2.824 (2)
2.967	2.778
2.933	2.737
2.923 (3)	2.726
2.833	2.698
2.778	2.697
2.700	2.652
2.697	2.640
2.667 (3)	2.611
2.583	2.596
2.555	2.542
2.539	2.513
2.500	2.506
2.359 (2)	2.500 (2)
2.334	2.485
2.333	2.457
2.267	2.417
2.222	2.404
2.200	2.395
2.133	2.378
2.111	2.375
2.100	2.341
2.000	2.333 (2)
1.834	2.278
1.667	2.238 (2)
1.333	2.205
1.167	2.133
1.000	2.056
0.834	1.867
0.667 (2)	1.815
	1.405
	1.349

| As: 21 | Cs: 50 | Fs: 9 | Ps: 36 |
| Bs: 74 | Ds: 9 | Ws: 0 | Is: 3 |

Figure 13.1. Learning Opportunities Program, Grade Report, Spring, 1990.

diagnostic testing before their first semester began. The purpose of this testing is to identify the students' strengths, areas for improvement, long-term instructional goals, and effective learning strategies.

The diagnostic information is used for preparing Individual Education Plans (IEPs) that are jointly developed by the student, LD specialist, and program director. Specific objectives, instructional materials, and strategies for remediating deficit areas are targeted in the IEPs. For example, an analysis of one student's math errors led to the conclusion that overcoming problems with understanding fractions was necessary in order to prepare the student for Introduction to Algebra. As a result, the LD specialist developed and implemented a program aimed at improving the student's understanding of fractions. (See Chapter X for examples and discussion of diagnostic reports and IEPs.)

At the end of each semester, students participate in two to three hours of post-testing to assess progress and to reevaluate goals. The type of post-testing is determined by the nature of the remediation and the requirements of coursework. If the student's coursework required a lot of reading and the focus of remediation was improving reading comprehension, the student's progress in reading would be measured. However, a student who has not worked on mathematics, with an LD Specialist or in a mathematics course, would not be post-tested in mathematics. Figure 13.2 summarizes two semesters of post-testing data for a student. In the first column, the results of the initial diagnostic testing are listed. The second and third columns present results of post-testing administered at the end of fall and spring semesters.

Improvement in basic skills is also reflected through students' overall grades and progress or grades in developmental courses in the areas of reading, written language (e.g., proofreading, sentence combining, grammar), mathematics, and vocabulary development. (See Chapter X for a discussion of developmental courses.)

Whereas post-testing at the end of each semester is relatively short and dependent on the intervention that took place, that is, on the specific areas of remediation, assessment of basic skills when the student leaves the program should be more comprehensive. A battery of tests at exit should include measures of reading, vocabulary development, written language (including an essay and tests of sentence structure, spelling and punctuation), mathematics, and study skills. Comprehensive diagnostic testing when students graduate provides important information that will help students make decisions about graduate school and/or employment (Adelman & Vogel, 1991; Adelman & Wren, 1990; Vogel, 1985).

Social/Emotional Adjustment

A very important outcome, but one that is more difficult to measure, is the social and emotional adjustment of students. This might be ac-

Learning Opportunities Program, Barat College, Progress Report

File Number _____ 0241

Measures	Date: 8/84 R.S. (Raw Score)	Session: Pre-test Grade/%ile (Grade Equivalent/ Percentile)	Date: 12/84 R.S.	Session: Post-test I Grade/%ile	Date: 5/85 R.S.	Session: Post-test II Grade/%ile
I. Reading						
A. Stanford Comprehension	29/30	11%ile			31/60	13%ile
B. PIAT Reading Comprehension	69/84	54%ile			70/84	57%ile
C. Stanford Fast Reading	8/30	10%ile				
D. WRAT Reading	8/26	2%ile	23/26	35%ile		
E. Woodcock-Johnson—Word Attack						
II. Written language						
A. Essay	11.2*				8.2*	
B. Sentence Structure	19/35	26%ile			28/35	50%ile
C. TOWL Style	17/25	16%ile				
D. Woodcock-Johnson Proofing	20/29	46%ile				
E. WRAT: Spelling	29/51	8.3 G.E.			36/51	9.7 G.E.
PIAT: : Spelling	63/84	10.4 G.E.				
Malcomesius Spelling						
III. Mathematics						
A. Key Math						
B. PIAT	24/35	39%ile	27/35	56%ile	30/35	70%ile
C. DTMS: Arithmetic Skills						
D. DTMS Algebra						
E. Woodcock-Johnson Quantitative Concepts	31/46	32%ile			37/46	76%ile
IV. Study Habits and Attitudes	105	55%ile				
V. PPVT	152	58%ile				
VI. Semester Grade Point Average	3,889				3,000	
VII. Cumulative Grade Point Average	3,889				3,533	

* The lower the score, the better.

FIGURE 13.2.

complished by looking at involvement in campus life (e.g., awards received, offices held on the Student Governing Board, and selection as resident assistants). The amount and intensity of parent contact may also be an indication of the students' adjustment to living away from home. However, measurement would be confounded by proximity as well as the parents' needs to contact their children.

Another way to measure whether students had been prepared for a responsible and independent life is to assess long-term social and emotional adjustment. Rogan and Hartman (1990) conducted a follow-up study of graduates from a private school for students with learning disabilities. Through questionnaires and telephone interviews, they determined the number of graduates who were living independently in their own apartments or with their spouses and assessed marital status, life satisfaction, and the need for ongoing therapy. Some studies have looked at social and interpersonal skills by assessing the ability to make and keep friends and the range of leisure activities in which individuals participated with peers (Blalock, 1981; Fafard & Haubrich, 1980; Haring, Lovett, & Smith, 1990; Scuccimarra & Speece, 1990).

Career Attainments

Another way to measure whether students had been prepared for a responsible and independent life is to determine educational and career attainment. Adelman and Vogel (1990) examined educational and career attainment of graduates who participated for at least one semester in the program at Barat College between 1980 and 1988. College transcripts and follow-up data were evaluated to identify Bachelor's degree completion, types of majors, and graduate studies. Career attainment was determined by (1) identifying the types of jobs students attained; (2) determining whether they were employed in their area of educational preparation; (3) determining whether they thought their learning disabilities affected their work; (4) determining whether they compensated for their learning disabilities and could articulate the ways in which they did so; and (5) determining their level of job satisfaction.

Adelman and Vogel (1990) found that the majority of graduates had majored either in education or business and management and held business-related jobs. Most graduates reported moderate to high levels of job satisfaction and responded that their learning disabilities did affect their work. Processing difficulties, including retention, amount of time required to complete work, and processing deficits (particularly number and letter reversals), were the most common difficulties. The most common compensatory strategies consisted of spending extra time to finish work, asking for assistance, and carefully monitoring work for errors.

Adelman and Vogel noted several important implications from the results of the study in which almost all of the graduates who completed the survey responded that their learning disabilities affected their work. First, their learning disabilities had not prevented them from completing their job responsibilities. Second, the graduates reported moderate to high levels of job success. Third, their success may be explained by their insight into how their learning disabilities affect them on the job and their understanding of how to compensate in order to fulfill their responsibilities successfully.

Several students mentioned that they applied the same compensatory strategies to work on assignments as those they used when completing school work such as spending additional time completing papers and taking tests, and/or asking for help to clarify verbal input and assignments. It appears that self-understanding may be a significant, long-term benefit of having received services when in college since it assisted these individuals in understanding their learning disabilities and in developing compensatory strategies they could use as they entered and progressed in the working world. Given these findings, Adelman and Vogel concluded that development of self-understanding should be a major goal of support programs for college students with learning disabilities.

Participant Evaluation

To assess properly the operation of the program, it is important to include all the individuals who are either participating in the program or are in some way affected by the program, that is, students, faculty, administrators, and service prviders.

Students' Perspective

From the students' perspective, two areas to be assessed include the individuals responsible for providing the services and the effectiveness of the specific services provided. Figures 13.3 and 13.4 are examples of evaluation instruments students at Barat College complete at the end of each semester in order to evaluate their LD specialists and the program director. The evaluation of the LD specialist focuses on whether the student feels comfortable with the LD specialist, finds the LD specialist accessible, and considers the sessions valuable. The evaluation of the director includes the students' overall evaluation of the program, communication, accessibility, and the effectiveness of advising.

Another approach to evaluating the effectiveness of the services provided is to ask students to rate the value of the services and to comment on the strengths and weaknesses of the program. This can be done at the end of each term or year, or as part of a long-term follow-up

Instructions: Please circle the correct response. Date _____

A. Sessions with _____ (LD specialist)

    1. I thought my LD specialist provided direction for dealing with my questions, problems, and/or concerns.

    Strongly Agree   Agree   Not Appropriate   Disagree   Strongly Disagree

Comments: _____

_____

    2. My LD specialist was reasonably accessible.

    Strongly Agree   Agree   Not Appropriate   Disagree   Strongly Disagree

Comments: _____

_____

    3. My LD specialits showed respect for me as an individual.

    Strongly Agree   Agree   Not Appropriate   Disagree   Strongly Disagree

Comments: _____

_____

    4. My LD specialist gave me an appropriate amount of guidance in my classwork—not too much, not too little.

    Strongly Agree   Agree   Not Appropriate   Disagree   Strongly Disagree

Comments: _____

_____

    5. Our sessions were worthwhile.

    Strongly Agree   Agree   Not Appropriate   Disagree   Strongly Disagree

Why or why not? _____

_____

    6. My LD specialist was sensitive to areas in which I needed help and recognized those in which I did not need help.

    Strongly Agree   Agree   Not Appropriate   Disagree   Strongly Disagree

Why or why not? _____

_____

    7. My LD specialist presented material in a clear, understandable manner.

    Strongly Agree   Agree   Not Appropriate   Disagree   Strongly Disagree

Comments: _____

_____

    8. Overall, the time we spent together was beneficial to me.

    Strongly Agree   Agree   Not Appropriate   Disagree   Strongly Disagree

Comments: _____

_____

Comments and suggestions for change will be *most appreciated*:

_____

_____

_____

FIGURE 13.3. Evaluation of LD specialist, Learning Opportunities Program, Barat College.

Instructions: Please circle the correct response. Date _____

1. From my experience, the design of the LOP seems appropriate and meets my needs.

   Strongly Agree   Agree   Not Appropriate   Disagree   Strongly Disagree

Comments: _____

_____

2. If not, which of your needs are not met?

Comments: _____

_____

3. From my experience, I can see that the director has recruited and hired competent staff.

   Strongly Agree   Agree   Not Appropriate   Disagree   Strongly Disagree

Comments: _____

_____

4. The director has trained the staff well.

   Strongly Agree   Agree   Not Appropriate   Disagree   Strongly Disagree

Comments: _____

_____

5. The LOP staff seem to be well supervised.

   Strongly Agree   Agree   Not Appropriate   Disagree   Strongly Disagree

Comments: _____

_____

6. The LOP staff and the director communicate frequently enough to be effective in meeting my needs.

   Strongly Agree   Agree   Not Appropriate   Disagree   Strongly Disagree

Comments: _____

_____

7. The LOP staff and faculty communicate frequently enough to help me to be effective in my courses.

   Strongly Agree   Agree   Not Appropriate   Disagree   Strongly Disagree

Comments: _____

_____

8. The LOP Director is available to discuss my concerns and needs.

   Strongly Agree   Agree   Not Appropriate   Disagree   Strongly Disagree

Comments: _____

_____

9. The advising process helps me to register in courses in which I have a reasonable chance of success.

   Strongly Agree   Agree   Not Appropriate   Disagree   Strongly Disagree

Comments: _____

_____

10. If not, please indicate your reasons.

_____

_____

_____

FIGURE 13.4. Evaluation of Director, Learning Opportunities Program, Barat College.

study. As part of the follow-up study of students who participated in the Learning Opportunities Program (LOP) at Barat College, 89 students were asked to rate the value of specific services and the entire program, to give their opinions of the strengths and weaknesses of the program, and to offer suggestions for improvement. Individuals who did not respond received reminders and additional surveys. A total of 57 (64%) of the students completed the questionnaire.

By examination of college transcripts and responses to the questionnaire, it was determined that 26 of the 89 students completed their Bachelor's degree at Barat, and an additional ten students transferred and graduated from other four-year institutions, resulting in a total of 36 graduates (G). Twenty students (the nongraduates—NG) withdrew (W) from the college due to academic failure (defined as below 2.0 on a 4.0 scale). Thirty-three students withdrew from the college to pursue non-academic goals or to transfer to another college. Thirty (83%) of the graduates completed the questionnaire. Of the 20 nongraduates, 8 (40%) returned the questionnaire. Eighteen (55%) of the students who withdrew returned the questionnaire. (See Table 13.1.)

Rating of Specific Services

Students were asked to rate the following services on a scale of one (least valuable) to five (most valuable):

1) Communication with faculty/staff to receive reasonable accommodations such as modified exam procedures, tape recording in class
2) Support in coursework from the LD specialist
3) Remediation, that is work on improving specific skills, also done with the LD specialist
4) Peer tutoring
5) Instruction in study skills, time management, and test taking
6) Modified exam procedures such as extended time, private room
7) Auxiliary aids such as books on tape, taped lectures, note takers, readers.

Table 13.2 delineates mean ratings of the seven services as perceived by graduates, nongraduates, and those who withdrew from the program. An interesting finding was that G and NG students ranked remediation as

TABLE 13.1. Percentage of questionnaires returned.

	Total number (N = 89)	Students who returned questionnaire	
	N	N	%
Graduates (G)	36	30	83
NonGraduates (NG)	20	8	40
Withdrawals (W)	33	18	55

TABLE 13.2. Mean ratings of program services.

Program services	G (N = 23)	NG (N = 8)	W (N = 17)
Communication with faculty/staff to receive reasonable accommodations	4.0	4.75	4.58
Support in coursework from the LD Specialist	4.38	4.38	4.74
Remediation with the LD specialist	4.60	4.75	4.21
Peer tutoring	3.40	3.25	3.94
Instruction in study skills, time management, and test taking	4.17	4.88	3.95
Modified exam procedures	4.21	4.50	4.37
Auxiliary aids	4.04	4.75	4.39

first and second, respectively, whereas W students ranked this service fifth. Students who had withdrawn considered support in coursework and communication with faculty as the most valuable services. Since a major goal of the program at Barat College is to provide remedial services so students have the opportunity to improve basic skills, the differences between W and G and NG students may reflect different program expectations. For the G students, there appeared to be a better match between the philosophy of the program and their own goals.

Another interesting finding was that all groups ranked peer tutoring as the least valuable service. The reason for the students' low ranking of this service may be due to the availability of faculty for assistance in coursework. Barat College is an undergraduate institution with an average class size of approximately 15 students. Not only do faculty provide additional assistance outside of class but the small size of most classes is very conducive to discussion and to asking questions of faculty during class. Because of the accessibility of faculty who are certainly the best qualified subject-matter tutors and of LD specialists, students in the Barat program did not find peer tutors as valuable as they may have found them at larger universities where faculty are less accessible, support services staff are not usually learning disabilities specialists, and graduate assistants are usually responsible for providing additional help. Given these findings, it was understandable that support in coursework provided by the peer tutors did not highly correlate with course support provided by the LD specialist for G, NG, and W students ($r = .3991$, $p = .03$; $r = .7467$, $p = .057$; and $r = .0446$, $p = .433$ respectively). It appears that students also recognized the value of working with a specialist in learning disabilities when receiving help in coursework over receiving assistance from a peer tutor.

Overall Rating of the Program

Students were asked their overall rating of the program on a scale of one (Poor) to five (Excellent). Table 13.3 compares the ratings of G, NG, and

TABLE 13.3. Overall rating of the program.

	Graduates (N = 30)		Nongraduates (N = 8)		Withdrawals (N = 18)	
	N	%	N	%	N	%
Excellent	16	53.3	1	12.5	4	22.2
Very good	9	30.0	4	50.0	6	33.3
Good	4	13.3	3	37.5	6	33.3
Fair	0	0.0	0	0.0	2	11.1
Poor	1	3.3	0	0.0	0	0.0

TABLE 13.4. Overall rating of program: mean rankings of program services.

Program services	Good (N = 13)	Very good (N = 19)	Excellent (N = 21)
Communication with faculty/ staff to receive reasonable accommodations	3.92	4.32	4.65
Support in coursework from the LD Specialist	3.92	4.58	4.75
Remediation with the LD specialist	4.23	4.47	4.76
Peer tutoring	3.08	3.68	3.71
Instruction in study skills, time management, and test taking	3.54	4.47	4.48
Modified exam procedures	4.31	4.22	4.57
Auxiliary aids	4.09	4.35	4.56

W students. Graduates gave the highest overall rating with 53.3% rating the program excellent compared with 12.5% for NG and 22.2% for W. Table 13.4 profiles the mean rankings of services according to how students rated the overall services of the program. Given earlier findings, it was not surprising that those students who rated the program "excellent" also considered remediation as the most valuable service, providing further evidence of the importance of making a "match" between the students' and the program's goals.

Program Strengths

Students were asked the question, "Generally, what was the major strength of the Learning Opportunities Program?" The results, shown in Table 13.5, represent the total number of responses (rather than number of respondents) since respondents often reported more than one program strength. For graduates, the greatest number of responses (37%) indicated that the major strength of the program was help with acquiring compensatory skills. Responses indicated that students had developed compensatory strategies as the result of gaining insight into their indi-

TABLE 13.5. Program strengths.

Program strengths	Graduates (NR = 65)		Nongraduates (NR = 9)		Withdrawals (NR = 39)	
	NR	%	NR	%	NR	%
Accommodations	5	8	1	11	2	5
Compensatory strategies	24	37	1	11	4	10
Course support	11	17	0	0	13	33
Remediation	5	8	0	0	1	3
Support and understanding of program faculty	16	25	6	66	12	31
None	2	3	0	0	6	15
No response	2	3	1	11	1	3

NR = Number of responses

vidual strengths, deficits, and learning styles. These compensatory strategies included acquiring organizational, time-management, and test-taking skills and were developed through an ongoing relationship with the LD specialist where self-understanding can grow and compensatory strategies were explored. For example, after receiving a disappointing grade on a test, the student and the LD specialist often discuss how the learning disability affected performance and how the strategies may or may not have been effective. One student, describing the benefits of receiving help from an LD specialist, said, "When my specialist pointed out to me exactly what my weaknesses were, I was aware of them and knew how to compensate and improve on them."

Since G students considered the help they received from their LD specialists in gaining self-understanding of strengths and weaknesses as the major strength of the program, it was not surprising that graduates considered the support and understanding of program faculty as the second most common strength (25%) of the program. NG and W students also considered the support and understanding of program faculty as major strengths of the program (66% and 31% respectively). Students not only indicated the importance of receiving help with understanding coursework and improving skills but also the emotional support provided by their LD specialists. One student responded, "I found my specialist extremely beneficial both with encouraging me when times were rough and helping me with classes. She gave me additional self-esteen where needed. She also answered questions when a subject was difficult before things became too confusing."

Program Weaknesses

Students were asked what they considered as the program's major weakness. Table 13.6 shows the results, representing the total number of responses. As illustrated, the most frequently reported weakness by G,

TABLE 13.6. Program Weaknesses.

Program Weaknesses	Graduates (NR = 46)		Nongraduates (NR = 9)		Withdrawals (NR = 23)	
	NR	%	NR	%	NR	%
Development of compensatory strategies	11	24.0	2	22	4	17.4
Specific problems with program faculty	8	17.0	1	11	4	17.0
Course support	3	6.5	2	22	3	13.0
Accommodations	4	9.0	1	11	1	4.4
Remediation	3	6.5	0	0	1	4.4
School environment	0	0.0	0	0	3	13.0
Cost	1	2.0	1	11	0	0.0
Too structured	2	4.0	0	0	0	0.0
No help after graduation	1	2.0	0	0	0	0.0
None	10	22.0	0	0	3	13.0
No response	3	6.5	2	22	4	17.4

NR = Number of responses

NG, and W students (24%, 22%, 17.4% respectively) was inadequate support in developing compensatory strategies. Several students emphasized the need to receive further help with developing self-understanding of their strengths and weaknesses in order to function more independently and to be better prepared for responsibilities after graduation. Perhaps the students' responses were due to the complexity of the task of developing compensatory strategies. This task not only requires understanding one's cognitive abilities but also identifying and then developing specific learning strategies that often must be modified for each learning situation, (e.g., instructional and testing modifications may change from course to course and also within each course).

G and W students identified problems with one of the LD specialist as the next most common program weakness (17% for both groups). They thought she lacked understanding, was condescending, or did not communicate adequately to meet the student's needs. The problems students noted with this faculty member suggest the importance of hiring faculty who not only understand the needs of adults with learning disabilities but also have the appropriate interpersonal skills to teach the students while always relating to them as adults.

Recommendations for Program Improvement

Students were asked, "In what ways could the program be improved?" Results are reported in Table 13.7. Given previous findings, it was not surprising that both G and W responded that the major recommendation was to improve the teaching of compensatory strategies (17% and 31% respectively). It was also understandable that G students who valued

TABLE 13.7. Recommendations for program inprovement.

Recommendations	Graduates (NR = 35)		Nongraduates (NR = 11)		Withdrawals (NR = 26)	
	NR	%	NR	%	NR	%
Improve development of compensatory strategtes	6	17	1	9	8	31
Improve course support	3	9	2	18	2	8
Improve remedial services	4	11	0	0	2	8
Improve access to accommodations	1	2.8	1	9	2	8
Foster independence	0	0	1	9	1	3.8
Improve program faculty	0	0	2	18	1	3.8
Stay current	1	2.8	0	0	1	3.8
Expand space	1	2.8	0	0	0	0
Improve communication	0	0	0	0	1	3.8
Start program for adults	1	2.8	0	0	0	0
Improve typing equipment	1	2.8	0	0	0	0
Eliminate additional fees	0	0	1	9	1	3.8
Gain support from school	0	0	0	0	1	3.8
None	8	23	2	18	1	3.8
No response	9	26	1	9	5	19

NR = Number of responses

remedial services so highly would recommend improvement of this program service. Other recommendations for improvement appeared to reflect specific concerns of individual students. For example, one student, unaware that the program also admitted older transfer students, suggested that a program for adults, or nontraditionally-aged students, be started. Others focused on specific problems they encountered while in the program such as the lack of space or the quality of the equipment.

Faculty's Perspective

An issue that concerned some faculty was the amount of additional time students in the Learning Opportunities Program may require of faculty. Another concern was the lack of understanding regarding what comprises "reasonable accommodations." Some faculty feared that providing reasonable accommodations to students with LDs would result in waiving requirements and/or lowering standards. To assess the validity of these concerns, faculty at Barat College were sent a questionnaire (See Figure 13.5) asking them to compare the amount of time spent outside of class with LOP students to the amount of time spent with non-LOP students, to indicate the modifications they made specifically for students with LDs and

Confidential

TO:

FROM: Dr. Pamela Adelman
      Director, Learning Opportunities Program

The LOP would appreciate your completing the following survey. We believe these data are necessary for our ongoing evaluation of our students' progress and of services offered by the program.

1. For each of the LOP students you have in your class, please indicate whether you spend less time, the same amount of time, or more time outside of class with her/him than you generally would spend with non-LOP students. If you checked "More Time," please estimate the number of additional hours during the semester.

Name	Less Time	Same Amount of Time	More Time	If More Time, Estimate Number of Hours

2. Extra time was spent in:
      _____ discussion of class materials.
      _____ discussion of reading.
      _____ discussion of assignments.
      _____ discussion of course progress.
Other: _____

      _____

Comments: _____

      _____

      _____

FIGURE 13.5. Faculty questionnaire, *continued*

3. What modifications, if any, did you make specifically for the LOP students?

_____

_____

_____

4. What suggestions or comments do you have to improve the LOP students' chances of success?

_____

_____

_____

Please return to Box 608 in the enclosed envelope. Thank you!

FIGURE 13.5. Faculty questionnaire.

to provide suggestions for improving the student's chances for success. Forty faculty who had students with LDs in their classes were sent the questionnaire. Twenty-four (60%) of the faculty responded.

Amount of Time

In response to the question asking the amount of time spent outside of class with students with LDs as compared to non-LD students in the same class, faculty reported that they spent the same amount of time with 74% of the students with LDs. For 7% of the students, they spent less time, and for 19% of the students, they spent more time. The most amount of additional time that a faculty member reported spending with a student with LDs with 1/2 hour each week, and that was for only one student.

Program Modifications

Faculty were asked, "What modifications, if any, did you make specifically for the LOP students?" The results, shown in Table 13.8, represent the

TABLE 13.8. Modifications ($N = 24$).

	Number of Responses (28)	
Modifications	NR	%
Additional help/counsel	9	32
Modification of exams/assignments	6	21
Tape recorder on front desk	1	4
No response	12	43

NR = Number of responses.

total number of responses (rather than number of respondents), since respondents often reported more than one modification. The major modification (32%) faculty reported was giving additional help on course material and suggesting ways in which to improve performance, e.g., consulting with the student's LD specialist, encouraging better attendance in class. Six responses (21%) stated that exam and assignment modifications were made. Only one response indicated that permission was given to tape record in class and that the tape recorder was placed on the front desk.

Suggestions for Improving LD Students' Chances for Success

Another question asked was, "What suggestions or comments do you have to improve LOP students' chances of success?" Table 13.9. shows the results, representing the total number of responses. The most common recommendation (28%) encouraged students to be more highly motivated. Perhaps this recommendation reflects the personal interest faculty at small colleges can take in their students and the emphasis on teaching as the faculty's primary responsibility. Encouraging the students to communicate more frequently with the faculty was the next most common recommendation (16%). Three (12%) responses suggested that students seek additional help. Only one response noted the importance of faculty being more understanding of students with learning disabilities.

The results of this faculty questionnaire were very helpful for several reasons. First, the results alleviated the concern that students in the program were requiring an excessive amount of the faculty's time. Second, the responses dispelled the concern that faculty would have to make modifications or accommodations that would result in lowering standards. In fact, the most common response (providing addition help/counsel) was neither a modification nor a reasonable accommodation. Third, the suggestions of faculty for improving students' chances for success highlighted a major reason for poor academic progress—inconsistent motivation. This faculty feedback provided important support for addressing students' motivational levels. A new service, Individual Support Meetings, offered by the Learning Opportunities Program, was initiated. During

TABLE 13.9. Suggestions for improving students' success ($N = 24$).

Suggestions	Number of Responses (25)	
	NR	%
Greater student motivation	7	28
Better communication with College faculty	4	16
Ask for additional help	3	12
Faculty need to be understanding	1	4
No response	10	40

NR = Number of responses.

students' first semester in the program, they met with a counselor in the College's Counseling Department for several sessions to help them make the transition from high school to college or from another college, to make them aware of the services offered by the Counseling Department, and to determine whether the student might benefit from counseling. A second major purpose of these meetings is to address nonacademic needs of the students in an attempt to prevent social and emotional issues from interfering with academic success.

Administrative Staff's and Service Providers' Perspectives

There are several ways to assess program effectiveness from the administrative staff's and service providers' perspectives. Following are some suggestions:

1) Administrators may want to evaluate the cost effectiveness of a program by assessing the effect on enrollment, retention, the number of resident students, and grants received as a result of offering a program for students with learning disabilities.
2) Administrators may also be interested in determining whether the program brought the institution into compliance with Section 504 and whether it contributes to fulfilling the school's mission.
3) In addition to post-testing at the end of each semester, LD specialists may evaluate their students by tracking attendance and documenting unusual behaviors.
4) LD specialists may also want to evaluate the process established for communication with faculty outside the program and within the program.
5) Program faculty should also evaluate the director and the overall administration of the program including admission procedures, staffings, services, and policies (e.g., for books on tape, notetaking, and attendance).
6) Peer tutors might be asked to evaluate sessions with the tutee and the effectiveness of support from the program faculty while working with the student with LDs.

Conclusion

Objective-oriented and participant-oriented evaluation offer a comprehensive approach to evaluating college programs for students with learning disabilities. Using this approach, it can be determined whether program goals are valid and whether the program is attracting the students for whom it was designed. By eliciting the opinions and concerns of all participants, their input is not only recognized and valued but it is ensuring the ongoing support of faculty and administrators, which is so vital for the success of these programs.

References

Adelman, P.B., & Vogel, S.A. (1990). College graduates with learning disabilities—Employment attainment and career patterns. *Learning Disability Quarterly*, *13*(3), 154–166.

Adelman, P.B., & Vogel, S.A. (1991). The learning-disabled adult. In B. Wong (Ed.), *Learning about learning disabilities* (pp. 563–594). New York: Academic Press.

Adelman, P.B., & Wren, C.T. (1990). *Learning disabilities, graduate school, and careers: The student's perspective.* Lake Forest, IL: Barat College.

Blalock, J.W. (1981). Persistent problems and concerns of young adults with learning disabilities. In W. Cruickshank & A. Silver (Eds.), *Bridges to tomorrow* (Vol. 2, The best of ACLD, pp. 35–55). Syracuse: Syracuse University Press.

Bursuck, W.D., Rose, E., Cowen, S., & Yahaya, M.A. (1989). Nationwide Survey of postsecondary education services for students with learning disabilities. *Exceptional Children*, *56*(3), 236–245.

Fafard, M.B., & Haubrich, P.A. (1981). Vocational and social adjustment of learning disabled young adults: A follow-up study. *Learning Disability Quarterly*, *4*(3), 122–130.

Haring, K.A., Lovett, D.L., & Smith, D.D. (1990). A follow-up study of recent special education graduates of learning disabilities programs. *Journal of Learning Disabilities*, *23*(2), 108–113.

Rogan, L.L., & Hartman, L.D. (1990). Adult outcome of learning disabled students ten years after initial follow-up. *Learning Disabilities Focus*, *5*(2), 91–102.

Scuccimarra, D.J., & Speece, D.L. (1990). Employment outcomes and social integration of students with mild handicaps: The quality of life two years after high school. *Journal of Learning Disabilities*, *23*(4), 213–218.

Vogel, S.A. (1985). Learning disabled college students: Identification, assessment, and outcomes. In D. Duane & C.K. Leong (Eds.), *Understanding learning disabilities—an international perspective* (pp. 179–203). New York: Plenum.

Vogel, S.A., & Adelman, P.B. (1990). Extrinsic and intrinsic factors in graduation and academic failure among LD College Students. *Annals of Dyslexia*, *40*, 119–137.

Worthen, B.R., & Sanders, J.R. (1987). *Educational Evaluation: Alternative Approaches and Practical Guidelines.* White Plains, Longman.

Author Index

344

Subject Index